4/92

CONFEDERATE
GOLIATH

CONFEDERATE GOLIATH

THE BATTLE OF FORT FISHER

Rod Gragg

HarperCollins*Publishers*

FIRST EDITION

Designed by Ruth Kolbert

Maps by Paul Pugliese (Fort Fisher map based on an original sketch by Jeff Smith)

Library of Congress Cataloging-in-Publication Data

Gragg, Rod.
Confederate Goliath: the battle of Fort Fisher/Rod Gragg.—1st ed.
    p.   cm.
  Includes bibliographical references
  ISBN 0-06-16096-9
1. Fort Fisher (N.C.)—Capture, 1865.   2. Fort Fisher (N.C.)—
Battles 1864–1865.   I. Title.
E477.28.G72   1991
973.7′38—dc20   90-38095

91 92 93 94 95 CC/MPC 10 9 8 7 6 5 4 3 2 1

For the Reverend Thomas Oakley Lunsford,
Mrs. Lula Bradley Lunsford, and their
daughter, Elizabeth Lunsford Gragg

LORENA

It matters little now, Lorena,
The past is in the eternal past;
Our hearts will soon lie low, Lorena,
Life's tide is ebbing out so fast.
There is a future, oh, thank God!
Of life this is so small a part—
Tis dust to dust beneath the sod,
But there, up there, tis heart to heart.

Contents

Illustrations follow pages 108 and 240.

Preface

I first saw Fort Fisher when I was a child. My family spent summer vacations at my grandparents' beach house, located about a mile north of the fort. More than ninety years had passed since the Battle of Fort Fisher, and most of the great fortress had washed into the ocean. Hidden from view beneath the area's dense thickets, however, lay the ruins of the fort landface, where much of the most desperate fighting occurred.

Occasionally, in those days, as I hiked along the beach or prowled among the thickets, I would discover rust-covered artillery shell fragments from Admiral Porter's bombardment. My teenage cousins, who lived at Fort Fisher year-round, had a repertoire of Fort Fisher stories. Along with tales of shark sightings and surf fishing, they told of finding cannonballs and bullets along the beach, and they spoke of Colonel Lamb, General Whiting, Admiral Porter, and General Terry as if they were neighborhood residents.

Immersed in such a heady historical atmosphere, and equally affected by my older brother's fascination with the War Between the States, I soon acquired an insatiable curiosity about the remarkable struggle that had taken place a century before on the site of my makeshift playground. When I was about ten, the state of North Carolina began restoration of the site and Ava L. Honeycutt, the site specialist, patiently answered all my childhood questions and fueled my interest in Fort Fisher. As I grew older and began to study the battle seriously, I was amazed that so little had been written about such a significant engagement. After a tour of duty as a news reporter and editor, I returned to graduate school and began serious research on the topic for a thesis. As a journalist, I knew this was an exceptional story and as a historian, I was impressed by the amount of available primary source materials.

More than thirty years after I first saw the ruins of Fort Fisher, and after almost a decade and a half of collecting historical evidence at every opportunity, I began to research the story systematically for this book. A wealth of information emerged. I was particularly impressed by three collections. The manuscript department of the Earl Greg Swem Library at The College of William and Mary has an incredible cache of primary source materials related to Colonel Lamb, including a diary for almost every year of his adult life. Housed deep in the National Archives are the deck logs for almost every Federal warship involved in the bombardment of Fort Fisher, including some that provide an almost minute-by-minute account of the battle and hourly weather observations. In the Terry Family Collection at Yale University's Sterling Memorial Library are the papers of General Terry's brother and aide, Captain Adrian Terry, who solicited private memoirs from a parade of Federal principals a few years after General Terry's death. Their accounts, not intended for publication, provide a candid, colorful, and invaluable behind-the-scenes glimpse into the Federal side of the 1865 battle.

Other collections build an almost flesh-and-blood profile of the engagement's principals. Admiral Porter has a voluminous collection of private papers in the Library of Congress. So does General Butler. Primary source materials from other participants provide precious pieces of the Fort Fisher puzzle. John Grattan, an aide to Admiral Porter, has a journal and a colorful memoir at the Library of Congress. Captain Kinchen Braddy, charged with a crucial role in the defense of the fort, left behind an immensely important account now in the holdings of the North Carolina Division of Archives and History. Daisy Lamb, the wife of Fort Fisher's commander, penned many of her wartime experiences in private papers now at The College of William and Mary. The somewhat controversial role of Hagood's South Carolinians is fairly documented in the James F. Izlar diary held by the South Caroliniana Library at the University of South Carolina. The manuscripts department of the William R. Perkins Library at Duke University has an immensely rich collection of private correspondence detailing soldiers' lives at Fort Fisher. A variety of valuable documents are held in the collections of the New Hanover County Public Library and the Lower Cape Fear Historical Society, both located in Wilmington. My fourteen-year sporadic search for Fort Fisher material produced a trunkload of archival treasures—thanks to the generous assistance of many people and institutions.

◆

Buz Wyeth, the executive editor of HarperCollins, offered sound advice which helped establish the style and approach of this history. Harper's Florence Goldstein always found the answer to every question I raised. Bob Spizer offered timely encouragement and went the extra mile in marketing the manuscript. Susan H. Llewellyn, Harper's production editor, provided indispensable technical advice.

Dr. Francis Lord, a friend and mentor, helped launch this project and generously shared his vast knowledge on the Civil War. Dr. Thomas L. Connelly and Dr. Clyde Wilson directed me to many of the primary sources that became the foundation of this work.

Torrey McLean of the North Carolina Department of Cultural Resources and Chris Fonvielle of East Carolina University, both experts on Fort Fisher, generously provided knowledgeable counsel on all areas of the fort's history. I'm especially thankful for their expertise and their willingness to share their knowledge. Gehrig Spencer, site specialist at Fort Fisher Historic Site, proofed the manuscript. So did Dr. Rich Gray of Montreat-Anderson College and David Perry of Conway, South Carolina. Margaret Locklair sacrificed her valuable time to make important copyediting suggestions. Her husband Ernie and her son Richard generously shared her time with me. Nick Allison provided timely, knowledgeable counsel on the manuscript. Jim Enos, Bill Edmonds, and David Parker provided valuable professional assistance in reproducing period photography.

Civil War expert Paul Fowler of Myrtle Beach, South Carolina, believed this work would be published when even I had begun to entertain a few doubts. He was a consistent source of encouragement throughout the research and production of the manuscript. His well-informed opinions on many matters greatly aided my research and writing. Author and historian Dr. Charles Joyner cheerfully gave me professional advice and thoughtful encouragement. Mrs. James K. ("Bud") Chandler was certain this was a story that deserved telling. Her cheerful reassurance and faithful prayers were an inspiration to me. Likewise, the positive influence of my friends and prayer partners at Grace Presbyterian Church, P.C.A., cannot be overestimated.

Mary Bull, the public service librarian at Coastal Carolina College's Kimbel Library engineered impressive feats of procurement through the University of South Carolina's interlibrary loan system. Other members of Dr. Lynn Smith's competent staff were always helpful and patient. My thanks to Linda Brumfield, Margaret Fain, Sallie Clarkson, David Wilkie, Joan Caldwell, Charmaine Tomcyk, Peggy Bates, Sharon Tulley, Edna Bellamy, Ann Wegner, and Quinn Jones. Beth Rogers, the only Southern belle from Blenheim and Bangkok, skillfully typed and retyped the most maddening portions of the manuscript and did so with characteristic skill and good humor. Jeff Smith, gifted artist and impressionist, generously shared a variety of creative ideas with me.

An important part of the research for this work was funded by a grant from the U.S. Army Military History Institute. Dr. Richard J. Sommers, archivist-historian at USAMHI, provided knowledgeable advice during my two-week research visit to the Institute. So did USAMHI staff professionals Randy Hackenburg and Michael J. Winey. I'm also grateful to these institutions and individuals: the Earl Greg Swem Library at The College of William and Mary; the manuscript department at Yale University Library; the manuscript department at Duke University's William R. Perkins Library; Charles Mann at the Pennsylvania State University Library; Michael P. Musick at the National Archives; Mary Ison and the staff of the Prints and Photographs Division at the Library of Congress; Martin L. Levitt of the American Philosophical Society; David Paynter and Steve McAllister of the New Hanover County Public Library in Wilmington, North Carolina; Ellen Stack and the Historical Society of Pennsylvania; the Filson Club Historical Society; the Chester County Historical Society; the Navy Historical Center in Washington, D.C.; Dr. Richard Knapp and others at the North Carolina Division of Archives and History; the U.S. Naval Academy Museum and Nimitz Library at the U.S. Naval Academy; the Western Reserve Historical Society, the Indiana Historical Society; Rosenberg Library in Galveston, Texas; the New Haven Colony Historical Society; the Southern Historical Society Collection at the University of North Carolina; South Caroliniana Library and Thomas Cooper Library at the University of South Carolina; the Museum of the Confederacy; the Marine Corps Historical Center in Washington, D.C.; the Lower Cape Fear Historical Society; the New Hanover County Museum; Dover Public Library and the Woodman Institute in Dover, New Hampshire; Eggleston Library at Hampton-Sydney College; the John M. Olin Library at Cornell University; Buncombe County Library in Asheville, North

Carolina; the Historical Foundation at Montreat, North Carolina; the Montreat-Anderson College Library; Richland County Memorial Library in Columbia, South Carolina; the U.S. Army Military Academy Library at West Point, New York; Oakdale Cemetery in Wilmington, North Carolina; Mecklenburg County Library in Charlotte, North Carolina; the South Carolina Historical Society; the Horry County Memorial Library in Conway, South Carolina; the South Carolina Department of Archives and History; Dr. Lawrence Lee of Charleston, South Carolina; Matthew Dowling of the history department at Yale University; Dr. Stanley South of the Institute of Anthropology and Archaeology at the University of South Carolina; Dr. Charles Perry of Charleston, South Carolina; the Grand Strand Civil War Roundtable; and the late Dr. Henry B. Wightman of Ithaca, New York.

Bobby Melton of Salisbury, North Carolina, and Charles Lunsford of Norman, Oklahoma, launched this work more than thirty years ago when they patiently included me on their adventurous treks around Fort Fisher. Even when weary from their backyard excavations at the green house inside the gates, they were always willing to do another tour of the fort. Likewise, my brother Ted was equally ready for another jaunt through the scrub oak and thickets of Federal Point, and his wife, Connie, shared him with me.

I'm also very thankful for the interest and encouragement I received from all my Outlaw inlaws: Bill and Margaret; Newt, Jimmy, and Gail; John, Joe, and Margaret; and from Doug and Jackie Rutt.

Never has there been a booster club quite as supportive as my parents, Skip and Elizabeth Gragg, who fueled my interest in history before I could even read. I love them very much. My father was always a history buff, and only a mother like mine would have patiently trudged up and down a sun-baked beach with a history-hungry son in tow.

My children—Faith, Rachel, Elizabeth, Joni, Penny, Matt, and Skip—were patient and loving throughout the production of this work, even when it attracted too much of my attention. My wife, Cindy, perhaps the last surviving Fort Fisher widow, served as my mentor, critic, and loving companion throughout the highs and lows of this long, long project. She is a true Proverbs 31 woman. Finally, and most important, I am eternally grateful for the enduring truth of II Corinthians 5: 17–21.

CONFEDERATE
GOLIATH

1

"Black Smoke and Moon Nights"

COLONEL WILLIAM LAMB STOOD IN THE COLD AND WAITED for the guns to fire. He was an impressive figure, tall and slim, erect and courtly, uniformed in Confederate gray. His woolen overcoat was lined in red—the color denoting an artillery officer. His brownish whiskers were neatly trimmed in the European style fashionable among military professionals of the day, and he carried himself with a proper military bearing. Standing atop the towering earthen gun battery, he could see the Atlantic Ocean on one side and North Carolina's Cape Fear River on the other. Nearby, for his benefit, a gun crew went through its drill, loading a large practice round into a monstrous seacoast cannon. Moments later, in a blast of smoke and flame, a melon-size shot arced through the winter sky and splashed harmlessly in the river.

If William Lamb looked confident throughout the demonstration, he had good reason: he was revered by his troops, respected by his superiors and viewed by many as an officer of unusual achievement. One more promotion would make him a brigadier general. His reputation had not come from the field of battle, however; in fact, he had seen little combat. Instead, William Lamb's prominence came from his post: At age twenty-nine, he commanded Fort Fisher—the largest, most formidable fortification in the Confederate States of America.

After almost four years, the American Civil War was grinding to an agonizingly slow and bloody conclusion. Few intelligent observers, North or South, doubted that the end was near. Already, the war had lasted much longer than most Americans had expected, and the carnage had exceeded their worst fears. Within a few more months, more than 600,000 Americans would have died in the bloodbath. More than a quarter-million of the dead would be citizens of Lamb's native South. In their quest for independence, Southerners had made a terrible sacrifice, costly beyond calculation, and still they now found themselves in a desperate plight. Despite the early, glittering victories and General Robert E. Lee's masterful maneuvering in Virginia, the Confederacy was dying—smothered slowly by the military and industrial might of the more mechanized, more populous North.

Federal forces now controlled the entire Mississippi River, splitting the Confederacy from north to south, and elsewhere the fledgling nation was being dismembered piecemeal, ravaged and conquered by invasion. General William T. Sherman and his overpowering columns had just laid waste to much of Georgia, and were now poised to strike at the Carolinas. In Tennessee, the once-proud Confederate Army of Tennessee, led now by General John Bell Hood, was ragged, reduced and hovering on the verge of destruction. In Virginia, the Confederate Army of Northern Virginia was stretched thinner almost daily, as Lee tried to hold his besieged line from Petersburg to Richmond, the imperiled Confederate capital. The powerful Federal naval blockade had steadily choked the Confederacy into isolation, stanching the flow of imported arms and equipment vital to the South's survival.

Dreams of Southern nationhood, so bright and so near reality two years earlier, were now but a faint, dimming hope held by only the most faithful. Nevertheless, Richmond officials believed that a slim chance for independence remained through negotiations with the war-weary North—if the beleaguered Confederacy could keep Lee's army in the field, successfully defend its capital and maintain its endangered lifeline to the outside world.[1]

These were the grim but unavoidable facts facing Colonel William Lamb this winter's day—December 13, 1864—as he watched artillery practice at his fort. Today, however, Lamb had other things on his mind. Christmas was less than two weeks away, and back in his quarters was a box of gifts awaiting shipment to his parents in Virginia. Somewhere he had to find a couple of holiday turkeys for his wife, and he wanted to get a new cloak made for his sister. Fortunately, he had just received a modest financial windfall from some wartime speculation. A few days from now, he would go to town with his wife's shopping list and he would need a small fortune—wartime inflation had driven prices in the South to outlandish levels. A turkey would cost him almost $40; he would have to pay $12 for a handful of pencils; and a new belt for his wife would cost $30. In his quarters, his wife and two small children were trying to live as normally as possible amid the war, and he had to think about Christmas. He had imported a sackful of European toys through one of the English ships that periodically docked at his fort en route to port. Tending to such pleasantries would have been routine in peacetime, but now it was troublesome and costly. Still, he was a dutiful husband and father, even in war, and he tried to give his family as many amenities of peacetime as possible. Despite his best efforts, however, the war was inescapable.[2]

Perhaps that was to be expected for the commander of Fort Fisher—the most fearsome fortification in the embattled Confederacy. Located 18 miles south of Wilmington, North Carolina, the giant, sprawling fort straddled Confederate Point, a long, tapering peninsula between the Cape Fear River and the Atlantic Ocean. On this day, a crisply cold Tuesday, Lamb was observing artillery practice at Battery Buchanan, a massive two-story earthwork whose four heavy artillery pieces anchored Fort Fisher's southern flank. Two large eleven-inch Brooke cannon had been mounted in the battery to complement its existing ten-inch Columbiads, and today the guns were being test-fired. Adding the Brookes to the fort's armament was Lamb's latest attempt to strengthen an already powerful fortification. Fort Fisher could not be too strong, he believed, for it was vital to the defense of Wilmington—and Wilmington was vital to the survival of the Confederacy. North Carolina's principal seaport, Wilmington was smaller than Charleston and was dwarfed in size by New Orleans, but now Wilmington was far more important than *any* Southern seaport. Now, in December 1864, Wilmington was the *only* Confederate seaport still able to supply the slowly strangling South with the quantities of imported arms and equipment deemed necessary for Southern survival. Wilmington had become the lifeline of the Confederacy.[3]

◆

The following Friday, Lamb made his shopping trip to Wilmington. He boarded the steamer *John Dawson* at Fort Fisher and made the voyage upriver to port with plenty of time left for shopping. Moored to Wilmington's wooden wharves when Lamb's riverboat arrived was a flotilla of sleek, grim-looking vessels—blockade runners—unloading the articles of war essential to the survival of the South. For more than three years, ships with names like *Wild Rover, Talisman, Vulture, Night Hawk, Banshee* and *R. E. Lee* had been slipping through the Federal naval blockade and into the mouth of the Cape Fear River near Fort Fisher. Then they would steam upriver to Wilmington to unload their precious cargoes: British Enfield rifles, bullets, bayonets, percussion caps, lead ingots for bullet making, sheet tin, bars of iron, leather accouterments, medical supplies, imported foodstuffs and high-profit civilian goods. From Wilmington, the imported war material was shipped by rail to the soldiers in the field—along with Carolina corn, Tarheel bacon and barrels of smoked fish.[4]

Entrenched at Petersburg, Lee's Army of Northern Virginia depended on Wilmington for essential munitions as well as for much of the army's meager rations. One by one, the Confederacy's Atlantic and Gulf seaports had been captured or, like Charleston, effectively blockaded by the Federal navy. With the capture of Mobile Bay in August of 1864, Wilmington had become the only major Southern seaport still open to European traffic and able to move the military imports to the Virginia front. An agricultural society poorly equipped to meet the demands of industrialized warfare, the Confederacy was desperately dependent on imported arms and equipment. Since the beginning of the war, the South had made an impressive attempt to develop an arms industry, but it was not enough. The loss of its seaports was slow death for the Confederacy, and keeping Wilmington open as a functioning port was vital to the Southern war effort. The North Carolina port had become as important as Richmond.[5]

In Wilmington, Lamb paid a call at district headquarters, located in the three-story DeRosset house a few blocks up Market Street from the riverside. He also spent some time with Captain Richard Gayle aboard the blockade runner *Stag,* where he learned that Sherman had taken Fort McAllister and had reached the Georgia coast. His socializing over and his shopping done, he spent the night at the home of a fellow officer. As he moved about Wilmington, Lamb could not help but notice the dramatic changes that had affected the port city since he had first arrived there three years earlier.[6]

Back then, in late 1861, Wilmington still retained much of its prewar flavor: it was North Carolina's largest city—a pleasant, orderly and moderately busy port trafficking in cotton, naval stores, rice and peanuts. The war—and blockade running—had changed everything. Wilmington now reminded some visitors of San Francisco at peak of the California gold rush. Most of the affluent, old Southern families who had directed the affairs of prewar Wilmington had closed or leased their homes and had left town. Middle-class wives, mothers and children had been sent inland to relatives in safer locations, and most of the city's adult males were either away in the army or buried beneath some distant battlefield or cemetery. Wilmington was now a city of men, and its business affairs were generally conducted by strangers. As he moved through Wilmington, Lamb was exposed to a population far different from the typical Wilmingtonians he had encountered in 1861. Roaming the streets and docks now were weathered British seamen, Confederate troops in ragged gray or butternut uniforms, black laborers, dockside toughs, cultured ships' officers and fuzz-faced farm boys. Once noted for its beauty and charm, Wilmington had acquired a seedy, neglected appearance. Paint peeled from formerly well-tended houses, the city's best brick avenues were dotted with potholes, uncollected garbage lined the streets, and lean, half-starved dogs nosed through the trash.[7]

Despite the harsh wages of war, Lamb knew that not everyone in Wilmington suffered. The immense profits available from blockade running had lured hordes of speculators, agents and traders to the port, and many had reaped fortunes equal to a gold strike. Wilmington's remaining old-time residents generally considered blockade running a disreputable business, a necessary evil at best, conducted by ruffians and foreigners. Lamb may not have shared that view—he knew and liked many of the blockade-running principals—but he undoubtedly knew plenty of high rollers who fit the stereotype, strolling about town in stylish, imported suits and partying lavishly in opulent, rented homes.[8]

"At every turn you met up with young Englishmen dressed like grooms and jockeys, or with a peculiar coachman-like look," recalled a wartime observer. "These youngsters had money, made money, lived like fighting cocks, and astonished the natives by their pranks, and the way they flung the Confederate 'stuff' about. . . . [One group] occupied a large, flaring yellow house on the upper end of Market Street. . . . A stranger passing the house at night, and seeing it illuminated with every gas jet lit (the expense, no doubt, charged to the ship), and hearing the sound of music, would ask if a ball was going on. Oh, no! It was only these young English Sybarites enjoying the luxury of a band of negro minstrels after dinner."[9]

The principals of some shipping firms did conduct themselves with more restraint, and while many Wilmingtonians may have sniffed in disdain at blockade running as a profession, the deprivation of war made most citizens eager for the rare consumer goods brought into Wilmington through the blockade. Public auction of goods salvaged from beached blockade runners or just the arrival of the latest ship could produce a carnival atmosphere in port.[10]

"Talk about Yankees worshipping the almighty dollar! You should have seen the adoration paid the Golden Calf at Wilmington during the days of blockade running," recalled a Confederate officer posted to the port.

> When a steamer came in, men, women, children rushed down to the wharves to see it, to buy, beg, or steal something. Everybody wanted to know if their "ventures"—the proceeds of the bales of cotton or boxes of tobacco—had come in. No people were more excited than the women, expecting gloves, parasols, hoop-skirts, corsets, flannels, and bonnets, silks and calicoes; for these things became frightfully scarce and dear in the South during the last year of the war. The first people aboard of course were the agents—on such occasions very big men. Then swarmed officials and officers, "friends" and "bummers" hunting after drinks and dinners, and willing to accept any compliment, from a box of cigars or a bottle of brandy down to a bunch of bananas or a pocketful of oranges.[11]

Colonel Lamb's associations with Wilmington's blockade runners provided some amenities normally unavailable to most Wilmingtonians. A couple of days earlier, for instance, a ship's captain had presented him with a handsome Adams revolver. For many civilians, however, consumer goods were unaffordable even when available through the blockade. And when he entered Wilmington's shops, Lamb too had to face the outrageous prices fueled by wartime inflation, which had rendered the Confederate currency practically worthless. A barrel of flour, which had sold for $8 in 1861, now cost $500; ground coffee, once 13¢ a pound, had soared to $100 a pound; a pair of shoes now cost $500, and a man's overcoat could cost $1,500. Like other Southerners, Wilmingtonians had learned to live with less. Instead of coffee, they drank boiled water seasoned with beans or potatoes, and a typical meal in Wilmington now consisted of a corn muffin, a serving of honey and maybe a single prized biscuit.[12]

The city was also plagued by a surge in violent crime. In dockside taverns, soldiers and seamen gambled and drank away their off-duty hours, and on Sundays Wilmington's clergymen often had to preach above the noise of nearby cockfights. At night, prostitutes trolled for customers and knife-wielding brawlers sometimes rolled in the waterfront streets, cheered by noisy onlookers. Murders were common and bodies were often found floating in the Cape Fear River on Sunday mornings. One citizen who saw a sailor shot dead in the street one night went aboard a blockade runner the next day and was aghast to discover the dead man's shipmates nonchalantly eating breakfast around the victim's corpse.[13]

Death was not limited to tavern brawlers: it came to Wilmington on a larger scale in August of 1862 with an epidemic of yellow fever. The origin of the deadly disease, a virus transmitted by the *Aedes* mosquito, was unknown at the time. Later, the blockade runner *Kate* would be blamed for bringing the epidemic to Wilmington. The first cases of the fever occurred among the ship's passengers; the proprietor of a dockside wood yard that had serviced the *Kate* was next; then the disease began to spread rapidly through the city's population. Those stricken became bedridden and severely weakened, were soon jaundiced, and then began vomiting a dark-colored fluid. The first fifteen victims died and Wilmington's residents began to flee the city, soon shrinking the port's population of 10,000 by two-thirds. Refugees crowded the roads and packed departing trains. Businesses closed, dock workers left the wharves, train and telegraph services ceased, the *Wilmington Journal* temporarily suspended publication, all troops were withdrawn from the city and the port was quarantined.[14]

Burning tar pots were placed on street corners to "purify" Wilmington's air, which was believed to transmit the disease. They spread a stench throughout the city and cloaked its roofs and spires with a dark, ominous-looking cloud of thick, black smoke. The 3,000 residents who remained in the city sequestered themselves inside, closing their doors, boarding their shutters and leaving the streets deserted. An eerie silence gripped the port, broken only by the clatter of doctors' buggies and the creaking of horse-drawn hearses. Daily, burial parties dug trenches in Wilmington's Oakdale Cemetery, and some feared the city's remaining residents would be annihilated. Finally, after 654 recorded deaths, a freak snowstorm hit the city in early November, ending the epidemic.[15]

The war had been hard on Wilmington in many ways, but at least the city had been spared the terror and destruction of combat. The enemy was nearby, however, just a few miles away at any time, aboard the Federal warships patrolling offshore. As he headed back to Fort Fisher on a Saturday steamer, passing the blockade runners docked along Wilmington's piers, Colonel Lamb may have pondered the latest odds of escaping the Federal patrols. It had been easy in the beginning, in July of 1861, when the Federal blockade of Wilmington was first enforced. Wilmington was infused by a giddy atmosphere in those days: young men in flashy uniforms were leaving for camp amid colorful celebrations and grandiose oratory, schoolboys toting wooden guns "drilled" in the streets and anxious businessmen of Northern loyalty were quietly leaving town. Wilmington was blockaded by a single Federal warship, the USS *Daylight,* and few people took the threat seriously. *"Daylight* is a little cock-a-hoop of a thing," scoffed the *Wilmington Journal,* "and a good sound shot from a rifled cannon . . . would soon open 'daylight' through her. We must get the thing up here to go a-fishing in."[16]

Southerners could afford to joke about the Federal blockade in 1861: equipped with a mere 35 warships, the U.S. Navy had to blockade 3,550 miles of Southern seacoast, 189 harbors or inlets and 9 major seaports. Now, however, neither Lamb nor most other Southerners saw anything humorous about the Federal naval blockade: almost 500 Federal warships patrolled the Confederate seacoast and rivers, and eluding capture was no longer an easy task for blockade runners. The odds of capture—one in ten in 1861—were now one in three.[17]

The risks were greater, but investors still considered the potential profits irresistible. If a blockade runner successfully completed one or two voyages, and most did, investors could afford to lose the ship on the next run and still make money. A profit of $150,000 on a single voyage was not unusual, and a shrewd investor could multiply his profits by investing in a round-trip venture. A ship's company could buy a ton of coffee for $249 in Nassau, for instance, sell it in a Confederate port for $5,500, then buy Southern cotton at 3¢ a pound for resale in Great Britain at $1 a pound. Not only did Southern and British shipping companies earn huge profits, but a ship's captain who would normally earn $150 a voyage in routine merchant service could make $5,000 or more in a single trip as captain of a blockade runner. Even a common sailor, shrewd enough to buy a half-dozen bottles of gin in Bermuda for $24, could resell his stock for $900 in Wilmington. By December of 1864, blockade runners had supplied the South with more than $200 million in goods and war matériel, and had carried more than 1.4 million bales of Confederate cotton back to Great Britain.[18]

Lamb and other coastal commanders had seen the blockade runner evolve into a unique vessel. At first, standard steamships had been employed, but as the blockade tightened, blockade runners adapted to the increasing risks with sophisticated specialization. Powerful side-wheel or double-screw steamers designed for high speed were built. Camouflaged with lead-gray paint, they were long, low, rakish-looking craft, often equipped with collapsible masts and smokestacks to reduce visibility. Canvas flaps were placed over the ships' paddles to muffle noise, and, when possible, smokeless anthracite coal was used to eliminate the telltale plumes that could be spotted from miles away. On a dark night, a well-camouflaged blockade runner was almost invisible, and that was when most ran the blockade. On moonless nights and in stormy weather navigation was hazardous, but capture was much less likely.[19]

Wilmington was 570 miles and 50 hours from Nassau, and 674 miles and 72 hours from Bermuda. British blockade runners bound for Wilmington usually refueled and added cargo at Nassau or Bermuda, then continued toward port, approaching the Carolina coast at night. Typically, about 30 miles offshore, lights were extinguished and the ship headed for the Cape Fear River at full steam. A blockade runner usually approached the coast above or below the targeted entrance into the river, then moved into the shallows and ran parallel to the beach. The maneuver was intended to hide the ship against the dark, wooded shoreline while the breakers muffled the engine noise and the splash of the ship's paddlewheels. Near the river entrance, the ship flashed a coded lantern signal, and received a countersignal from Confederate lookouts ashore. Range lights were then illuminated, directing the ship into the river, and, hopefully, the blockade runner would safely speed into the inlet. Afterwards, out of danger, the ship could leisurely steam upriver to Wilmington. The guns of Fort Fisher and the surrounding Cape Fear fortifications prevented Federal warships from pursuing blockade runners into the river.[20]

The Federal warships patrolling the Cape Fear coast were part of the navy's North Atlantic Blockading Squadron, and duty was routinely mundane except on "moon nights"—the dark, moonless period favored by blockade runners. Then the Federal blockaders went to their night stations at dusk, forming a large semicircular blockade around the two entrances to the Cape Fear River. With artillery ready, lanterns covered and sailors forbidden to speak above a whisper, the warships waited. Aboard each ship, a deck officer posted aloft in the bosun chair scanned the dark horizon, straining to spot the silhouette of a blockade runner or a distant plume of ship's smoke. If a blockade runner was sighted, a signal rocket would streak through the night and the chase would begin. Steam up and guns manned, the blockaders would pursue their quarry, firing rocket after rocket to mark the blockade runner's direction. Most pursuits occurred at night, but sometimes a tardy blockade runner would be spotted at dawn. "Black smoke!" the deck officer would shout, sending seamen to their battle stations. Hurriedly shoveling pitch pine

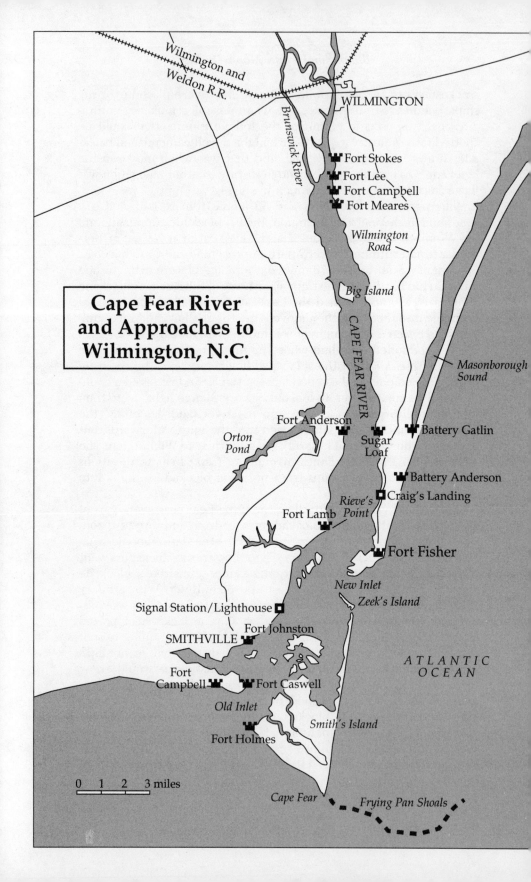

Wilmington and
Weldon R.R.

Brunswick River

WILMINGTON

Fort Stokes
Fort Lee
Fort Campbell
Fort Meares

*Wilmington
Road*

Big Island

CAPE FEAR RIVER

**Cape Fear River
and Approaches to
Wilmington, N.C.**

*Masonborough
Sound*

Fort Anderson

*Orton
Pond*

Sugar
Loaf

Battery Gatlin

Battery Anderson

Craig's Landing

*Rieve's
Point*

Fort Lamb

Fort Fisher

New Inlet

Zeek's Island

Signal Station/Lighthouse

SMITHVILLE Fort Johnston

ATLANTIC
OCEAN

Fort
Campbell Fort Caswell

Old Inlet

Smith's Island

Fort Holmes

0 1 2 3 miles

Cape Fear *Frying Pan Shoals*

and rosin chunks into the ship's furnace, the warship firemen would stoke a hotter fire to build speed for the chase.[21]

Aboard the harried blockade runner, firemen would sometimes fuel the ship's furnace with sides of bacon or turpentine-soaked cotton, trying to gain enough speed to outdistance the enemy. If the chase was close, the ship might be lightened by tossing cargo overboard. Narrow escapes were common, and sometimes, when capture or sinking seemed imminent, a captain would heave to and surrender his ship and cargo. More often, he would turn toward shore and try to beach his vessel in the breakers, hoping the cargo could be salvaged later under Confederate protection.[22]

Colonel Lamb had heard of chases that lasted for hours—and the Federal pursuers had an equal share of tales. Commander John Almy of the USS *Connecticut* once pursued a Wilmington-bound blockade runner for seventy miles before overtaking the ship and boarding it. As his sailors rummaged through the captured cargo, Almy came aboard and greeted its captain. "Good morning," the Federal officer cheerfully barked, "glad to see you." "Damned if I'm glad to see you," replied the dejected captain.[23]

Blockade running could be profitable on the Northern side as well. Confiscated cargo was auctioned in Northern ports, and while half the profit was claimed by the Federal government, the rest was awarded as prize money to the officers and crew of who made the capture—minus a 5 percent cut for the commander of the blockading squadron. By war's end, naval personnel would have earned more than $10 million from confiscated cargo. Seamen blockading Wilmington, where traffic was heavy throughout the war, could hope to amass a small fortune. In 1864, for example, capture of the blockade runner *Hope* produced more than $13,000 in prize money for the master of the USS *Eolus,* almost $6,700 for the ship's engineer, $1,000 for each crewman—and a prize of $532.60 for the ship's cabin boy.[24]

By December of 1864, 33 Federal warships maintained the Wilmington blockade. Lamb had no way to make an exact count, but he could tell their numbers had dramatically increased. Despite the sightings made by his lookouts and the numbers reported by the blockade runners, he was constantly reminded of the Federal naval threat by the long line of skeletal-looking shipwrecks littering the beach near his fort. Of the estimated 100 blockade runners that steamed in and out of Wilmington during the war, approximately 60 had already been captured or forced aground by Federal blockaders. Despite the losses and the best Federal efforts to close the port, however, more than $3.2 million in imported munitions and goods had flowed into Wilmington in a one-year period ending in the fall of 1864. The Confederate lifeline thus remained intact and effective.[25]

Wilmington's survival was no accident—Lamb knew that better than anyone. And he knew the reasons: for starters, the port's location was perfect for blockade running. Located some 20 miles upstream from the mouth of the Cape Fear River, it was out of bounds for Federal warships and could not be reached by an offshore bombardment. Nor could it be bottled up like Charleston to the south— thanks to the geography of the Cape Fear River. From the heart of North Carolina the cloudy Cape Fear drained toward the Atlantic, sweeping past Wilmington and flowing south, past the mainland on the west and Confederate Point on the east, heading steadily toward the ocean. At its mouth, the Cape Fear split around Smith's Island, a 10-mile-long body of sand dunes, sea oats and marshland, then spilled surging and foaming into the Atlantic through two inlets— New Inlet to the north and Old Inlet to the south. This geographical feature meant that the Federal navy had to blockade two entrances to the Cape Fear River, and to do so the warships also had to dodge a 25-mile-long finger of shallows called Frying Pan Shoals. A simultaneous blockade of New Inlet and Old Inlet meant the Federal warships had to patrol a 50-mile-long arc to bottle up Wilmington. It was too much territory to cover effectively and the Wilmington blockade leaked like a sieve.[26]

However, geography was not the main reason the port of Wilmington remained open when all other major Southern ports had fallen or were sealed. The real reason undoubtedly seemed obvious to Colonel Lamb as his steamer brought him back downriver from Wilmington that Saturday in December, chugging past fort after fort along the Cape Fear. The crucial lifeline was preserved by Southern steel and shot: Wilmington was protected by one of the most formidable defense systems in the world. And the anchor of that system— the key to Wilmington's survival—was Fort Fisher.[27]

2

"They Will Never Get Us Alive"

THERE HAD NEVER BEEN A FORT LIKE THIS ONE. LAMB WAS certain of it. From Wilmington to Nassau, from London to Washington, Fort Fisher was described with awe. It was the anchor of the Cape Fear defense system, a remarkable network of fortifications that encircled Wilmington and extended downriver on both banks of the Cape Fear. The waterway bristled with artillery—along both riverbanks, on Smith's Island, along the beach overlooking Old and New Inlet, and at Smithville, a little fishing village on the mainland downriver from Fort Fisher.[1]

Fort Caswell, perched on a peninsula overlooking Old Inlet, was a formidable-looking masonry fort built more than thirty years earlier by army engineers. The rest of the Cape Fear fortifications were composed of earthworks—huge mounds of dirt reinforced by timbers and sandbags, and armed by wide-muzzled heavy artillery pieces. Like Fort Fisher, most of the fortifications were named for Southern patriots, either famous or local, and bore names like Fort Lee, Fort Meares, Fort Anderson, Fort Campbell, Fort Holmes— even Fort Lamb. Most of the earthen forts had been designed by Confederate engineers and built with pick and shovel by slaves impressed from nearby plantations. Earthen fortifications were more practical than masonry forts, which could be bombarded into rubble by the latest heavy artillery. Earthwork fortifications like Fort Fisher simply absorbed the pounding.[2]

Stretching across and down the southern tip of Confederate Point and heavily armed throughout, Fort Fisher was the ultimate earthen fortification. Federal warships kept well out of range, acknowledging the giant fort's dominance of New Inlet and making that channel the preferred approach to the Cape Fear for most blockade runners. Political leaders in Richmond and Washington alike spoke of Fort Fisher with respect, and military leaders often compared the fort to the impregnable British post that loomed over the entrance to the Mediterranean. Fort Fisher, they would say, was "the Gibraltar of the South."[3]

Colonel William Lamb was Fort Fisher's creator as well as its commander. No one knew the fort like Lamb. No one knew its capabilities more than he. No one had more confidence in its ability to defend Wilmington and the Cape Fear. Yet, in December of 1864, Lamb was seriously worried about Fort Fisher's survival.[4]

He was not one to worry much. Handsome and affable, he was optimistic by nature—a romantic man who had spent the hours prior to his wedding searching for just the perfect shirt ruffle to adorn his bridegroom's suit. He was an addicted diarist who had begun keeping a pocket journal while in college and had regularly recorded entries almost every day since. Nor was his normally positive attitude simply an expression of youth. His was a personality trained in optimism, born of privilege and carefully cultivated in that rare social greenhouse: the home of a nineteenth-century Southern gentleman.[5]

Unlike most Southerners, he was a city boy—a product of the Virginia Tidewater—born in Norfolk in 1835, in the city that had been home to his family since before the Revolution. His father, a prominent lawyer and three-term mayor of Norfolk, gave his son a gentleman's education: a sound primary program, the Rappahannock Military Academy at fourteen, a preparatory school up North, then the bachelor of law program at The College of William and Mary. There he studied the classics, history, and biography as well as law. Under such tutelage, he could have grown effete and aloof, but his parents balanced privilege with an emphasis on discipline and priorities. His father taught him riding, rowing, boxing and fencing, and at military school he chopped wood and toted water like every other cadet. Through his mother's influence, he became a devout Christian and also acquired a deep love for books.[6]

Much of his boyhood was spent immersed in military biographies, and at age fourteen he repeatedly waded through a voluminous history of Virginia. He pondered biblical and theological issues and eventually grew so confident in his faith that he would at times end military dispatches with references to the Almighty. At age nineteen, he graduated Phi Beta Kappa from William and Mary, equipped with a law degree but too young to practice. He came back home unemployed, but he wasn't idle long—his father bought him a half-interest in a Norfolk newspaper.[7]

At age twenty, Lamb found himself editor and half-owner of the *Southern Argus.* It was an ideal post for a young man with political ambition, and some people expected Lamb to follow his father as mayor of the city. He liked politics, and in 1856, as a Virginia delegate to the Democratic National Convention, he watched as James Buchanan was knighted as the party's presidential nominee. A year later Lamb ran for mayor of Norfolk, but was defeated by the Whig candidate. The loss did not dampen his political interests and he continued to use his editor's post to lobby for Democratic positions.[8]

"Government without Oppression—Liberty without Anarchy," proclaimed the *Argus* as Lamb pounded the Know-Nothings and the newly born Republicans in his regular editorials. The *Argus* lamented the growing influence of the Federal government and denounced the emerging "Republican host," which Lamb viewed as the "real and true foe of Democracy." Once his editorial enthusiasm almost landed him in a duel with a volatile North Carolina editor, but the dispute was peacefully resolved at the last moment.[9]

Lamb's concern about a rising Republican menace in the North apparently had little impact on his romantic notions—in 1857 he wed a Yankee. She was a delicate, dark-haired nineteen-year-old named Sarah Anne Chafee—called Daisy—whom Lamb had met two years earlier in Providence, Rhode Island. His family had gone there to escape a yellow fever outbreak in Norfolk and Lamb instead was stricken by love. Well-educated, articulate and attractive, Daisy was a compatible match. She shared Lamb's affection for reading, loved the South and its people, fretted about "those meddlesome Fanatics at the North," and was equally devout—reluctant even to write a letter on the Lord's Day. Typically, the sentimental Lamb chose September 7—his birthday—as the wedding day. "I have been blest with health & comfort, & the most devoted wife that ever a husband had," he confided to his diary. "He is everything I could wish," she wrote a cousin, "and oh so kind and devoted to me. I have always desired a lover husband, and I have one now."[10]

A year later, in 1858, Lamb's military interests took a practical turn when he helped organize a Norfolk militia company called the Woodis Rifles. He was elected captain and in 1859 was present with his troops at John Brown's hanging. "Sooner or later," Lamb later wrote in the *Argus*, "the ties which now link together the North and the South must be sundered." The sundering occurred, thought Lamb and thousands of Southerners, when Abraham Lincoln was elected in 1860—an event many Southerners believed would ensure Northern domination of the South. Some Virginians were timid about secession, but not William Lamb; earlier than most he embraced the dream of Southern nationhood.[11]

When war erupted, he saw combat quickly. Less than a month after Virginia seceded, Lamb and the Woodis Rifles assisted a Confederate battery in skirmishing with the USS *Monticello* at Sewall's Point on Hampton Roads. For more than three years, that would be his only serious combat experience. The Woodis Rifles was taken into the Sixth Virginia Infantry and Lamb, promoted to major, was ordered to Wilmington as chief quartermaster for the District of Cape Fear.[12]

Daisy liked Wilmington in 1861. "It is a pretty place and the people are very refined and polite," she wrote her parents soon after arriving in the port. She lived in "a delightful neighborhood," she reported, and enjoyed the pleasures of a "cozy" rented house graced by a shrub garden and a row of towering sycamore trees. It was handsomely furnished and even had a new piano. "I never enjoyed anything more than I do my sweet cheerful home," Daisy wrote. "Will comes home to his meals and at night so I am really blest in these troublesome times."[13]

The idyllic family life vanished as the war grew serious. Lamb was transferred from quartermaster to commander of Fort St. Philip, a small cluster of earthworks on the Cape Fear River north of Smithville. The couple already had three small children, two girls and a boy, and when Daisy became pregnant with a fourth, Lamb convinced her to take the children and live in Norfolk with his parents. Soon afterwards, the city was occupied by Federal forces and the Yankees temporarily imprisoned Lamb's father, who was again serving as mayor. Daisy and the children then went North to her family in Providence.[14]

Lamb, meanwhile, was transforming his fledgling "fort" into a strong defensive work. Renamed Fort Anderson, it would become an anchor for the west bank of the Cape Fear defense system. Lamb's ability as a military engineer must have surprised his superiors. Although obviously intelligent, well-educated and energetic, he had come to them as a volunteer quartermaster officer with no regular army training—a newspaper editor–turned–soldier who had attended military school as a teenager and had served a brief stint as a militia officer. He may have been an efficient quartermaster, but when he was sent to Fort St. Philip, William Lamb's genius emerged. Typically, he consumed every book on military engineering he could find, and as he strengthened the riverside earthworks, his skills became obvious to his superiors. Up the coast from Wilmington, the Federals had easily captured the Confederate defenses on Roanoke Island, had occupied New Bern and had turned Beaufort into a coaling and supply point for the blockade. Wilmington might be the next target, and Lamb undoubtedly seemed the perfect choice to build up the lower Cape Fear's weak defenses.[15]

He was made colonel of the Thirty-sixth North Carolina Artillery and on July 4, 1862, the twenty-six-year-old Lamb was ordered across the river to command Fort Fisher. He took over at noon and by sundown had conducted his first official inspection. What he found was a collection of earthworks consisting of six artillery batteries mounting seventeen guns. The fortification had been honorably named, memorializing a North Carolina officer—Colonel Charles F. Fisher—who had died in battle at First Manassas, but it was hardly a fortress nor was it formidable enough to deter attack or withstand invasion. The morning after he assumed command, his first full day at the post, Lamb was surprised to see a Federal warship anchored within easy range of the fort. He called for a junior officer, inquired about the position of the enemy vessel and was informed that Federal warships often anchored within range and sometimes even shelled the fort's work crews. Garrison orders, the officer explained, prohibited firing on an enemy warship unless the enemy fired first. The astounded Lamb promptly issued his first combat order: Fire on that ship, he commanded. Moments later a round from the fort splashed dangerously near the Federal blockader, which quickly weighed anchor and steamed out of range.[16]

When he looked at Fort Fisher, perched on Confederate Point between the river and the ocean, Lamb had a vision. "I determined at once," he later recalled, "to build a work of such magnitude that it could withstand the heaviest fire of any guns in the American Navy." What Lamb envisioned was a massive fortress, able to protect blockade runners coming in and out of adjacent New Inlet, strong enough to deter any attempt to close the river, and formidable enough to resist assault. Lamb's vision was larger than even his departmental commander, General Samuel G. French, could appreciate, but French allowed the young colonel to proceed.[17]

Using the fort's garrison and impressed slaves, Lamb kept as many as 1,000 men steadily at work on Fort Fisher's defenses. For two years he kept up the pace, until Fort Fisher was the largest seacoast fortification in the Confederacy. Built in the shape of an upside-down L, the fort stretched almost a half-mile across Confederate Point, from the river to the ocean, then snaked more than a mile down the beach, heavily armed with artillery all the way. The "landface" section, running from river to sea, was a bumpy line of 15 huge earthen mounds, called "traverses" in the military jargon of the day. Each was approximately 30 feet high, about 25 feet thick, and was "bomb-proofed" with a hollow interior to shelter the garrison during a bombardment. Between the traverses, heavy artillery was mounted in elevated "gun chambers" surrounded by sandbags. By late 1864, the fort's landface was armed with 20 heavy seacoast artillery pieces—mostly large Columbiads—and was supported by three mortars and several field pieces. The landface gun chambers were accessible from the rear by wooden stairs, and a long interior passageway connected all the bombproofs.[18]

For almost a half-mile north of the landface, the peninsula had been cleared of trees and foliage to provide a clear field of fire. Running parallel to the landface from the river to the ocean was a newly erected palisade fence made of nine-foot-high sharpened pine logs. Halfway down the landface, a tunnellike "sally port" cut through the earthen wall so field artillery could be rushed from bombproofs to an elevated sally-port gun battery during an enemy attack. On the river side of the landface, where a narrow wooden bridge spanned a patch of marsh, the sandy road from Wilmington entered the fort through a gate in the palisade. The gate had no doors; instead, it was barricaded with sandbags and guarded by a section of field artillery.[19]

At the angle of the L, where the landface intersected the seaface, Lamb had constructed a massive earthwork called the Northeast Bastion. Its sloping, sodded walls towered forty-three feet above the beach, providing a magnificent, sweeping view. From his combat headquarters in the Pulpit Battery, a crescent-shaped eminence adjacent to the Northeast Bastion, Lamb would be able to see an enemy fleet miles away. From there he could also see both walls of his sprawling fort, the treeless plain to the north and the Cape Fear River to the rear. He could even see Battery Buchanan, rising hump-like more than a mile and a half away at the tip of Confederate Point. The huge bombproof beneath the Pulpit would serve as a field hospital during battle. Although combat headquarters would be located in the Pulpit, the fort's official headquarters were located just to the rear of the battery in a pine cottage built twenty-seven years earlier for the keeper of a nearby government lighthouse. The old wooden lighthouse was gone now, but it had given the peninsula its name, Federal Point—known as Confederate Point since the beginning of the war.[20]

From the Northeast Bastion, the fort's seaface ran along the beach—another line of bumpy, sodded traverses and armed gun chambers. Midway down the seaface in the Armstrong Battery was the pride of Lamb's armament, a colossal, 150-pounder Armstrong Rifled Cannon—said to be a gift to President Jefferson Davis from the gun's British manufacturer. The long-range Armstrong was perfect for Fort Fisher, where it could keep blockaders at bay. However, ammunition for the weapon was hard to get, so Lamb hoarded his limited supply for battle.

A telegraph station had been erected at the lower end of the seaface and lines had been strung on poles all the way to district headquarters in Wilmington. At the southern end of the seaface, a full mile from the Northeast Bastion, Lamb's greatest single engineering feat towered above the Atlantic. It was a mountainous, sixty-foot-high artillery emplacement known as the Mound Battery. For more than a year and a half, construction crews shoveled tons of beach sand onto a steadily rising hill until they could go no farther. Then they tore down the old lighthouse and built scaffolding for an inclined railway, so a small steam engine could haul load after load of sand up the hill. Finally, when it reached a height of sixty feet, the Mound was fortified and armed with two heavy seacoast artillery pieces.[21]

Atop the Mound, gunners could lob shells through the decks of any enemy ship attempting to enter nearby New Inlet, and a beacon was mounted to signal blockade runners. The Mound was visible for miles at sea. It was the talk of seafarers on both sides of the Atlantic and became a Confederate landmark. During an 1864 tour of the fort, President Davis was escorted to the Mound's summit, where he received a twenty-one-gun salute.[22]

By December of 1864, Fort Fisher's seaface was armed with twenty-four pieces of heavy artillery which, combined with the twenty on the landface, gave the fort forty-four heavy guns. Still Lamb kept strengthening the fortress. He built Battery Buchanan on the tip of the peninsula almost as an afterthought, adding it to protect New Inlet and the fort's rear. A rear attack seemed unlikely: the inlets were believed too shallow for the deep-draft Federal warships. Even so, Lamb hurried to finish Battery Buchanan, recruited a detachment of Confederate seamen to man its guns, and reinforced the rear of the fort with a line of rifle pits. Fort Fisher appeared impreg-

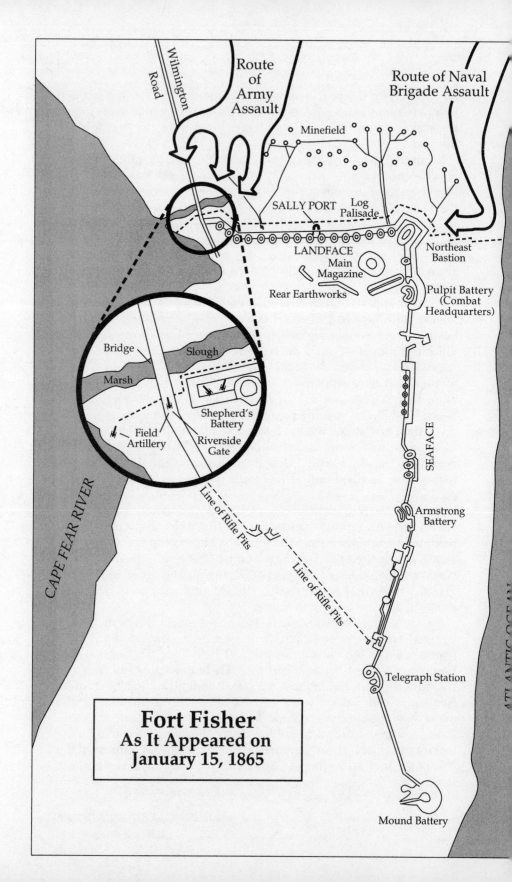

Route of Army Assault

Route of Naval Brigade Assault

Wilmington Road

Minefield

SALLY PORT
Log Palisade

LANDFACE

Northeast Bastion

Main Magazine

Rear Earthworks

Pulpit Battery
(Combat Headquarters)

Bridge

Slough

Marsh

Field Artillery

Shepherd's Battery

Riverside Gate

SEAFACE

CAPE FEAR RIVER

Line of Rifle Pits

Line of Rifle Pits

Armstrong Battery

Telegraph Station

Fort Fisher
As It Appeared on
January 15, 1865

Mound Battery

ATLANTIC OCEAN

nable. Its thick earthen walls could absorb the impact of the largest artillery rounds of the day and its numerous bombproofs provided more than 14,500 square feet of protection and storage. Behind the Northeast Bastion, in the fort's main magazine, a 60-foot-wide bombproof earthwork, Lamb had stored 13,000 pounds of black powder.[23]

In addition to the conventional defenses, Fort Fisher was also defended by the latest technology—an electrically detonated minefield. Confederate ordnance experts from Mobile, Augusta and Richmond had planted twenty-four explosive devices from the river to the beach north of the fort landface. Some were specially wired artillery shells; others were "torpedoes"—iron cylinders filled with 100 pounds of black powder. They were connected by an underground network of wires to a primitive electric battery inside the fort. The experts believed an enemy ground assault on the fort landface could be shattered by detonating the minefield.[24]

Lamb had built one of history's greatest fortresses, but at least one weakness remained. It was the same problem that endangered Confederate commands everywhere: a shortage of troops. Fort Fisher's garrison had doubled in the two and a half years since Lamb assumed command, but even so, the fort was now defended by fewer than 600 troops. More would be pulled in from nearby positions during an attack, but Lamb knew his great and heralded fortress was woefully undermanned. Equally troubling, the fort's garrison was inexperienced, composed primarily of the Thirty-sixth North Carolina, an artillery regiment recruited from the eastern part of the state. The Thirty-sixth had spent most of the war on Confederate Point and had had no serious combat experience. "The garrison," an officer bluntly observed, "consisted of one raw, inexperienced regiment that had never smelled powder."[25]

The soldier's life at Fort Fisher did have its challenges. Rations were often inadequate, drinking water was brackish and the "fever" was a serious threat in warm weather. "I am afraid this place is going to be very unhealthy this summer," one soldier wrote home from the lower Cape Fear. "Our supply of water from the cistern is getting very small and what there is is scarcely fit to drink. The rats got into the cistern in such quantities that the water tastes and smells very strong of the little devils which everybody knows is far from being pleasant. Our well water is also of the worst description, worse than any mud hole in the cypress ponds."[26]

Whipped by ocean winds and soaked by northeasters, Confederate Point could be miserable in the wintertime. "We have the most disagreeable weather down here I ever saw," complained one Tar Heel soldier. "It is so cold I can hardly keep away from the fire. The wind seems to be vying with the cold in rendering everything as miserable as possible." Summers could be equally uncomfortable; the temperature sometimes topped 100 degrees. "The weather is not to say warm, it is absolutely hot, hot enough to cook eggs—if we had any of that article down here," reported another Johnny Reb one August. "We've about quit work drills and everything else. We do nothing of a day but lounge about in the shade, when we can find anything like a shade. There are no trees and when night comes, instead of getting cooler, it positively gets warmer and the mosquitoes come in swarms. They attack on every side—some of them as large as hummingbirds, with bills a half an inch long. With the heat and the mosquitoes there is not such a thing as sleeping thought of. I go on the sick list every day so that I can sleep in the day, but I don't gain much by that game for there is too much noise for even a soldier to sleep."[27]

Garrison duty at Fort Fisher was often monotonous. A soldier considered himself lucky if he drew duty tending the post garden north of the landface or engaging in occasional target practice. Most troops spent day after day building up the fort's defenses. "Levelling sand hills," fretted a weary Johnny Reb, "is the worst work I ever did, standing in the sunshine, which is hot enough to roast an egg." The boredom was at times interrupted by skirmishes with the Federal navy. In June of 1863, Lamb's artillerymen traded fire with enemy warships after the vessels forced the blockade runner *Modern Greece* ashore near the fort. Two months later, in a skirmish over the blockade runner *Hebe*, the Confederates captured a landing party of 15 Federal seamen who were trapped while trying to fire the ship. Later, in the spring of 1864, Rose O'Neal Greenhow, the famous Confederate espionage agent, was returning from a mission to Great Britain when her ship, the *Condor*, was run aground off Fort Fisher by enemy blockaders. Afraid of capture, the determined Mrs. Greenhow insisted on trying to reach shore in a ship's launch and was drowned when the boat capsized in rough seas. Her body washed ashore and was prepared for burial by Daisy Lamb.[28]

Such excitement was rare at the fort, although routine garrison duty could be demanding. "Work, work—all the time and no rest except Sabbaths," complained another soldier. "Every man that is able to work has to go from morning til night preparing to receive Uncle Abraham." Soldiers who worked all day laying sandbags and shoveling sand for gun emplacements often had to spend the night on picket duty. "Tonight I will have to walk on the beach close to the water all night and listen to the roaring of the sea," grumbled a Confederate scheduled for picket duty in 1862. "I have spent some lonesome hours standing guard by the sea. Many a thought passes my mind while I am on guard. My mind is about home and the happy hours that I have spent and hoping that it would be so again, but everything looks mighty gloomy."[29]

A similiar sentiment was expressed by Sergeant Thomas McNeil, a college-student-turned-soldier, when he wrote home from Fort Fisher in late 1862. "The morality in the Army is terrible," he observed. "What a great thing peace would be, but there is so much wickedness among the soldiers, that it is no wonder we are scourged so terribly. I do not think the blessing of the Almighty will rest on our armies as long as the officers and soldiers are so wicked."[30]

In the atmosphere of war, human life could seem to lose its value, even among garrison troops. "We had three men killed two or three weeks ago by the bursting of a cannon," wrote a perceptive soldier posted to the Cape Fear defenses. "They were scarcely noticed, not near as much sorrow was felt as you would feel if your Ma would kill your pet chicken. When men are looking for their lives to be taken every day, they become indifferent as to the security of their lives and have a sort of don't care feeling whether they or anybody else is killed."[31]

Desertion was not uncommon among the troops serving on the Cape Fear. If caught, deserters were put to work at hard labor, forced to wear a ball and chain or publicly flogged. Three of Fort Fisher's soldiers were convicted of desertion and executed by firing squad while Lamb was in command—a duty he disliked, but conducted as ordered. A lesser offense would put a soldier in the post stockade or keep him on his knees pulling weeds all day.[32]

Off-duty diversions were few but welcome at the fort. Soldiers were sometimes allowed to take a steamer to Wilmington for a night in town, but most spent their free time at the fort. They played cards and shot marbles, attended the Sunday worship services conducted by chaplain Luther McKinnon, and went fishing with homemade rods and Minié ball sinkers. "I wish you could be down here some time to see us catch fish," wrote one soldier to a friend back home. "Sometimes we fish in the sea and catch from 15 to 20 barrels. At a channel we are getting good oysters to eat. You can get them anytime you go after them." Garrison life was occasionally enlivened with performances by the fort band or homegrown musicians from the ranks. "All the boys appear to enjoy themselves very well," wrote an optimistic young Reb. "Singing and playing the fiddle and dancing is the way we let our idle hours slip."[33]

Although Colonel Lamb normally forbade liquor on the post, some of Fort Fisher's troops somehow managed to pass their idle hours with a bottle. Inside the whitewashed post barracks, an occasional drinking spree might be uneventful. When a beached blockade runner yielded a cargo of spirits, however, the effect on the garrison could be dramatic. "A wreck was a most demoralizing affair," recalled a Confederate officer, who may have been given to exaggeration. "The whole garrison generally got drunk and stayed drunk for a week or so afterward. Brandy and fine wines flowed like water; and it was a month perhaps before matters could be got straight."[34]

Even an occasional skirmish or unauthorized binge did not relieve the monotony of garrison duty, and some soldiers eventually yearned for combat. The danger of battle, they argued, was preferable to constant boredom. "If the Yankees ever get this place they will never get us all alive," boasted one defender. "We are going to fight until they disable us and then we will look vengeance at them."[35]

Duty at Fort Fisher did have some benefits, however. Blockade runners sometimes rewarded the garrison with gifts of coffee, fruits and other commodities rarely available in the wartime South. Some soldiers also realized that they could be spending the war in far worse circumstances. "You can see the sun go down as if into the waves of the dark blue sea, which will create feelings of the most sublime nature," wrote a young soldier posted across the river at Fort Caswell. "In another direction you may see the most beautiful forest of live oak, so thick that it resembles a solid mass of green. The beach of the sea is also beautiful, being lined with the most beautiful shells you ever saw."[36]

In many ways, garrison duty was easier for Colonel Lamb, although his responsibilities were far greater than those of the soldier in the ranks. The continuous construction projects at the fort were constantly demanding, and on "moon nights" he was often at his post all night. Even so, he enjoyed some benefits of rank, including the presence of his wife and children. Daisy had left her parents to return South in 1863, after Sallie, the couple's third child, died of illness in Rhode Island. Aided by her parents, Daisy had persuaded Federal authorities to let her pass through the lines and rejoin her husband. Maria and Richard, the two oldest Lamb children, had come with her, but she had felt it best to leave her infant son, Willie, up North with her parents.[37]

She had been offered quarters across the river at palatial Orton Plantation, but she wanted to be closer to her husband. So, Lamb had ordered post carpenters to erect a rustic but comfortable pine cottage north of the fort at Craig's Landing, a dock overlooking the Cape Fear, near the post hospital and commissary. "I am at last settled in my little new home and am very comfortable indeed," Daisy wrote home, sending the letter North on a circuitous route through Bermuda. "I suppose to you just coming from our sweet beautiful home everything would look homely and plain enough, but to me . . . this looks quite charming. It is a dreary situation having no trees about it, but the beautiful view we have of the river nearly compensates for the want of them."[38]

In his off-duty hours, Lamb planted peach trees at the cottage and sowed grass, and he and Daisy found ways to entertain each other. They dined outside on their back porch, roughhoused with their children, read aloud to each other at night and took frequent horse-back rides across the peninsula to the beach. It was a family life unavailable to most Confederate officers and troops—even though Daisy and the children had to endure occasional gunfire from the Federal blockaders. At the little cottage north of the fort, the Lambs hosted a parade of colorful and influential guests—Confederate army and naval officers, renowned sea captains, British army officers, foreign correspondents and others. Guests often came calling with hard-to-find gifts, and although she sent much of the bounty to the post hospital, Daisy kept an unusually well-stocked wartime pantry. "Let me tell you the presents I had from captains in two days," she wrote home, "a large bag of white sugar, four bottles of rum, two jars of pickles, a large cheese, six boxes of sardines, a quantity of limes and two pineapples, a box of toilet soap, half a dozen bottles of claret, 1 doz. bottles of sherry and 1 doz. of port, two bottles of brandy and two of Madeira—and two beef tongues. Isn't that doing very well?" Charmed by Daisy's cheerful hospitality, travelers spread the word about the gracious hostess at Fort Fisher and eventually Daisy Lamb became known as "the heroine of Confederate Point."[39]

While serving as commander of Fort Fisher, William Lamb occasionally invested in cargo going through the blockade. It was a common practice among officers at coastal posts, although it carried a stigma of tawdriness—at least among professional soldiers. "It was the small fry generally who engaged in this discreditable business," commented a Confederate officer posted to Wilmington. "[They were] men who had been either in the retail grocery or dry goods business before the war, and who could not keep their hands from such pickings, or get over their old store habits. It was seldom you caught a West Pointer at this trading business, poor as most of them were. . . ." Lamb's investments hardly made him rich, but they could yield a welcome profit—in 1864, a single sale of wine and champagne netted him $1,070.[40]

He had little time for business, however; his duties kept him busy seven days a week, especially as the war progressed. As the Southern ports were sealed or captured one by one, and Wilmington became increasingly important, tension rose at Fort Fisher. Lamb kept the troops and slaves working feverishly. For three weeks in the fall of 1864, a general alarm was declared and the garrison was supposed to be in a state of readiness. On Monday, October 24, Wilmington headquarters received warning of an impending attack on Fort Fisher. It would be a joint army-navy expedition, due to appear offshore unannounced any day, Richmond advised. The report also came with an odd twist: an anonymous letter had arrived at Wilmington headquarters, reporting an alleged plot by Lamb's troops. They would supposedly spike their guns, cut the telegraph wires to Wilmington, then surrender to the enemy. Headquarters had treated the tip seriously, but Lamb considered the idea ludicrous. His garrison was untested, but he was convinced of their loyalty. When the time came, he believed, they would fight.[41]

But now he had another, more serious worry—his new commanding officer, General Braxton Bragg. The solemn-faced, gray-bearded Bragg had been sent to Wilmington by President Davis to replace the longtime commander of the district, General W. H. C. Whiting, who had helped Lamb create his military masterpiece on Confederate Point. Whiting was more than Lamb's superior; he was a mentor, a friend, the man for whom Lamb would name a son. Whiting inspired loyalty among subordinates and affection among the troops. Bragg was nothing like Whiting. Soon after he took command, Bragg made an inspection of Fort Fisher. He routinely examined the post, trailed by his staff and accompanied by North Carolina's governor, Zebulon Vance. Lamb was not favorably impressed. Bragg was cold, formal, aloof. Lamb would never enjoy a warm and productive relationship with the new commander as he had with Whiting for the past two years. But Lamb's concern transcended personalities— Braxton Bragg brought with him a record of controversy and failure.[42]

He had come to the Confederacy with all the right credentials: fifth in West Point's class of '37; combat experience in the Seminole War; three brevets and a lieutenant colonelcy from the Mexican War; prominent family ties in North Carolina; a notable career as a planter and state official in Louisiana—and the friendship of Jefferson Davis. In the Confederate army his ascent in rank and command had been impressive; he had risen from brigadier to major general to lieutenant general to full general in just over a year. In 1862, Davis had placed him in command of the Confederate Army of Tennessee. Skillfully outmaneuvering Federal forces in Tennessee, Bragg invaded Kentucky, taking a Southern army farther North than any other commander in the Western Theater.[43]

Then came the failures. He was forced to retreat from Kentucky, fought a costly, inconclusive action at Murfreesboro, and afterwards suffered a nervous breakdown. His defense of Chattanooga in 1863 ended in the loss of that vital rail center, and when he successfully counterattacked at Chickamauga, he failed to follow up the victory. Davis resisted high-ranking calls for Bragg's removal, but after receiving a humiliating defeat at Missionary Ridge, Bragg resigned his command. Davis ordered him to Richmond—not for censure, but for appointment as chief of staff.[44]

He may have been the most unpopular officer in the Confederacy. No one doubted his loyalty—he was steadfastly devoted to "the Cause"—but as a commander he was often timid and indecisive, and he stubbornly refused to admit error. He was a stern disciplinarian—some claimed he executed a deserter a day—but he was seen by many as an inept loser who was reluctant to fight and quick to retreat. When other generals passed through the ranks, the troops might cheer; not so with Bragg. Instead, the men would derisively yell, "Bully for Bragg, he's hell on retreat!"[45]

Much of the controversy stemmed from his personality. Plagued by migraine headaches, chronic indigestion and a nervous temperament, Bragg was often quarrelsome and niggling. One officer who knew Bragg insisted that once, while simultaneously serving as quartermaster and company commander, Bragg fell into a dispute with himself and finally had to summon his superior officer to settle the disagreement. "And to be entirely frank," confided a fellow officer, "there were some who did not hesitate openly to say he was simply muddle-headed. . . ." Contemporaries described him as unfriendly, unpleasant and vengeful, and subordinates spoke of repulsive personal habits and the absence of a social life. Few people liked Braxton Bragg. However, he continued to benefit from the president's confidence—and it was the president who wanted Bragg in command at Wilmington when an attack there seemed imminent.[46]

"Bragg has been sent to Wilmington," editorialized the *Richmond Examiner.* "Goodbye Wilmington!" Not all Wilmingtonians shared the newspaper's opinion—General Whiting had offended some locals—but Bragg's appointment as commander of the Department of North Carolina worried some Confederates. They feared Wilmington now awaited the same fate that had befallen Chattanooga. Colonel Lamb viewed Bragg's appointment as "a bitter disappointment," but he refused to believe Bragg's shadow of defeat would necessarily follow him to Wilmington. However, Fort Fisher's garrison received the news as a calamity. General Whiting was popular among the troops and they were troubled to learn he had been replaced by the hapless Bragg. Lamb could not help but wonder how untried troops would be affected by such disappointment if the current alert ended in battle.[47]

General Bragg was not the only officer who worried Lamb. He was involved in a long-running personality clash with his immediate superior, Brigadier General Louis Hebert. A forty-four-year-old officer with a distinguished service record, Hebert was artillery commander for the Cape Fear District and was headquartered across the river at Smithville. Lamb and Hebert were a study in contrasts. Hebert was a West Pointer and Lamb was a volunteer officer. Hebert was at times given to depression; Lamb was an optimist. Hebert occasionally indulged in off-duty drunkenness; Lamb was critical of such behavior. The contrasts rankled, and in October of 1864, Lamb officially requested permission to report directly to General Whiting, bypassing Hebert. The act incensed Hebert, who immediately ordered Lamb placed under arrest and removed from command of Fort Fisher. The punishment lasted only a few days, but it was too much for Lamb. He asked Whiting for a transfer, stating that he was "unwilling to stay under Brig. Gen. Hebert." Whiting had no intention of letting the gifted Lamb go elsewhere and he denied the request. By then it was November and rumors of a pending attack on Fort Fisher were circulating. Lamb decided to drop the issue.[48]

Yet it was almost certainly part of the equation he had to consider as he stood in the bitter cold on December 13 and watched Battery Buchanan's gunners go through their practice drill. Fort Fisher had been placed on alert, warned that the long-awaited enemy attack could come at any time. Yet he still had to answer to General Hebert, and General Whiting, the commanding officer he most trusted, had been replaced. Now, in overall command of the Cape Fear District, including Fort Fisher, was Braxton Bragg with his terrible record of failure. And then there was the current state of Fort Fisher. A large portion of the fort garrison was absent, sent across South Carolina to face Sherman in Georgia. A Yankee attack might be imminent, but Fort Fisher had been left undermanned, garrisoned by inexperienced, unhappy troops and equipped with an inadequate amount of ammunition. It was a troubling analysis, even for a positive thinker like William Lamb. Yet he knew he had built one of the most formidable military bastions in the world and he was confident it could withstand anything the Federal navy could throw at it. He had devoted the last two and a half years to building and strengthening Fort Fisher. Everything—all his time, all the planning, all the construction, all the resources the Confederacy could spare—everything had gone into creating an impregnable fortress strong enough to keep the Southern lifeline open. All along he had known that some-day the enemy would come. He had built the Confederate Goliath, and now perhaps the time of testing was near.[49]

3

"Something Must Be Done to Close Wilmington"

As COLONEL LAMB WATCHED PRACTICE ROUNDS SPLASH into the Cape Fear River, a giant fleet of Federal warships was steaming southward to attack Fort Fisher. At daybreak that morning—December 13, 1864—the fleet had been anchored at Hampton Roads, Virginia, where the James River spilled into Chesapeake Bay. As the sun lightened the eastern horizon, the USS *Malvern* fired a signal gun and hoisted a multicolored flag. Every ship's captain in the fleet understood the order: "Prepare to get under way."[1]

One by one the warships fell into line and headed seaward. On the nearby wharves and lining the shore, throngs of spectators shouted cheer after cheer for the departing warships. So large was the fleet that almost four hours passed before the last vessel was out of sight. Those on shore who cared to count recorded the passage of 56 ships of war, plus numerous tugboats, support vessels and supply ships. Included in the oceangoing parade were the huge 3,400-ton *Colorado* with its 52 guns and crew of 626, the 48-gun *Minnesota*, the 46-gun *Wabash*, the famous iron-plated steam frigate *New Ironsides* and four ironclad monitors: the *Canonicus*, the *Mahopac*, the

Monadnock, and the *Saugus.* The fleet carried 619 guns—more than ten times the amount of artillery at Fort Fisher.[2]

Last to weigh anchor and steam seaward was the *Malvern,* the fleet flagship, a 627-ton side-wheel steamer which served as a floating command post for the fleet commander, Rear Admiral David Dixon Porter. Anyone watching Porter direct the departure of his fleet surely would have considered him the ideal image of a naval commander—erect, dignified, serious and impressively uniformed in navy blue with gold lacing. At fifty-one, Porter retained a young man's muscular build, shaped by four decades of rigorous life at sea. He was actually a bit shorter than average, but it was easily overlooked; he carried himself like a much taller man. His thick, dark beard reached his chest and he often wore a deep-set scowl, giving him the look of a man constantly squinting into the sun.[3]

Authoritative and decisive, he barked orders with the bold self-confidence of a seasoned leader. He could be gruff, caustic and opinionated, but his cocksure attitude was tempered by a genuine sympathy for the common sailor, deeply ingrained by years in the ranks. Among subordinates, he inspired loyalty and respect, but his ways often grated upon fellow officers and superiors. He was ambitious and boastful—"vain, arrogant and egotistical to an extent that can neither be described nor exaggerated," reported a newspaper correspondent who knew him. "David . . . had no hesitation in trampling down a brother officer if it would benefit him," observed Gideon Welles, the U.S. secretary of the navy, who considered Porter "boastful of his own powers, given to exaggeration in everything relating to himself."[4]

Yet even his critics acknowledged Porter's abilities: as a naval commander he was bright, resourceful, energetic and competent. Welles readily credited Porter for having "stirring and positive qualities" and praised his "great energy, great activity and abundant resources." He was a fourth-generation naval officer. His great-grandfather had been a merchant seaman, his grandfather had commanded an American privateer in the Revolutionary War and his father and namesake had been a naval hero in the War of 1812. The sea was in David Porter's blood. He had taken his first cruise with his father at age 10. At 13, he did a brief stint in the Mexican Navy, and by age 15, he was a midshipman aboard the USS *Constellation.* He married a commodore's daughter, met and wooed aboard ship, and was promoted to lieutenant at 27. Despite commendation as a "brave and zealous officer" in the Mexican War—he led a daring landing party assault at Tabasco—he remained stalled at lieutentant's rank for almost 20 years. In 1861, he was hours away from leaving the navy

in frustration when he received an important command and chose
to remain in the service, anticipating the prospects of wartime duty
and advancement.[5]

Promotion came quickly. He commanded a mortar flotilla during
the 1862 campaign against New Orleans, received the surrender of
Forts Jackson and St. Philip, and in October of the same year assumed
command of the navy's Mississippi Squadron. He earned the official
thanks of Congress for his role in the joint army-navy victory at
Arkansas Post in early 1863, and when Federal forces captured
Vicksburg later that year Porter's role was cited by both Grant and
Sherman. For his part in opening the Mississippi, Porter was jumped
from commander to rear admiral, skipping the ranks of captain and
commodore and leaving in his wake a parade of embittered older
officers.[6]

A new command on the Mississippi put him in charge of more than
3,000 miles of waterways, and although he was prominently involved
in the ill-fated joint Red River Campaign, he was credited for salvaging the navy's reputation with a skillful retreat. His fame was in no
way comparable to that of his adoptive brother, Vice Admiral David
Farragut—the conqueror of New Orleans—who had carved a niche
in American history and folklore with his dramatic "Damn the
torpedoes!" victory at Mobile Bay. Even so, Porter had become the
second-most-famous naval figure of the war and, with a single spectacular victory, his fame could conceivably eclipse even Farragut's.
Earlier, Porter jealously had tried to convince Navy Department
officials that Farragut, then in his sixties, should be retired from
service due to old age. The Department rejected the suggestion, so
Porter was left to hope that the Fort Fisher Campaign would propel
him into the ranks of American naval heroes. "I intend to write my
share of the history of this rebellion," Porter privately boasted, and
he hoped his share of history would be boosted by his operation
against Fort Fisher.[7]

At precisely eight o'clock on the evening of December 13, Admiral
Porter and his flagship passed the Cape Henry lighthouse on the
Virginia coast, entered the Atlantic and headed southward. It was a
clear, starlit night, temperature about 36 degrees, and the sea was
calm, barely ruffled by a light breeze. The flagship easily overtook the
convoyed fleet, and when Porter retired to his stately quarters that
evening, he undoubtedly did so with a satisfaction he had not felt for
a long time. Such a mood was not simply the product of his environ-
ment, although his stateroom was renowned for its opulence. Porter
knew how to enjoy the benefits of rank—his flagship cuisine was
almost legendary and he had been known to stow horse-and-buggy

and hunting dogs aboard ship for use when needed. This night, however, the satisfaction he unquestionably enjoyed was produced by the long-awaited departure for Fort Fisher.[8]

For months, Porter had waited impatiently for this moment. He had been given command of what was probably the largest fleet in U.S. naval history and the charge of bombarding the Confederacy's most fearsome fortress into submission. But instead of steaming into action, he and his warships had been forced to lay idly at anchor for week after week. Patience was not a quality normally associated with David Porter, but neither had it earned him this very desirable assignment. He had been chosen, instead, for his proven ability at combat command, and perhaps because of some high-powered connections—and also, he would have to admit, by process of elimination.[9]

The opportunity had come back in August, while he was in Washington on navy business. Assistant Navy Secretary Gustavus Fox, who happened to be Porter's brother-in-law, had invited him to a prearranged meeting at the home of Postmaster General Montgomery Blair, who lived just over from the Navy Department, across the street from the Executive Mansion. Navy Secretary Welles—"Father Neptune," Lincoln called him—presided over the discussion. Spreading charts and maps on Blair's table, Fox and the white-headed, bewhiskered Welles had given Porter a top-secret briefing on plans for a long-delayed army-navy expedition against Fort Fisher. Admiral Porter, Welles revealed, was his choice to head up the navy's crucial role in the campaign—if Porter wanted the assignment. His answer did not require much thought: the next day Porter told Welles he would take the job. A day later, the two visited General Grant to begin plans for the expedition.[10]

The admiral undoubtedly congratulated himself on receiving the important assignment, but Welles had no reasonable alternative. Farragut had been his first choice, but the sixty-three-year-old naval hero was in poor health. He would eventually return to active duty, but he had declined the offer to head the navy's attack on Fort Fisher. Rear Admiral John A. Dahlgren, commander of the South Atlantic Blockading Squadron, had been briefly considered. The inventor of the Dahlgren cannon and other naval ordnance, Dahlgren was a bright, aggressive officer, but Welles felt Dahlgren had too little combat experience for such an important command. Rear Admiral Samuel F. Du Pont was out of the question. He had a distinguished record and impressive combat experience, but he had resigned his command in a dispute with Welles over an unsuccessful operation against Charleston the year before. Nor could Welles give the command to Rear Admiral Samuel P. Lee, who had been an earlier choice for the job. Welles had finally convinced General in Chief Ulysses S. Grant to supply the necessary troops for the Fort Fisher Campaign, and Grant's approval was conditional: he wanted a naval commander more aggressive than Lee.[11]

That left Porter. Among the navy's top-ranking combat commanders, Porter was the best available choice, Welles believed, despite the admiral's boastful nature and unrestrained ambition. "Porter is young," Welles confided in his diary, "and his rapid promotion has placed him in rank beyond those who were his seniors, some of whom it might be well to have in this expedition. But again personal considerations must yield to the public necessities. I think Porter must perform this duty." Porter was acceptable to Grant, and Welles needed Grant's support.[12]

Since 1862, Welles had been lobbying for a joint army-navy operation against Wilmington, but he had received little support from War Department officials, who had other priorities. In December of that year, at his urging, the idea had reached the planning stage: a flotilla of warships would bombard fledgling Fort Fisher, while ironclads ran past the Cape Fear batteries to support an army drive on Wilmington from New Bern. When they learned that the navy's gunboats were deemed too heavy to enter shallow New Inlet, however, army officials canceled the operation. Another expedition proposed in 1863 had met a similar fate.[13]

Still, Welles had stubbornly continued to push for an expedition against Wilmington. Finally in 1864, when Wilmington's increasing importance to the Confederacy had become obvious, War Department officials began to listen. By then, however, Colonel Lamb had transformed Fort Fisher into a world-class fortification—an unavoidable obstacle to Federal operations against Wilmington. Closing the port now meant capturing Fort Fisher. If it could be done at all, it would require a huge fleet of warships and a major commitment of troops. Up to 50,000 men would be necessary for a successful campaign against Fort Fisher, according to some officials, and such estimates made Grant reluctant to commit the army.

That summer, the determined Welles decided his best chance was to get President Lincoln's endorsement. Accompanied by Fox, he went to the White House. There he laid out his plan before Lincoln and Secretary of War Edwin M. Stanton. "Something must be done to close the entrance to Cape Fear River and the port of Wilmington," Welles argued. "I have been urging a conjoint attack for months. Could we seize the forts at the entrance of Cape Fear and close the illicit traffic, it would be almost as important as the capture of Richmond on the fate of the Rebels, and an important step in that direction."[14]

Lincoln and Stanton caught the vision, but neither wanted to force Grant into the project. Through the muggy summer of 1864, Welles continued his White House lobbying, and finally, in August, Lincoln gave his blessing to the proposal—but only if Grant felt he could spare the men. Grant approved of Porter, and he agreed to commit troops—preferably no more than 7,000 men. Grant approved of Porter, but he vetoed the War Department's choice for army commander, General Quincy A. Gilmore. A West Pointer and a veteran combat commander, Gilmore had been blamed for bungled operations against Richmond earlier that year, and was still recuperating from a battlefield accident. He was also quoted as saying that an operation against Fort Fisher would require at least 12,000 troops. Grant wanted no such pessimism. His choice for commanding officer was General Godfrey Weitzel, a twenty-nine-year-old corps commander and chief engineer for the Army of the James.[15]

The son of German immigrants, the Cincinnati-born Weitzel was a gifted West Pointer who had been appointed to the academy's engineering faculty at age twenty-three. He had begun the war as a lowly lieutentant, was cited for his conduct in operations against New Orleans and Port Hudson, made corps commander at age twenty-eight, and would end the war as a major general. His association with a couple of controversial political generals had caused some official muttering, but Grant liked him, considered him competent and named him as army commander of the Fort Fisher Expedition.[16]

Grant believed the fort could be taken with far less than 12,000 troops and to do it, he designated almost 7,000 soldiers from the 39,000-man Army of the James, entrenched near Richmond. The Army of the James was a recent invention, created in April of 1864 by the merger of the U.S. Army's X and XVIII Corps. Named for Virginia's James River, its principal area of operations, the Army of the James was notable for its lack of success. It had failed to take Richmond or Petersburg during the Bermuda Hundred Campaign, had been badly drubbed at Drewry's Bluff, and had failed to capitalize on its single big victory at Chaffin's Farm. Despite such a spotty record, Grant planned to put the Army of the James to further use—including action against Fort Fisher. As plans were being laid for the campaign, the Army of the James was reorganized to include a corps composed entirely of black soldiers. By late 1864, the Army of the James was already noted for its large concentration of black troops, officially known as the U.S. Colored Troops. Reorganizing all the black regiments into a single corps, the XXV Corps, created the largest force of black troops assembled during the war. The first-line troops in the Army of the James were white, however, and the principal force chosen for the Fort Fisher Campaign was the Second Division of the all-white XXIV Corps, commanded by General Adelbert Ames. It would be supported by soldiers from the Third Division of the all-black XXV Corps, under General Charles J. Paine. The expedition would include approximately 6,500 veteran infantry. Two batteries of artillery were also scheduled to go, along with contingents of engineers, signal corpsmen, couriers, carpenters and a small string of horses and mules. Colonel Cyrus B. Comstock, Grant's aide-de-camp, would serve as chief engineer of the expedition.[17]

While army officials hurriedly assembled a flotilla of troop transports, General Weitzel was ferried south by the navy to make a personal reconnaissance of Fort Fisher from the sea. Offshore Confederate Point, he studied Fort Fisher's bumpy profile for two days and interviewed naval officers who had blockaded the Cape Fear for more than three years. He also heard from several naval pilots who were Wilmington natives, and met with a local spy—the president of Wilmington's clandestine Loyal Union League—who had been secretly brought aboard. The general described the unidentified agent as a savvy intelligence operative who "knew every green pine tree between Wilmington and New Inlet." When he reported back to Grant, Weitzel was still confident Fort Fisher could be taken, but he had acquired a new respect for the fortification's awesome strength.[18]

Porter meanwhile had delivered a farewell speech to the assembled seamen of the navy's Mississippi Squadron and had officially relieved Admiral Lee as commander of the North Atlantic Blockading Squadron. Porter promptly reorganized the squadron's 120 ships into four divisions, each ordered to patrol a section of the coast from Wilmington to the Chesapeake Bay. From each of the four divisions he selected warships for the Fort Fisher Expedition and ordered all to report to station at Hampton Roads. There he organized one of the largest fleet of warships ever assembled. Finally, the Fort Fisher Expedition appeared to be nearing reality.[19]

Then the unexpected occurred. In a surprise move, General Weitzel's immediate superior, Major General Benjamin F. Butler, assumed field command of the expedition's army force. Butler commanded the Federal army's Department of Virginia and North Carolina, in which the expedition would be staged and conducted. He was therefore officially in charge of the operation, although responsibility for the army's part in the expedition belonged to Weitzel as field commander. When Butler exercised the privilege of rank and announced his intention to accompany the expedition, it meant command responsibilities automatically fell to him. Butler's decision was a shock to every principal in the operation, for Ben Butler was almost certainly the most controversial officer in the Northern army.[20]

"I always think of old Ben as a cross-eyed cuttle fish swimming about in waters of his own muddying," observed one general. "[Butler] is as helpless as a child on the field of battle and as visionary as an opium-eater in council," said another. Enemies were more affected by his presence: when Butler visited Point Lookout prison, his mere appearance caused a near riot among the captive Confederates.[21]

In wartime America, almost everyone had heard of Ben Butler, and most—North and South—had definite opinions about him, including many who saw him as an imaginative visionary and a champion of the public good. A savvy Massachusetts lawyer and a flamboyant politician, Butler was perhaps the best-known volunteer general in the Northern army. At forty-six, he was fat and balding, with a sagging face, puffy eyes and a drooping mustache. He wore his hair long in back and was ever ready with a quick witticism or a biting retort. "A vivacious, prying man, this Butler," observed a British correspondent, "full of life, self-esteem, revelling in the exercise of power." An awry left eye invited jokes about "Old Cockeye," but Butler's cleverness could turn even that affliction to his advantage. Once an opposing attorney accused him of eyeing the jury while addressing the judge; said Butler, "You can't tell which way I am looking."[22]

He was undeniably eccentric: at times he had been known to ride about on horseback, late at night, reciting poetry aloud, and in the field he sometimes galloped about attired not in the customary cavalry boots, but in white jean slippers adorned by heavy brass spurs. Even in childhood he was audacious. Denied his dream of attending West Point, he grudgingly enrolled at a Baptist college in Maine, where his mother hoped he would become a clergyman. Instead, the seventeen-year-old Butler was considered insolent by teachers and arrogant by students, who generally disliked him. Even as a pupil he could be vengeful, once deliberately misstating a Greek recitation in order to block his instructor's promotion to professor. When he so wished, he could be equally endearing, and once memorized the entire text of Matthew's Gospel—including the genealogy—just to please his mother.[23]

He was brilliant, few denied that. He became an acclaimed attorney and a richly successful businessman, although controversy followed him into both professions. He was admitted to the Massachusetts bar at twenty-two, set up a practice in Lowell, and quickly acquired a widespread reputation. He was known as a wily, sometimes unscrupulous foe, who attracted big clients, but was willing to defend low income millworkers. His thriving practice and some shrewd investments enabled Butler and his wife Sarah, a former theater actress, to live lavishly in an opulent home overlooking Lowell's Merrimack River.[24]

He built a strong political base by stumping statewide for a shorter working day for textile workers. At one rally, he whipped mill hands into a frenzy with a threat to torch the city if mill owners blocked the reform. He won his fight and established his constituency, but he also created some powerful enemies. Ben Butler was a "notorious demagogue and political scoundrel," raged an opposing newspaper. "The only wonder is that a character so foolish, so grovelling and obscene, can for a moment be admitted into decent society anywhere out of the pale of prostitutes and debauches."[25]

Despite the fervor of his critics, Butler was elected to a seat in the Massachusetts House of Representatives as a Democrat in 1852. Six years later he was elected to the state senate, but failed in the first of numerous campaigns for governor. At the 1860 Democratic National Convention, he created a convention spectacle by bolting from party favorite Stephen Douglas and voting fifty-seven times for Mississippi's Jefferson Davis, believing that Davis was the one man who could hold the Union together.[26]

Although he had no formal military training, Butler was fascinated by the military, perhaps because his father had been a dragoon officer in the War of 1812. While building his law practice, Butler had served as a colonel in the state militia, rising to brigadier by the eve of the war. Despite the urging of secessionist friends to come South, he fiercely supported the Union and raised a regiment of volunteers, the Eighth Massachusetts, which became the first regiment of troops to reinforce the nation's capital. Fearful of a secessionist takeover, tense government officials celebrated Butler's arrival and the Massachusetts politician-turned-general was catapulted into national fame, matched in headline space by President Lincoln alone. Butler did not mind the association; he had his own ambitions for the presidency.[27]

He became the first major general of volunteers appointed by Lincoln, but his spectacular wartime debut quickly dissolved into controversy—sparked by his cocky independence and military inexperience. "I never read the army regulations," he boasted, "and what is more I shan't, and then I shall never know I am doing anything against them." His first command ended in a minor but humiliating debacle at Big Bethel, but he recovered with a highly publicized victory at Hatteras Inlet. While the Lincoln administration delayed dealing with the escaped slaves pouring into Northern lines, Butler boldly declared them "contraband of war," thereby establishing a wartime precedent. He also became one of the first to muster black regiments, although he initially doubted their abilities as soldiers.

His ethics remained questionable: he reportedly asked army contractors for payoffs and authorized army purchases from his brother-in-law at inflated prices. As military governor of Louisiana, headquartered in conquered New Orleans, he was accused of illegally seizing $1 million from the French consulate, and was accused of stealing Southern silverware—an allegation that caused him to be dubbed "Spoons" Butler.[28]

He ordered a New Orleans man hanged for allegedly desecrating a U.S. flag, and inflamed the South by ordering his troops to arrest the women of New Orleans as prostitutes if they showed disrespect toward Federal soldiers. Known as the "Woman's Order," the controversial decree was issued after a New Orleans woman leaned out an upper-story window and emptied a chamber pot on Admiral Farragut's head. President Davis declared Butler an outlaw, to be hanged if captured, and throughout the South chamber pots were adorned with the image of "Beast Butler."[29]

In late 1862, Butler was removed from command at New Orleans under rumors he had amassed a fortune through his office. As the North's most prominent Democrat in uniform, however, he seemed immune to punishment. "Butler can do the most atrocious things— steal or murder—and be let alone," observed an amazed fellow officer. He was a constant source of frustration to Lincoln and the War Department, but his political influence usually prevailed. When removed from command at New Orleans, he was given command of the Department of Virginia and North Carolina, which later included the Army of the James. In May of 1864, Butler ineptly allowed the enemy to bottle up his army at Bermuda Hundred—a fiasco that brought him substantial disgrace. Again, however, he escaped serious disciplinary action: his forces were reduced and in late October, he was temporarily dispatched to New York City to oversee voting in the 1864 presidential election.[30]

By then, planning for the Fort Fisher Expedition was well under way and Butler had come up with what he thought was an ingenious idea for the campaign—a scheme he perhaps thought capable of salvaging his waning reputation. Butler had a fascination with military innovations: he had experimented with a battery of Gatling guns, although the weapon had been rejected by the Bureau of Ordnance, and once he had hired a balloonist to make aerial reconnaissance of enemy positions. Other ideas were bizarre: he had proposed using jets of water from fire engines to blast down enemy earthworks, and for a while he had promoted a plan to tunnel under Richmond and launch a surprise attack from beneath the city. His latest idea came from a newspaper article about the accidental explosion of two gunpowder barges at the British port of Erith. Reports said the blast leveled nearby buildings, caused substantial damage and inflicted numerous casualties.[31]

Why not fill an old ship with gunpowder, Butler reasoned, tow it close to Fort Fisher and ignite it? Such a huge floating bomb would surely level the enemy fort or at least paralyze its garrison. On his way to New York City for the election, Butler stopped in Washington and unveiled his powder boat scheme to government leaders, including President Lincoln. Lincoln was dubious, but the concept was "readily embraced" by the navy secretary, according to Butler. Ordnance experts from both branches of the service were ordered to make immediate studies of Butler's idea.[32]

The U.S. Army's chief engineer, General Richard Delafield, studied the plan, produced a detailed research document and predicted failure. "I consider that the explosion of a vessel load of gunpowder at the nearest point it can approach Fort Caswell or Fort Fisher can produce no useful result," he concluded. Privately, Delafield told Grant that the proposed explosion "would have about the same effect on the fort that firing feathers from muskets would have on the enemy." Lieutenant Commander William Jeffers of the Navy Ordnance Yard agreed, but Butler found a supporter in Major James G. Benton, commander of the Washington Arsenal. If a boat could be packed with 200 tons of powder and ignited within 100 yards of the fort, Benton believed, "the work will be seriously damaged by the explosion of its principal magazines, and the traverses and bombproofs may be shattered or overturned."[33]

Unlike General Delafield's findings, Major Benton's brief report cited no evidence and concluded with an admission that it was based on "little attention and thought . . . and the absence of all practical experience." Still, it was what Butler and others wanted to hear. Even Admiral Porter, normally skeptical and ever-critical, warmed to the idea. Within a few weeks of Benton's report, Porter was acting like the idea was his own. "I propose running a vessel . . . as near to Fort Fisher as possible with 350 tons of powder, and exploding her by running her upon the beach outside and opposite Fort Fisher," he explained to a subordinate. "My calculations are that the explosion will wind up Fort Fisher and the works along the beach, and that we can open fire with the vessels without damage."[34]

By the time Major Benton presented his opinion, President Lincoln had been reelected and General Butler was back in Virginia, where he arranged a meeting with Grant and Porter aboard the *Malvern.* There witnessed by General Weitzel and a stenographer, he dramatically unveiled his powder-boat scheme. The blast would unleash the force of a tornado, Butler enthused, and the resulting shock wave would flatten Fort Fisher's walls and kill most of its garrison. Any Confederates who survived the explosion would probably suffocate from poisonous gases, he predicted, and the army could merely walk in and claim the fort for the Union. His secret weapon, Butler confided, would revolutionize naval warfare.[35]

Grant was unenthusiastic, but he agreed to let the experiment proceed. Porter saw potential glory and readily agreed to furnish the ship, the explosives and transportation to the detonation site. After the meeting, one of his aides was openly skeptical. "Admiral, you certainly do not believe in this idea of a powder boat?" the officer scoffed. "It has about as much chance of blowing up the fort as I have of flying." Porter disagreed: "The names of those connected with the expedition will be famous for all time to come," he predicted, and ordered subordinates to find a suitable ship for the experiment.[36]

Selected for the job was the USS *Louisiana,* an aging, flat-bottomed vessel doing service as a blockader off the North Carolina coast. The 295-ton *Louisiana* had the required shallow draft necessary to run in close to shore. Taken to Hampton Roads and placed under the care of Major Thomas Lincoln Casey, an explosives expert with the Army Corps of Engineers, the ship was carefully camouflaged. She was quickly stripped of armament and masts; her deckhouse was moved forward to make more room for the explosives, and a 70-foot framework was erected on deck to hold more powder. That done, Casey ordered a fake smokestack erected near the ship's single stack and had the vessel painted a dull gray. When finished, the old ship easily could have passed for a blockade runner on a dark night—a deception that might be necessary to get the floating bomb close to Fort Fisher without drawing enemy fire.[37]

When finally refitted, the *Louisiana* was towed far away from the fleet Porter had assembled and was carefully loaded with approximately 200 tons of gunpowder. The powder was brought on board in barrels and 60-pound bags shipped in from as far away as Brooklyn and Boston, and was packed into every available space aboard ship. When Casey and his men finished, the vessel had become a giant seagoing powder keg. So that the barrels and bags of powder would explode simultaneously, Casey designed an intricate ignition system that employed timing devices, fuses and a "slow-match" to insure ignition. Then, as almost an afterthought, he stored a pile of "fat lighter"—rosin-filled heart pine—inside the ship's cabin to be set afire when the demolition crew abandoned ship.[38]

Despite all the planning, the Fort Fisher Campaign almost suffered the same fate as the earlier attempts to organize an expedition. At one point, Grant quietly decided to postpone the expedition: he felt Porter had been too obvious about assembling his fleet and too talkative about the intended target. Grant was certain that the numerous Confederate spies lurking around Hampton Roads had reported the huge fleet and its suspected destination, so he decided to let the rumors cool a bit before launching the expedition. The delay frustrated Porter, who was impatient to get under way. He was generally critical of the army anyway, believing the war had been needlessly prolonged so that greedy and glory-seeking officers could benefit themselves. The admiral also could be harshly critical of Grant, claiming that the lieutenant general's rapid rise in fame and rank was due at least in part to the combat support Porter and the navy had provided. "I never worked so hard in my life to make a man succeed as I did for him," he grumped to Welles. At one point, Porter wondered aloud if Grant would ever give the expedition the go-ahead. "I am afraid Grant is not sufficiently interested in this business," he confided to a friend. The navy was ready, he boasted, and was "full of zeal and full of fight."[39]

Then Grant saw reports in Southern newspapers that General Braxton Bragg and an estimated 8,000 troops had been transferred from Wilmington to face Sherman's army near Savannah. The reports were confirmed by independent intelligence. Grant responded quickly. He sent orders for General Weitzel and his troops to leave immediately for Fort Fisher in hopes of attacking the fort while Bragg and much of the region's troops were away. Weitzel's orders were sent through General Butler. Go now, Grant ordered, while good weather prevailed. But days passed and still the expedition did not depart: work on the powder boat was not complete. "I think it advisable for you to notify Admiral Porter, and get off without delay, with or without your powder boat," Grant wired Butler on December 4. "I feel great anxiety to see the Wilmington expedition off," he urged, "both on account of the fine weather, which we can expect no great continuance of, and because Sherman may now be expected to strike the sea coast at any day, leaving Bragg free to return."[40]

Finally, on December 12, the powder boat was ready. Next day, in the early morning darkness, Butler ordered the transports under way. They steamed out of the James River into the Chesapeake Bay, then turned northward and went up the Potomac in a feint to confuse any Confederate spies watching the army flotilla. During the night the transports reversed course, steamed downriver, entered the Atlantic and followed Porter's fleet southward. Not until the transports were underway did Grant know for sure that Butler planned to accompany the expedition. A few days earlier, during a visit with Grant, Butler had talked about going; then, on December 13, while en route downriver with the transports, he had stopped at Grant's City Point headquarters and confirmed his plans. Weitzel was a good general, Butler explained, but he was young and the Fort Fisher Expedition demanded a mature commander. Besides, Butler added, he wanted to make sure the powder boat experiment was properly conducted.[41]

Grant did not object—at least he did not prohibit Butler from going. It was customary for the departmental commander to remain with the main portion of his army—and the larger part of the Army of the James was staying in Virginia. However, Butler had the right and the rank to assume command of the troops dispatched for the expedition, and Grant let him. He was reluctant to prevent a departmental commander from accompanying his troops on such an important expedition—especially the controversial, influential General Butler. Privately, however, Grant was worried. "He did not have much confidence in General Butler's military abilities," a subordinate tactfully put it.[42]

Porter had no confidence in Butler whatsoever: the two despised each other. The hostilities had begun in 1862, when Butler publicly criticized Porter's role in the capture of New Orleans. It would be a lifelong feud, and from the campaign's beginning it affected the Fort Fisher Expedition. A few weeks earlier, Porter and Grant were walking along the bustling wharves at City Point, discussing Fort Fisher, when Porter looked up and saw Butler ambling toward them. "Please don't introduce me to Butler," he whispered to Grant. "We had a little difficulty at New Orleans, and although I attach no importance to the matter, perhaps he does." Grant waved away Porter's whispered concern. "Oh! You will find Butler is quite willing to forget old feuds," he replied, "and as the troops who are to accompany you will be taken from his command, it will be necessary for you to communicate with him from time to time."[43]

Grant then greeted Butler and introduced him to Porter. To the admiral's surprise, Butler invited him to lunch and, a few days later, took him on a cruise downriver aboard the *Greyhound,* Butler's headquarters ship. It was a voyage both would regret. The *Greyhound,* a former blockade runner, was regarded as the fastest ship on the James River. Porter despised his own flagship—the aging, slow-moving *Malvern*—so he quickly seized the opportunity to examine Butler's coveted vessel. As the *Greyhound* steamed downriver, Porter toured the vessel and was disturbed at the lax security aboard ship. He was making his way to the bridge to report a suspicious-looking group of civilians loitering in the ship's lounge when a violent explosion shattered the *Greyhound*'s engine room. The ship was enveloped in flames and sank in five minutes. Porter, Butler and others aboard barely escaped. Investigators blamed the explosion on Confederate saboteurs and Porter blamed it on Butler—another example of the general's blundering incompetence, he thought. Porter now wanted nothing more to do with the flamboyant general. "It requires great patience to deal with fools," he complained to friends, "and I have no patience to spare."[44]

Now, as the *Malvern* plowed through the dark Atlantic on the night of December 13, Porter felt confident the Fort Fisher Expedition would produce a great victory for him and the navy, hopefully with little interference from the canny, posturing Butler. That was Porter's primary complaint about this expedition—he would have to exercise at least some contact with Butler. For that, he blamed General Grant. "I expressly told him that I wanted nothing to do with General Butler," Porter would grouse, "and he promised me faithfully that he should not have any connection with the expedition." But Grant had allowed Butler to come after all, Porter privately griped. "Butler is too cunning for Grant and will make him do what he pleases," the admiral confided to friends. Meanwhile, the flotilla of army transports was preparing to follow the *Malvern* south, led by the headquarters ship *Ben De Ford* and General Benjamin F. Butler. Aboard the troopships, at least some soldiers shared Admiral Porter's opinion of the expedition's army commander. "Old Butler is here," a New York soldier wrote home, "and will perhaps command the expedition—in order to insure its failure."[45]

4

"There's a Fizzle"

ONE OF THE SOLDIERS KNEW WHERE THEY WERE GOING.
The flotilla of army transports entered the Atlantic on the
afternoon of December 14, one day behind Porter's fleet. The soldiers cheered as the ships got under way and regimental bands on
various vessels broke into spirited tunes. Watching Virginia's Cape
Henry recede into the distance, the troops could only guess where
they were headed. Speculation about their destination ranged from
Wilmington to Texas, and most apparently believed they were heading toward Savannah to reinforce Sherman's army.

"I wished you was here to tell me where we are going," wrote a
Federal soldier aboard the transport *Demolay.* "We think we will
bring up in South Carolina. Some say that we are going to Mobile,
but I guess not. I would like to know, but the opinion is that we are
going to Sherman."[1]

Seas remained calm, the weather clear, but it was still an uncomfortable voyage for some of the troops. "Five hundred soldiers are
crowded on the *Weybossett,*" complained one New Yorker. "Part are
on the decks, part between, and part of them are half smothered in
the lower hold, where they remain day and night, making their bed

on the coal. Coffee is made for them twice a day by steam, a caskful at a time. This, together with raw pork and hardtack, constitutes their rations."[2]

En route the troops learned of their destination, and the army flotilla reached its anchorage off the Cape Fear region the night of Thursday, December 15. General Butler had selected his own rendezvous site, a point off Masonboro Inlet—about 18 miles north of Fort Fisher—and had ordered the flotilla to anchor about 20 miles offshore, so the transports would not be detected by the enemy. He took the *Ben De Ford* and a courier tender farther south to make contact with Porter's fleet, which he expected to find at the fleet's rendezvous point 25 miles off Fort Fisher.

The fleet had not arrived. Butler hailed one of the blockaders stationed off the coast and questioned the captain, but no one had seen the admiral or his fleet. The *Ben De Ford* steamed back and forth at the rendezvous point all night, waiting for the fleet to appear at any moment. At dawn on Friday the 16th, Porter still had not arrived. Butler anchored and waited all that day and the next without any sign of the admiral or his fleet. The weather was beautiful and the ocean looked like a placid lake. Seas were so calm that Butler had his personal gig lowered and rowed himself over the smooth waters, savoring the exercise after days aboard ship.[3]

The wait was less enjoyable for the troops. The soldiers were restless, the crowded conditions were tiresome and the wait was monotonous. "We still float in the same place," one soldier penned in his diary. "Everybody wonders why we lie here, but no one, with the exception of General Butler and Admiral Porter, knows." They played cards and dominoes, wrote letters, swapped stories and fished off the sides of their ships, dubbing any catch a "Lincoln sardine." Aboard the troopship *C. W. Thomas,* the officers and their staff passed the time with some high-stakes, all-day poker games, and on the *Weybosett* troops improvised a variety show. "In the cabin where I was fortunate to be quartered, the evenings were enlivened by music and dancing," reported a grateful soldier. "We have a violin, good singers, and contrabands without number, whose performances would make you laugh yourself into an apoplexy." Fish chowder improved the rations and the pastimes helped, but the wait wore on the soldiers. "Tired! Tired! Tired!" one complained to his journal. "Oh! How I long to feel solid ground again. Inclined to the belief that my former fondness for the ocean was bosh. Oh when will this tiresome floating about end."[4]

Butler dispatched General Weitzel and Colonel Comstock in the *Chamberlain* to make an offshore reconnaissance of Fort Fisher. The

Chamberlain steamed within sight of the giant fort and the two officers studied its bumpy outline, now familiar to Weitzel, and then returned to the anchorage. By Sunday, December 18, the army flotilla was in its third day of wait—in excellent weather. Butler and his officers lamented the lost opportunity to make an easy landing, and even the troops began to wonder why they were not taking advantage of the perfect conditions to go ashore. "Weather fine, calm and warm, yet all unused," a sergeant observed. "And here we are without one thing to relieve the monotony and sameness."[5]

On Sunday, December 18, the naval tug *Du Pont* appeared, came alongside the *Ben De Ford,* and delivered a dispatch to Butler from Admiral Porter. The message made no reference to the fleet's delay, but reported Porter's intention to have left Beaufort on Saturday. The admiral expected even greater results from the explosion of the powder boat, and advised Butler to take his flotilla even farther out to sea, lest the explosion cause the ships' boilers to rupture.

Admiral Porter and the fleet finally arrived at the rendezvous point on Sunday night. The two old adversaries made no attempt to meet, communicating instead by dispatch. The delay had been caused by the powder boat: loading the extra explosives had taken longer than Porter had expected, and then the fleet had to wait on high tide to leave Beaufort. To Butler's surprise, Porter reported that he had just sent the powder boat toward shore for immediate detonation. Still avoiding face-to-face contact with Porter, Butler quickly dispatched Weitzel and Comstock to the admiral's flagship to protest the unilateral decision. The wind was up and a gale might be on the way, they told Porter. That would prevent the troops from landing and would give the Rebels time to recover from the explosion. General Butler advised detonating the *Louisiana* when a landing was imminent and that meant waiting another day to see if good weather would hold. The admiral complied and dispatched a fast tug to recall the powder boat.[6]

Next morning the wind picked up and light swells replaced the calm waters. A storm seemed likely, making an immediate landing impossible. Porter signaled his plans to Butler's ship: since a landing was impractical, he would "exercise" the fleet, putting the warships through battle formation and rehearsing the plan of attack against Fort Fisher. The fleet steamed into battle lines about five miles offshore from Fort Fisher, moving for the first time within sight of the fort.

By dusk, the wind was blowing hard from the northeast, the sea was rolling in whitecaps and experienced seamen knew a strong gale would soon strike. The landing would have to be postponed until the storm ended. By now the troop transports were low on water and coal, so Butler took the flotilla to Beaufort, where they could recoal, resupply and ride out the storm closer to safety. The troops remained aboard ship as the transports tried to weather the gale.[7]

It was a fierce northeaster, lasting two days and striking the flotilla with stunning violence. Seasickness seemed epidemic and even the cockiest soldiers appeared unnerved by the ferocity of the storm. Army Chaplain Henry M. Turner of the First U.S. Colored Troops recorded the ordeal in his diary:

> About twelve o'clock the ocean was covered with white foam and rolling waves, but still the wind increased, and higher did the billows roll until great mountains, towering apparently up to heaven, came dashing along in sublime vengeance. . . . Many, for a while, tried to laugh and shake off their fears, but about eight o'clock we ceased laughing. I had been praying all the time, and I believe many others were. Now all began to feel serious and solemn. Even the crew looked and spoke apprehensively. Finally, an awful sea came and broke in our wheel-house. Still the raging waters and howling winds grew worse.
>
> At last many of us gave up all hope. I lay down and bade my mother, wife, and children farewell, and after asking God to protect them and bring us together in heaven to be separated no more, I begged the Lord to put me to sleep, and that if it was His will that the ship should be dashed to pieces, I should remain asleep and be spared the heart-rending spectacle of nearly fifteen hundred men launched into eternity in one moment.[8]

When Turner and the other troops awakened the next morning, the storm was finally over and not a man had been lost. There were other victims, however; on the transports *Salvo* and *Charles Thomas,* the expedition's small string of horses had panicked, kicking down their stalls and doing such damage that troops on the vessels had to load their rifles and shoot the animals. Some soldiers, tossed about during the gale or struck by fallen objects, were left with minor wounds and bruises. "Everything movable was dashed and slammed around in the most confused manner," reported one man. "The officers rushed across the cabin like locomotives off the track. One shut the door of his stateroom on his coattails and then pitched forward and tore the tails clean off. The poor darkies dove around, butting their hard heads through the panels and howling like demons in pain." Aboard the *Baltic,* the prolonged officers' poker game continued just as it had throughout the gale. On the transport *Montauk,* however, the gale had produced at least a temporary change in behavior among the troops that Sergeant-Major Christian Fleetwood found commendable. "[I was] amused at the sudden conversion of the boys by the storm," he observed. "A night of prayer for once— quite an agreeable change from the usual swearing."[9]

With seas calmer, the flotilla docked at Beaufort, but few of the weary troops were allowed ashore. General Butler did not want some land-happy, half-drunken soldier to reveal the expedition's destination. His attempt at secrecy did little more than inconvenience the troops: the "secret" was already out. Although the War Department had jailed one newspaper reporter who discovered the expedition's target, news of the expedition was already public. Newspapers in Boston and Philadelphia had reported the expedition's departure and by the time the flotilla docked in Beaufort, newspaper readers in Richmond knew Fort Fisher was the target.[10]

While at Beaufort, Butler wired Grant a terse, coded telegram: "Have done nothing—been waiting for navy and weather." He followed it with a detailed report, sent by mail, which outlined the expedition's activity—or lack of it—since leaving Virginia. On Friday morning, December 23, Butler dispatched an aide with a message to Admiral Porter, reporting the army's plans to return to the rendezvous site the following night, Christmas Eve. The naval bombardment and the landing could take place the next morning, Christmas Day.[11]

Porter had other plans. The naval fleet had ridden out the storm at the rendezvous site without loss of life or vessel. Despite high seas and gale-force winds that struck the fleet with the violence of a hurricane, even the low-riding ironclads and the heavy-laden *Louisiana* had survived without serious damage. With his fleet intact, Porter decided not to wait for General Butler or his army—the navy would unilaterally take the honor for exploding the powder boat against Fort Fisher. When Butler's aide arrived with his dispatch on the afternoon of December 23, Porter informed him of his plans: he would have the *Louisiana* towed into shore late that night and exploded at 1 A.M. The naval bombardment would begin sometime the next day. The aide immediately reversed direction and steamed full speed back toward Beaufort to report Porter's intentions, but rough seas kept him outside Beaufort's harbor until the next morning.[12]

When Butler received the news, he was furious. "The Admiral supposed he would blow the fort all to pieces, and be able to land with his marines and take possession of it," Butler fumed. His officers agreed. That was "fine cooperation," they groused sarcastically— Porter wanted to destroy Fort Fisher in the army's absence so he could claim all the credit for himself. Immediately, Butler ordered his headquarters ship to head for Fort Fisher, leaving orders for the transports to follow as soon as the recoaling was finished. He knew, however, that by now his secret weapon—the powder boat—had been exploded for better or worse.[13]

◆

A rosy hue colored the western sky when Porter ordered the fleet to move farther out to sea. He had announced his plans to General Butler's aide earlier that day, and now began to prepare for the explosion he hoped would level Fort Fisher. Tomorrow was Christmas Eve and if the powder boat experiment worked as planned, there would be few survivors to celebrate Christmas in Fort Fisher. He took the fleet to an anchorage twelve miles farther out to sea and ordered all the ships to release the steam from their boilers—so the boilers would not be ruptured by the distant explosion. Left behind to tow the *Louisiana* to shore was the USS *Wilderness*.[14]

The dangerous task of detonating the giant floating bomb belonged to a small contingent of volunteers led by Commander Alexander C. Rhind, an experienced veteran of numerous risky ventures on the coasts of the Carolinas and Virginia. "Great risks have to be run and you may lose your life in this adventure," Admiral Porter bluntly advised Rhind, "but the risk is worth the running, when the importance of this object is to be considered and the fame to be gained by this novel undertaking. . . ." If Rhind and his volunteers could successfully detonate the powder boat, Porter believed, the damage to Fort Fisher would be worth all the dangers involved in the mission. "I think that the concussion will tumble magazines," he predicted, "and that the famous Mound will be among the things that were, and the guns buried beneath the ruins. I think that houses in Wilmington and Smithville will tumble to the ground and much demoralize the people, and I think if the rebels fight after the explosion they have more in them than I gave them credit for. . . . I expect more good to our cause from a success in this instance than from an advance of all the armies in the field." Rhind readily accepted the assignment and chose as his second-in-command Lieutenant Samuel W. Preston, a handsome young officer with a reputation for coolness under fire. For his crew, Rhind picked twelve volunteers from his ship, the USS *Agawam*. They would ride the floating bomb to its final destination, set the charges and abandon ship, rowing back to the *Wilderness* in launches.

At 10:30 on the night of December 23, the *Wilderness* began towing the *Louisiana* toward shore with Rhind and his crew aboard the powder boat. Towing the ship meant its engines did not have to be fired until the last moment, reducing the chance of a premature explosion. As the two vessels cruised through the darkness toward Fort Fisher, Acting Master's Mate Henry Arey, commanding the *Wilderness*, warily watched for any sign of the enemy. His ship's guns were loaded with grapeshot and canister, just in case Confederate boarding parties appeared from out of the night. The two ships continued shoreward without interruption, however, until Arey estimated they were 500 yards offshore from Fort Fisher. Then seamen aboard the *Wilderness* flashed a green lantern three times and cast off the tow lines. It was the signal to go.

The *Louisiana*'s engines were fired, and at 11:30, with a full head of steam in her boilers, the old ship moved slowly toward the beach and the distant, towering walls of Fort Fisher. Rhind wanted to take the craft to within 150 yards of the target, but when he could see the fort walls silhouetted in the darkness, he began to worry that the powder boat would be spotted by Fort Fisher's sentries. As he pondered his next move, a ship suddenly approached. It was a blockade runner, the *Little Hattie*, making her run toward New Inlet in the darkened shallows. Quickly, Rhind ordered the *Louisiana*'s pilot to steer the ship behind the *Little Hattie*'s wake, hoping that if sighted the powder boat would be mistaken for another blockade runner. The camouflaged *Louisiana* followed the blockade runner down the shoreline until Rhind judged they were about 300 yards offshore Fort Fisher's Northeast Bastion. Then he killed the engines and dropped anchor in the quiet darkness. He wished he could have taken the ship closer to the fort, but he felt he had pushed his luck far enough—300 yards would have to do. Actually, he had misjudged the distance. The *Louisiana* was no closer than 600 yards from the fort.

The ship seemed to be drifting, so Rhind dropped a second anchor, then dismissed all the crew except Lieutenant Preston and a volunteer engineer, Anthony Mullin. After the other crewmen rowed away in the night toward the *Wilderness*, Rhind and his two companions began setting the powder boat's ignition devices. On the starboard and port bows and in the engine room, they set three clock devices to simultaneously activate the ignition fuses at 1:18 A.M. Then they lit backup candles and a slow-match, which would eventually burn their way to the powder if the fuses somehow failed. Finally, as they prepared to lower their escape launch, Rhind tarried long enough to set fire to the pile of "fat lighter" stacked beside the ship's cabin. As a small blaze began to spread through the woodpile, Rhind joined Preston and Mullin in the launch. With clocks ticking, candles burning, slow-matches slowly hissing and the "fat lighter" ablaze, they rowed furiously toward the *Wilderness,* out of sight in the distant darkness. It was almost midnight.[15]

Minutes later they reached the *Wilderness* and were taken aboard. The warship promptly weighed anchor and steamed away at full speed, firing rockets to signal the other warships that the great bomb was prepared to explode. When the ship joined the rest of the fleet at anchorage forty-five minutes later, Admiral Porter was steaming up and down the lines in the *Malvern,* signaling his ships to stand by for the explosion. The air was a mild 45 degrees, a slight breeze blew from the west and the night sky was clear and starry. Toward shore, a distant red glow appeared above the ocean horizon—Rhind's "fat lighter" was flaming on the *Louisiana.* Everything else was dark. Aboard the warships, sailors lined the rails and crowded the rigging, joking and talking as they waited for the distant explosion Porter believed would herald a new era in naval warfare. The newspaper reporters the admiral had brought along to publicize the event stared intently at the flickering glow to the west, occasionally checked their pocket watches, and waited to record history.[16]

At 1:18 Christmas Eve morning, the deadline arrived—but nothing happened. Porter, Rhind and the fleet's sailors braced themselves for the blast, but saw nothing. The newspaper men rechecked their watches. One-thirty arrived, then 1:45. The explosion was almost a half-hour overdue. Still, except for the distant red glow, the ocean horizon remained dark and silent. Then, at 1:46 A.M., the powder boat exploded.

In the darkness to the west—toward Fort Fisher—a huge, brilliant geyser of flame erupted, quickly followed by a gentle vibration. As the trembling increased, the masts and spars on the vessels began to rattle. A distant, thunderlike rumble began to swell and quickly became a loud, rolling roar, punctuated by a series of *booms.* Ensign John W. Grattan, an aide to Porter, described the explosion in his shipboard diary: "Suddenly a bright flash was observed and a stream of flames ascended to a great height and spread out in an immense sheet of fire, illuminating for an instant the whole horizon." *New York Times* correspondent W. H. Whittemore said the explosion produced a deep, heavy blast that sounded something like "the discharge of a 100-pounder." Standing at the rail of the USS *Montgomery* with an Associated Press reporter, Whittemore watched a colossal wall of pale gray smoke rise from the shoreline and roll silently toward the fleet like a massive thundercloud. "As it rose rapidly in the air, and came swiftly toward us on the wings of the wind, [it] presented a most remarkable appearance," he reported, "assuming the shape of a monstrous waterspout, its tapering base seemingly resting on the sea. In a very few minutes it passed us, filling the atmosphere with its sulphurous odor, as if a spirit from the infernal regions had swept by us."[17]

Then there was silence—and darkness. Commander Rhind had expected a much larger explosion. Aboard the *Wilderness,* he turned to the officers lining the rail beside him. "There's a fizzle," he said. Then he went below.[18]

At first light, the USS *Rhode Island* steamed toward Fort Fisher. Aboard was Major Thomas L. Casey—the man who had armed the *Louisiana.* From a safe distance, Casey studied the fort through binoculars, searching intently for damage. He found none. "The edges and crests of the parapets remained as sharp and well-defined as ever," he reported to Admiral Porter. The fort's barracks were still standing, apparently undamaged. The log palisade was still intact. The fort's walls appeared as strong as ever. Even the rusting smokestack of an abandoned blockade runner beached nearby appeared to have escaped any damage. The powder boat experiment Porter expected to revolutionize naval warfare had proved to be a loud and spectacular failure. Fort Fisher would have to be reduced by naval bombardment.[19]

◆

Colonel William Lamb had just gone to bed when the *Louisiana* blew up. Fort Fisher was undamaged—not even the marsh grass on the fort's sloping walls was displaced—but the fort's sentries immediately sounded the alarm, alerting Lamb and the garrison. Most affected by the explosion was a battalion of teenage soldiers, the North Carolina Junior Reserves, which was camped on the beach near the blast site. Although unharmed, they were jarred from their blankets "like popcorn from a popper," one said—and were frightened senseless by the blast. Some said the explosion was heard as far away as Beaufort, some seventy miles north of Fort Fisher. It was particularly loud in Wilmington, where it startled officers at army headquarters. General W. H. C. Whiting quickly telegraphed a query to Fort Fisher. Colonel Lamb replied with his best guess: an enemy blockader apparently ran aground in the night, was set afire and abandoned by its crew, then blew up when the fire reached the ship's magazine.[20]

If Lamb's explanation relieved General Whiting, it did so only temporarily. For two years, since he had assumed command of Wilmington and the Cape Fear region, Whiting had worried about an enemy attack. He knew it would come someday and he had tried to be ready. He was a skilled engineer—perhaps the best in the South—

and had been mentor as well as commander for young Lamb. Whiting's extensive professional knowledge complemented Lamb's natural gifts. It was this combination of knowledge, talent and zeal that had made Fort Fisher so formidable and so famous—and had kept the Wilmington open to blockade running.

Whiting had transformed the Wilmington defenses, molding the crucial port's light and spotty defense system into a model of military protection. He had assumed command just as the 1862 yellow fever epidemic was ending in Wilmington and upon arriving he found the port almost defenseless. "I find everything in confusion," he reported to Richmond, "owing to the pestilence, and works in many cases [have been] stopped or left unfinished." The city's defenses were inadequate; the area's largest fortification, Fort Caswell, was obsolete and isolated; Colonel Lamb had just begun expansion of Fort Fisher; and the command was dangerously lacking in troops. Whiting immediately began to fortify Wilmington and the entrance to the Cape Fear River, concentrating especially on Fort Fisher, which he and Lamb considered to be the anchor of the Cape Fear defense system. He dramatically improved Wilmington's defense capabilities, but even so, he was destined to exercise a two-year command marked by strife and controversy.[21]

For William Henry Chase Whiting, strife and controversy were nothing new: such was the nature of his wartime career. That was ironic, for Chase Whiting had been viewed by many as the rising star in the "old army's" prewar engineering corps. He was literally a soldier's soldier—the son of Lieutenant Colonel Levi Whiting, a forty-year career army officer. His parents were Massachusetts natives, making him a Northerner by heritage, but Whiting was born in Biloxi, Mississippi, while his father was on duty in the South, and it was the South that won Chase Whiting's devotion. An exceptional student, he graduated from Boston High School in his mid-teens and finished first in his class at Washington's Georgetown College, completing a two-year program in a single year. He was named to West Point by President John Tyler, and graduated first in the class of '41—holding a scholastic record that would not be surpassed until the graduation of Douglas MacArthur more than sixty years later.[22]

At posts on the Atlantic, Gulf and Pacific coasts, he quickly distinguished himself. He helped construct engineering projects at Pensacola, Florida; supervised work at Georgia's Fort Pulaski; and dodged Comanches while surveying a military road across Texas. He was transferred to the Cape Fear region a few years before the war and was posted to Fort Caswell, which would later fall under his command. While there, he met Katherine Davis Walker of nearby

Smithville and in 1857, they were married. It was a bond that further strengthened his deep Southern sympathies. At the outbreak of war, he quickly resigned his captain's commission and joined the Confederate army.[23]

He achieved prominence rapidly, rising from major to general in six months. He was present for the war's opening shots in Charleston, assisting his close friend, General P. G. T. Beauregard. For a month, he commanded the Southern forces at Wilmington, but was called to the Virginia front before he could really begin work. Appointed chief of staff to General Joseph E. Johnston, he was promoted to brigadier on the field at First Manassas, saw action as a divisional commander at Seven Pines, served in Stonewall Jackson's 1862 Valley Campaign and was a brigade commander at the Seven Days Battles. Some considered him the best engineer in the Confederacy, and his conduct in combat won praise from Johnston, Jackson and Beauregard. His rapid rise in Confederate service abruptly halted, however, when he fell into a personal feud with President Davis.[24]

Although he was short, Whiting was an aristocratic-looking officer—a slim figure with a well-trimmed mustache, graying hair and dark eyes. "He was a small man, but his bearing was military and his manners most courtly," recalled a fellow officer. "He was a man of wide reading and great scientific knowledge, and was capable of adorning a court of royalty." He drilled his troops thoroughly, was equally attentive to their needs in the field and earned widespread affection among soldiers under his command, who nicknamed him "Little Billy." While he enjoyed the affection of his troops and the respect of fellow officers, Whiting rankled some of his superiors, who considered his self-confidence close to insubordination. He was brusque at times, and was quick to express disdain for ideas and orders he deemed foolish. Such testiness was usually tolerated because of his obvious talent, but when Whiting offended President Davis, "Little Billy's" career became clouded.[25]

The fateful slight came early in the war, when the president ordered General Johnston's army reorganized so the troops could be brigaded by states. Davis claimed that the system would create a healthy rivalry among the brigades; others believed the order was designed to enable troops from Davis's home state of Mississippi to distinguish themselves more easily. Whiting had been chosen to command one of the new Mississippi Brigades, but he opposed reorganization. In a blunt report to the War Department, he described the president's plan as "a policy as suicidal as foolish . . . inconceivable folly . . . solely for the advancement of log-rolling, humbugging politicians." Said Whiting: "I will not do it."[26]

The president was incensed. He promptly ordered the War Department to send Whiting "a stern rebuke," and only Johnston's intervention protected Whiting from an immediate and humiliating demotion to the backwaters of the war. Still, Jefferson Davis was viewed by critics as one who never forgot a friend and never forgave an enemy, and the president had clearly lost faith in Chase Whiting. When Johnston recommended Whiting for a promotion in May of 1862, Davis denied the request. That summer Whiting performed an act that might have put him back in the president's good graces: while searching for field headquarters, Davis accidentally took a wrong turn and was heading straight for enemy lines when Whiting overtook the chief executive and prevented his possible death or capture.[27]

The gesture did no good. Davis heard rumors that Whiting had publicly referred to Stonewall Jackson as a fool; that he was drunk on the field at the Battle of Gaines Mill; that he wanted to overthrow the presidency and install General Johnston as dictator. The president mentioned the rumors to Acting Secretary of War Gustavus W. Smith, a friend of Whiting's, who asked how Davis received such information. "I am not on the witness stand," Davis hotly replied. Whiting, he said, was infecting the army with a "mutinous and disorganizing spirit."[28]

Certain his career was in a permanent stall, Whiting unloaded his frustrations to Robert E. Lee, who had replaced Johnston as commander of the Army of Northern Virginia. Later, in the fall of 1862, when room was needed in the officer corps for the promotion of John Bell Hood, Lee diplomatically suggested that the War Department find a post in need of an engineer of Whiting's superior skills, citing him as "an officer of great ability."[29]

And so it was, in November of 1862, that General W. H. C. Whiting came to command Wilmington and the eight-county Cape Fear District upon orders of the War Department. Although perhaps disappointed to be posted to Wilmington for the third time in his military career, he was at least far away from the displeasure of the president—and he immediately set about the task of fortifying his command with typical zeal. For the next two years he oversaw the construction of a model coastal defense system second to none in the Confederacy, regarded with awe by blockade runners and viewed with uneasy respect by the enemy.[30]

Even so, Whiting believed his famed defense system was paper-thin due to lack of troops. He relentlessly petitioned the Confederate War Department for more men and more ordnance. "My first and last request," he wired his superiors as bluntly as ever, "will be for

troops the instant they are available. The Department is undoubtedly aware of the imminent need for them for the defense of Wilmington." Whiting was granted more troops, not the 10,000 he asked
for, but all Richmond believed it could spare. Repeatedly, he called
for reinforcements—more men to garrison the Cape Fear forts, a
sizable body of cavalry to patrol the beaches, relocation of winter
camps from the war's front lines to Wilmington. The Cape Fear
fortifications grew ever more formidable, and Whiting's accomplishments won him promotion to major general in 1863, but his repeated
requests for reinforcements were consistently ignored. When an
enemy attack was imminent, the War Department promised, he
would receive the troops he needed.[31]

The assurances did not alleviate Whiting's concerns: his troops
were generally inexperienced. His garrisons were too small to make
an adequate defense. He had few infantry and only a sprinkling of
cavalry, and he was afraid the South's poor rail system would fatally
delay the arrival of reinforcements, leaving him to defend the vital
port with reduced garrisons and support troops composed of the
Junior and Senior Reserves—young boys and old men of the Home
Guard. "The little boys are prostrate with all the diseases of children
and are too weak to bear arms," he complained. "Their officers, made
by election, are entirely ignorant." When an attack came, he believed, it would be made in force and the defenders would have to
endure a gruesome pounding. "Defenders here must go through an
ordeal that only old soldiers can stand," he prophesized. "I have
nothing but a few hundred boys and old men, utterly inefficient and
unreliable, as experience has shown, and totally inadequate." No
matter how eloquent or demanding he made his pleas, Richmond
was adamant—no sizable reinforcements would come until attack
was imminent. Whiting could only seethe in frustration.[32]

Even in Wilmington, far from the front, he became embroiled in
controversy. Within a few weeks of assuming his new command, he
was feuding with Wilmington officials, the city's naval commander
and North Carolina's governor. Whiting was accused of bullying city
officials and administrating his command like a dictator. A dispute
with the local naval commander over control of the blockade-running trade eventually resulted in a reprimand from the War Department. And his attempts to shut down a state-owned saltworks, which
he believed was a base for Unionist spies, earned him the enmity of
the state's powerful governor, Zebulon B. Vance.[33]

Vance had asked the War Department to post Whiting to Wilmington because of the general's reputation as an engineer, but complaints from city officials and the clash over the saltworks soured the

governor's enthusiasm for Whiting. The general had acquired a reputation for heavy drinking—an accusation Whiting steadfastly denied—and Vance openly discussed the rumors with other state officials. Whiting fired off a letter to Vance, chastising him for spreading the rumor, and Vance replied with a catalog of charges against Whiting. "I have even swallowed in silence some very rough and discourteous remarks of a personal character more than once reported as having fallen from you," he retorted.[34]

Not content merely to spar with Whiting, Vance took his complaints to Robert E. Lee in September of 1864, lobbying for Whiting's removal. The timing of the governor's demand was unfortunate: just four months earlier General Beauregard, who knew Whiting was chafing at his backseat post, had arranged for him to assume an important command near Petersburg. There, at the Second Battle of Drewry's Bluff, Beauregard tried to surround and demolish General Butler's army. The attack floundered in a heavy fog, Butler's forces escaped destruction and Whiting was saddled with much of the blame for failing to bring up his force on time. One of Beauregard's subordinates, Brigadier General Henry A. Wise, accused Whiting of drunkenness on the field. A politician–turned–soldier, Wise was somewhat of a bumbler with several notable defeats on his own record, but he was also a most influential Virginian—former governor, U.S. congressman and diplomat—and his accusations carried weight.[35]

Whiting, who had been ill and sleepless at the time of battle, swore "on his honor as a gentleman" that he had drunk nothing stronger than coffee during the engagement, a statement strongly supported by his staff. In fact, abstinence was the problem, some of Whiting's friends were said to have confided. "He was afraid of getting drunk & therefore did not touch any liquor," one officer reported. "His nerves, accustomed to have a stimulant, were upset by the lack of it." There was no proof of any wrongdoing, but even his friend Beauregard gently cited Whiting for a poor showing. In response, Whiting resigned his Petersburg command and returned to Wilmington in humiliation. Ironically, his questionable performance occurred on the day President Davis had chosen to visit the battlefield, reinforcing the president's distrust.[36]

By the time Governor Vance petitioned for Whiting's removal, even Lee had doubts about Whiting. "I share [your concern] to an equal degree," Lee confided to Vance, "but I can find no one whom I deem better. He is a man of unquestionable ability, versed in the particular knowledge suited to his position, but whether he would be able at the required time to apply the qualifications and to maintain the confidence of his command is with me questionable."[37]

President Davis had no doubts. When the War Department learned that a Federal fleet was being assembled for an attack on Fort Fisher, Davis ordered General Bragg to relieve Whiting and assume command over the troops and defenses of the Cape Fear region. Bragg may have lost battle after battle, but he had not lost the president's friendship or support. He arrived in Wilmington by train on October 22, assumed command of the department but kept Whiting as district commander. He also drafted a confidential report on Whiting for the president, describing the general as industrious and zealous, but needlessly excited about a possible enemy attack. Publicly, Whiting accepted his demotion gracefully. Privately, he feared Bragg would allow the region to fall to the enemy. "I acquiesced with feelings of great mortification," he confided to a friend.[38]

When the inevitable attack came, Whiting believed, a Federal fleet would bombard Fort Fisher and put troops ashore on the peninsula north of the fort. Then the Federal navy would try to "run the bar," placing warships in the river behind the fort and thereby closing Wilmington to blockade running—with or without the fall of Fort Fisher. If the warships could not get through the shallow inlets, the Yankee army would storm the fort or put it under siege. The fort would have difficulty withstanding a prolonged siege, and the Yankees would no doubt come in vastly superior numbers. They would have to be stopped while landing on the beach, when they were most vulnerable, and that would require an assault by a large Confederate support force.[39]

Bragg dismissed Whiting as a worrier, and on November 23, at President Davis's suggestion, left for Augusta, Georgia, to assume temporary command of a Confederate force being assembled near there to face Sherman. Undoubtedly, Whiting did not mind being left in charge of his old command in Bragg's absence, but he was dismayed to learn that half of Fort Fisher's garrison was going with Bragg. Adding to his concern, Whiting received orders soon afterwards to send 1,500 more troops from the Cape Fear region north to Weldon to oppose a Federal diversion near there. Fort Fisher and the rest of the Cape Fear defenses were left with a skeleton force of defenders.[40]

In Richmond, meanwhile, Confederate officials were being peppered with rumors that the enemy's Fort Fisher Expedition soon would be under way. A Confederate spy at Hampton Roads had even reported Yankee sailors splashing ashore in a practice landing as preparation for the expedition. President Davis suggested that Bragg return to Wilmington, and on December 17, the general arrived back at Cape Fear headquarters to resume command—without the troops he had taken with him. The next day, General Lee dispatched an urgent telegram from the Virginia front: Confederate intelligence agents reported that the Yankee expedition against Fort Fisher was now en route, commanded by Admiral Porter and General Butler.[41]

With half its garrison still hundreds of miles away, Fort Fisher was in desperate need of reinforcements—a fact no one now denied. With the attack perhaps hours away, General Robert F. Hoke's division, composed of some 6,500 veteran troops, was ordered out of the Richmond-Petersburg line and dispatched, one brigade at a time, by rail to Wilmington. It was welcome news to Whiting: Hoke was a seasoned field commander and his troops—North Carolinians, South Carolinians and some Georgians—were battle-tested combat veterans. They knew how to fight, they were ably led and they were on their way. They were coming on the unreliable Confederate rail system, however, and were forced to use a time-consuming, roundabout railway route. A crucial question remained unanswered: would they arrive in time?[42]

◆

At dawn on December 20, Fort Fisher's lookouts sighted what they believed was the enemy fleet on the distant horizon. A few minutes later, an aide knocked on Colonel Lamb's cottage door and reported the news. Lamb dressed, left Daisy and the children in bed and went to the fort, where he climbed atop the Pulpit. The sky was an ugly gray and a gusty wind whipped across his face from the northeast—a serious storm was obviously brewing. He stared seaward toward the brightening horizon and there, through the gray morning light, he could make out five Federal warships. Perhaps they were the enemy blockaders that regularly patrolled the Cape Fear, he thought, but soon there was no mistaking the sight. One by one, more warships appeared on the Atlantic horizon until the distant sea was dotted with them. Lamb began to count, stopping with a tally of twenty-five warships. Those were the ships he could see. Others no doubt lay out of sight. For a while, he studied the sprawling enemy fleet, then he sent word to Wilmington headquarters—the enemy had arrived.[43]

The next four days were a blur of activity, as Fort Fisher's defenders readied themselves for the impending attack. Lamb pleaded for more rations, and Whiting managed to scrape together a ten-day supply of hardtack for the fort's troops, but it was hardly enough to withstand a prolonged siege. Lamb sent the fort's impressed slaves home to safety, so every available soldier had to go to work shoring up the fort's defenses. A detachment of seamen was drafted from the CSS *Chickamauga*, berthed at Wilmington, to man a battery of Brooke rifled cannon on the fort's seaface. The guns had been salvaged from the sunken gunboat CSS *Roanoke* and were unfamiliar to the fort's artillerists. Like the Confederate seamen posted at Battery Buchanan, the *Chickamauga*'s sailors were disliked by some of the Cape Fear's army officers, who considered them drunkards and rowdies. Still, they were needed now. The fort was also reinforced by two companies of the Tenth North Carolina Artillery sent from across the river and by the Seventh Battalion of Junior Reserves—a unit of teenagers commonly called "The Seventeen-Year-Olds." Governor Vance, meanwhile, issued an emergency call for volunteers, urging "all good people who may be able to stand behind the breastworks and fire a musket, of all ages and conditions, to rally at once to the defense of their country and hurry to Wilmington." Vowed Vance: "Your governor will meet you at the front and will share with you the worst." Despite the dramatic oratory, no army of civilian volunteers showed up for battle, and neither did Vance.[44]

The violent storm that followed the sighting of the fleet and postponed the Federal attack had bought time for troops to be recalled and for Hoke's reinforcements to wind their way south from Virginia. By the time the muffled growl from the powder boat explosion rumbled through Wilmington, every man who could be spared had been moved to Confederate Point and the train carrying the advance brigade of Hoke's division had rolled into town. Whiting was no doubt relieved to see them: despite his best efforts, Fort Fisher was manned by fewer than 800 troops.[45]

Daylight on December 24 revealed good weather. The storm was over and Whiting knew the attack would soon begin. Who knew how it would end? The defenses were unsurpassed, he was confident of that. But Fort Fisher's thin garrison of inexperienced soldiers would be facing a vastly superior force of battle-hardened Federal troops. A successful defense, Whiting knew, would depend on Hoke's division—most of which was still en route from Virginia. Would enough reinforcements arrive to throw the invaders back into the ocean? If so, would Bragg commit them when the Yankees tried to land? Whiting had no answers, just a lot of anxiety. "It's an ungrateful duty, this, and no bed of roses," he complained, "and the prospect is not particularly cheerful ahead. . . . Between Bragg and Lee, Sherman and Grant, old North Carolina is in a pretty fix."[46]

5

"A Storm of Shot and Shell"

ENSIGN JOHN GRATTAN OF THE USS *MALVERN* thought he might die in the coming battle. The powder boat explosion had accomplished nothing, so when Porter's sailors awakened to more good weather Christmas Eve morning, they knew the fighting would soon begin. "This is the night before the battle," Grattan had written in his journal. "As I sit here my thoughts wander to home and to the fair girl who I have promised to make my wife. If I should be killed in this engagement, my last breath will be to echo her name, and to bid my father and mother, sisters and brothers goodbye."[1]

By daylight of the 24th, Grattan and the other seamen of the fleet had little time to think about the hazards of combat—they were too busy. Except for one boatload of troops, Butler and the army had not yet returned from Beaufort, but Admiral Porter had decided to do battle anyway. The sailors had been roused to duty before dawn and by eight o'clock the fleet was under way, heading due west toward Fort Fisher. A sudden rise in the wind prompted Porter to order an anchorage at 10 o'clock, but skies were clear, the wind soon died down and the fleet resumed course. A slight breeze swept shoreward, puffing the canvas on the masted steamers. The mighty armada steamed steadily westward, arrayed in tight formation, trailing white, foamy wakes. Those who could pause from their duties long enough to gape at the line of advancing warships were left impressed. "The sunlight flashed on their numerous polished guns," one admiring seaman observed, "and the scene was very grand and imposing."[2]

At about 11:30, as the fleet neared the coast, ships' drummers beat "to quarters for action." Aboard each warship, gunners manned their batteries, shot and shell stood charged and ready, and the ships' youthful powder monkeys spread ashes around each gun, so no one would slip on a bloody deck during battle. All cooking fires had been extinguished in the galleys hours earlier, so coffee for the hands' noon meal was heated in the boiler rooms, then passed with hardtack to the men at their battle stations. The sailors sipped the dark brew, munched on the dry crackers and watched the fort's bumpy outline grow nearer.[3]

Each warship had orders to shell an assigned area of the fort. Porter planned a general bombardment, designed to pound each of the fort's gun batteries as well as the interior of the huge fortification. Battle formation called for four lines of warships in position opposite the fort and the ironclad division anchored a little closer to shore. The three forward lines would bombard the fort, and the fourth line, the reserves, would replace seriously damaged vessels, cover the troop landing and carry dispatches. At about 12:30, the warships steamed within range of the giant fort and prepared to open fire.[4]

◆

Private Arthur Muldoon was first to see the enemy fleet reappear. Posted as lookout atop Fort Fisher's Pulpit, he saw the Federal warships slip one by one into sight. The ocean, calm after the recent storm, looked as placid as a lake, flat and dark blue under the clear winter sky. Visibility was excellent, and as Muldoon peered oceanward toward the morning sun, he could see dozens of enemy vessels coming into view as if on parade. As ordered, he sent for Colonel Lamb. When Lamb arrived, he stood in the Pulpit for a long moment, staring over the parapet at the distant, approaching line of ships. Then he ordered the fort's drummer to beat "the long roll," calling the fort's troops to battle quarters.[5]

The drum roll echoed across the sandy peninsula from ocean to river, and the fort's soldiers hurried to their battle stations. Artillery ammunition lined the walls of each gun chamber, within easy reach of gun crews. But Lamb had only 3,000 rounds for the fort's 44 guns, fewer than 70 rounds per gun, and for the huge Armstrong cannon, he had a mere 13 rounds. To preserve the limited ammunition he had issued strict orders: only the long-range artillery would be fired regularly and no gun would be fired more than once every half-hour, unless a concentrated fire on a single target was ordered. The gunners understood the purpose of the order: every shot must count.[6]

Now, as the long-awaited battle approached, an eerie silence cloaked the fort. Along the land side of the fort from the river to the beach, then down the seaface from the Northeast Bastion to the Mound, the gun crews stood stoically beside their artillery. By Lamb's order, no artillery would be fired until the discharge of the fort's signal gun, a huge ten-inch Columbiad mounted in the Pulpit. In the bombproof beneath Lamb's observation point, Chief Surgeon Spiers Singleton and his two assistants prepared the fort's field hospital for the expected casualties.[7]

Behind the fort's walls, the soldiers in gray and butternut watched the enemy warships as they approached in battle formation. Like Ensign Grattan on the *Malvern,* some of Fort Fisher's troops thought of death. "We are all in readiness and I think and hope that we will be successful," one soldier had written his wife on the eve of battle. "I shall stand to my post and go wherever duty calls me. I shall never disgrace my wife and child. If I should fall, however, weep not for me; your dear brother and uncle have gone before me and I hope I will be prepared to meet them in a peaceful land." At their posts, the fort's soldiers quietly watched the giant fleet approach. Only the crash of the nearby surf broke the grim silence. On flagpoles above the Mound, the Pulpit and the riverside gun battery, the red, white and blue banner of the Confederacy flapped in the westerly breeze.[8]

◆

The honor of opening the battle went to the USS *New Ironsides.* The iron-plated warship was one of the U.S. Navy's first ironclads and, with the USS *Monitor* and the USS *Galena,* had revolutionized naval warfare. She had survived several Confederate attempts to sink her, including a torpedo attack by the Confederate submarine *David,* and now led the Federal fleet into battle. Approaching the coast just north of the fort, the warships veered to port when within range and steamed to their battle stations in three long lines, trailed by the reserves. The *New Ironsides* and the ironclads *Monadnock, Saugus, Canonicus* and *Mahopac* reached anchorage first, about three-quarters of a mile off the beach. The fort appeared strangely quiet as the fleet reached battle stations, and some sailors began to wonder if perhaps the powder boat explosion had done some damage after all.[9]

Commodore William Radford was commander of the *New Iron-*

sides. When he saw that his ship was directly northeast of the Confederate flag fluttering above the fort's Northeast Bastion, he gave the order to drop anchor and open fire. It was exactly 12:45. The *New Ironsides'* dark body spat flame and smoke, and the first shot of the battle, an eleven-inch shell, made a high, shrieking arc over the ocean shallows, whistled past the headquarters flagstaff and exploded loudly behind the Pulpit. From his position atop the Pulpit, Colonel Lamb could see the enemy shell as it hurtled over the ocean. When it exploded, he ordered the fort's signal gun fired. The huge Columbiad bellowed a deep roar and sent the fort's first round whizzing toward the fleet. The missile, a ten-inch solid shot cannonball, ricocheted off the smooth sea, regained altitude, passed over the rail of the USS *Susquehanna* and punched a gaping hole in the ship's smokestack. The fort's gunners now jumped to action and the long line of batteries on the fort's seaface belched fire and smoke.[10]

Anchored at their battle stations, the long line of Federal warships replied with a stunning barrage. A fiery, mile-wide swarm of shot and shell screamed toward the fort, exploding overhead, plowing up the fort's sandy interior and splashing into the Cape Fear River in the rear. Businesslike, the fleet's gun crews methodically sponged, swabbed, reloaded and fired again and again, while a great white cloud of powder smoke drifted slowly shoreward.[11]

Inside Fort Fisher, shells tore into the fort's eastern walls, raising geysers of sand. Others burst overhead in showers of spinning iron or exploded among the garrison barracks, ripping jagged holes in the whitewashed structures. "What with the continuous roar of the firing and the scarcely less frequent reports of bursting shells, the aggregate noise was not unlike that of a rolling, volleying, long-sustained thunderstorm," recalled one of the Confederates forced to endure the bombardment. "The hostile missiles which showered into the fort . . . were of all sorts and sizes, from the big XV-inch spherical shot or shell, and the 100-pounder rifled Parrott, down through the list, and the whiz or whistle of each variety seemed to strike a different and more vicious note."[12]

"It was a magnificent sight," a Federal naval officer observed, "and one never to be forgotten. [The ships'] sides seemed a sheet of flame and the roar of their guns like a mighty thunderbolt . . . Nothing could withstand such a storm of shot and shell as was now poured into this fort." From the vantage point of the USS *Mohican,* sailor B. F. Blair was equally impressed: "It was a splendid yet a wicked sight— what a shower of shell we must have pounded down on their devoted heads. Our shells would bury themselves in the sand and earthworks and hum there in all directions. . . . One continual roar like the heaviest thunder—and the smoke so thick at times to completely hide the sun. I got so deaf after awhile as to be most entirely indifferent to it. My ears are singing yet. Oh! It was a sight never to be forgotten."[13]

Admiral Porter took a position atop the *Malvern*'s wheelhouse, directing signals to the warships through his flag officer, while the flagship steamed up and down the battle lines. "Excellent," he would signal a ship after a well-placed broadside. "A beautiful shot, do it again." Prowling up and down the fleet battle stations, its pennants flying in the breeze, the *Malvern* was an obvious target and drew extra fire from the fort. Once shell fragments peppered the wheelhouse inches below Porter's feet, and one round from the fort splashed into the ocean alongside the *Malvern*'s bow, dousing a gang of gawking seamen crowded on the ship's forecastle. Otherwise, the flagship remained undamaged.[14]

◆

Meanwhile, Fort Fisher's garrison remained inside the dimly lit bombproofs, protected from the enemy fire. As planned, they emerged occasionally to fire their guns. The bombardment blanketed the interior of the fort, but the fire was not concentrated and much of it landed harmlessly in the Cape Fear River behind the fort—obscured from the fleet by distance and the smoke of battle. Even so, the unprecedented bombardment took a toll on the fort.[15]

Oddly, the first serious damage was self-inflicted. In one of the seaface gun chambers, Lieutenant Thomas Arendall and troops of the Tenth North Carolina trained an eight-inch Columbiad toward one of the distant warships and fired their first round. Recoil from the charge jarred the huge cannon tube from its carriage, sending the gun crew stumbling and scrambling out of the way. The stunned gunners watched helplessly as the heavy weapon came to rest uselessly in the sand.[16]

The Confederate sailors manning the fort's Brooke Battery apparently took the first serious casualty, when a well-placed round from the fleet exploded in their midst. Seaman J. F. Higgins was flattened by the exploding shells, which severed his left leg and sent it spinning across the sand. Nearby, one of the fort's young couriers was struck by fragments from a huge eleven-inch shell as he sprinted across the fort's interior with a dispatch. He died instantly, horribly dismembered. Gunners from a nearby battery braved the bombardment long enough to hastily dig a shallow grave, where they quickly buried the teenaged soldier.[17]

About an hour after the bombardment began, an exploding shell set fire to a stable behind the fort's seaface. Fort Fisher's main stables were north of the fort, but a string of officers' horses were kept in this small barn, which was soon ablaze. The horses managed to escape the flames, only to be caught in the midst of the bombardment. Mad with fright, the animals galloped wildly through the fort until, one by one, were killed by the artillery fire. Soon afterwards, the fort barracks were set afire by the barrage. Built of combustible Carolina pine, the buildings blazed quickly, and within minutes flames were clawing at the sky beneath a huge, billowing column of black smoke. The dense smoke provoked a resounding chorus of husky "hurrahs" from the sailors of the fleet. The cheers rolled down the long line of warships and echoed shoreward above the roar of battle.[18]

Restricted by orders to infrequent fire, the fort's gunners had difficulty adjusting their range, and many of their shells overshot the warships. One gun crew disregarded orders, however, and fired round after round at the USS *Powhatan,* until they found the range. Then they put five rounds through the ship's hull in quick succession, knocking a jagged hole in the vessel and forcing its seamen to shift some of the guns to port to prevent a serious starboard list.[19]

◆

One of the *Powhatan*'s ensigns, eighteen-year-old Robley Evans, was handed a pair of binoculars and ordered up the ship's rigging as an artillery spotter. In place high above the deck, he pulled a piece of leftover hardtack from his pocket, stuck it between his teeth and peered through the binoculars. As he scanned the fort's walls through the smoke, he spotted the Confederate battery that was pounding the *Powhatan.* He watched the gray-clad artillerists elevate their gun until he seemed to be looking directly into the weapon's muzzle. As he watched, his view was suddenly obscured by a puff of white smoke, and something resembling a lamppost crossed his field of vision. At that instant he realized *he* was the target. The enemy shell clipped the rigging below his feet, knocking him off his perch. He fell hard against the mast, frantically clutched a handful of rigging and somehow managed to hold on. He climbed down from his post, trying to control his wobbly knees, then realized with a start he was missing something—the hardtack he had held between his teeth. He looked around the deck in vain, then began to wonder if he had swallowed the big cracker.[20]

Aboard the USS *Pontoosuc,* a round from the fort ripped through the ship's hull, narrowly missing the engine, punched through an iron bulkhead, tore through a wall of mess lockers, splintered a heavy wooden beam and exploded in the paymaster's storeroom. Incredibly, no one was wounded by the wild shell, but it set fire to the ship. The *Pontoosuc*'s crew managed to extinguish the blaze and the ship remained at its station.

Seamen aboard the USS *Osceola* were less fortunate. A ten-inch shot from the fort penetrated the vessel's hull, perforated the starboard boiler and exploded, bursting the boiler. Six sailors were scalded and the boiler room flooded. Listing sharply starboard, the *Osceola* hoisted the "sinking" signal and retired from the battle. A boatload of repairmen finally managed to plug the big hole in the hull and staunched the flooding.[21]

The USS *Mackinaw* suffered a similar fate while engaging in a duel with Fort Fisher's Mound battery. As ordered, the Mound's fire was sporadic, but the battery's high elevation gave the battery's two guns a plunging fire which finally took its toll on the *Mackinaw*. All afternoon the warship traded fire with the Mound until just after three o'clock, when a Confederate round tore through the ship and into the engine room, exploding a boiler and scalding eight sailors and two marines. The *Mackinaw*'s commander tried to take the ship out of line—until he received a signal from Porter: "Remain where you are and fight." Meanwhile, the commanders of the *Monticello, Keystone State* and *Quaker City* concentrated all available firepower on the Mound. A deadly torrent of shells tore into the towering battery, sending the Mound's gunners to their bombproof and silencing the battery for the rest of the afternoon.[22]

Ironically, the navy's worst casualties on the first day of battle were not caused by the fort's fire, but instead by a series of deadly accidents. Aboard the USS *Juanita,* Lieutenant David D. Wemple commanded a starboard battery that pounded the fort with a huge 100-pounder Parrott. The Parrott had a bad reputation—it would sometimes explode in action. A popular young officer, Wemple stood behind the massive weapon as the gun crew sponged, swabbed, reloaded and fired again. Suddenly the gun exploded in a deafening blast of flame and smoke, spraying jagged pieces of the broken gun tube in all directions. Wemple's head, chest and legs were crushed—killing him instantly. The blast also killed Marine Second Lieutenant Jonas Pile, whose mangled body was blown through a gunport into the ocean. Seaman Henry Payne, disemboweled, quickly died of shock. Fireman Thomas Abos bled to death, and James Ennels, a young powder monkey, was so badly mangled that the best efforts of the ship's surgeon could not save him. The exploding Parrott killed five and wounded eight, including Seaman Thomas Mahoney, who survived the blast to discover an odd silence cloaking the frantic rescue attempts that followed: he had been deafened by the explosion.

The *Juanita* lurched out of formation, retiring from the line. Admiral Porter spotted the retreating warship and ordered the *Malvern* alongside, plucking Marine Pile's broken body from the sea en route. "My 100-pounder has exploded!" shouted the *Juanita*'s commander. "Then why in hell don't you go back and use your other guns?" Porter shouted back. Obediently, the *Juanita*'s commander took the ship back to its battle station. Later, Porter challenged another retreat by one of his warships with a threat: "Go back to your place or I will send you and your boat to the bottom!" The fleet remained at battle stations and the bombardment continued, while the wounded were transferred to hospital ships, anchored in the rear under red and yellow flags.[23]

As Porter's flagship moved away from the *Juanita,* signal flags appeared on the *Yantic* and the *Ticonderoga* reporting the explosion of Parrotts on both those ships as well. They were not alone; before the bombardment ended, Parrotts would also explode on the *Mackinaw* and the *Quaker City.* The *Ticonderoga* suffered the most from the malfunctioning Parrotts. Lieutenant Louis Vassallo was sighting one of the guns when it exploded. He suffered facial cuts, but somehow survived. Others were less fortunate. When the screams ended and the smoke cleared, eight seamen were dead and twelve were wounded. Seeing their shipmates sprawled dead and dying on the bloodied deck, some of the surviving gunners began to panic. Coxswain William Shipman rallied the seamen back to their battle stations. "Go ahead, boys," he shouted. "This is only the fortune of war!" The *Ticonderoga* remained in line, its batteries still firing. However, with thirty-seven casualties on five ships from exploding Parrotts, Porter ordered all the 100-pounders retired from the battle.[24]

◆

Casualties were actually lighter inside the fort. Much of the fearsome barrage continued to fall behind the works and none of the naval fire penetrated the bombproofs that sheltered the garrison. Still, when the soldiers manned their guns, casualties occurred. At a five-gun battery on the fort's seaface, Lieutenant Daniel Perry saw his gunners felled one by one by the enemy fire. A spent shell knocked Sergeant J. M. Benson unconscious in the sand; Corporal G. L. Birt went down with a side wound; and six other soldiers in Perry's battery were hit. Others, exposed to the same dangers, endured the hail of artillery fire without a scratch. Such was Lieutenant George Parker's experience: he had left his sickbed to command a landface battery near the Northeast Bastion. At regular intervals all afternoon he and his gun crews lobbed shot at the Federal ironclads, without harm to a single man or gun.[25]

The battle had its odd moments. The Confederate sailors at the Brooke Battery had no bombproof available, so they huddled under the seaface wall. At one point, they broke out a carefully hoarded bottle of imported rum, but as one of the men raised the coveted container to his lips, a sabot from an exploding shell smashed the bottle in his hand. Momentarily oblivious to the danger around them, the stunned sailors stood looking at the shattered glass, cursing their fortune and fretting over the spilled spirits.[26]

At one point during the day, the warships concentrated their fire on the fort's seaface flagstaffs, trying to knock down the garrison flags. Round after round whizzed past the Confederate national flag flying above the Pulpit and exploded to the rear. Colonel Lamb's brick headquarters building—the old lighthouse keeper's cottage—was soon pounded to rubble and the exterior of the fort's huge magazine was pockmarked with shell craters. Finally, a direct hit splintered the Pulpit flagstaff and sent the colors twisting to the ground. The flag atop the Mound gave the fleet's gunners more trouble, but eventually it too was shot away. One of the Mound's officers called for a volunteer to replace the fallen banner, and the challenge was accepted by Private Christopher ("Kit") Bland, a twenty-year-old soldier from the nearby fishing village of Calabash. Bland stepped forward, took the flag and coolly shinnied up the flagstaff. For a moment, as if awed by the sight, the fleet's fire appeared to slacken, then it quickly resumed with greater intensity. By then, however, Bland had attached the flag to the top of the staff and was back down—with the Confederate colors again whipping in the breeze. An even more determined barrage followed, leaving the banner hanging limply by one corner. Bland repeated his feat, but this time his heroics brought him closer to death. As he slid down the pole this time, a Federal shell whooshed by close enough to brush his hair. But for a while at least, the fort's colors remained in place above the Mound.[27]

At about 4:30 that afternoon, at the height of the bombardment, Colonel Lamb was surprised to discover General Whiting and three of his staff officers climbing the path to the Pulpit. Lamb had notified Wilmington headquarters by telegraph when the bombardment began. In response, Whiting promptly put a steamer on standby, received permission from General Bragg to join Lamb at Fort Fisher, then set out for the fort aboard ship. While Whiting and his officers were still far upriver, the roar of the bombardment became audible, and as they drew closer they could see the dark column of smoke from the fort's burning barracks. At about four o'clock, their steamer arrived at Battery Buchanan, where the general normally would have been met with saddle horses. Now the post's mounts were dead or scattered, so Whiting and his staff had to walk from Battery Buchanan to Fort Fisher—braving the naval bombardment for more than a mile and a half as they hurried across the fort's sprawling interior.[28]

Lamb immediately offered to relinquish command to Whiting, but the general declined the offer. He had come merely to assist and observe, he said. He did bring Lamb some good news: two companies of reinforcements had been ferried across the river from Fort Caswell to Battery Buchanan and would be placed on line as soon as it was dark. More importantly, part of Hoke's division had arrived and by now was probably in place at Sugar Loaf, a sprawling, fortified earthwork overlooking the Cape Fear about six miles upriver from Fort Fisher.[29]

◆

General William W. Kirkland trotted his horse over the sandy ruts that passed for a road on Confederate Point, heading toward the beach. Kirkland and two regiments of his brigade, the advance force of Hoke's division, had been up and moving early that morning, despite a long, cold and punishing train ride that had ended in Wilmington at midnight. Their march down to Confederate Point through the deep coastal sands had been exasperatingly slow, and Kirkland had ridden ahead on horseback. He had arrived at Sugar Loaf, where his brigade would anchor its line, shortly before the fleet began its bombardment. Turning his horse to the east, he had ridden, as soldiers were supposed to do, toward the sound of the guns.[30]

Kirkland had spent five years in the U.S. Marines; he understood landings and he wanted to see what kind of support troops would be facing the Federal forces when they came ashore. What he found was not encouraging. He was a gutsy soldier, known as a field officer who would go into the thickest of a fight at the head of his troops. Despite a somewhat genteel appearance—jowly cheeks and a Beauregard-style mustache and goatee—he was a veteran of some of the war's bloodiest combat, from First Manassas to the Wilderness, and he had survived three severe wounds over the course of the war. He had West Point training, even though he had left without graduating, and he knew what kind of force would be needed when the Yankees came ashore. What he found instead was about 1,200 Junior and

Senior Reserves—schoolboys and old men, who could hardly be expected to stop Butler's veterans.[31]

The Reserves were deployed around Battery Gatlin, a large earthwork constructed about five miles north of Fort Fisher near Myrtle
Sound—the northernmost fortification on the oceanfront of Confederate Point. The battery mounted a thirty-two-pounder, manned by
a handful of troops from the Tenth North Carolina, and was reinforced by field artillery. In command of the support troops was Colonel John K. Connally. General Kirkland assumed command from
Connally, conferred with the colonel for a few moments, then rode
down to the beach—just as the Federal fleet opened fire. He watched
the impressive spectacle for a few minutes, then, with shells beginning to fall around him, he moved his horse through the woods and
returned to Sugar Loaf to await his troops.

Several hours later, at about the time General Whiting joined
Lamb in the Pulpit, Kirkland's weary soldiers reached Sugar Loaf
after what had turned out to be an all-day march through the deep
sand. The troops—the 42nd, the 17th and a portion of the 66th North
Carolina—were immediately deployed despite their exhaustion.
Some 500 of the Junior Reserves and part of the 17th North Carolina
were sent down to Fort Fisher at General Whiting's command, although troop dispositions outside the fort normally would be made
by General Bragg. Kirkland put the rest of his 1,300-man force on a
line across the peninsula from Sugar Loaf to Battery Gatlin, with a
small force of reinforcements at the battery and about 80 more two
miles down the beach at another one-gun earthwork called Battery
Anderson.[32]

As Kirkland's jaded veterans advanced through the woods toward
their battle line, they encountered several dead from the Senior
Reserves. The men had been killed by the naval fire. Captain Charles
G. Elliott, a twenty-four-year-old staff officer, had seen lots of battle
dead during the war, but these were different—all were gray-haired.
As he moved through the woods with the troops, Elliott felt deep pity
for the dead men; they were so old to have been killed in battle. His
troops were in line, but Kirkland knew his force was too thin to
withstand a major enemy force; he just hoped the Yankees would not
land until the rest of Hoke's division arrived. Meanwhile, as the
afternoon light melted into dusk, he established field headquarters
at Sugar Loaf and waited for orders from General Bragg.[33]

◆

At 5:30 P.M., Porter signaled the fleet to cease firing. A thick, white
pall of smoke hung over the fort from beach to river, and the setting

sun appeared blood red through the sulfurous haze. Following the tide out to sea were acres of empty ammunition boxes, tossed overboard from the warships during the day. A sudden silence cloaked the coast and for the first time in almost five hours that day, troops manning Fort Fisher's batteries could hear the nearby surf breaking on the beach. As the long lines of warships began to retire, the last shot of the day boomed from the fort and a final round splashed harmlessly in the ocean.[34]

Shortly before the fleet retired, General Butler arrived aboard the *Ben De Ford*. Butler waited until the fleet began to retire, then pulled alongside the *Malvern* and sent a staff officer aboard with a message for the admiral. General Weitzel and Colonel Comstock would come aboard later that night to discuss landing troops the next day, he advised. Butler was incensed that Porter had exploded the powder boat and engaged the enemy before the army had returned. Obviously, the explosion had accomplished nothing and Butler was certain Porter and the navy had botched the experiment—*his* experiment. He made no attempt to see Porter in person; instead, he would let his staff handle the face-to-face communications with the admiral. That was fine with Porter—he had no desire to see Butler. Indeed, he was in no hurry to meet with the general's staff either and at first declined the request for an evening meeting, claiming to be too sore from a fall he had taken aboard ship the day before.[35]

Later, he relented and met that night with Weitzel and Comstock. They were briefed on the day's action and arranged naval assistance for the next day's troop landing, which would begin in the morning. Even if the powder boat had accomplished nothing, Porter was certain his bombardment had rendered Fort Fisher defenseless. If the fort's guns were not destroyed, he asserted, they were at least disabled—their muzzles filled with sand from the navy's pounding. The limited return fire from the fort was proof enough that most of Fort Fisher's guns had been rendered useless by the bombardment, Porter believed. "There was not a blade of grass or a piece of stick in that fort that was not burned up," the admiral would boast. The army would merely need to walk inside the fort and claim it for the Union.[36]

Butler and his officers thought otherwise. Weitzel had commanded assaults on Port Hudson and against entrenched positions in Virginia, and he believed the fort's garrison would make a strong defense despite damage by the naval bombardment. If the fort's commander fought by the book, Weitzel believed, he would simply keep his main force safely inside the fort's bombproofs, maintain a steady but limited return fire until the bombardment ceased, then order his troops out to fight when the Federal forces launched their assault. Weitzel and Comstock suggested that Porter have his warships "run the bar" and get into the river behind the fort, as Grant had indicated. With the navy in the Cape Fear River, Fort Fisher would be useless and the port of Wilmington—like New Orleans and Mobile—would be put out of operation with little loss of Federal troops. Porter said no. The channel was too shallow, too intricate for his deep-draft warships, he said, and the Rebels probably had placed torpedoes and obstructions in the river. Weitzel then suggested using warships that had been converted from blockade runners; they were certainly light enough to get through the channel. And if the fort was now as defenseless as Porter claimed, getting into the river would be an easy task for the navy. But the admiral was adamant. It could not be done, he declared.[37]

Back on the *Ben De Ford* that night, Weitzel, Comstock and Brigadier General Charles K. Graham met with Butler in the general's opulent cabin and discussed the army's options. Butler was ready to quit. By exploding the powder boat early and beginning the bombardment without the army, Porter had destroyed all chances for success, Butler believed. His staff officers agreed: Porter wanted all the glory for the navy—and he had sacrificed the expedition in a futile attempt to get it. Landing troops now was useless, Butler argued, because the element of surprise was gone. The Confederates would be ready and waiting. His strategy for victory had been wrecked, he believed, and he favored an immediate return to Fort Monroe. Weitzel and Graham agreed—the landing should be canceled. But Comstock urged restraint: Why not put part of the force ashore in the morning, reconnoiter, *then* decide what to do? Eventually, Butler and the others acquiesced: they would put enough troops ashore to test the enemy defenses.[38]

"Fine cooperation," Comstock sarcastically confided to his diary that night. Thousands of men and dozens of ships had come hundreds of miles to launch a combined attack on the Confederacy's great fortress and the joint commanders were not even speaking to each other. Their longtime personal feud had spilled over into their professional lives, affecting their military judgment and undermining the expedition. The admiral had begun the "combined" attack unilaterally and the general was ready to quit and go home. The navy should have been ready when the army first arrived off Fort Fisher, Comstock believed, instead of wasting three days of sunny weather, perfect for a landing. A combined operation depended on cooperation, and that commodity appeared to be in short supply on the Fort Fisher Expedition. This was *not* the way to overcome a stronghold like Fort Fisher, and Comstock went to bed Christmas Eve unsure of what the next day would bring.[39]

◆

Inside Fort Fisher meanwhile, Colonel Lamb had taken stock of the damage and had sent a telegram to General Bragg: although blanketed with shell craters, Fort Fisher had survived the bombardment with limited damage. Two artillery pieces were disabled, four were damaged but serviceable. Most of the garrison barracks were now smoldering ashes and the post headquarters building was destroyed; otherwise, damage was minor—and casualties were surprisingly light. Crowding the garrison into the bombproofs had kept the fort's casualties to twenty-three, including probably no more than four dead or mortally wounded. Most of the enemy barrage had fallen on the fort's open interior or in the Cape Fear River. The bombardment had been fierce, but like the powder boat, it had failed to destroy Fort Fisher.[40]

"The Enemy Has Landed"

O N CHRISTMAS DAY, ACTING MASTER'S MATE JOSEPH SIMMS
awakened aboard the USS *Minnesota* with a case of prebat-
tle jitters. He didn't like going into combat on Christmas. As he
joined his shipmates for an early breakfast in the ship's mess, he
pondered the irony of it: while he should be celebrating the birthday
anniversary of Jesus Christ, the Prince of Peace, he and his shipmates
would soon be trying their best to kill their fellow man. His thoughts
were interrupted when the noisy mess quieted for moment; one of
the seamen was saying grace aloud. Simms and the sailors around
him bowed their heads in silence and listened respectfully to the
prayer of thanks. Afterwards, Simms realized, most of his jitters were
gone.[1]

On the USS *Fort Jackson,* Captain Benjamin F. Sands watched
solemnly as the fleet's dead and wounded were brought aboard his
ship. Later, whenever the battle ended, Sands's orders were to take
the *Fort Jackson* northward, depositing the dead at Beaufort for
burial and carrying the wounded on to Hampton Roads for further
treatment. For Sands and the seamen of the *Fort Jackson,* it was a
grim way to greet Christmas morning, but the hospital ships might

need extra room for the carnage expected that day.[2]

At 10 o'clock, the fleet got under way, heading back to the battle lines off Fort Fisher. At 10:48, led by the *New Ironsides,* the fleet resumed the bombardment, unleashing another hail of shot and shell on the fort. The troop transports, which had arrived at the offshore rendezvous site during the night, stood by in the rear of the warships, awaiting orders to put troops ashore. The navy would land the troops at a point north of the fort between Battery Gatlin and Battery Anderson. The troops would come ashore safely out of range of the fort's guns, but Battery Gatlin and Battery Anderson would have to be silenced before the landing, and a detachment of warships was detailed to bombard the two oceanfront batteries into silence. Meanwhile, the fleet would continue to pound Fort Fisher.[3]

The naval bombardment resumed Christmas Day with the same fury as that of the day before. "It was a sublimely grand spectacle, such as one has but few opportunities to behold in a lifetime," penned one Yankee witness to the barrage. "Broadside followed broadside with great rapidity and the terrible discharges of the gunboats made it one continuous roar . . . [the] heavy ordnance making the shores of the Old North State reverberate the deafening roar."[4]

From the deck of the transport *Herman Livingston,* Chaplain Henry Turner had a front-seat view of the bombardment, which he described in his diary: "Broadside after broadside was fired, until the reports became so continuous that, in many instances, it was one unbroken roar, which seem to be awful enough to shake the world. From that time until night did the lurid flash and the grim roar mutter while everything trembled as if it were rocked in the cradle of consternation."[5]

"The ironclads and their consorts thundered away at Fort Fisher with such stunning violence that the ocean fairly trembled," reported another observer. "I can imagine nothing like the bellowing of our fifteen inch guns. The belching of a volcano with accompanying explosions may suggest a corresponding idea. The din was deafening. Above the fort the countless flashes and puffs of smoke from bursting shells spoke for the accuracy of our guns while occasionally columns of sand heaved high in the air suggested that possibly the [bombproofs] were not so safe and cozy after all."[6]

Neither were the warships. Aboard ship, conditions were almost intolerable for the sailors working the guns. The sustained bombardment produced a roar and vibrations that were almost maddening. "Every particle of flesh upon one's bones seemed to be slipping off," observed Acting Master's Mate Simms, who described conditions aboard the *Minnesota* as a "truly thundering, hellish rattle—indescribable torture." The gunners fired, sponged, swabbed, reloaded and fired, again and again. Inside the ships' batteries, the air was thick with powder smoke and residue from the charges. The gun crews coughed and choked on the fumes, and tears caused by the smoke ran down their blackened, grimy faces. Many of the men suffered nosebleeds; others were partially deafened. A thick coat of saltpeter settled on the batteries like fine chalk dust, turning the sailors' blue uniforms a powdery white.[7]

Aboard the transport *Weybossett,* a crusty veteran of the Third New York Infantry watched the shells burst above Fort Fisher and drawled philosophically to a fellow soldier, "I'd rather Johnny'd be where them eggs is breaking than me." Nodding thoughtfully, his comrade shifted his chewing tobacco to one side and replied, "Them's my sentiments."[8]

Inside Fort Fisher, the "eggs" were breaking as furiously as the day before, but most of the barrage still missed the fort's main works, falling again on the interior plain and plunging into the river. Colonel Lamb, assisted by General Whiting, continued to direct the fort's defense. He had kept troops working to repair damages throughout the night, shoveling in shell craters on the fort walls, filling and stacking sandbags, and performing maintenance on the guns. The work had continued on Christmas morning, ending only when the fleet resumed the bombardment. Again, Lamb restricted his batteries to a limited fire of one round every half-hour, conserving the fort's ammunition for the troop assault certain to come.[9]

It was a harrowing Christmas for Fort Fisher's troops. The bombardment set fire to the fort's remaining barracks, again knocked down the garrison flag and carpeted the fort's interior with solid shot and shell fragments. Lieutenant Richard Armstrong, a Confederate naval officer who had volunteered for the Brooke Battery, was awed by the scope of the bombardment. "Never since the foundation of the world was there such a fire," he told a friend in amazement. "The whole interior of the fort . . . was as one XI-inch shell bursting." Armstrong was certain he could have crossed the wide interior of the fort without touching the ground, just by stepping on the countless cannonballs and shell fragments.[10]

"I never saw shells fall so thick," Private Junius Cromartie reported in a letter home. "They came down like hail. I thought every shell would get me. We did not enjoy Christmas." Captain John M. Sutton of the Third North Carolina Artillery commanded Shepherd's Battery, which consisted of two heavy artillery pieces and two seacoast howitzers near the river—where most of the enemy barrage was falling. Sutton's battery took a severe pounding. The fire dismounted two of his guns and, one by one, ten of his soldiers went down, including three who were injured by one of the falling guns. In a seaface battery commanded by Captain Samuel B. Hunter, a shell exploded near the muzzle of a huge ten-inch Columbiad, igniting the powder charge inside and jarring the mammoth gun off its carriage.[11]

At one point during the bombardment, a round landed in the midst of a Confederate gun crew commanded by Captain Daniel Patterson. For a long second the shell lay half-buried in the sand, smoking and hissing, while the gun crew stood in frozen terror, bracing for a deadly explosion. Then, one of the men, Private John Turner, pounced on the shell and quickly smothered its fuse. Another soldier, Private J. H. Brisson, grabbed the projectile and heaved it outside the gun chamber. Captain Patterson would later cite Turner and Brisson for bravery.[12]

◆

Across the Cape Fear River at Orton Plantation, Daisy Lamb sat on a high wall overlooking the river and watched the battle through a powerful pair of binoculars. She and the children had been evacuated from their cottage to safety, but she could still see the smoke of battle and the shells bursting above the fort. She knew her husband was over there in the thick of the fight. The day before, she had watched the bombardment from the same spot all day, once becoming so overwhelmed that she laid her head on the fence and sobbed aloud. At one point during her vigil, she was interrupted by young Dick, the colonel's preschool son. "Mama," he said, "I want to pray to God for my papa." Daisy knelt with the child and prayed earnestly for his father's safety. Later, she took her carriage down to one of the nearby fortifications to get the latest report from Fort Fisher, but en route she turned back, unable to bear the thought of bad news. Finally, after watching the bombardment for hours on Christmas day, she bundled up the children, took them aboard a steamer and retreated to Wilmington. There, away from the sights and sounds of battle, she waited for word on the fate of her husband and Fort Fisher.[13]

◆

Standing behind the sandbagged earthworks at Battery Gatlin, Lieutenant Colonel John P. Read watched with mounting concern as a flotilla of enemy warships moved away from the fleet and anchored in a battle line opposite the beach between Batteries Gatlin and Anderson, which he commanded. Read was worried: he figured the

Yankee troops would come ashore a few miles north of Fort Fisher, out of range of the fort's guns—and just about where his batteries were located. Read thought Battery Gatlin was a trap, bounded by the ocean to the east, a swamp in the rear, and the lower end of Myrtle Sound to the north. He knew his skeleton force could not defend it against a serious assault. So he planned to pound away at the enemy with his field pieces and the battery's one heavy thirty-two-pounder, then retreat when the Yankees came ashore.[14]

When the flotilla was in place opposite his position, at about 11 o'clock, the warships opened fire. A barrage of artillery fire began falling around the two batteries and on the beach in between, with most of the fire concentrated on Battery Gatlin. The shells screamed in and exploded, knocking up giant geysers of sand and hurtling deadly shell fragments in all directions. Read ordered his guns to open fire and called for reinforcements. The gunners manning a 12-pounder Whitworth stood firm under the barrage and plugged away at the distant warships. So did some of the other field artillery crews, but the gun crews working the 32-pounder and a 6-pounder Whitworth cowered under the hail of enemy fire and refused to man their guns. The battery's return fire was slow and hesitant, and as the barrage continued, the other gunners began to wilt under the heavy fire. Read did everything he could to keep his men at their guns, but most were clearly terrified and some simply ignored all his commands.[15]

As he tried to compel the frightened soldiers to do their duty, an enemy round exploded overhead, pelting Read and one of the Whitworth crews with shell fragments. The Whitworth's lieutenant went down and so did Read, his left arm mangled and almost severed from his body. As he was being carried to the rear, more field artillery arrived, commanded by Captain Thomas Southerland of the Tenth North Carolina. Southerland reined in his horse and bent down from the saddle to take orders from the blood-soaked Read. Take command, Read ordered, warning that the troops were "behaving very badly." As he was carried off to have his arm amputated, Read gave his final command to Southerland: "Repel the landing, if made, at all hazards." Southerland did not protest, but he knew the order would be impossible to execute—Battery Gatlin was practically out of commission. Meanwhile, the battery's shaken gun crews had new cause for alarm: the Yankees were coming.[16]

◆

In the offshore shallows, a crooked line of navy launches snaked through the lightly rolling surf, heading toward the beach. In the first wave were 500 New Yorkers from Curtis's Brigade—450 troops from the 142nd New York and a detachment of 50 from the 112th New York. Captain Oliver S. Glisson of the USS *Santiago de Cuba* commanded a flotilla of 17 warships charged with covering the landing. As the longboats headed for the beach, the warships increased their fire, pounding the fort and flailing the wooded shoreline at the landing site with a hail of iron.[17]

Perched in the bow of the lead launch was Colonel Newton Martin Curtis, the officer charged with establishing a beachhead on Confederate Point. At six-foot-four, the twenty-nine-year-old Curtis towered over the soldiers and sailors around him. He was a volunteer officer whose higher education had been conducted at a Wesleyan seminary, not a military college, but what he lacked in formal military training he made up in fearlessness. A native New Yorker, he had been a law student, a school teacher, a farmer and a small-town postmaster, and when the war began he had helped organize the Twelfth New York Volunteers, becoming one of its captains. Sporting an unruly chest-length beard, he was bright, aggressive and eager for combat. Early in the war he was seriously wounded in fighting on Virginia's Peninsula and upon recovery had spent most of the war on desk duty. Now he was a commissioned colonel and a breveted brigadier general—commander of the First Brigade, Second Division, of the XXIV Army Corps—and he was ready for battle and promotion. When the boats hit the beach, Curtis was the first man ashore.[18]

Splashing through waist-deep surf, their rifles held high, the New Yorkers charged ashore about 400 yards north of Battery Anderson and deployed into a skirmish line behind the sand dunes. As the troops rushed onto the beach, thousands of soldiers aboard the transports broke into a chorus of cheers. Moments later, when Curtis and some of his blue-clad soldiers unfurled a United States flag atop one of the dunes, the cheering increased and a brass band aboard one of the transports struck up a spirited rendition of "Yankee Doodle." General Weitzel, who came ashore with Curtis's brigade, was relieved the landing force suffered no casualties. He had feared the troops would have to come ashore under fire, then battle Hoke's veterans to establish a beachhead. So far, however, Bragg had made no attempt to stop the invasion. The Federal forces had come ashore unopposed.[19]

Curtis secured the landing site with a strong skirmish line, then led a force down the beach to assault Battery Anderson, which was still under fire from the naval support flotilla. Behind the battery's sandbagged walls, Captain Jacob Koonts of Kirkland's brigade watched what appeared to be an overwhelming force of Yankees moving on his position in battle formation. Koonts and his thin command—Company A of the Forty-second North Carolina Infantry—had been sorely tested by the naval gunfire. Considering the pounding they had taken, their casualties were surprisingly light, but Koonts could see his troops were hopelessly outnumbered and had lost their zeal to fight. The Yankees were still far up the beach and advancing cautiously when a white flag began to wave back and forth above Battery Anderson.[20]

Aboard the USS *Britannia,* lying offshore, Lieutenant Samuel Huse spotted the flag of truce, ordered a cease-fire and dispatched a landing party to accept the surrender: it would be a welcome Christmas present for the admiral. Commanders of three other nearby warships—*Tristam Shandy, Howquah* and *Santiago de Cuba*—did likewise. The exercise quickly became a rowing contest as the landing parties raced each other to be first ashore. When the troops advancing on the battery realized the navy was coming ashore to take the surrender, the soldiers broke into a run, prompting the seamen to row even harder—and suddenly an interservice race was on to see who would capture the first prisoners of the campaign.[21]

The sailors won. While the soldiers were still more than a hundred yards away, one of the *Britannia*'s boats reached the surf and its crew hurriedly splashed ashore. Led by Acting Ensign William H. Bryant, who carried a U.S. flag, the seamen sprinted across the beach, scaled Battery Anderson's battered walls and confronted the dejected North Carolinians. As Captain Koonts surrendered his company, Ensign Bryant erected his flag atop the captured earthwork and the Federal sailors emitted three rousing cheers. Curtis's winded New Yorkers arrived seconds afterwards, but they were too late and were left with nothing to do but watch grumpily while the Confederate prisoners were rowed out to the *Santiago de Cuba.*[22]

Seeing Curtis and his force safely ashore and moving down the beach without opposition, Butler allowed more troops to go in. The rest of Curtis's brigade was landed, followed by the Second Brigade under Colonel Galusha Pennypacker and Colonel Louis Bell's Third Brigade. As hundreds of Federal soldiers massed on the beach, the troops extended their skirmish lines north and south of the landing site. Finally, as the Federal forces moved off the beach and began to spread out through the woods, they encountered the Confederate skirmishers of Kirkland's brigade and the staccato pop of small arms fire rose over the peninsula.[23]

◆

General Kirkland was surprised by the Yankee landing. He did not expect the enemy to come ashore so quickly and he had expected them to land farther north, near Battery Gatlin, where he had anchored the eastern end of his thin line of troops. He had just left Battery Gatlin and was riding south through the woods to check on Battery Anderson when he heard the distant cheering that signaled the successful enemy landing. Moments later he was stopped on the sandy road by an excited courier who reported the surrender of Battery Anderson. Kirkland immediately galloped back to his main line and brought forward skirmishers to probe the enemy advance. Nearing the beach, the Confederate skirmishers sighted Federal troops moving slowly through the woods and opened fire. The opposing lines traded volleys and the Federals slowly backed out of the woods, withdrawing cautiously toward the landing site. Kirkland was trying to analyze the situation when his scouts reported the size of the Federal force: what appeared to be three full brigades were either ashore or landing. The rest of Hoke's division still had not arrived, leaving Kirkland with a single regiment to oppose three brigades—odds he knew would never succeed. His sparse line could easily be flanked by the enemy, or the Federals could put more troops ashore near Battery Gatlin and drive a wedge between his force and Wilmington. Kirkland ordered his skirmishers to halt. Then, posting a small force of pickets, he withdrew his troops back to his main line, stretching across the peninsula from Sugar Loaf bluff on the river to Battery Gatlin on the beach. "It would have been madness to have advanced further," he later lamented. He could do nothing more until reinforcements arrived. Meanwhile, with the landing site now heavily defended, Curtis and General Weitzel ordered a troop movement south toward Fort Fisher. Led by Curtis's New Yorkers, the Federal soldiers moved through the woods toward the fort, encountering no resistance on the way.[24]

◆

While the infantry landed unopposed north of the fort, a party of Admiral Porter's seamen was facing an ordeal by fire. Although still opposed to sending his warships into the Cape Fear River, Admiral Porter had ordered a sounding party to chart and mark the entrance to the river at New Inlet—just in case the navy decided to run by the enemy batteries. The admiral had access to prewar charts of the area, but new sandbars could have formed over the years, and he also feared running aground on the uncharted wreck of a blockade runner or striking a submerged torpedo. Porter wanted New Inlet charted and the channel marked with buoys. The orders were issued to Commander John Guest of the USS *Iosco*. He took his warship and eight others to an anchorage off New Inlet, where they unleashed a heavy, sustained fire against Fort Fisher's Mound Battery and nearby Battery Buchanan. Sounding and marking the channel would have to be done in small boats in open water within easy range of the fort's guns. It was a potentially suicidal mission, but Porter had no trouble finding a volunteer to lead it.[25]

Lieutenant William B. Cushing was the man for the job and he eagerly accepted it. He was only twenty-two years old. In normal times, he would have just graduated from college or would have been laboring at an entry-level post in his chosen profession. Instead, his recklessly courageous wartime exploits had made him an almost legendary figure in the navy and a national hero in the North. He had earned headlines by steaming into New York harbor with a captured blockade runner. He had led numerous nighttime raids behind enemy lines, and once he had almost single-handedly fought off a Confederate boarding party. His most celebrated feat had occurred on the night of October 27, 1864, however, when he led a small party of volunteers on a commando raid against the powerful ironclad CSS *Albemarle*, lying in coastal waters near Plymouth, North Carolina. Cushing and his men took a steam launch up the Roanoke River, rowed up to the *Albemarle* and shoved a spar torpedo under the ship's hull. The torpedo exploded, the Rebel ironclad sank and Cushing and a companion somehow escaped. Navy Secretary Welles praised the youthful officer as a "brilliant example of courage and enterprise," and President Lincoln commended him before Congress. He had just completed a congratulatory tour of major Northern cities when he joined the Fort Fisher Expedition as commander of the admiral's flagship. Hazardous duty on the Cape Fear River was nothing new for Cushing—two of his behind-the-lines raids had taken him up the river in the dark of night. Now his daredevil's skills were being put to the test in daylight.[26]

Cushing boldly led a ten-boat sounding party of sailors into New Inlet. For a long moment, the fort's guns were silent. Then Battery Buchanan and the Mound Battery opened fire. Commander Guest's detachment of warships bombarded the two batteries with cannon fire, but the Confederates remained at their guns, concentrating their fire against the little flotilla of launches. Rounds from the fort fell all around the boats, whizzed overhead and splashed into the river inches away, but the sailors coolly took their soundings. So thick was the fire of grapeshot and canister that Coxswain Asa Betham of the USS *Pontoosuc* felt like he was working in a hailstorm. Cushing made an especially inviting target, seated in the stern of his launch under a blue and white officer's pennant. At one point, Cushing brazenly stood up in his launch, defiantly studying the fort's towering batteries. Incredibly, no one was hit, although Cushing's crew had to bail the water splashed into their launch by near misses.[27]

The sounding expedition did produce casualties—beginning in the fort. At about 2:30 that afternoon, as Confederate Midshipman Clarence Cary fired one of the seaface Brookes, the big artillery piece exploded, spraying the gun crew with jagged iron fragments. When the smoke cleared, Cary stared in horror at the carnage around him. One artilleryman lay headless near the wrecked cannon, another was twisted knotlike in the sand with a huge piece of iron embedded in his stomach, and sprawled nearby were a half-dozen other wounded. About an hour later, the other Brooke exploded. Afterwards, the Brooke battery was abandoned.[28]

By 3:30, Cushing and his seamen had sounded and marked the channel without sustaining any serious casualties. Cushing decided he had pushed his luck far enough and prepared to withdraw. Before the launches could retreat, however, one of the gunners in Battery Buchanan, Midshipman William R. Mayo, carefully trained his gun on a launch from the USS *Tacony* and fired another round. The shot arched over the inlet, passed within inches of the launch commander, Acting Master Rudolph Sommers, and neatly clipped the boat's stern pennant. Sommers fished the pennant out of the water, tied the banner to its broken staff, then ordered his crew to carry on. Mayo fired again. This round was a direct hit. It ripped through Sommers's launch, cutting the boat in half. One seaman was hit by flying splinters and another, twenty-six-year-old Seaman Henry Sands, collapsed in the boat, his legs severed at the knees by the shot. As the launch sank, other boats rescued its crew, including Seaman Sands, who later died. Cushing ordered a speedy withdrawal and the launches returned to their ships. The channel had been sounded and marked, but Admiral Porter still considered it unnavigable for his deep-draft warships. The sounding party's report had changed nothing: the fleet would not enter the river.[29]

◆

As the Federal troops moved down Confederate Point toward Fort Fisher, General Whiting dispatched a flurry of telegrams to Wilmington headquarters, urging General Bragg to reinforce the fort and attack the enemy from the rear. But Bragg seemed paralyzed. In Wilmington, the city's churches remained full long after Christmas services ended. The city's congregations stayed in their pews, praying for the protection of Wilmington and its defenders, as the distant bombardment rumbled like thunder and rattled church windows. At headquarters, Bragg appeared indecisive and shared little of his intentions with his staff. Finally, in an alarming display of pessimism, he made arrangements for his wife, Elisa, to flee the city by train. Word of her departure provoked a mass exodus by many of Wilmington's citizens. Despite pleas by Whiting and Lamb, Bragg issued no orders for an attack on the Federal rear. Some of the headquarters staff began to wonder if their commanding officer had lost his nerve. At one point, one of Bragg's subordinates later reported, the general's hands were trembling.[30]

At 4 P.M., with a superior enemy force now on the beach unopposed and the naval bombardment still pounding his works, Whiting sent Bragg an urgent plea for help. "A large body of the enemy has landed near the fort, deploying as skirmishers," he wired. "May be able to carry me by storm. Do the best I can. All behaving well. Order supports to attack." But no help came and it was Whiting's last dispatch: moments after the telegram was tapped to Wilmington, the line went dead.[31]

◆

Less than a mile north of the fort, Lieutenant George Simpson of the 142nd New York had just cut the telegraph wire connecting the fort and Wilmington. Federal skirmishers moving across the peninsula toward the river discovered the telegraph poles erected along the Wilmington road, and Colonel Curtis promptly ordered the line cut. Lieutenant Simpson obediently shinnied up the pole and severed the wire. Simpson and three companies of his regiment composed the Federal advance force led down Confederate Point by Colonel Curtis and General Weitzel. After posting a strong advance skirmish line from the river to the beach, Curtis cautiously moved his New Yorkers forward to within about 2,200 yards of the fort's landface. From there, he and Weitzel used a pair of binoculars to study the sprawling fort. Both were impressed. Curtis thought the fort's high earthen walls and towering palisade fence were formidable obstacles, and he counted at least seventeen landface cannon that still looked serviceable. Assaulting the fort might be costly, but it could be done, Curtis believed. Weitzel, however, had serious doubts. Porter's bombardment had not done the job, he concluded: from close range the fort did not appear to be seriously damaged. As a military engineer, Weitzel was trained to think defensively. When he saw Fort Fisher up close, he decided the giant fortress was intact and impregnable. At the Battle of Sabine Pass on the Texas coast the year before, he had seen how a small but aggressive body of Rebels could repel a superior force. He had also heard the horror stories about the disastrous Federal assaults on Battery Wagner near Charleston, and he figured the chance of a similar disaster at Fort Fisher was four times more likely. After a long look at the fort, he told Curtis not to engage the enemy without orders. Then he headed back to the landing site to commandeer a launch and report his observations to General Butler.[32]

Meanwhile, Curtis led his New Yorkers forward again until they occupied an abandoned line of Rebel earthworks about 150 yards north of the fort. He then ordered the right side of his skirmish line to move in even closer. The soldiers double-quicked across the sandy, open plain, hastily scooped rifle pits in the sand near the river and flopped on their stomachs about 75 yards from the fort. In front of them the Wilmington road stretched across the plain, crossed the riverside marsh over the fort's wooden bridge and entered Fort Fisher through the gate in the palisade fence. Moments later, a Confederate courier on horseback suddenly galloped through the gate, clattered across the plank bridge and headed up the sandy road toward the distant woods. The courier was nineteen-year-old Private Amos Jones of the Thirty-sixth North Carolina, and he was carrying a dispatch from Major William Saunders, the fort's chief of artillery. Saunders had no authority to order troops to leave the fort, however, he needed field artillery from the support force at Sugar Loaf. With the fort telegraph down he decided to send a courier on a horse someone had rounded up, unaware that the enemy was so close.[33]

Jones did not get far. As he neared the hidden Federal skirmishers, one of the New York infantrymen rose up from his rifle pit and shot the teenaged soldier from the saddle. Jones tumbled from his mount and fell dead in the sand. The Northern marksman knelt beside the fallen form, searching the body, and discovered Major Saunders's dispatch. Excited to find enemy documents, the soldier left the dead courier where he fell, caught the riderless horse and galloped back to Curtis with the captured dispatch.[34]

The colonel had been studying the fort from his new position and had decided it easily could be taken by assault—an opinion shared by his advance skirmishers. Sergeant John White of the 142nd New York had crawled close to the fort's log palisades, inching his way forward in the deep ruts of the Wilmington road, and from his position he could see that the bombardment had left sized gaps in the palisades. He was certain a charge up the road would capture the fort. Private Henry Blair had worked his way to within a stone's throw of the palisade. The fort walls were deserted. Not a single sentry was in sight, Blair noted. Surely, he thought, a column of troops could easily take this fort.[35]

Lieutenant William Walling, an officer in Company C of the 142nd, got close enough to the fort to capture a coveted trophy—and did so unscathed. Walling and a handful of troops were behind rifle pits near the river when they saw a shell take down Fort Fisher's riverside flag, dropping it between the landface wall and the palisade fence. "I'll go and get the flag," the lieutenant shouted to his men. "You keep a sharp lookout for riflemen on the works! Let every man have his gun in position to fire!" Covered by his troops, Walling sprang forward and raced toward the battered palisade. A stray shell exploded nearby, momentarily stunning him, but he recovered and dashed on. He darted through a splintered gap in the palisade timbers, grabbed the fallen flag and raced back to his position.[36]

A hundred yards away, Curtis watched the lieutenant dash back to safety with the captured flag. Walling's act convinced Curtis that Fort Fisher could be taken if an assault in force was made promptly. His aide-de-camp, Lieutenant George Ross, agreed. Like General Weitzel, the lieutenant had been present at the disastrous assault on Charleston's Battery Wagner. Unlike Weitzel, he thought an assault on Fort Fisher could succeed. Curtis needed no more encouragement; he was confident his troops could take the fort. He sent an orderly back to the rear guard to summon reinforcements, so he would be ready when he received the order to attack.[37]

◆

By now General Butler had approximately 2,500 troops ashore or landing, with another 4,000 held in reserve aboard ship. The troops had landed unopposed. At Battery Anderson, the nearest Confederate resistance had surrendered without a fight, and the thin force of Confederates under General Kirkland had been withdrawn to a distant defensive line. The rest of Hoke's division had yet to arrive at Confederate Point, permitting Curtis and his New Yorkers to advance on Fort Fisher without resistance. However, while Curtis waited for reinforcements and orders to assault the fort, General Butler was making plans to retreat.[38]

Butler needed little encouragement to pull out. He was still fuming about Porter's decision to explode the powder boat without the army, still convinced proper detonation of the *Louisiana* would have devastated the fort and allowed a successful ground attack. The Fort Fisher Expedition had been doomed, Butler believed, the moment the navy prematurely and improperly detonated the powder boat. Now Weitzel was saying that the navy's great bombardment had failed to seriously damage the fort's artillery and advised against an army assault, at least until the navy had silenced the fort's landface guns. "It would be butchery to order an assault on that work under the circumstances," Weitzel reported. He suggested allowing the navy one more day to bombard the fort and silence the landface artillery, then the army could mount an assault.[39]

Butler mulled it over. As army commander for the expedition, the decision to assault the fort was his. However, Grant had ordered him not to withdraw once his troops had landed. Still, only part of his force had gone ashore, so he could argue that a successful landing had not been completed—he had merely been conducting a reconnaissance-in-force. As Butler weighed his options, he was handed a report on the interrogation of a Confederate deserter who had come into the Federal lines. The soldier, one of Kirkland's troops, presented a disturbing message: General Hoke and a whole division of veterans from Virginia were due to arrive at any moment, and then the Yankees would have a real fight on their hands. Butler's vision of flattening Fort Fisher with a giant explosion and walking in unopposed to claim victory was now displaced by an ominous possibility: suppose he did assault the fort and failed—as General Weitzel predicted— then was bottled up against the ocean by Hoke's hard-driving Confederates? It could be a military and political disaster.[40]

As Butler studied Fort Fisher's distant walls and wrestled with his decision, General Charles Graham, the officer in charge of the landing, presented what amounted to an ultimatum. A storm appeared to be brewing, the seas were becoming rough and Butler's army was divided between the troopships and the beach. "General," Graham advised, "you have either got to provide for those troops on shore some way tonight, or get them off—because it is getting so rough that we cannot land much longer." Weitzel weighed in with a decisive opinion: building forts was his profession and he believed Fort Fisher was as strong as Fort Monroe, the giant, impregnable Federal fortress near Norfolk. Butler believed him. He had heard that the Rebel General Whiting was the architect of Fort Fisher, and Whiting, Butler lamented, "had been brought up at the foot of a cannonball." He was said to be a superb engineer—no wonder Fort Fisher was so powerful. Finally, Butler's mind was made up: he and his troops were leaving.[41]

◆

The order to withdraw was slow reaching Curtis at the front. After sending the orderly back for reinforcements, he had waited impatiently at his forward position, but no more troops arrived. Gradually, his impatience turned to frustration: It was almost five o'clock and soon it would be dark. Who knew how conditions might change? The assault should be made soon. Finally, exasperated with the delay, he recalled his skirmish line and stomped through the sand back to his rear guard.[42]

There, he found more troops *had* arrived. Finding the senior officer present, Curtis demanded to know why the reinforcements had not been sent forward. The answer was simple: General Butler was withdrawing all troops. Curtis was stunned. He knew Weitzel had doubts about assaulting the fort, but a retreat was out of the question. There had to be a mistake. He summoned another courier and scrawled a message to General Butler. "Your order is held in abeyance that you may know the true condition of the fort," he wrote. "The garrison has offered no resistance; the flagstaff of the fort was cut by a naval shot and one of my officers brought from the rampart the garrison flag. Another cut the telegraph wire connecting the fort with Wilmington. My skirmishers are now at the parapet." Soon after Curtis sent the courier hurrying to the rear, General Adelbert Ames arrived. He had landed with the second wave, and although he was the division commander, he too was ignorant of an order to retire. With Ames's permission, Curtis returned to his forward position and redeployed his troops.[43]

Sent by Curtis to secure the Wilmington Road, Colonel Rufus Daggett of the 117th New York had just gotten his troops in place when he looked up to see one of his men coming through the woods with a Confederate officer in tow. The prisoner identified himself as Major John M. Reece, commander of the Eighth North Carolina Junior Reserves, and to Daggett's astonishment, the major announced that he would like to surrender his command—more than 200 troops of the Fourth, Seventh and Eighth North Carolina Junior Reserves.[44]

◆

That morning Reece had been forced to lead his "Seventeen-Year-Olds" through the harrowing fire of the Federal naval bombardment all the way from Battery Buchanan to Fort Fisher's landface. It had been an unnerving experience. Several of the boys had been wounded and one was killed and dismembered by an exploding shell. By the time they had reached the shelter of the fort bombproofs, they were thoroughly terrorized. At one point General Whiting had spotted them, calling out encouragement. "These are North Carolina's pets," he had yelled to them. "She's got a damned bad way of showing it," one demoralized youngster had shouted back. Later, to relieve crowding in the bombproofs, Reece and the Junior Reserves had been ordered out of the fort and up the peninsula. Away from the bombardment, Reece had put the boys under the cover of the riverbank and had gone looking for the Yankees—apparently determined that no more of his boy soldiers would die.[45]

Reece wanted to surrender, but his offer raised suspicions among the New Yorkers. Colonel Daggett and his staff officers held a quick conference. How did they know Reece wasn't trying to lead them into an ambush? In response, Reece asked Daggett if he happened to be a member of the secret international order of Freemasonry. "No, but he is," Daggett replied, nodding to a subordinate, Captain Arnold Stevens of the 117th New York. Stevens challenged Reece to reply to a secret Masonic code, and when Reece replied correctly, Stevens turned to Daggett and vouched for the Confederate. Daggett remained skeptical, so Stevens volunteered to go with the major to bring in his surrendered troops. Moments later, the two officers—one in blue, one in gray—passed the Federal skirmish line and disappeared into the woods. They moved across the peninsula until near the river, when Stevens was startled to hear the chilling sound of 200 muskets cocking in a cacophony of clicks.

"What does that mean?" he demanded in a hushed voice.

"The boys are preparing to fire on us," Reece whispered back. "Wait a moment."

Moving forward several steps, he yelled a password and shouted, "Don't fire, boys!"

"We won't!" a dozen voices shouted back.

"Come on, captain," Reece called to Stevens. "It's all right."

Cautiously, Stevens followed Reece out of the woods and onto the riverbank, where he saw what looked like a large crowd of schoolboys in Confederate uniforms, crouching near the water. Immediately, an aggressive young officer, Lieutenant F. M. Hamlin, confronted Reece and began to report that the Yankees were nearby. Reece interrupted and announced, "Well boys, I've surrendered."

"Not by a damn sight," snapped Hamlin.

"Yes, I have," Reece told the baffled youngsters. "We are surrounded and can't get away."

Stevens then spoke for the first time. "We've got you, boys," he stated authoritatively. "You may as well give up."

The young soldiers looked confused, and some began to peer at Stevens's uniform. "Are you a Yankee officer?" asked one, wide-eyed.

"Yes," Stevens stated flatly, and the boy gasped.

Lieutenant Hamlin and a handful of followers slipped wordlessly away from the crowd and followed the river upstream until they passed into Confederate lines, encountering no opposition along the way. The rest of Reece's Junior Reserves surrendered without complaint. "We can't be worse off," one youngster told Stevens. "We have never received a cent of pay nor scarcely anything to eat except what we picked up." Minutes later, led by Captain Stevens, 237 Confederate officers and troops marched in order through the woods and into the Federal lines, where they were surrendered to an incredulous Colonel Daggett. Counted and questioned, the boy soldiers were marched to the landing site, then ferried as prisoners to the troopships. Not until they were aboard ship did anyone tell them to hand over their loaded muskets.[46]

◆

Meanwhile, Colonel Curtis waited at the front with mounting frustration. It was almost dark and still he had heard nothing. Finally, the first orderly returned and reported what Curtis already knew—General Butler had ordered a withdrawal. Curtis turned the man around and sent him back with the same message: The fort could be taken with proper reinforcements. The courier slogged off through the deep sand again, and Curtis turned back to face the darkening, bumpy outline of the fort. Surely he would get the orders and the troops he needed to assault Fort Fisher before it was too dark.[47]

Soon afterwards, Colonel Comstock joined Curtis at the front. Comstock had reconnoitered the fort from aboard ship with General Butler, then had come ashore to make his way down to the front. Now, for the first time, Comstock was able to view the monster fortress up close. When he studied Fort Fisher's defenses, he did so with expertise second to none on this expedition. The thirty-three-year-old engineer had graduated first in his class at West Point, had helped build prewar forts in Florida and Maryland, and had returned to the Point as an instructor. When the war began, he was assistant to the Army Chief of Engineers, and during the past three-and-a-half years of bloodshed, he had become an expert on Confederate military engineering in places like the Peninsula, Fredericksburg, Vicksburg and Mobile Bay. He had seen strong works, but none quite like this one. However, he listened as Curtis made his case, proposing a quick charge while the fort appeared undermanned. Comstock believed the fort only appeared lightly defended because the garrison was waiting out the bombardment in the fort bombproof. It was standard procedure in a siege to keep your troops safely undercover, then rush them forward to defend the post when the bombardment ceases. When the naval fire ended—and it had to stop to allow the Federal assault—then Fort Fisher's walls would fill with enemy marksmen.

Comstock accompanied Curtis as he moved his men back to their forward position near the fort. There, when he was within a stone's throw of the fort, Comstock began to think perhaps Curtis was right after all. They had come so close to the huge fort with no opposition, and the fort seemed deserted for the moment. It was almost dark, time was running out and the fort did indeed present an inviting target at close range. As they studied the fort's irregular outline, just yards away, Curtis resumed his refrain. He could take the fort with just fifty men, he boasted to Comstock. But this time he received a different response: he ought to do it, Comstock replied, now convinced. Curtis hesitated, then revised his estimate: he could do it with a brigade—his brigade. Yes, do it, Comstock urged, warming to the idea. Do it despite the orders—go ahead. Curtis hesitated again: if he just had positive orders from General Butler, he complained. Comstock made an offer: he'd go back himself and try to get permission from Butler.[48]

As they spoke, the troops they had brought up were deploying into battle position, throwing up breastworks on the open plain before the fort. Dusk was deepening into darkness and suddenly the fleet ceased fire. The day's bombardment was over: it would soon be too dark to keep up a sustained fire and, with practically no coordination established between the army and the navy, Porter assumed the army would attack the next morning. Therefore he had ordered an evening cease-fire as planned and the bombardment ended. Almost immediately, the chilling Rebel yell echoed over the plain. Fort Fisher's landface walls filled with riflemen, artillery crews manned their pieces and the fort unleashed a fusillade of cannon and small arms fire in the direction of Curtis's New Yorkers. Comstock stayed put—there was no chance of Curtis's sole brigade assaulting the fort under such heavy fire. An assault under these conditions would require several thousand troops. Now, it was certain, they would have to be reinforced in substantial numbers.[49]

◆

The Confederates who raced cheering out of the crowded bomb-proofs were following Colonel Lamb's prearranged orders: he knew the naval bombardment would have to cease to allow the enemy ground assault, so he had ordered his officers to move the garrison to the battle lines as soon as the naval fire ended. When the barrage stopped, Lamb and his officers assumed the ground assault was imminent. They quickly hustled the garrison out of the bombproofs and into line behind the sandbagged walls of the landface gun chambers. Lamb sent about 800 troops through the landface sally port double-quick, deploying them into a skirmish line behind the palisades, where they were supported by the sally-port field artillery. More troops were summoned from the seaface, and the Junior Reserves were ordered out of the bombproofs, their safe positions. Many of the "Seventeen-Year-Olds" had to be forced out of the bombproofs by their officers, who scolded and swore the boy-soldiers into action, swatting the backsides of those who tarried. "Don't be cowards, boys," Lamb urged as he hurried them into line.[50]

With most of the garrison deployed on the landface, the fort was able to pour a heavy, sustained fire into the darkness toward Curtis's troops. Even so, Whiting and Lamb were worried. They were afraid the Federals would carry the fort with an overwhelming assault, unless Bragg distracted them with a full-scale attack on their rear. Lamb was especially worried that the Federal naval forces might be able to enter the river and mount a ground assault from the rear while the main enemy force assaulted the landface. Regardless of how the enemy launched his attack, however, Lamb was determined to do everything possible to repel it. He would open a heavy fire of grapeshot and canister from the landface artillery, have the fort electrician detonate the field of buried torpedoes, then hope to stop the enemy survivors with massed rifle fire. It could work, he believed, if Bragg ordered a simultaneous attack on the enemy rear, forcing the Federals to deplete their reserves.[51]

General Whiting, meanwhile, sent Bragg a roundabout telegram, dispatched across the river to Confederate forces, then north to Wilmington. "If you send reinforcements for Kirkland to attack in the rear we can hold out," he told Bragg. The implied alternative was obvious. Bragg eventually responded, telling Whiting to bring in more Junior Reserves and to request all available troops from across the river. The commanding general reported that he was sending the rest of Hoke's division down to General Kirkland as quickly as they arrived, but he suggested Whiting consider an evacuation procedure in case Fort Fisher had to be abandoned—a proposal that infuriated the beleaguered Whiting.[52]

Darkness soon cloaked the peninsula and the muzzle flashes of the opposing troops flared brightly in the night. The exchange of fire continued for more than an hour. Then, shortly after seven o'clock, the Federal fire sputtered, then ceased. Whiting and Lamb waited tensely for the assault, but it did not come. They could see very little in the smoky darkness, but it appeared that the Yankees were withdrawing.[53]

◆

Colonel Curtis was furious—the army *was* retreating. He had been confident the report of a withdrawal was a misunderstanding. Even as darkness settled over his position and his New Yorkers traded fire with the Rebels in the fort, he had expected at any moment to see reinforcements arrive with orders to assault Fort Fisher. Instead, he had received a definite and final order to withdraw, issued from the commanding general and forwarded through General Ames. Reluctantly, he recalled his troops, formed them in line and retired up the peninsula to the landing site. As they moved through the darkness in retreat, some men cursed Ben Butler aloud.[54]

When they reached the landing site, the cursing increased: they were stranded. Naval launches were ferrying the last of the Second and Third brigades through choppy seas to the troopships and some gutsy sailors managed to disembark some of Curtis's First Brigade, but the seas were too rough to move any more. The surf had become ferocious, overturning launches and splitting their hulls against the beach. The remainder of Curtis's troops were stranded on Confederate Point without adequate drinking water, rations or ammunition—and they were now outnumbered by the enemy.[55]

They had not been issued blankets, the engineers had departed with all the entrenching tools and it began to rain. By 10 o'clock, a fog had settled over the peninsula, the temperature had fallen and the rain had turned to sleet. The troops were miserable. Using gun butts, tin plates, discarded oars and planks ripped from the wrecked launches, they wearily dug rifle pits and entrenched themselves in a defensive line facing the woods. Offshore, the ironclads began to fire sporadically through the fog, lobbing shells into the woods to discourage the Confederates from attacking the stranded soldiers. Curtis knew the tables had been turned on him and the advantage now lay with the men in gray. He now had less than a single brigade ashore—about 700 men—and they would be no match for an attack by thousands of Hoke's veteran Confederates. During the day the fleet's immense firepower could probably prevent the Rebels from massing for an attack, but what if the storm continued, making it impossible for the fleet to brings its guns to bear? Or what if the Confederates launched a night attack, when the fleet would be unable to direct its fire against the enemy without endangering Curtis's men? As the sleet fell on his soaked and shivering troops, Curtis knew he was in a precarious position.[56]

◆

In reality, he had no need to worry. General Bragg had no intention of launching an attack. Inside Fort Fisher, Colonel Lamb kept the garrison in line and at their guns all night, calling for reinforcements and trying to repair his damages in the flickering glare of the fort's burning barracks. Alarmed by a jittery sentry who mistakenly thought he saw the Yankees landing at about 3 A.M., the garrison poured rifle and cannon fire into the darkness for several minutes until they realized nothing was there. In the foggy morning light, Lamb and Whiting studied the distant Federal landing site through a telescope and concluded that the Yankees were still ashore, massed at the landing site and presumably still in the woods. Up the peninsula, General Kirkland maintained his thin defensive line, waiting to see what the Yankees would do. He received no orders to advance from General Bragg, who was presumably waiting for the rest of Hoke's division to arrive on the 26th. Kirkland's troops did capture a Federal officer, Lieutenant Charles Smith of the 142nd New York, who somehow wandered into Kirkland's picket line during the foggy night. When interrogated, Smith proved quite willing to talk: keeping a straight face, he told his Confederate captors that they were facing a full Federal division—up to 12,000 troops.[57]

◆

Curtis's New Yorkers remained stranded all day on the 26th. Rough seas continued to prevent their removal. The expedition's quartermaster filled water casks with hardtack and beef and tried to float the rations ashore on a raft, but the experiment failed. The hungry soldiers stayed in line, watching for the expected Rebel attack, and prepared to spend a second night on the beach—knowing they were pushing their luck. Late that day the bulk of Hoke's division finally arrived in Wilmington and was immediately marched south to Sugar Loaf. Accompanied by his staff, General Bragg came downriver by steamer and officially assumed command of the 6,000-man force. He reinforced Kirkland's defensive line and discussed strategy with Hoke—then did nothing. Even with Hoke's veterans now present, Bragg was certain the Yankees still outnumbered him.[58]

The second night on the beach was worse than the first for Curtis's stranded soldiers. Now they were as jittery as the raw troops in Fort Fisher. A heavy rain continued to fall and the weary Federals thought they saw the Rebels in every shadow. Several times during the night, the pickets sounded the alarm and the fleet was signaled by torchlight. The ironclads would then rake the nearby woods with gunfire as the New Yorkers lay in their trenches, hoping they would not be killed by their own navy.[59]

Finally, at dawn on December 27, Curtis's troops were cheered to see a flotilla of naval launches bucking through choppy but manageable seas. Bearded, wet and worn, the New Yorkers happily waded waist-deep into the icy surf and greeted the bluejackets with cheerful appreciation, relieved to be off the enemy beach. "The boys had a lively time getting off," one observer wrote home, "but they made a joke of the whole thing. As soon as a boat came to them, five or six men grasped it on each side and turned its prow to the sea. Then throwing aboard their bundles, muskets and equipment, they waded out until breast deep in the water, where a final shove was given and all climbed in. Very often the boats swamped, but the boys came up laughing to renew their effort."[60]

Curtis was among the last to leave the beach. He climbed into a launch from the USS *Nereus* and was soon pulling away from Confederate Point. As the beach slowly receded in the distance, he and his staff made no attempt to conceal their contempt for Butler. If his troops had been reinforced, Curtis grumped to a nearby naval officer, Fort Fisher would have been captured. When safely aboard ship, Curtis's troops learned they had even more to fume about: while they had been enduring their unnerving ordeal on the beach, General Butler had already left for Hampton Roads. He had gone the day after Christmas, ready to be rid of the frustrating Fort Fisher Expedition and certain, he would later proclaim, that his subordinates would be able to rescue his stranded troops. In a dispatch to Admiral Porter, he had described Fort Fisher as "substantially uninjured as a defensive work by the navy fire" and therefore still too strong to carry by ground assault. The fort could only be taken by siege, he asserted, and he had not planned to conduct a siege. "I shall therefore sail for Hampton Roads as soon as the transport fleet can be got in order," he had announced. And then he had gone. It was the final peculiarity in an expedition riddled with controversy—and it earned Butler the enduring enmity of his own troops. "Curses enough have been heaped on Butler's head to sink him in the deepest hole of the bottomless pit," one of the New York soldiers wrote home. "Everybody is disgusted. Officers and men express that the fort was ours and that no one but Butler prevented them from taking it."[61]

The navy was even more critical. A *New York World* reporter accompanying the expedition heard prominent naval officers condemning Butler as "either a black-hearted traitor or an arrant coward," who had ruined all chances of success against Fort Fisher. "He was determined to have his own way," one naval officer griped, "and seeing that he could not, he was bent on thwarting everything." Porter was stung by Butler's declaration that the navy had failed to effectively silence the fort and had botched the powder boat experiment. The admiral considered the navy's role in the campaign to have been a complete success, unrecognized by the army, and he was incensed that Butler dared blame the navy for the expedition's failure. "Great heavens, what are we coming to?" Porter confided to a friend. "God save me from further connection with such generals." He had poured more than one million pounds of iron on Fort Fisher—20,271 artillery rounds, to be exact—he told Navy Secretary Welles, and all Butler had to do was walk in and possess the battered fort the navy had won for him. "I feel ashamed that men calling themselves soldiers should have left this place so ingloriously," he confided privately to Welles. "It was, however, nothing more than I expected when General Butler got himself mixed up in this expedition. . . ."[62]

As soon as the stranded troops were rescued, the fleet and the troopships headed north—the troopships back to Hampton Roads and the warships to Beaufort. After all the preparations, after all the waiting, after two days of the war's greatest bombardment, after landing almost 3,000 troops, after advancing to within yards of the fort—the expedition was over, aborted at the very last moment. It was a humiliating failure for the Army of the James and a frustrating ending for the seamen of Porter's giant fleet. Aboard the troopship *Weybossett*, steaming back to Hampton Roads, Lieutenant William Walling took a last look at the Confederate flag he had risked his life to capture. Then he and his fellow soldiers cut the colorful banner into tiny red, white and blue squares—souvenirs from the unsuccessful Fort Fisher Expedition.[63]

◆

As the Federal warships disappeared one by one over the horizon, Fort Fisher's garrison watched with surprise and relief. Suddenly, it seemed, the battle was over and Fort Fisher was still theirs. They had endured an incredible barrage. They had traded fire with enemy troops. And they had survived. As the garrison realized the enemy was gone, a holiday atmosphere arose. "Our brave boys gave the Yankees a good thrashing and they left," one Johnny Reb boasted to the folks back home. When the battered survivors of the detachment from the CSS *Chickamauga* limped down to Battery Buchanan, towing their wounded in an oxcart, their fellow seamen ushered the detachment into a hollow square and saluted them with cheer after cheer. Colonel Lamb felt he had good reason to celebrate: the unprecedented two-day bombardment and the Christmas Day skirmishing had produced a mere sixty-one casualties, including six dead—surprisingly light casualties for such a pounding. The garrison's barracks were destroyed and the fort's traverses were badly battered, but no more than four of the fort's heavy artillery pieces were destroyed. Fort Fisher was still standing—and strong. Most importantly, with the fort's guns still protecting New Inlet, the Cape Fear was still open to blockade runners. The day after the Federal fleet departed, the blockade runners *Banshee* and *Wild Rover* slipped safely through the inlet in the early morning darkness, then steamed upriver and deposited their crucial cargo at Wilmington. The Confederacy's lifeline to its European suppliers was still open.[64]

Following the enemy withdrawal, General Whiting promptly recommended Colonel Lamb for promotion to brigadier general. The recommendation was endorsed by Bragg and Confederate Secretary of War James Seddon, who routed it through government channels for routine approval. Lamb, relieved that his fort had survived its ordeal by fire, praised his troops for what he officially described as a "great victory." General Bragg was even more effusive, touting the Yankee withdrawal in an official proclamation. "The successful defense of Fort Fisher against one of the most formidable naval armaments of modern times proves that the superiority of land batteries over ships of war has been reestablished by the genius of the engineer," Bragg proclaimed, "and the weaker party on the defensive may still defy the greater numbers and mechanical resources of an arrogant invader." The proclamation carried no hint of Bragg's indecision, his reluctance to attack the enemy or the lack of confidence with which he was viewed by subordinates.[65]

Indeed, General Bragg seemed to feel Fort Fisher and Wilmington were no longer endangered. He declined an offer of additional ammunition from General Lee, suggested that North Carolina's governor disband the Junior and Senior Reserves so they could be reorganized, and made plans to return Hoke's division to Virginia. General Whiting was shocked by Bragg's relaxed mood. Fort Fisher had been saved because the gale that arose Christmas night prevented further enemy landings, Whiting believed. The Yankees had come ashore just as he had predicted and the attack had come after the fort's garrison had been depleted—over his strong objections. The enemy had been unwisely allowed to move down the peninsula largely unopposed—and had not been seriously attacked while ashore. The enemy's tactics demonstrated the need for a permanent support force to attack the Federals as they came ashore, he argued. Bragg demonstrated little interest in Whiting's concerns; instead, he began planning a victory review for Hoke's troops before sending them back to Virginia.[66]

Meanwhile, Whiting and Lamb concentrated on strengthening Fort Fisher in case the enemy returned. Lamb ordered a day of rest for his garrison and directed Luther McKinnon, the post chaplain, to conduct a thanksgiving service. Otherwise, he kept the troops working at a frantic pace. Aided by some 200 slaves impressed from nearby plantations, they rebuilt the fort's battered traverses, repaired gun carriages, mounted new artillery, removed wagonloads of unexploded enemy shells, laid a new underground telegraph line across the fort's interior and underwater to a point across the river, and put in an order for enough lumber to reconstruct the post barracks. They also began moving logs from across the river to build a palisade in the rear of the fort between the Mound Battery and the landface.[67]

While he tried to oversee the work, Lamb also had to play host to a parade of visitors, who came to tour the site of what was now being reported throughout the Confederacy as a great victory. Government officials, journalists and a boatload of women from the Ladies Soldiers Aid Society visited the fort. The ladies were naturally the most popular visitors, if for no other reason than the fact that they came armed with a bounty of home-cooked food. They marveled over the fort's high walls, stepped gingerly over the enemy shell fragments carpeting the fort and paused for a moment of silence beside the grave of slain courier Amos Jones. Before they left, Colonel Lamb told the ladies they had done what the Yankees had failed to do—take the garrison by surprise and successfully storm the fort.[68]

On January 8, 1865, less than two weeks after the enemy expedition had departed, General Bragg ordered Hoke's troops to withdraw from their lines on Confederate Point and retire to Wilmington for a dress parade. Whiting and Lamb were dismayed by the order. They did not want Hoke's troops removed; they wanted several thousand of them posted near the Federal landing site, so the Yankees could be met on the beach if they returned. *That* was where the Federals had to be beaten, Whiting believed, and not on the walls of Fort Fisher. Bragg dismissed the advice. The prevailing wisdom at Wilmington headquarters predicted no more enemy action against Fort Fisher until late spring—if even then. Hoke's troops were withdrawn from Confederate Point and Bragg went ahead with his grand parade in Wilmington. Attired in a new uniform presented to him by some grateful citizens, he watched as Hoke's soldiers marched shoulder to shoulder in step with martial melodies. Later, the troops were dismissed to enjoy the comforts of town. At Bragg's direction, a military band serenaded ladies and gentlemen of the city with popular tunes of the day.[69]

The exercise left General Whiting frustrated and embittered. His urgent warnings had accomplished nothing, except probably to alienate him further from the commanding general. He and Lamb had worked furiously for the past two weeks, trying to prepare for another attack. Whiting was certain the Yankees would return—and that they would not wait until spring. He had tried to sound the warning, but Bragg apparently did not share his concerns. As second-in-command, Whiting could do only so much. Still, he was gravely worried about the fate of Fort Fisher and the South's sole surviving port. Meanwhile, far to the north near Richmond, a Federal deserter crossed into Confederate lines with some ominous news: the same army-navy force that had tried to take Wilmington a few weeks earlier had just left Hampton Roads and was sailing South again—to attack Fort Fisher.[70]

7

"The Fort Will Soon Be Ours"

Tʜᴇ Yᴀɴᴋᴇᴇs ᴡᴇʀᴇ ʙᴀᴄᴋ.

Colonel Lamb could see the lights of their warships as he stood on Fort Fisher's ramparts and peered seaward into the darkness. It was just after midnight on the evening of January 12, 1865—barely two weeks since the Federals had retreated north. Now they were back, just as he and Whiting had feared, and this time who knew what the outcome might be? One thing was almost certain: the Yankee fleet would resume its awful bombardment in the morning and in the hours before dawn. Lamb had a lot to do.

He dictated a telegram, alerting Wilmington headquarters, then ordered a drummer to beat the "long roll," summoning the garrison to battle stations. The fort's sleepy troops poured out of the bomb-proofs, their makeshift barracks, and fell into line. When all were assembled, there were just over 700 soldiers. The garrison now consisted of the 36th North Carolina; the rest of the fort's troops had been relocated following the Christmas battle. Again, Lamb ordered his men to prepare for combat. They had little time and they had to be ready. Out there in the darkness, Lamb knew, thousands of well-equipped Northern troops were waiting for the dawn—and the orders that would send them charging against the walls of his fort.[1]

◆

They were out there all right, resting in the night for the battle soon to come. They had been escorted down to the Cape Fear coast again by the U.S. Navy and Admiral David Dixon Porter. Even before the troops had returned to their campsites in Virginia, Porter had begun lobbying for resumption of the Fort Fisher Campaign. "Fort Fisher can't be held half an hour against the attack of the navy and land forces at the same time," he had boasted to Navy Secretary Welles a few days after the Christmas attack was aborted. "Well, sir, it could have been taken on Christmas with 500 men, without losing a soldier; there were not 20 men in the fort, and those were poor, miserable, panic-stricken people, cowering there with fear. . . ." He had distanced himself from the unsuccessful explosion of the powder boat, ignoring his initial enthusiasm for the idea and his rush to explode the powder boat before Butler and the army arrived. "I did not care a fig for the powder-boat," he assured Welles. He had heaped scorn on Benjamin Butler—publicly as well as privately. With the obvious approval of the Navy Department, Porter had released his official report of the Christmas battle, tactfully but clearly blaming the expedition's failure on Butler. Porter described Fort Fisher as "so blown up, burst up, and torn up that the people inside had no intention of fighting any longer." In his private correspondence, he was even harsher, claiming the failure of the Fort Fisher Expedition "will be a blessing to this nation" if it kept General Butler from gaining the White House. "Had he succeeded," predicted Porter, "it would have made him our next president, the greatest calamity that could have happened to the country."[2]

The Northern press, led by the *New York World,* was quick to join the fray. A few Democratic newspapers defended Butler, but most papers attacked the peculiar, controversial general, using Porter's official reports as evidence of Butler's military blundering. The Fort Fisher Expedition became a national scandal and the powder boat experiment—"Butler's powder-boat"—became a national joke. Navy Secretary Welles stated publicly that General Grant never should have allowed Butler to command the expedition. Veterans of the ill-fated campaign fashioned a mocking medallion to commemorate the expedition—a general's insignia mounted on a pair of running legs—and dedicated it to Butler for his "heroic conduct before Fort Fisher." In Washington, the powerful Joint Committee on the Conduct of the War launched a Congressional investigation into the Fort Fisher fiasco, and President Lincoln demanded to know who was responsible for the expedition's embarrassing failure.[3]

Typically, Butler mounted a vigorous, eloquent defense—before both his superiors and the public—and blamed the expedition's failure on Admiral Porter. The navy should have been at the rendezvous on time so a coordinated landing could have been made in good weather, he argued, and should have exploded the powder boat at the right time and in the proper way. Furthermore, Butler countered, Porter refused to force his way into the Cape Fear and failed to weaken the enemy fort enough to allow a successful ground attack. The allegations stung Porter, but this time even Butler's wiliest lawyer's skills could not save him. The fatal blow came from General Grant. Butler had disobeyed orders, Grant told the president, the congressional committee and the public. "General Butler came away from Fort Fisher in violation of the instructions which I gave him," Grant later testified at a Congressional hearing. "My instructions were very clear, that if they effected a landing there above Fort Fisher, that in itself was to be considered a success; and if the fort did not fall immediately upon their landing, then they were to intrench themselves and remain there and cooperate with the navy until the fort did fall."[4]

Grant asked for permission to remove Butler from command. President Lincoln carefully weighed public opinion, decided that even the Radicals and abolitionists who were Butler's strongest supporters could no longer defend him, then took decisive action. Four days into the new year, down from the White House came Executive Order No. 1 for 1865: General Benjamin F. Butler was officially removed as commander of the Army of the James and was replaced by General E. O. C. Ord.[5]

The army's black regiments were angered by Butler's dismissal, but the general's demotion was welcomed by others in the military. "We all believe Butler to be a rank traitor and a coward and everything but a gentleman," confided a young officer to his family. Observed another, "I think that the removal of Gen'l Butler will give very general satisfaction in the army. It may be for the best that Butler did not have the honor of capturing Wilmington, as he has killed all his plans for the presidency."[6]

Defiant to the end, Butler assembled the Army of the James at Fort Monroe for a final review and subjected them to a parting speech. "I have refused to order the useless sacrifice of the lives of such soldiers," he told them, "and I am relieved of your command. The wasted blood of my men does not stain my garments. For my action I am responsible to God and my country." To his black troops, Butler added a special salute: "With the bayonet you have unlocked the iron-barred gates of prejudice, opening new fields of freedom, liberty and equality of right to yourselves and your race forever."[7]

It was an emotional departure. "Comrades of the Army of the James," Butler concluded, "I bid you farewell! Farewell!" He then turned over command to General Ord and was escorted to the army ship *Chamberlain,* where his family waited unhappily in his stateroom. With all the dignity he could muster, the portly Butler saluted his escort and boarded ship. While walking to his stateroom for the trip North and home, he passed one of the ship's coal heavers and instinctively grabbed the surprised crewman's hand, shaking it vigorously in habitual political style, eager for acceptance amid the humiliation of the moment. And then he was gone, his military career ended.[8]

◆

Even before Butler was removed from command, Admiral Porter had been politicking earnestly for a new army commander for a second Fort Fisher expedition. Porter's first choice was General William T. Sherman, who had just burned his way across Georgia to capture Savannah as a Christmas present for President Lincoln. A few days after Christmas, Porter had dispatched an aide on a fast ship to Savannah with a message for Sherman, urging him to take his victorious army up the coast to Wilmington and join the navy in another combined assault on Fort Fisher. "I invite you to add to your brow the laurels thrown away by General Butler after they were laid at his feet by the Navy," Porter wrote. "Take this place and you take the *crème de la crème* of the rebellion. With you I feel sure of success," he lobbied, "and shall bless the day when I shall once more see your esteemed self in our midst. A host of old friends are here to welcome you, and show you the most magnificent naval fight you ever laid your eyes on."[9]

Sherman wanted the assignment. He immediately sat down with Porter's emissary and outlined a plan: "I propose to march my whole army through South Carolina," he wrote, "tearing up the railroads and smashing things generally, feign on Charleston and rapidly come down on Wilmington from the rear, taking all their works in reverse." He was already urging Grant to support the march to Wilmington, Sherman reported, and hoped to move northward within the next two weeks—if he received Grant's permission. He did not. Grant had other plans for Sherman—plans that would indeed result in a fiery, devastating march through the heart of South Carolina—but Grant had already decided who would be the army commander for the second expedition.[10]

Alfred Howe Terry was his name. He was a thirty-eight-year-old brigadier general from Connecticut, and at first thought he seemed an odd choice for Grant, who had his pick of practically any officer in the U.S. Army. Terry was not a professional soldier. He had not attended West Point. Instead, he was by profession a lawyer—the clerk of New Haven County Superior Court—who spent his spare moments in peacetime playing the flute or singing bass in a local choral society. But Grant had good reasons for choosing Terry. Although not a West Pointer, Alfred H. Terry was a veteran combat commander, a disciplinarian and a dramatic contrast to the flamboyant, controversial Ben Butler. Tall, dark-haired, with a neatly groomed beard, he was a quiet, mild-mannered man who got along easily with superiors and subordinates alike. He was serious-minded and dependable, determined to succeed when assigned a task, and too busy even for marriage. "Although the General was a very modest man, we could all see he was a brave soldier," observed one officer upon meeting Terry. "Pomposity, arrogance, cowardice and self-conceit seemed to be elements foreign to his character."

One of ten children and a descendant of early New England settlers, he was a Yale Law School alumnus who had left school before graduation in order to practice law. Like many young men of the antebellum era, he had a fascination with the military. He had been active in the state militia for years and by 1861, he had risen to commander of the Second Connecticut Militia. When Lincoln called for Northern volunteers to force the South back into the Union, Terry and the Second Connecticut responded. He took the 90-day regiment into action at First Manassas, then, when the enlistments expired, he helped organize the seventh Connecticut Volunteers and was made its colonel. He saw more action in the Port Royal Campaign, helped take Fort Pulaski, commanded the Federal forces on Hilton Head for a while, then led his troops in various operations near Charleston in 1863. After two disastrous Federal assaults on Battery Wagner near Charleston, Terry was scheduled to lead a third assault—but the Confederates withdrew before the planned attack. He was later transferred to the Army of the James, serving as one of Butler's corps commanders in operations against Petersburg and Richmond. His rise in rank was rapid—brigadier in 1862, corps commander a year later, and brevet major general by the summer of 1864.[11]

Terry exuded a quiet competence that others found striking. "He was an ideal soldier and gentleman, whose honest, truthful, and upright life gained him the highest esteem of all who knew him," reported a contemporary. Even Lincoln, exposed to a constant stream of officers, was impressed by Terry's bearing when introduced in Washington. "Why have we not seen you before?" the president asked. "Because my duties have kept me at the front," Terry modestly replied. Grant's aide-de-camp, Lieutenant Colonel Horace Porter, mentioned Terry to Grant as a likely commander for the renewed Fort Fisher Expedition. Upon examination, Grant found Terry to be the perfect choice: a seasoned combat commander whose proven competence in joint operations reduced the worrisome risk of another failure at Fort Fisher. His easygoing nature would ensure cooperation with the volatile Admiral Porter, and Terry was respected and liked by the officers and men of the Army of the James. His reputation was a dramatic contrast to Butler's, and replacing Butler with another volunteer officer would enable Grant to demonstrate his continued faith in volunteers. On January 2, 1865, Terry was summoned to Grant's City Point headquarters for a conference with the general in chief. Grant was determined that the second campaign against Fort Fisher, unlike the first, would remain secret as long as possible. Therefore he concealed the expedition's destination even from Terry, revealing only that Terry had been chosen to lead more than 8,000 troops on a land-sea operation. The expedition would sail under sealed orders, Grant explained, and Terry would learn the target of the campaign only after departure. Rumors of a return to Fort Fisher were already being bandied around the campfire, but Terry apparently believed the expedition was meant to reinforce Sherman's Carolinas Campaign—mainly because Grant posted orders citing Savannah as the destination.[12]

Terry learned differently three days later, on January 5, when the expedition left Bermuda Hundred. Terry's headquarters ship, the *McClellan*, docked en route at City Point for a final conference with Grant, who finally revealed the expedition's destination. "The object is to renew the attempt to capture Fort Fisher, and in case of success, to take possession of Wilmington," he told Terry. "It is of the greatest importance that there should be a complete understanding and harmony of action between yourself and Admiral Porter," he emphasized. "I want you to consult the admiral fully, and to let there be no misunderstanding in regard to the plan of cooperation in all its details." Grant was determined that the army would not be blamed for failing to cooperate with the navy this time. A second embarrassment at Fort Fisher would be scandalous, as emphasized by a dispatch he had just received from the Navy Department. "The country will not forgive us for another failure at Wilmington," Assistant Navy Secretary Fox had written, "and I have so informed Porter."[13]

The Admiral needed some encouragement. He was surprised and irritated that *his* choice—the famous Sherman—had been rejected in favor of a virtual unknown. Even worse, Porter fumed, the new army commander was one of Ben Butler's subordinates. How could he be expected to work with such a selection? "The man Grant is going to send here, a volunteer general, is one of Butler's men," Porter carped to Gustavus Fox, "who will likely white-wash Butler by doing just as he did." The admiral also wanted the U.S. Colored Troops left behind on the next expedition. "We want white men here—not niggers," Porter confided to Fox. The failure of the Christmas expedition was primarily Grant's fault, Porter believed, because he "permitted the most inefficient men in the country to come here." Grant was uninterested in the Fort Fisher Expedition, Porter theorized, because the idea had originated with someone else. "I am not one of those who consider him the military genius of the age," Porter told Fox. As for Grant's choice to replace Butler, this Alfred H. Terry: "Don't be surprised if I send him home with a flea in his ear," the admiral boasted.[14]

Porter came face to face with Terry for the first time a few days later, when the troop transports made rendezvous with the naval fleet at Beaufort, North Carolina on January 8. As the troopships entered the harbor, sustained cheering rolled from the decks of the naval warships. Aboard the transports, the troops returned the salute with wild hurrahs, and an atmosphere of celebration affected soldiers and sailors alike. The reason for the involuntary cheers was obvious to all—the Fort Fisher Expedition was again under way and this time all believed there would be a victory. Amid such an atmosphere, even the temperamental Porter found it difficult to be grumpy—especially after he met General Terry. During the first expedition, Butler and Porter had no official personal contact—not a single personal conference. This operation would be different: Terry's first act upon arriving at Beaufort was to come aboard the *Malvern* to confer with Porter. The general climbed aboard, came face to face with the admiral and offered his hand. The two warmly clasped hands, amid the chorus of cheers. "At first sight, both appeared to be pleased with each other," noted Adrian Terry, the general's brother and adjutant. Actually, Porter initially thought Terry to be "cold and formal" and lacking "the frankness of the true soldier"—perhaps because Terry initially rejected Porter's advice. The two soon warmed to each other, however, and Terry found Porter to be "a frank, straightforward, courteous gentleman." Terry's forthright character seemed to affect Porter just as positively as it had influenced Lincoln and others. "Terry had no staff, wore no spurs, and we do not think he owned a sword," Porter later noted. "He had a well-formed head, full of sense, which served him in lieu of feathers, sword, boots, spurs and staff—of which a general can have too many." From this moment

A law school graduate at nineteen and a newspaper editor at twenty, William Lamb of Virginia immersed himself in military biographies as a child. Bright, energetic, and devoted to the cause of Southern independence, he excelled in the army and eventually commanded the greatest fort in the Confederacy. *(College of William and Mary)*

At twenty-six William Lamb was promoted to colonel and placed in command of Fort Fisher, guardian of what would become the Confederacy's most important seaport. "I determined at once," he said, "to build a work of such magnitude that it could withstand the heaviest fire of any guns in the American navy."
(Museum of the Confederacy)

Noted for her beauty and charm, Daisy Lamb shared her husband's loyalty to the South despite her Northern birth and education. She was devoted to her "lover husband," as she called Lamb, and ignored the hazards of warfare to make her home with him at Fort Fisher.
(College of William and Mary)

Flamboyant, innovative, and politically powerful, Gen. Benjamin F. Butler was the most controversial volunteer officer in the U.S. Army. Described as a "notorious demagogue and a political scoundrel" by Northerners, the general was known as "Beast Butler" in the South, where chamber pots were decorated with his image. The Fort Fisher Campaign would be the climax of his military career. *(Library of Congress)*

Comfortably attired in his bedroom slippers, General Butler *(seated, left)* posed for an official photograph with his staff officers prior to the Fort Fisher Expedition. Seated beside Butler in knee-high cavalry boots is his protégé, Gen. Godfrey Weitzel, Grant's first choice to lead the army expedition. *(USAMHI)*

Gen. Godfrey Weitzel was chief engineer of the Army of the James when picked to command army operations against Fort Fisher. It was a promising command for Weitzel, but as the expedition got under way his assignment took an unexpected turn. *(USAMHI)*

Gen. W. H. C. Whiting was a Northerner by heritage and a Confederate by choice. Few doubted his brilliance and he enjoyed the devotion of his troops, but his wartime career was plagued by rumors and frustration—and he had incurred the wrath of President Davis. Without orders, he chose to cast his fate with the defenders of Fort Fisher. *(Library of Congress)*

The president's friend, Gen. Braxton Bragg held one important wartime command after another, but trouble and controversy seemed to follow him everywhere and some described him as "simply muddle-headed." Ultimately, the defense of Fort Fisher and survival of the South's last major seaport would rest upon him. *(Library of Congress)*

Gen. Robert F. Hoke of North Carolina was poised in the Federal rear with 6,000 Confederate combat veterans. If allowed to unleash a full-scale attack, Hoke's Rebels could shatter the Federal strategy for capturing Fort Fisher. *(USAMHI)*

Confederate General Alfred H. Colquitt came downriver in a rowboat to take command of Fort Fisher's defense at the climax of the battle. His war record was commendable, but Colonel Lamb had little faith in an officer he viewed as a mere "Georgia militia general." *(USAMHI)*

Assertive, strong-willed, and eager for fame, Admiral David Dixon Porter "had no hesitation in trampling down a brother officer," observed U.S. Navy Secretary Gideon Welles. Even so, when he had to select a commander for naval operations against Fort Fisher, Welles chose Porter. *(Library of Congress)*

Standing ramrod straight in a no-nonsense pose, Admiral Porter was photographed at the center of his staff officers. Those around him who survived Fort Fisher knew they had witnessed the war's greatest naval bombardment. *(USAMHI)*

"Why have we not seen you before?" President Lincoln asked Gen. Alfred H. Terry. Modest, easygoing, and unwarlike by nature, Terry was a Connecticut clerk of court whose favorite pastime was playing the flute. The war turned him into a combat officer, and eventually he was charged with command of army operations against Fort Fisher. *(author's collection)*

"He was an ideal soldier and gentleman," a contemporary said of General Terry, seated here in the center of his staff in Virginia. When General Butler failed to capture Fort Fisher, Grant replaced him with Terry, hoping the easygoing Terry could successfully cooperate with the navy. "The country will not forgive us for another failure at Fort Fisher," predicted a high-ranking U.S. official. *(USAMHI)*

An expert on military fortifications, Colonel Cyrus B. Comstock was appointed as chief engineer for the Fort Fisher Expedition. He had helped direct operations against Confederate fortifications in two theaters of the war, but he had never encountered a fort like this one. His advice would crucially affect Federal operations against the fort. *(USAMHI)*

The Federal troops selected to lead the assault against Fort Fisher were drawn from the Second Division of the XXIV Army Corps, commanded by Gen. Adelbert Ames. A general at twenty-seven, Ames boasted a distinguished war record, but a personal quarrel with one of his brigade commanders may have affected his combat judgment at Fort Fisher. *(USAMHI)*

A former schoolteacher, Colonel Newton Martin Curtis of New York had been forced to sit out much of the war due to a serious wound. Upon recovery, he was eager to see more combat. His wish was granted when he was chosen to lead the Federal assault against Fort Fisher. *(USAMHI)*

Promoted to colonel two months after his twentieth birthday, Galusha Pennypacker was believed to be the youngest brigade commander in the United States Army. He had entered service at sixteen, suffered numerous wounds, held a distinguished combat record—and was too young to vote. Fort Fisher would be his last battle. *(Pennsylvania State University)*

The son of a prominent New Hampshire politician, twenty-seven-year-old Colonel Louis Bell was intelligent, athletic, and perfectly suited for a postwar political career. At home he had an infant son he had never seen. At Fort Fisher, he and his troops would be called in when the fighting became desperate. *(USAMHI)*

Capt. Albert G. Lawrence, aide-de-camp to Gen. Adelbert Ames, posed for this photograph in his civilian finery. Fond of all-day poker games with the other young officers on Ames's staff, Lawrence would gamble his life in a race to lead the army assault at Fort Fisher. *(USAMHI)*

Col. Joseph C. Abbott and his brigade defended the Federal rear during the battle. Before the fighting ended, however, they would be needed at the front. *(USAMHI)*

One of Admiral Porter's favorite young officers, Lt. Comm. K. Randolph Breese often drew the choice assignments. At Fort Fisher, the admiral bypassed senior officers to put Breese in command of the naval assault force; but instead of enhancing his career, this assignment would end in tragedy. *(U.S. Navy Historical Center)*

Lt. Comm. James Parker of the USS *Minnesota* was the senior officer in the naval assault force, but he was denied a major role in the assault— until the unexpected occurred. *(USAMHI)*

Flag Lt. Samuel W. Preston had spent a year in a Confederate prison camp before joining the Fort Fisher Expedition. Competent, dignified, and popular, he volunteered for a chance to fight his former captors. *(USAMHI)*

Despite his schoolboy appearance, Lt. Benjamin F. Porter was a five-year navy veteran at age nineteen. Like his close friend Sam Preston, Porter had spent time in a Confederate prison camp and he too volunteered for hazardous duty. When it was time for the Federal Naval Brigade to storm Fort Fisher, Lieutenant Porter would carry the admiral's flag. *(USAMHI)*

A national hero at twenty-two, Lt. William B. Cushing was famous for sinking the Confederate ironclad *Albemarle.* At Fort Fisher, Cushing would again put his life on the line with a daredevil exploit. *(Library of Congress)*

Naval Ensign Robley Evans was a Virginian who had chosen to fight for the Union. A cocky, courageous eighteen-year-old, he found all the fight he could handle at Fort Fisher, where he suffered four battle wounds. *(A Sailor's Log)*

Ready to kill each other in battle, Colonel William Lamb *(right)* and Colonel Newton Martin Curtis became close friends after the war. By the time they posed for this photograph at Curtis's New York home, Lamb jokingly referred to Curtis as "my friend the enemy." *(College of William and Mary)*

onward, the Fort Fisher Campaign would be a model of army-navy cooperation.[15]

The expedition left for Fort Fisher on the morning of January 12, after riding out a punishing gale that tossed sailors from their bunks, washed at least one sentry overboard and infected thousands of soldiers with rail-hugging seasickness. Throughout the Beaufort layover, Terry tried to keep their destination a secret. It was too large an operation not to spawn rumors, but Terry, Grant and the War Department tried hard to maintain adequate security. In fact, when the *Philadelphia Inquirer* broke a story about the expedition on the eve of departure, military officials persuaded President Lincoln to jail the source of the leak and to censor any other newspapers planning to report the expedition's destination. The Associated Press and the *Baltimore American* also had the story, but suppressed it under threats from the White House.[16]

Led by the *Malvern,* the great fleet steamed south toward Fort Fisher in two long, precise lines with the troopships in between. There were 59 warships, 3 more than in the first expedition, mounting a total of 627 guns. Aboard the 21 transports were 8,897 officers and men—the troops from the first expedition plus reinforcements. The Second Division of the XXIV Army Corps under General Adelbert Ames was returning, along with the Third Division of the XXV Army Corps under General Charles J. Paine. Going too was the 2nd Brigade, First Division, of the XXIV Army Corps under Colonel Joseph C. Abbott. Grant had decided to equip this expedition for a siege if necessary, so Terry's command also included artillery—three companies of the 1st Connecticut Heavy Artillery, a battery of the New York Light Artillery and a battery of the Third U.S. Artillery. Two companies of engineers completed the army force, and Grant had 4,000 more troops standing by in Baltimore if Terry needed additional reinforcements.[17]

Most of the troops in the XXIV Corps were Northeasterners: soldiers from New York, New Hampshire, Pennsylvania and Connecticut, supplemented by one regiment of Midwesterners—the Thirteenth Indiana. The XXV Corps had again sent along its Third Division, composed of nine black regiments led by white officers. The bulk of the XXV Corps again remained in Virginia—along with its corps commander, General Godfrey Weitzel. Like all blacks in the Federal army, the troops of the XXV Corps were paid less than white soldiers, endured prejudice from their white comrades and were generally used as support forces, although by 1865 they had proved themselves in numerous combat situations. "You must not turn up your nose when I say they fight splendidly," a Federal soldier wrote home about the XXV Corps. "We have to give it up and say the old nigger will fight."[18]

As the immense fleet headed south toward Fort Fisher at eight knots, trailed by a motley collection of tugboats, tenders, coal carriers and supply ships, a gentle breeze fluttered the pennants and flags atop each vessel. The day—Thursday, January 12—was cheerfully sunny with clear blue winter skies. The long line of ships resembled a giant, waterborne parade. "It was a grand and inspiring sight to see the long lines of vessels," recalled a veteran of the voyage. "The placid beauty of the sea and sky had banished our sea-sickness and raised our hopes—a grand display of naval beauty and symmetry and power."[19]

The task force reached anchorage five miles north of Fort Fisher at about 10 o'clock that evening, and Terry immediately went aboard the *Malvern* for a conference with the admiral. The two had prepared for a night landing, but arrived so late they decided instead to allow the troops a full night's rest before going ashore. The landing would begin first thing next morning. More than eighty vessels dropped anchor in the darkness off Fort Fisher. Aboard the *McClellan,* General Terry's flagship, the ship's masthead glowed with red, white and green signal lights, marking Terry's headquarters, and in a cocky display of confidence, Porter's warships were allowed to display their normal lamps. These were the lights, flickering brightly above the dark Atlantic, that alerted Colonel Lamb to the ordeal he would soon face.[20]

◆

Inside Fort Fisher, Lamb dispatched an urgent plea to Wilmington headquarters for reinforcements and called for the return of General Hoke's division. Lamb believed the Federals would probably try to come ashore at first light. Hoke's troops needed to be on the move immediately, so they could be in place to stop the landing in the morning. Lamb had another message to send—this one to Daisy. He dispatched a courier up the peninsula to his cottage with instructions to wake Daisy and the children so they could pack for evacuation. He ordered his barge manned and held in readiness at Craig's Landing, near his cottage, to take the family across the river to safety. He would give Daisy and the children a little time to gather the family's most important belongings—after all, they might never return. About an hour later, he called for his horse and hurried up to his cottage, where he was shocked to discover Daisy had simply gone back to bed. He hurriedly roused the family, helped them pack, then escorted everyone to Craig's Landing. It was 2 A.M., when he bade them goodbye, and watched as they disappeared into the darkness across the river.[21]

◆

Upriver at Wilmington, General Braxton Bragg was having a rough night. This was supposed to have been a pleasant evening, marked by martial pomp and music—the prelude to a new offensive. Bragg was keeping it top secret, but it was said he had issued rations and ammunition for a Confederate drive against Federally held New Bern to the north. Now that the Yankees had reappeared, however, his plans would have to be scrapped. The Federal fleet had been sighted up the coast earlier in the night, but the news was delayed by a drunken telegraph operator in Wilmington. It was past midnight when Bragg learned of the fleet's return. Now he was trying to react appropriately. He wired the news to General Lee at Petersburg, issued orders to round up all the troops around town, suspended all furloughs, recalled the Senior Reserves and ordered General Hoke to head back immediately to Confederate Point with the bulk of his force. Hoke's orders were simple: "Make every effort to prevent a landing of the enemy." If the Yankees landed before Hoke could get his troops back to Confederate Point, then he should establish a defensive line to block any enemy advance. This time Bragg did not evacuate his wife, as he had done when the fleet first appeared. There would be plenty of time to make such arrangements if Fort Fisher fell, so there was no need to panic the civilians or provoke unnecessary criticism. Besides, the Yankees had failed to take Fort Fisher in their first attempt, and Bragg did not expect them to succeed this time either.[22]

◆

Admiral Porter expected the fort to fall—he was determined it would. He had his seamen up early on Friday, January 13. The *Malvern* fired a signal gun at 4:15 A.M. and hoisted signal number 1218—red and green lanterns—ordering the fleet's seamen to duty doublequick. Soon afterwards, the shrill call of the bosun's whistle echoed across the darkened fleet, summoning the sleepy-eyed sailors to their stations. An hour later, at 5 o'clock, new lanterns were raised above the *Malvern,* signaling the fleet to get under way. Outside, a panorama of stars in the dark morning sky promised good, clear weather. Throughout the huge fleet, anchors were being hauled glistening wet from the ocean depths, steam was up in the ships' boilers and the crews were at their stations. Battle would soon begin.[23]

The eastern sky was beginning to lighten as the warships steamed toward Fort Fisher. Porter's plan of battle was similar to that of the Christmas bombardment. Three lines of warships backed by reserves would pound the fort, with the five ironclads positioned just in front of the first line. For the first few hours, most of the fleet would bombard the woods around the landing site to clear the area of enemy troops. Each ship's commander had his battle orders: "Fire deliberately. Fill the vessels up with every shell they can carry, and fire to dismount the guns and knock away the traverses. . . . Concentrate fire always on one point. With the guns disabled the fort will soon be ours." No shells were to be wasted by firing at the fort flagstaffs this time, Porter ordered. He intended for the bombardment to concentrate solely on the fort's artillery and to be much more accurate this time.[24]

By 7 A.M., the warships were nearing their battle stations. The sun was ascending into a cloudless sky. A light breeze blew from the west and the temperature was 40 degrees. At 7:19, the USS *Brooklyn* led the first line of warships to temporary anchorage off the landing site and opened fire with a broadside directed at the wooded coastline. The other warships followed the *Brooklyn*'s example, hurling a barrage of shot and shell into the pines and scrub oak behind the landing site.[25]

◆

Inside Fort Fisher, Colonel Lamb stood behind the sandbagged parapet of his Pulpit headquarters and watched the fleet move into position. One by one the warships and transports appeared over the eastern horizon as the sun rose behind them. It was a most impressive spectacle. Surely, Lamb thought, this must be the most powerful armada that ever floated on the sea. His gun crews were at their battle station, prepared to return the fleet's fire at regular half-hour intervals, taking shelter in the bombproofs between rounds. Out to sea, Lamb could clearly see the hulking form of the *New Ironsides* and the squat, flat monitors as they slowed their speed, then dropped anchor offshore. As soon as the *New Ironsides* stopped, Lamb gave the command and the fort's long line of guns expelled smoke and flame.[26]

◆

It was 8:30 when the ironclads dropped anchor. Commodore William Radford, commander of the *New Ironsides*, held his fire and allowed Fort Fisher to begin the battle. There was nothing chivalrous about his act: he was counting the fort's guns as they fired and marking their approximate range. That done, he ordered his crews to open

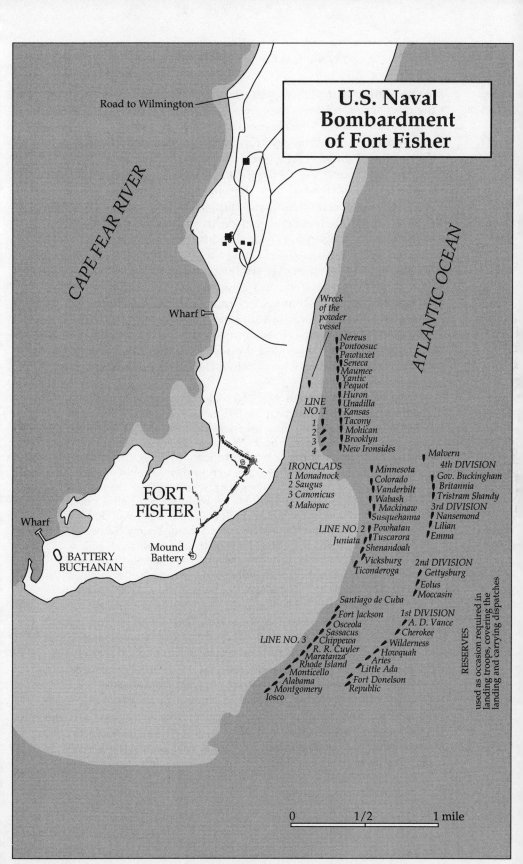

Road to Wilmington

CAPE FEAR RIVER

U.S. Naval Bombardment of Fort Fisher

ATLANTIC OCEAN

Wharf

Wreck
of the
powder
vessel

Nereus
Pontoosuc
Pawtuxet
Seneca
Maumee
Yantic
Pequot
Huron
Unadilla
Kansas
LINE
NO. 1
1   Tacony
2   Mohican
3   Brooklyn
4   New Ironsides

Malvern

4th DIVISION

IRONCLADS
1 Monadnock
2 Saugus
3 Canonicus
4 Mahopac

Minnesota
Colorado
Vanderbilt
Wabash
Mackinaw
Susquehanna
LINE NO. 2   Powhatan
Juniata   Tuscarora
Shenandoah
Vicksburg
Ticonderoga

Gov. Buckingham
Britannia
Tristram Shandy
3rd DIVISION
Nansemond
Lilian
Emma

2nd DIVISION
Gettysburg
Eolus
Moccasin

FORT
FISHER

Wharf

BATTERY
BUCHANAN

Mound
Battery

Santiago de Cuba
Fort Jackson
Osceola
Sassacus
LINE NO. 3   Chippewa
R. R. Cuyler
Maratanza
Rhode Island
Monticello
Alabama
Montgomery
Iosco

1st DIVISION
A. D. Vance
Cherokee
Wilderness
Howquah
Aries
Little Ada
Fort Donelson
Republic

RESERVES
used as occasion required in
landing troops, covering the
landing and carrying dispatches

0   1/2   1 mile

fire. Beginning with the aft battery, the ship's guns were methodically discharged until the range was verified by hits. Then the *New Ironsides* unleashed a terrible barrage of flame, smoke and flying iron. The monitors *Mahopac, Canonicus, Saugus* and *Monadnock* did likewise, pummeling the fort with a sustained, accurate fire. This time Radford found the fort's fire to be equally accurate. A freak round from the fort, a ten-inch shot, passed through the *New Ironsides'* starboard porthole into the ship's sick bay, where it smashed the ship's dispensary cabinet and destroyed the vessel's medicine supply. The ship's lightning rod and rudder pennant were shot away, her railing was cut up, a deck cutter was badly damaged and her ironclad hull was battered. Aboard the monitor *Mahopac,* the second round fired from the ironclad's number-one gun prematurely exploded, blowing away four feet of muzzle. The blast flattened the gun crew, wounding four, but somehow no one was killed.[27]

The damages did not seriously impede the fire from the ironclads. Hour after hour they pounded the fort with their heavy guns. Recalled a Federal soldier who watched the ironclads at work:

> The day was bright and clear and cold and crisp, which made the smoke light and the wind from the northwest quickly lifted the smoke so the flash of each gun could be seen clearly. To me it seemed like meteors were being fired out of a volcano. . . . I would watch the turrets of the monitors through my glass. They would turn their iron backs on the enemy to reload and I could distinctly see the big rammer staves come out of the ports. Then they would wheel around toward the fort. There would be two puffs of blue smoke, then I could see the big shells make a black streak through the air with a tail of white smoke behind them. Then would come over the water not the quick bark of the field gun, but a slow, quavering, overpowering roar, like an earthquake—then away among the Rebel traverses would be another huge ball of mingled smoke and flame as big as a meeting house.[28]

Meanwhile, the army was going ashore. Terry had chosen to land a little north of Butler's landing site, putting the troops ashore near the lower end of Myrtle Sound. Batteries Gatlin and Anderson were nearby, but both were now abandoned. Terry hoped the sound would give the troops some protection from a Confederate attack as they landed—their most vulnerable moment. To discourage the enemy from attacking, the fleet would continue to bombard the woods around the landing area until everyone was ashore. Terry's orders forbade any straggling: officers would form their troops as soon as they were on the beach, and the first ashore would quickly establish protective skirmish lines around the landing site. Each soldier was equipped with forty rounds of ammunition and a three-day ration of hardtack. More rations and ammunition were held in reserve aboard the accompanying supply ships.[29]

At 8:45 A.M., the landing began. It moved quickly. "The transports had hardly anchored when the water was covered with the small boats of the navy, varying in size from the small cutter to the huge launch, the former pulling six oars and the latter between twenty and thirty," observed an army officer. "[They] pulled rapidly up to the transports and were quickly filled with the soldiers, who evidenced the utmost eagerness to reach the shore as soon as possible, more I fear to get on solid land once more than from their desire to meet the enemy. . . ." Cheer after cheer rang from the transports as the line of landing craft quickly stretched to the beach and the first troops splashed ashore. "The landing was made in a heavy surf," recalled a veteran of the exercise, "and not a few of us got our first salt water bath that forenoon, though without bathing suits. There were no serious mishaps, however, [thanks to] the rough kindness of the sailors who were manning the boats. They jeered at us for land lubbers, but they gave us a helping hand where it was needed. A soldier astride a sailor's neck and being carried to land through the surf was a common sight."[30]

Launch after launch ferried the blue-clad troops to the beach. Usually, the soldiers remained seated aboard their landing craft until they reached knee-deep water, where they would wait for the waves to recede. "Jump now!" a sailor would then shout, and the troops would stumble from the boat and splash through the surf, carrying knapsacks and cartridge boxes on fixed bayonets. Occasionally a soldier would hesitate when ordered out, then try to gingerly climb from his craft—only to be toppled by an incoming wave. He would surface seconds later, capless and spitting seawater, his uniform, ammunition and equipment thoroughly soaked. Another might disembark properly, holding his rifle and knapsack high above the surf, then suddenly step into a hole, stumble, and temporarily disappear beneath the waves.[31]

No one drowned, however, and the first wave of soldiers sprinted over the sand dunes and formed a skirmish line in the edge of the woods between the beach and the sound. The beach was quickly filled with Federal troops and the landing site secured. "For the space of two miles the beach was occupied by our troops," observed a naval officer. "The beach was black with men with the bayonets glittering in the sunshine and their regimental flags floating in the breeze."[32]

Overjoyed to be off the transports, the troops gathered driftwood and scrub oak for campfires. Soon the beach was covered with half-naked soldiers wringing salt water from their socks and drying their uniforms over the flames. In the woods behind the beach, skirmishers discovered about thirty-five head of cattle. Within minutes, the troops were grilling steaks. Some soldiers gathered oysters in Myrtle Sound and roasted them in the campfires. Others rolled in the sand in boyish horseplay. A regimental band struck up a series of spirited tunes, accompanied at times by outbursts of laughter from the troops, who howled at every soldier dunked by the surf. When a pompous-looking officer in an obviously new uniform stumbled head-first into the waves, some men collapsed on the beach in hilarity. The reaction was the same when two company cooks from the Seventh New Hampshire stepped out of their launch with huge bags of sugar and coffee tied around their necks—and momentarily sank like stones beneath the surf. Any soldier who made it ashore relatively dry was enthusiastically cheered, and one sailor swore the laughter was loud enough to muffle the roar of the ocean.[33]

Troops who landed later had it easier. Watching the soldiers clumsily disembark, Acting Master Zera L. Tanner of the USS *Rhode Island* had an idea. He ordered a line secured between a beached launch and the transport then preparing to disembark troops. The launches could then follow the line to shore, and when there, the soldiers aboard had a handhold to guide them through the surf. The innovation proved to be a popular success and the troops dubbed it "Tanner's Ferry." General Terry used it, sitting with characteristic dignity upon an ammunition box as he was rowed ashore. Colonel Curtis was not so fortunate: he was tumbled by a wave, much to the amusement of his troops and, probably, to the satisfaction of General Ames, the division commander. Curtis and Ames were feuding. Relations between the two had been tense since the first expedition: Curtis thought Ames had not tried hard enough to prevent the withdrawal. Now the feud was even worse. General Ames had made his quarters aboard Curtis's troopship, but was absent when Curtis received the order to depart. Curtis ordered the transport to sea anyway and Ames was left ashore. Enraged when he discovered his plight, the general commandeered a hospital ship, overtook the troopship, stormed aboard and charged Curtis with "a shabby trick." Curtis hotly denied the accusation and demanded an apology. Ames eventually did apologize, but now the two were not speaking to each other.[34]

By three o'clock Friday afternoon, almost 8,000 Federal troops were on the beach. To replace any ammunition and rations lost in the landing, Terry ordered 300,000 rounds and a six-day supply of rations brought ashore. It was late afternoon by the time the troops were resupplied and ready to move off the beach, but Terry ordered the army forward anyway. Now that the troops were ashore, his first task was to establish a strong entrenched line across the peninsula to protect the army's rear as the main force advanced on Fort Fisher. He had planned to anchor his main line at the lower end of Myrtle Sound, hoping the sound would provide some protection against an enemy attack. The area proved too shallow for that purpose, however, so Terry ordered the army to move south toward Fort Fisher with orders to put an entrenched line across the peninsula near what was believed to be a large pond. On Terry's map, the pond looked large enough to provide a natural barrier against a Rebel assault. In reality, the "pond" was little more than a swampy depression that would provide scant protection.[35]

◆

Meanwhile, Hoke's Confederates had finally arrived. If Bragg had left them on the peninsula instead of ordering them to Wilmington for a parade, the 6,000 Confederates would have been available to disrupt the Federal landing. Instead, they were too late, or at least Hoke felt they were too late, and the Federals had come ashore unopposed. Hoke made no attempt to attack the Federal landing site. Instead, he simply deployed his troops across the peninsula so as to block any Federal advance northward toward Wilmington. His troops were a fair match for the Federal infantry, but Hoke received no new orders to attack, so he simply maintained his defensive line. That was more than some of the Confederate pickets had been able to do when the Federals began moving inland.[36]

Asa King, a soldier in the Sixty-sixth North Carolina, lay on his stomach behind a forward rifle pit near Myrtle Sound and watched the Yankees begin their advance. He was part of a thin forward skirmish line deployed close enough to the beach to observe the Federal landing, and had wondered why no attempt had been made to oppose the enemy troops as they came ashore. Perplexed, he finally had sent for his captain. The officer offered no explanation. "We did nothing," King later recalled, "just lay quiet . . . and let the enemy land. We could have repulsed them if we had fired on them as they landed, which we were anxious to do before they got a force together. We received no orders from our officers, just let [the Yankees] assemble a force together, then they commenced firing on us."[37]

Looking through the trees toward the beach, King could see the

Yankees advancing in his direction. He could not know that he was facing the men of Colonel Joseph C. Abbott's brigade, who had been ordered forward to probe the Confederate defenses. Heavily outnumbered, the Confederate pickets fell back, firing as they withdrew. For a few moments the firing was brisk, but Hoke did not move his main force forward to support his skirmishers. Moments later, the Confederate pickets were in trouble.[38]

King and his fellow soldiers hunkered down behind their makeshift breastworks. Heavy small arms fire peppered their position and incoming artillery rounds exploded around them. Then two regiments of Yankee troops suddenly rose up and charged. King saw his captain turn and run, then the rifle pit was suddenly surrounded by a mass of blue uniforms. "Do you surrender?" one of the Yankees yelled. "Of course we do," a nearby lieutenant calmly replied, and King realized he had become a prisoner of war. Hustled to the beach with the other prisoners, he found himself being interrogated by a group of Federal officers, headed by General Terry. "He asked where our army was," King recalled. "I said, 'Just as soon as you get through that [swamp] they will answer.' He looked at me sour and said sternly, 'You have not answered my question.' I did not reply. He said, 'It will not hurt you to tell me.' Again I was silent. I would have died in my tracks before I betrayed my people. Then Gen. Terry smiled and said very kindly, 'Johnnie, I admire a man true to his country.'"[39]

King was dismissed, but other Confederates were more cooperative. Terry learned he was facing Hoke's division, the same Rebel force the Army of the James had battled in Virginia. Federal intelligence specialists had reported Hoke's division to be in line against Sherman—but here they were facing Terry and his army. It was troublesome news: Terry and his troops had managed to land unopposed, but now they had to worry about Hoke's men attacking their rear as they moved against Fort Fisher. "While the landing was going on, the situation began to dawn upon us," one Federal officer observed. "We were soldiers of long acquaintance with the enemy's way of doing things: there we were on an open beach with the big fort on one side and a veteran division of Confederates on the other. We had learned in Virginia that Confederate soldiers could always be counted on to make trouble if there was an opportunity to do it, and we were not sure that an attack from Fort Fisher with one at the same time from the direction of Wilmington would not be tried."[40]

To keep Hoke's Confederates on the defensive, Terry ordered Colonel Abbott's brigade to dig entrenchments near the landing site and to make a vigorous demonstration—as if preparing to move north against Wilmington. Terry hoped the feint would keep Hoke's division tied down while the main Federal force moved south toward Fort Fisher. As soon as it was dark enough to conceal his troop movements, Terry would advance down the peninsula, leaving Abbott's brigade in line near the landing site. Abbott's troops would be ordered to build a host of campfires on the beach, so the enemy would think the Federals were encamped at the landing site.[41]

Terry actually had little to worry about from Hoke's division—Bragg had no intention of trying to drive the Federals into the sea. His mentality was defensive, and, in Whiting's opinion, self-defeating. Bragg believed nothing could be done to stop the Yankees from landing, that the enemy fleet's firepower was just too awesome. The Yankees outnumbered him two to one, Bragg incorrectly assumed. He could only hope the fort could withstand the threat as it had done before. Whiting, meanwhile, worried that Fort Fisher would soon be added to Bragg's list of failures—his most stupendous disaster. Bragg moved about Wilmington headquarters like a man already defeated, ordering arms and ammunition relocated as if preparing for evacuation. Alarmed by the headquarters atmosphere, Whiting became increasingly frustrated and dismayed. He wanted to take command of Hoke's division, throw Hoke's veterans against the Federals before they could fully organize, attack them before they deployed away from their beachhead—but Bragg ignored his pleas.[42]

As the day wore on, and he received no orders, Whiting seethed. Desperate, he telegraphed Richmond, asking Confederate Secretary of War James A. Seddon for orders. Seddon instead reaffirmed Bragg's command with a terse reply: "Your superior in rank, Gen. Bragg, is charged with the command and defense of Wilmington." Finally, Bragg began to trace a proposed line on the headquarters map—a point of retreat in case Fort Fisher fell. It was too much for Whiting: he had not spent two years of his life overseeing construction of one of the world's greatest forts to see it sacrificed by a man he considered an imbecile.[43]

Followed by two of his young staff officers, Major James H. Hill and Lieutenant J. S. Fairley, Whiting stormed out of Wilmington headquarters and down Market Street to the docks. There he commandeered a steamer to take him to Fort Fisher—without orders. On the street he stopped a headquarters aide and left word of his destination. If he were killed or captured, Whiting told the startled officer, he wanted it known he had gone to Fort Fisher without orders simply because he knew there would be fighting and he would be needed. Another youthful staff officer, Major Benjamin Sloan, learned Whiting had left for Fort Fisher and hurried to the docks to join him. As Sloan stepped from the gangplank onto the deck of the steamer, Whiting spotted him. "Where are you going?" he asked Sloan. "With you," the young officer replied. Whiting would not hear of it. "You can serve me better here than in Fort Fisher," he said, and ordered the aide ashore. Moments later, Whiting's ship cast off its lines and moved down the Cape Fear. Sloan, who idolized Whiting, remained on the dock, immobile, watching mournfully until the vessel was out of sight.[44]

As the steamer chugged downriver toward the fort, the rumble of the naval bombardment became louder with every mile. Whiting was angry. And he felt defeated, betrayed. It had all come to this: two years of a thankless command. Two years of pleading for reinforcements, cajoling and demanding more men. Two years of building the Confederacy's greatest fort—famous in two hemispheres—built with grueling effort, one spadeful at a time. Two years of unfulfilled hopes for a resurrected reputation. Two long, bitter years of waiting for an enemy he knew would come someday, an enemy whose every move he had predicted, an enemy whose fortitude had already failed once in the face of the great fort. And what of Lee's army—and the beleaguered Confederacy—dependent on this fort, *his* fort, for the last supply line, the final link with the outside world? They would be lost. It would all be lost—"sacrificed," that was the word for it—sacrificed by General Braxton Bragg, the president's friend, with his dark, gloomy countenance and his depressing record of defeat. Even so, Lamb and the garrison would not be left to fight alone. General William Henry Chase Whiting would be there with them—Whiting of West Point honors, of great and unrecognized talent. He would be there to face the enemy with them and to share their fate.[45]

In this fatalistic mood, Whiting steamed downriver past the waterside landmarks that had become so familiar on his cruises to and from Fort Fisher—past the spires and houses of Wilmington, past the bluffs and marshes, the cypress and pine, the long line of earthen batteries topped by cavernous cannon muzzles, heading southward, making what he believed would be his last cruise on the Cape Fear River, heading toward what he expected to be his final battle.

By the time his ship reached Battery Buchanan, the bombardment was at its deadliest. A reserve line of warships had been charged with protecting the landing site and the others had resumed bombardment of the fort. The *Minnesota* had entangled her propeller in a hawser, so the USS *Colorado* led the way to battle stations. The hail of shot and shell falling on the fort increased, carpeting the fort with deadly missiles, keeping Lamb's gun crews in their bombproofs and doing great damage to the landface artillery.[46]

Into this storm of falling iron strode General Whiting, accompanied by Major Hill and Lieutenant Fairley. They boldly crossed the long open plain between Battery Buchanan and the fort's Northeast Bastion, and surprised Colonel Lamb at his battle headquarters. Lamb did not see Whiting until the general was at his side. Making no attempt to hide his feelings from his friend and protégé, Whiting delivered a frank and pessimistic greeting. "Lamb, my boy," he said, "I have come to share your fate. You and your garrison are to be sacrificed." It was not the greeting Lamb wanted to hear. "Don't say so, General," he protested. "We shall certainly whip the enemy again." Whiting disagreed. "The last thing I heard General Bragg say," he told Lamb, "was to point out a line to fall back upon, when Fisher fell." And there, under the hail of Federal naval fire, he told Lamb the whole story—how Bragg showed no determination to rush Hoke's veterans against the enemy, how he seemed to accept defeat before the battle had hardly begun. When he left Wilmington headquarters, Whiting lamented, Bragg was frantically issuing orders to evacuate ammunition and equipment, as if the fort and the city had already fallen. Apparently at a loss for words, Lamb offered to yield command of the fort to Whiting—the same offer he had made in the first battle. Again, Whiting waved him away. He would offer advice and counsel, but he did not want Lamb's command—that was not why he had come. "I have come to share your fate"—*that* was Whiting's intention.[47]

At the moment, the fort's fate did not look promising. The naval bombardment was far more accurate, far more destructive than during the previous battle. No shells were wasted on the fort flagstaffs, nor did much of the barrage fall harmlessly in the river. This time the warships concentrated on doing damage to the fort's landface artillery and their fire was on target. Lamb tried to maintain a slow but deliberate return fire as he had done during the Christmas bombardment, but this time the barrage kept the gun crews pinned in their bombproofs for long intervals, interrupting the fort's return fire. One by one the fort's artillery pieces were being dismounted or battered into useless junk, and the toll of dead and wounded was mounting steadily.[48]

Private James Montgomery, a twenty-year-old volunteer from nearby Brunswick County, had joined Company B of the Thirty-sixth North Carolina with friends he had known from childhood. Now he saw the fort's white sands stained with their blood. "Shot and shell rained on us," he reported. "We could not repair our displaced guns, cook or eat or bury our dead lying around us. We were helpless. . . . Our guns were disabled and our front shot to pieces." Seaman

Robert Watson was one of the Confederate sailors manning the Brooke Battery on the fort's seaface. "Several of us were knocked down with sand bags," he wrote in his diary. "We were all nearly buried in sand several times. This was caused by shells bursting in the sand. Whenever one would strike near us in the sand it would throw the sand over us by the cartload." From atop Battery Buchanan a detachment of army signal corpsmen had a spectacular view of the bombardment. "I assure you it was the most terrible storm of iron and lead that I have ever seen during this war," reported one corpsman. "[The shells were] exploding so fast that it would seem to be but one roaring sound—and the sand and water rising in great clouds—so that you could not see ten feet in any direction and the atmosphere was filled it seemed by sulfur."[49]

Amid this fiery storm, Chase Whiting moved about like a man with a death wish. He walked casually along the parapet as if out for an afternoon stroll, puffing calmly on his pipe as the shells exploded nearby. Lieutenant E. L. Hunter watched Whiting with amazement: "I saw him stand with folded arms, smiling upon a 400-pounder shell, as it stood smoking and spinning like a billiard ball on the sand not twenty feet away until it burst, and then move quietly away." At one point, when a fort courier hesitated to expose himself to the Federal fire, Whiting accompanied him through the barrage. Incredibly, Whiting was not injured as he strode about the fort during the bombardment. Soldiers who saw him as they hurried to and from their guns were impressed and encouraged by his behavior. "I saw him fight, and saw him pray," reported Hunter, "and he was all that a general should be in battle."[50]

Whiting requested reinforcements from the forts across the river. The bombardment had severed Fort Fisher's telegraph line, even though it had been buried following the first battle, so dispatches had to be sent by boat across the river to Smithville, then telegraphed to Wilmington headquarters. Whiting sent his first telegram to Bragg shortly after arriving at Fort Fisher. He was typically blunt: "The enemy have landed in large force," he wired Bragg. "Garrison too weak to resist assault and prevent their advance. You must attack them at once." Several hours later, he tried again: "Enemy are on the beach, where they have been all day," he told Bragg. "Why are they not attacked?"[51]

By then General Bragg was on his way south to Confederate Point to personally oversee Hoke's division. He had ordered the Senior Reserves sent down to Sugar Loaf to reinforce Hoke and he had called out the Home Guard to help protect Wilmington. Then he had taken a steamer downriver to Sugar Loaf. It was almost dusk when he arrived. He immediately went into conference with Hoke to discuss the situation. Hoke had placed most of his force in a defensive line from the river to the ocean, opposing any Federal advance toward Wilmington. A detachment of the Second South Carolina Cavalry, placed in the woods between the fort and the Federal lines, was ordered to immediately report any sign of an enemy advance on the fort. Bragg approved the disposition. He feared moving close to the enemy would attract the fleet's fire and was afraid that if he divided Hoke's force the Federals would overrun his field headquarters at Sugar Loaf. Whiting and Lamb hoped Bragg would assault the Federal rear at night, when the fleet could not fire on Hoke's troops for fear of hitting the Federal forces. Instead, Bragg told Hoke, stay put and attack only if the Yankees advance from the landing site.[52]

♦

At sundown, Porter ordered most of the fleet to cease fire. The ironclads would continue to shell the fort throughout the night, but the wooden warships were allowed to retire. Friday's good weather had held: the first day of battle ended with a pastoral sunset that contrasted oddly with the day's violence. "The sky was clear, air balmy, and the sun cast the shadows of the fort and its batteries seaward," recalled Acting Master's Mate Joseph Simms of the USS *Minnesota.* "The sombre hues in purple and dark grays softened and blended into the brilliant sun-tints upon the edges of the battle smoke." Looking to the beach, the fleet's sailors could see the army forming for an advance.[53]

♦

Just after dark, Terry ordered the bulk of his 8,897-man army to move toward Fort Fisher. As ordered, the men of Abbott's brigade stayed behind and built countless campfires around the fortified landing site, creating the false impression that the army was encamped there for the night. The ruse worked—even General Whiting believed the Yankees were still massed where they had come ashore. Leaving Abbott's brigade to defend the landing site, Terry took the rest of the army down the beach past Battery Anderson, now abandoned, and across the peninsula toward the river. They were searching for the pond that appeared on the army maps, but soon discovered that there was no "pond"—only a low, swampy area of thick underbrush. Led by the black troops of Paine's division, presumably brought forward to clear the brush, the army moved through the marshy thickets toward the Cape Fear. The troops reached higher ground as they neared the river, but the dense undergrowth only worsened, breaking up the advance skirmish lines and leaving the troops to push through the thickets in single-file formations. Every few minutes the officer leading the advance would have to halt and check his compass by matchlight to confirm direction. Finally, after almost four hours of struggling through the jungle-like thickets, Paine's skirmishers emerged from the woods and found themselves standing on the banks of the Cape Fear River, which gleamed in the moonlight.[54]

They were not there long. A reconnoitering party reported better ground closer to the fort, and Terry ordered the troops to resume the march down Confederate Point toward Fort Fisher. At about 2 A.M., they reached a point approximately two miles north of the fort. There, on high ground, Terry ordered the troops to establish a fortified line of entrenchments from the river to the beach. Eight hundred spades were issued and for the next several hours the troops shoveled away in the darkness. Logs were dragged to the line, placed on the trench bank and covered with dirt. "All night long the troops labored most vigorously, the tools passing from hand to hand," reported an officer, "until by sunrise we had a line of breastworks across from the river to the sea, behind which our men could easily repel the attack of double their force." Meanwhile, the 142nd New York under Colonel Joseph McDonald was ordered to establish a skirmish line as close to the fort as possible. They moved cautiously through the darkness and established an advance skirmish line within rifle range of the fort landface. Before dawn, Terry surveyed his main line and was convinced that this time the army was here to stay.[55]

◆

Inside Fort Fisher, meanwhile, there was little rest for the garrison. The ironclads pounded the fort through the night—and the day's bombardment had already taken a severe toll. The landface was seriously damaged—guns dismounted, carriages battered, earthworks chewed up—and the shells continued to fall. Damages went untended: it was just too risky to make repairs. Dozens of men were already dead or wounded—Lamb could not be sure yet just how many—but sending out burial parties only produced more casualties. No meals could be cooked: the troops just huddled in the bombproofs and hoped for an end to the barrage. Lamb knew an end *would* come eventually—and with it would come the inevitable Federal assault. He also realized that at the rate his artillery was being destroyed, he would have little artillery support when the enemy assault finally occurred. He knew too that his limited force could not repel the thousands of Federal troops out there in the darkness. His only hope was General Bragg. If Bragg would aggressively attack the Federal rear with Hoke's 6,000 veterans, the fort—and Wilmington—might be saved. Lamb could only hope, and wait for the dawn.[56]

8

"I Will Hold This Place"

GENERAL BRAGG WAS SHAKEN. FIRST THING SATURDAY morning, January 14, he had ordered General Hoke to move a reconnaissance force toward Fort Fisher and make contact with the Second South Carolina Cavalry, charged with patrolling the peninsula between Hoke's division and the fort. During the night nothing had been heard from the South Carolinians, who had been ordered to report any enemy movement toward the fort, so Bragg had presumed the Federals were still encamped at their landing site. However, when Hoke's skirmishers moved through the woods toward the fort—led by Hoke himself—they stumbled into the Federal main line and were surprised by a brisk scattering of small arms fire. Hoke had immediately reported the news to Bragg: somehow the Yankees had moved down the peninsula during the night and were now entrenched between Hoke's forces and the fort.[1]

It was bad news for the Confederates. Bragg had chosen not to attack the Federal army while it was massed at the landing site, choosing instead to depend on a vague defensive strategy. He had intended to keep the Federals from advancing on Fort Fisher—that was why he had posted the cavalry between Hoke's lines and the fort.

126

Yet, somehow, thousands of enemy troops had moved down Confederate Point during the night and had entrenched themselves in a mile-long fortified line between the river and the ocean. Bragg had no idea how they had gotten past the South Carolina cavalrymen unnoticed or at least unreported. Apparently, the South Carolinians had simply failed in their mission. But now the enemy was in position to assault the fort in force. What was to be done?[2]

Bragg did not ponder the problem long. From his field headquarters at Sugar Loaf, he sent Hoke decisive orders: move upon the enemy—attack and drive the Yankees from their works. Hoke promptly ordered his division to come up and form in line of battle. Bragg left Sugar Loaf and hurried to the front. There, he could see the Federal line: it was well entrenched and looked strong. Thousands of Yankees were out there, outnumbering his troops by far, Bragg concluded. In reality, the Federals had at most a total superiority of about one-third, and the enemy force covering the landing site, Abbott's brigade, was much smaller than Hoke's division. Still, Bragg was certain he was hopelessly outnumbered and would surely draw the full fire of the fleet if he assaulted the enemy. His determination began to fade. In sight of the enemy line, he countermanded his order and canceled the attack.[3]

◆

An assault like the one Bragg almost launched was General Terry's gravest fear. All night he had kept his troops at work digging entrenchments and in the morning he ordered them to keep at it, strengthening the line of Federal breastworks that now stretched across Confederate Point. From the Confederate prisoners, Terry knew that Hoke's division was poised in his rear, and he believed that sooner or later they would attack. They had not done so during the landing, when his force was vulnerable, nor during the night. He figured the Confederates were waiting for the moment he launched his assault against the fort. With a major part of his force committed, he would be vulnerable to a rear assault. He felt better knowing that his main force was now well-entrenched. He knew, too, that he could count on the firepower of Porter's fleet, but he also knew the navy had limitations—darkness or heavy seas could render all that firepower useless. He was almost certain Hoke's division would attack his rear when he assaulted the fort, but it was a risk he had to take.[4]

At first light on Saturday the 14th, Colonel Henry L. Abbot, Terry's chief of artillery, was trying to land the expedition's siege train. It would be no small accomplishment: he had to land twenty 30-pounder Parrott artillery pieces, four 100-pounder Parrotts, and twenty Coehorn mortars—plus caissons, mule teams, rations and forage, three companies of heavy artillery, two batteries of light artillery and a company of engineers. The caissons and artillery pieces were disassembled, then brought ashore piece by piece via "Tanner's Ferry"—rigged again between ship and shore. The hardest task proved to be the mules. They kicked and bit, tangled their tow lines, tried to climb into the launches and sometimes just sat on the deck of the transports, refusing to budge. One of the first mules landed was tethered on the beach as a decoy to lure the others ashore, but the remaining mules ignored him. One animal kicked a hole in the launch towing him, almost sinking the boat, then swam more than a mile out to sea before he could be recaptured. Acting Master Zera Tanner again solved the problem: at his suggestion the mules were blindfolded and then towed to shore with a minimum of resistance. It would be dusk before all the caissons would be landed and reassembled, but by midday some of the field artillery was ashore and ready for action.[5]

At Admiral Porter's direction, designated warships had continued to fire on the fort throughout the night, and shortly before 11 o'clock Saturday morning, the ironclad division resumed the bombardment while the rest of the fleet remained at ease and out of range. The *New Ironsides* pounded the fort with her port battery, and the ship's officers were certain the huge ironclad was inflicting serious damage. "We had found completely the range of the enemy," Lieutenant Henry Blake wrote in the ship's deck log. "We dropped our shells in the fort with precision, the monitors also firing slowly and accurately. The fort did not reply to our fire."[6]

The return fire from the fort was now infrequent, but it could still be troublesome. Aboard the USS *Canonicus,* Chief Quartermaster Daniel Stevens was posted topside to direct signaling and soundings when a round from the fort shot away the ship's flag. Stevens quickly replaced the fallen banner. Twice more the flag was shot away and both times Stevens replaced it under fire. For his act, he would later receive the Congressional Medal of Honor. Less fortunate was his fellow crew member, Seaman Robert Ludbig, who was at his post in the monitor's turret when an enemy shell fragment spun freakishly through the turret sight hole and wounded him in the chest.[7]

◆

Despite an occasional well-placed round, Fort Fisher was in trouble—that fact was obvious to Lamb and Whiting. The fort's landface artillery was systematically being destroyed by the navy barrage. Less artillery support meant more dependence on small arms fire, leaving the fort's understrength garrison in a serious predicament. During the night, the steamer *Pettaway* had ferried in some reinforcements—the troops Whiting had had requested from the forts across the river. Company D of the 1st North Carolina Heavy Artillery had come over. So had Company F of the 10th North Carolina Artillery, four companies of the 40th North Carolina, and a contingent of about 50 Confederate sailors and marines. By Saturday morning, the fort's garrison had almost doubled in numbers, but still numbered no more than 1,500 troops—facing almost 9,000 Federals.[8]

It was now clear to Lamb that Fort Fisher's fate lay with General Bragg. If Bragg attacked the enemy and put the Federals on the defensive, Fort Fisher might stand. If he left the garrison to defend itself, Fort Fisher would need even more reinforcements—a lot more. Lamb and Whiting agreed: they had to know Bragg's intentions. So early Saturday morning, Whiting went to Battery Buchanan, boarded a steamer and went across the river to Smithville to contact Bragg by telegraph. A code of signals had been established to communicate by flag and lantern between Battery Buchanan and Smithville, but the smoke of battle often obscured the messages. Besides, Whiting wanted to personally oversee these crucial telegrams.[9]

Soon the Smithville telegraph operator was tapping out Whiting's message to Bragg. He had counted seventy-six enemy vessels off Fort Fisher earlier that morning, Whiting reported. He had expected the Yankees to assault the fort all night, but they had not done so. The garrison had been manning the guns day and night and needed reinforcements. "I must have a regiment to do duty at night," Whiting wired. The telegram was transmitted up to Wilmington and down to Bragg's Sugar Loaf headquarters. After a while, Bragg's response made the return trip. In the exchange that followed, Bragg promised to send 1,000 of Hoke's troops into the fort Saturday night, but wanted the reinforcements already sent to the fort to be returned to their commands. Whiting objected—he could spare no troops and instead wanted more. Bragg relented. All the troops could remain in the fort and he would send a thousand of Hoke's veterans anyway. Bragg also reported the enemy's position—in line across the peninsula about two miles north of the fort. He said nothing about his decision not to attack the Federal rear. Whiting, however, addressed the subject in a terse telegram he dispatched before he returned to Fort Fisher. "We hold Fisher," he wired Bragg. "Sooner you attack the enemy the better." Bragg did not respond.[10]

◆

Meanwhile, Saturday morning Federal troops from Curtis's brigade moved forward along the river's edge, occupying Craig's Landing and taking possession of Lamb's cottage. Studying the distant movement with a telescope from atop the fort parapet, Lamb could see the blue-uniformed soldiers swarming around the house and yard where his wife and children so often played together. He immediately ordered the remaining land-side artillery to open fire on the enemy troops, but the naval bombardment soon drove his gun crews back into their bombproofs.[11]

As he studied the distant enemy troops, Lamb was shocked to see a Confederate supply ship approaching Craig's Landing. It was the steamer *Isaac Wells*, loaded with much-needed ammunition and rations dispatched to the fort by General Bragg. The steamer was headed straight for Craig's Landing, now occupied by Yankee troops. Lamb ordered one of the landface cannon manned and fired, and a round splashed in the river near the ship. The vessel's captain ignored the warning, however, and foolishly pulled alongside the wharf to tie up. Instantly, the steamer was mobbed by Federal soldiers. The gleeful troops had lost their race with the navy to capture Battery Anderson during the first battle. Now they could taunt Porter's sailors with a new boast: the first Confederate vessel captured during the campaign had been taken by the army. The soldiers had little time to celebrate, however. Soon afterwards, the Confederate gunboat CSS *Chickamauga* came into view and opened fire on Craig's Landing. Earlier that day Bragg had sent a dispatch to Confederate Flag Officer Robert F. Pinkney in Wilmington, asking for support from the *Chickamauga*. A refitted British-built blockade runner, the *Chickamauga* carried at least three batteries of Brooke artillery—the reason some of her crew had been sent to man the Brooke Battery at Fort Fisher—and Flag Officer Pinkney had readily complied with Bragg's request. Before arriving off Craig's Landing, the ship had already fired on the Federals upriver, killing and wounding several. Now the ship's big Brookes expelled a broadside of iron, scattering the Federals aboard the *Isaac Wells* and lacing the ship's hull with holes. Within minutes, the steamer settled to the bottom of the river—her lines still secured to the dock.[12]

Seeing the enemy deprived of the fort's supply ship gave Lamb some grim satisfaction, but the event upset him, and what troubled him was far worse than the loss of a cargo of supplies. For General Bragg to have sent a supply ship to Craig's Landing showed he was unaware of the enemy's troop dispositions—he really did not know what was happening on Confederate Point. It would have been easy, Lamb thought, for Bragg to have taken a steamer downriver, where, in relative safety, he could have observed the movements of the enemy and the condition of the fort. But Bragg had not done so. For the first time since the enemy fleet reappeared, Lamb felt deserted. For the first time, he was convinced Whiting was right—Bragg was leaving them to their fate. "You and your garrison are to be sacrificed," Whiting had warned. Now Lamb believed him.[13]

After returning to Fort Fisher, Whiting conferred with Lamb. Now that Federal troops were securely entrenched across the neck of the peninsula in force, they concluded, Admiral Porter would next try to enter the river. Once behind the fort, the enemy warships could exploit the fort's vulnerability: it had practically no defenses against a riverside attack. While enemy troops stormed the landface, Federal warships could blast the fort and its defenders from the rear. Again, Whiting and Lamb agreed that the fate of the fort depended on Bragg. Whiting therefore decided to again try and rouse Bragg to action. He sent the steamer *Cape Fear* upriver with a message for the general. Again, Whiting was blunt.[14]

"The game of the enemy is very plain to me," he wrote Bragg. "They are now furiously bombarding my land front; they will continue to do that, in order, if possible, to silence my guns until they are satisfied that their land force has securely established itself across the neck and rests on the river; then Porter will attempt to force a passage. . . . I have received dispatches from you stating that the enemy had extended to the riverbank. This they never should have been allowed to do; and if they are permitted to remain there the reduction of Fort Fisher is but a question of time." Driving home his point, Whiting almost issued the commanding general an ultimatum: "I will hold this place til the last extremities; but unless you drive that land force from its position I cannot answer for the security of this harbor."[15]

Again, Bragg made no immediate reply. However, he did have an opinion of Whiting's dispatches—he didn't like them. Their tone offended him, he told others, and he claimed the fort was capable of mounting an adequate defense without any support from Hoke's troops. With a thousand more reinforcements soon to be added to the 1,500-man garrison, Bragg said, Fort Fisher should be "impregnable against assault." Hours later, he finally formed a response to Whiting. Signed by his assistant adjutant-general, it was as terse as Whiting's dispatches: "General Bragg desires you will report at these headquarters early to-morrow morning for conference." There it was—in the middle of battle, the commanding general wanted to see Whiting face to face at Wilmington headquarters.[16]

◆

Friction between commanders also existed on the Federal side. General Ames and Colonel Curtis were still feuding. Ames came to General Terry Saturday afternoon, asking that Curtis be denied command of the Federal advance. He had little confidence in Curtis and his brigade, Ames explained. Terry listened, but ignored the advice. Curtis and his New Yorkers had led the advance in the first battle and they would do so again. In fact, after Curtis's brigade was in line near the fort, Terry borrowed a pair of binoculars from one of his aides, Captain George F. Towle, and summoned Curtis and Colonel Comstock for an official reconnaissance of the fort.[17]

The three studied the fort from an abandoned Confederate battery anchoring the Federal front line. Fort Fisher's landface was only 500 yards away. During the first battle, when Curtis and Comstock had advanced this far, they had counted sixteen artillery pieces on the fort's landface. Now they could only see nine; the rest had been knocked down or destroyed by the naval bombardment. The fort's traverses were torn up and pockmarked with shell craters, and huge gaps had been blown in the fort's palisade fence. Through Captain Towle's binoculars, Terry carefully studied the approach to the fort. An assault against the eastern half of the landface would take the attacking troops over a long stretch of high ground, exposing them to Rebel fire from the entire length of the landface. However, on the western side of the landface the terrain sloped toward the river, especially where the Wilmington road approached the fort's riverside gate. Troops attacking on a route closer to the river would be less exposed to fire from the eastern half of the landface. Terry noticed the bridge crossing the swampy area that drained from the riverside marsh. Some of the troops could charge across the bridge, even though much of its flooring was gone, but most of the attacking force would have to wade through the marshy depression on both sides of the bridge. The patch of marsh would slow them down, but Terry believed this was still the best route of attack. Comstock and Curtis agreed, noting that once across the marsh, large numbers of troops could charge quickly through the palisade gate and the gaps blown in the fence.[18]

He wanted to give the navy more time to inflict heavier damage to the enemy artillery and the palisade, Terry concluded, but tomorrow afternoon he planned to order a full-scale assault against Fort Fisher's landface. Curtis and his brigade would lead the charge, followed by the rest of Ames's division. "Do you still believe the fort can be carried by an assault with such force as I can spare from the line

established last night?" Terry asked. Curtis was sure he could take
the fort with three brigades. "It has already been decided," Terry
revealed, "that in case an assault is ordered you will make it."[19]

At 8:30 that night, while Curtis built more entrenchments along
the advance skirmish line, Terry was rowed out to the *Malvern* for
a battle conference with Admiral Porter. In the darkness he passed
Porter's warships, riding at anchor in battle formation. The general
bombardment had ceased at sundown, but Terry could hear the
monitors lobbing shells into the fort with a slow, steady fire. He
arrived alongside Porter's flagship at precisely nine o'clock and was
escorted to the admiral's stateroom. Porter greeted him warmly and
the two moved quickly to a professional discussion of the battle.
Porter was generally pleased with the navy's performance and his
casualties were light. Most were again caused by accidents. Parrotts
had exploded on the *Pequot,* the *Saugus* and the *Susquehanna.* The
Huron's mainmast had been shot away and the *Unadilla* had suffered some serious damage, but the fleet had generally fared well
during the battle—and Porter was confident the navy had done severe damage to the fort. During the December battle, the fleet had
fired 20,271 artillery projectiles at the fort, and Porter was sure his
ships were well on the way to equaling or surpassing that record—
and with more accurate, more damaging fire. Terry too was impressed with the damage inflicted by the fleet, but he wanted more.
He wanted the remaining artillery on the fort's landface destroyed
and he wanted the palisade blown apart so his troops could charge
through the fence quickly. Could the navy do that?[20]

Porter assured him it could be done, noting that Terry still did not
fully appreciate the fleet's capabilities. Throughout the night, the
warships would continue a slow, deliberate fire on the fort. Sunday
morning, the bombardment would resume in full and would continue until noon. Then Porter would send in "every ship which could
find a place to anchor and open upon the fort with every gun that
could be brought to bear, firing as rapidly as was consistent with
accuracy of aim." Part of the bombardment would concentrate on
destroying the landface artillery, and part would focus on the palisade. Using the army code, signal corpsmen would direct the fleet's
fire from the shore, shifting the navy's fire to any point Terry wanted
to bombard or calling for a cease-fire if needed.[21]

At precisely three o'clock Sunday afternoon, Terry would signal for
the fleet to shift its bombardment from the landface, and the ground
assault would immediately follow. Led by Curtis's Brigade, General
Ames's division would assault the western end of Fort Fisher's landface, aiming for a breakthrough at the fort's riverside gate. At the

same moment, a 2,000-man navy "boarding party" would launch a ground assault against the eastern, oceanside end of the landface, targeting the fort's Northeast Bastion as the point of assault. Porter was determined that the navy's role at Fort Fisher would equal or surpass the army's. Days earlier he had called for volunteers and he had received plenty: the "boarding party" would be composed of 1,600 sailors and 400 marines. Equipped with Sharps rifles and carbines, the marines would provide cover fire while the sailors stormed Fort Fisher's high walls in boarding party style—armed with Colt revolvers and cutlasses. He was determined to write his share of the history of this war, Porter had vowed, and soon his sailors would make history at Fort Fisher.[22]

General Terry, like Porter, was anxious to avoid the kind of interservice conflict that had marred the first expedition against Fort Fisher. "No disagreement or discord occurred," commented an onsite observer, "both the Admiral and Alfred being willing to yield everything that would prevent the most perfect harmony of action." For that reason, perhaps, General Terry recorded no official opinion about Porter's plans for the naval ground assault. No doubt Terry was grateful that another 2,000-man force would be thrown at the fort as his troops made their charge, expecting as he did that Hoke's veterans would come screaming against his rear as soon as the ground assault began. Still, as an experienced combat officer, he must have thought Porter was either incredibly foolish or utterly fearless to send 1,600 sailors charging across an open beach armed with nothing more than handguns and cutlasses. If the bombardment eliminated Confederate resistance, such a dramatic, extraordinary "boarding action" would certainly grab headlines and history; but if Fort Fisher's defenders were still there in strength, Porter's dramatic naval ground assault could result in a bloody disaster.[23]

◆

The moon was full Saturday night, the evening sky was clear. From their ships Porter's sailors could see thousands of campfires where Terry's troops were massed on shore. In contrast, Fort Fisher's silhouette loomed dark and gloomy, lit only occasionally by the flash of an exploding shell. In camp, aboard ship and in the fort, men on both sides thought about tomorrow and the fighting that was sure to come. "I feel tonight as though there was a dark shadow hanging over me," Captain Solon Carter of Paine's division wrote to his wife up North. "I trust that it is all superstition, and that the same Power that has protected me through dangers past will protect me tomorrow, and restore me ere long to my wife and darling baby. . . . I want to spend my last days with you. I cannot endure the thought of closing my life among strangers when there is one who loves me far away."[24]

Aboard the USS *Powhatan,* Seaman James Flannigan, a sailor from Philadelphia, looked up Ensign Robley Evans, the young officer who had survived being shot off the *Powhatan*'s mainmast during the Christmas bombardment. Both had volunteered for the assault party and knew they would be charging the fort tomorrow. Now Flannigan sought out Evans and handed him a small box. "Mr. Evans," Flannigan asked, "will you be kind enough to take charge of this box for me—it has some little trinkets in it—and give it to my sister in Philadelphia?" Why did he not deliver it himself, Evans asked. "I am going ashore with you tomorrow, and will be killed," Flannigan calmly replied. Evans tried to dismiss the notion, but Flannigan would not be dissuaded. Finally, Evans took the box and promised to deliver it if anything happened to Flannigan.[25]

Major Leonard Thomas of the Ninety-seventh Pennsylvania was certain there would be bloody fighting tomorrow, but he had no forebodings. Curtis's First Brigade, which had been moved to within 500 yards of the fort, was kept in place at the front for the night. The troops of the Second Brigade—to which Thomas' regiment belonged—had been pulled out of line along with the Third Brigade and had been ordered to replenish their ammunition, draw more rations, fill their canteens and clean their muskets. That done, they were supposed to get all the rest they could. To Thomas, those signs were unmistakable: they would see combat tomorrow.[26]

◆

Inside Fort Fisher, conditions were grim. Already the garrison had suffered more than 200 casualties among the 1,500 defenders. No more than three or four artillery pieces were still serviceable on the landface. The troops had little to eat and nothing to protect them from the nighttime temperatures, which dropped to near freezing Saturday night. In the darkness, eleven- and fifteen-inch shells from the monitors exploded overhead or bounced along the fort traverses like wild bowling balls until they burst in showers of iron.[27]

With the Yankee infantry in position close to the landface Saturday night, a ground assault the next day seemed certain, Lamb thought. Surely Bragg would attack that night, when darkness restricted the fleet's fire. Lamb persuaded Whiting to contact Bragg once more, urging him to launch a night attack on the Federal rear, while Lamb led an assault on the enemy's front line. Whiting sent the message, but received no reply from Bragg. Even so, after burying the day's dead, Lamb ordered ten companies of the garrison to stand by for action. He then took Captain Daniel Patterson and Company H of the Thirty-sixth North Carolina through the landface sally port, through the battered palisade and down toward the beach, where he deployed them as a skirmish line to determine the exact location of the enemy. They proceeded carefully across the open plain from the beach to the river, probing for the Federal skirmish line. They found no enemy troops along the beach, but near the river they drew fire from the Yankee pickets. With the Federal line thus located, Lamb deployed Patterson's company in a skirmish line and waited for the sounds of battle from the north—the signal that Bragg had attacked the Yankee rear. When that happened, Lamb would call the other nine companies forward and lead them in an assault on the Federal front line.[28]

Lamb and his skirmishers waited in the darkness. Hour after hour passed, but nothing happened. No word came from Bragg and no heavy firing was heard to the north. Except for the Federal naval fire exploding over the fort, Confederate Point remained quiet. They waited all night, but nothing happened and Bragg sent no word. Finally, just before dawn, Lamb and his weary troops quietly withdrew and reentered the fort through the sally port.[29]

Back inside Fort Fisher, he was dismayed to learn that only a small portion of the 1,000 reinforcements promised by Bragg had arrived in the fort. Bragg had picked some of Hoke's best troops for reinforcements—four regiments and a battalion from Hagood's brigade. Led by South Carolina's General Johnson C. Hagood, now home on leave, the troops had seen heavy fighting near Charleston, at the Wilderness and at Petersburg. In a two-month period of sustained fighting at Petersburg, for instance, Hagood's brigade had suffered a casualty rate of more than 60 percent. Now commanded by Colonel Robert F. Graham, Hagood's brigade appeared to be just what Lamb needed, but where were they?[30]

◆

Graham had tried to move the brigade to Fort Fisher during the night, but had encountered a bizarre series of delays. The troops had boarded three transport steamers near Sugar Loaf at about eight o'clock Saturday night. The three ships—the *Sampson,* the *Harlee,* and the *Pettaway*—had been delayed by one mishap after another. The *Pettaway* had run aground almost immediately. Part of her troops were transferred to the *Sampson,* which freed the *Pettaway,* but when the two ships moved downriver to catch up with the *Harlee,* they found that ship had run aground. The *Harlee*'s troops were then transferred to the *Pettaway,* but with the additional weight the *Pettaway* again ran aground. Only the *Sampson* made it to the fort Saturday night, disembarking its troops at Battery Buchanan after midnight.[31]

◆

Dawn was now fast approaching and with the day, Lamb knew, would come the Federal ground assault. Almost all his artillery had been destroyed. His garrison was understrength, hungry, cold and worn out from two days of enemy bombardment. Only a fraction of the promised reinforcements had arrived and the commanding general, poised up the peninsula with thousands of fresh veteran troops, appeared to be doing nothing to help. Out there in the diminishing darkness, practically within shouting distance, were almost 9,000 combat-seasoned Yankee troops, well armed, well fed and supported by a gigantic fleet of warships. Lamb had but one consolation: the enemy had found Fort Fisher too tough to take the first time, and maybe the fort would be too tough once more. One thing was certain—Lamb was determined the Yankees would have to fight to take his fort.[32]

9

"Like Sheep in a Pen"

T HE 15TH DAY OF JANUARY DAWNED CRYSTAL CLEAR—A BEAU-
tiful Sunday morning. Like a giant, luminous orange ball, the
sun slowly appeared over the Atlantic horizon, brightening a cloudless blue sky. A slight breeze blew from the northwest and the temperature hovered just above freezing, giving the air a crisp chill
despite the emerging sun's early brilliance. Aboard the Federal warships, the morning routine was well under way. The fleet's sailors had
risen in the early morning darkness to quaff their coffee and move
to their stations. Now, they awaited the call to battle.[1]

Up the peninsula from Fort Fisher, behind the main Federal line,
smoke from countless small campfires drifted seaward in the breeze,
as Terry's troops heated coffee to wash down their hardtack. Farther
up Confederate Point the cooking fires were also smoking inside the
Union rear line, as the black soldiers of Paine's division prepared for
breakfast on the line. Hot coffee was a luxury unavailable to the New
Yorkers of Curtis's brigade, manning the Federal advance skirmish
line. They had slept in turns, cradling their firearms, dug in behind
the advance rifle pits just north of the fort. There had been no serious
action during the night on either line—front or rear—just some spo-

radic small arms fire rippling along the lines from time to time in the darkness.[2]

◆

Hoke's Confederates had not attacked. Like their enemy counterparts on the Federal skirmish line, Hoke's front-line troops had also slept with loaded weapons. They were still in line at sunup, still waiting for orders to attack from General Bragg—but Bragg had no plans for an attack. Hoke's division was severely outnumbered, Bragg still believed, and would be annihilated by the fleet's firepower if he ordered an attack. Fort Fisher was capable of defending itself, he professed, especially since he had bolstered the garrison with reinforcements. If the weather turned bad and the ocean became rough enough to disrupt the fleet's fire, then Bragg might consider an assault on the Federal rear. Otherwise, he would use Hoke's division to block any Federal advance on Wilmington and he would leave Fort Fisher to defend itself.[3]

Inside Fort Fisher, Colonel Lamb braced for another day of battle. He *looked* ready—uniformed in his red-lined greatcoat with his saber at his side—but Lamb was concerned about his men. They had spent a miserable night without blankets on the sand floors of the crowded bombproofs. Rations were still scarce and the unrelenting bombardment had undoubtedly left the men strained and weary. And there was no relief in sight. Most of the thousand-man force of South Carolinians Bragg had dispatched to reinforce the fort were still stranded on their troopships, waiting to be ferried to the fort. To provide whatever rest was possible, Lamb rotated some of the troops manning the seaface batteries. The naval contingent from the *Chickamauga* had spent the night huddled under the rim of the fort's Brooke Battery, hoping not to be killed or dismembered by a stray Federal shell. At daylight, they were replaced by another gun crew and returned to Battery Buchanan, where they scrounged up some breakfast, downed some whiskey, then tried to get some sleep.[4]

◆

Sleep would be difficult at Fort Fisher this day. At 7:16 A.M., the *New Ironsides* reopened the bombardment with a round from her number-one port battery and continued firing her port guns in rotation. The monitors also resumed firing, joined at 9:30 by five wooden warships—the *Colorado*, the *Minnesota*, the *Wabash*, the *Mohican* and the *Susquehanna*. Then, at 11:30, the entire fleet came to battle. "The uproar of the cannonade kept sea and shore in a tremor, which was fainter or stronger as lighter or heavier guns were discharged," reported a Federal observer. "Occasionally a jar like an earthquake shook the ground [from] the enormous guns of the iron-clads, lying very near the shore. The huge projectile itself was quite visible, leaping from the rolling masses of smoke at the gun's muzzle, through its deliberate rush to the end of its flight—an explosion near the fort, or silent burial in the soft sand. The noise of its slow passage through the air was a deep, hoarse roar that drowned the shriller scream of the smaller missiles."[5]

Seas were calm, the fleet had the range of its targets and now the bombardment was even more accurate. "A steady rain of great shells fell upon the fort, searching for every spot on its parapets and in its interiors," reported a Federal observer. "They came from every side except the west and they were falling and bursting faster than the ticking of a watch. The Confederate artillerists tried in vain to stand to their guns. One by one, these were broken or dismounted, and the garrison driven to their bombproofs."[6]

One eyewitness to the destructive power of the naval fire was Frank Vizetelly, artist and correspondent for the *London Illustrated News.* A heavy-set, dark bearded adventurer, the thirty-four-year-old Vizetelly had covered many of the war's bloodiest engagements. He had an uncanny knack for being at the scene of action, and he had wanted to be present for the battle of Fort Fisher. Now he had a front-row seat. It may have been more than even Vizetelly bargained for and it surely matched any combat he had ever experienced. Leaving the safety of the bombproofs, Vizetelly came outside amid the full fury of the bombardment to make a preliminary sketch for his paper. He recorded a maelstrom of destruction: exploding Federal shells knocked up great geysers of sand, burst in violent clouds of flame and smoke and sent deadly shell fragments spinning in all directions. One shell exploded near the Northeast Bastion, killing two soldiers and an officer. Stretcher-bearers toted the wounded to the fort's bombproof hospital, but the fleet's fire continued to add more casualties and cause more destruction. As Vizetelly watched, a Federal solid shot hit, bounced and struck a stack of artillery ammunition, scattering cannonballs like a billiard break. Gun crews came forth to fire the fort's remaining cannon, but the scene Vizetelly sketched was quickly becoming common on the land-face: a wooden gun carriage stood abandoned in its gun chamber, the carriage timbers shattered and the huge cannon tube resting immobile on the fort's sand floor, dismounted by the Federal bombardment. Around the wreckage lay the bodies of the gun's crew.[7]

Most of the seaface artillery was still serviceable and maintained a slow but steady fire, although lack of ammunition rendered the highly touted Armstrong Battery virtually useless. The seaface still drew fire from the fleet, but the naval bombardment was concentrated on the landface—and it was both accurate and effective. By noon on Saturday, Fort Fisher's once-mighty landface artillery was practically destroyed. Colonel Lamb surveyed the destruction and found a single landface cannon still fully serviceable—a Columbiad located in a somewhat sheltered position near the Northeast Bastion. Elsewhere, cannon tubes were shattered. Guns were dismounted. Carriages were pounded into splinters. Elevation mechanisms were battered into disrepair. All the work, all the maintenance that had kept the landface guns ready for action for almost three years— lacquering the tubes, lubricating the works, painting the carriages— now mattered not at all. The guns were useless. The fort's formidable-looking landface wall was virtually devoid of artillery protection.[8]

The landface palisade had also suffered. Wide, yawning gaps now marked the big fence in many places. Now, Lamb thought, the palisade might actually protect an assaulting enemy instead of deterring him. Casualties continued to increase among the fort's garrison. On the fort's seaface, for instance, one gun crew took a direct hit from a Federal naval shell. One moment the half-dozen artillerists were methodically training their cannon on a distant enemy warship, a moment later—after a violent explosion of flame, smoke and iron— all lay dead around their smoke-shrouded battery. Lamb figured his troop strength was now less than 1,200 and diminishing steadily under the enemy bombardment.[9]

◆

General Terry spent the morning carefully making arrangements for the afternoon assault. It was important that all his divisional commanders understood the battle plan. Ames's division would make the assault, led by Curtis's Brigade, already entrenched at the front. General Paine and his division would protect the Federal rear, standing by to repulse the expected attack by Hoke's Confederates. Abbott's brigade was ordered forward from the landing site to provide support if needed. The Federal field artillery was now ashore and a battery of it was now in place on the river to keep the CSS *Chickamauga* away. If the assault failed, Terry would bring up the artillery and resort to a siege. Late Sunday morning, the Second and Third brigades of Ames's division were ordered forward to within supporting distance of Curtis's brigade.[10]

◆

Meanwhile, on board the *Malvern,* Admiral Porter decided it was time to put his 2,000-man boarding party ashore. Moments later a signal was hoisted: "Arm and away all boats." Soon a flotilla of launches was in the water, manned by sailors and marines. As they rowed toward shore, wild cheers rose from the fleet: One after another, thirty-five warships cast off their boats, sending a steady stream of launches pulling through the calm Atlantic toward the beach. It was just past noon by the time all were ashore, milling around the beach about two miles north of the fort. The force numbered 2,261 officers and men, including approximately 400 marines.[11]

In charge of the naval brigade was Lieutenant Commander K. Randolph Breese. At thirty-three, Breese was practically an "old salt." He had gone to sea at fifteen, served under Farragut in the Mexican War, and was aboard Commodore Perry's ships on the famous voyage to Japan in 1853. A favorite of Porter's, Breese was the admiral's fleet captain and had served under Porter for most of the war. He had commanded a division of naval mortars in the New Orleans and Vicksburg campaigns and had spent two years in hazardous duty along the Mississippi. When Porter assumed command of the North Atlantic Blockading squadron, he brought Breese along as fleet captain. Dark-headed, with a neatly trimmed beard and a receding hairline that camouflaged his youthfulness, Breese was bright, aggressive and quick-witted—character traits Porter valued. When he assembled volunteers for the naval brigade, Porter had put Breese in charge—even though he had to jump him over senior officers.[12]

It was a difficult command for Breese. Sailors were out of their element on land, were unfamiliar with the maneuvers necessary to move large bodies of men from point to point, and in this case, their attack had to be precisely coordinated with the army assault. As ordered by Porter, most were armed with Colt revolvers and cutlasses. Porter had conducted target practice at Hampton Roads before the Christmas expedition, and the sailors had proven to be terrible shots. However, the admiral was determined the navy would have a major role at Fort Fisher and he was impressed by Colonel Curtis's report of the fort's vulnerability. His sailors did not have to be good marksmen, Porter decided: they could scale the fort's walls the old-fashioned way—armed with cutlasses and revolvers.[13]

A lot had to be done before the assault was launched, and Breese had come ashore early. Even so, his assignment was marked by confusion from the beginning. As he tried to assemble the first sailors ashore, he was confronted by Lieutenant Commander James Parker, the executive officer of the *Minnesota*. Parker was Breese's superior and somehow had the idea that he had been given command of the naval brigade. When Breese produced written orders from the admiral, Parker submitted gracefully, but it was not the best way to begin a difficult command. As if he did not have enough headaches just carrying out his orders, Breese also had to keep an eye on Admiral Porter's son, Carlisle, who had been allowed to leave his duties as the admiral's secretary to join the action ashore. Breese put young Porter to work as a courier, then concentrated on bringing some order to the growing force of sailors and marines massing on the beach. "The sailors as they landed from their boats were a heterogeneous assembly," observed one of their officers. "[There were] companies of two hundred or more from each of the larger ships, down to small parties of twenty from each of the gunboats. They had been for months confined on shipboard, had never drilled together, and their arms—the old-fashioned cutlass and pistol—were hardly the weapons to cope with the rifles and bayonets of the enemy. Sailor-like, however, they looked upon the landing in the light of a lark. . . ."[14]

Breese first organized an entrenching detail. A handful of men from each ship had been issued spades, so he called them up and sent them forward under the command of Flag Lieutenant Samuel W. Preston, an aide to Porter and one of the most popular young officers in the fleet. A Canadian by birth, he had moved to Illinois as a child and had been appointed to the U.S. Naval Academy. His studies had been interrupted in 1861, when he and his class had been called to active duty. Preston had risen quickly in rank and responsibility, serving as an aide to Admirals Du Pont and Dahlgren and seeing action aboard the *Wabash* and the *New Ironsides*. He had led a naval assaulting party in an ill-fated attack on Confederate-held Fort Sumter—an action that landed him in a South Carolina prisoner of war camp for more than a year. Exchanged and returned to duty in time for the Christmas expedition against Fort Fisher, he had served as second-in-command of the volunteer detail that took the powder boat *Louisiana* to its final anchorage. He was only twenty-three, but he conducted himself with a cheerful competence that endeared him to subordinates and superiors alike.[15]

Preston took his detachment down the beach, threw up a breast-work about 600 yards from the fort, then, under sporadic enemy small-arms fire, moved forward and dug two more lines of rifle pits—the last one only about 200 yards from the fort palisade. Breese meanwhile rounded up the first detail of marines to come ashore and sent them down the beach to man the skirmish line Preston's sailors were digging. Led by Lieutenant Louis E. Fagan, the marines hus-

tled down the beach until they were about a mile from the fort,
where they began to draw fire from Confederate sharpshooters.
Fagan ordered his men to spread out and continued forward until
they reached Preston's first line of entrenchments. There they took
cover behind the makeshift breastworks, used their hands and bayonets to strengthen their rifle pits, then dug in to wait for the rest of
the marine force.[16]

Back up the beach, Breese was trying to form the 2,000-man force
of sailors and marines into some kind of battle formation. They had
beached their launches and were now milling around on the strand
in a light-hearted mood, glad to be off ship. Breese had no orders for
organization of the force, so he and several other officers stood
around on the sun-bathed beach and discussed how to form their
men for the assault. What emerged was a plan to attack in four
divisions. The first division would be commanded by Lieutenant
Commander Charles H. Cushman of the USS *Wabash*. Leading the
second division would be Lieutenant Commander Parker, who apparently stifled any resentment he may have felt about serving under
Breese, and in charge of the third division would be Lieutenant
Commander Thomas O. Selfridge, Jr., of the USS *Huron*. A fourth
division, composed of the marine force, was commanded by the
senior marine officer ashore, Captain Lucien L. Dawson.[17]

The battle plan called for the marines to go forward to the rifle pits
dug by Preston's entrenching detail, dig in and lay down a covering
fire against the fort in advance of the naval assault. Then, with the
fort walls presumably cleared of Rebels by the marine fire, the naval
brigade would charge. As the assaulting party passed, the marines
would fall in and bring up the rear—all the while continuing to fire
upon the fort with their Sharps carbines. Breese explained it all to
Captain Dawson: the sailors would make the assault in their three
newly organized divisions, thereby charging the fort in three waves.
The route of attack would take them straight down the beach to the
fort palisade; it was low tide and they could charge around the end
of the big fence—or rush through the gaps blown in it by the naval
fire—then they would scale the fort's walls and go after the Rebels.[18]

The naval charge would be coordinated with the army assault:
when the army was ready, General Terry would alert the fleet by
signal flag, then Admiral Porter would order all the warships to
simultaneously blow their steam whistles. The bombardment would
cease or at least shift away from the fort's landface, so none of the
Federals would be endangered by their own fire, and, it was hoped,
the fort would be quickly carried by storm. It was important, Porter's
orders stressed, that the naval brigade delay its assault until Terry's

troops could be seen charging up the riverside wall of the fort.[19]

Dawson did not like the way things were going. Breese had sent Lieutenant Fagan and his detachment of marines forward to the skirmish line even before Dawson had reached shore. The naval brigade seemed disorganized. The sailors were going to have to make a long charge over an open beach with no cover. They obviously would come under enemy fire before they were close enough to use pistols or cutlasses. And Breese was hurrying him. It took time to organize his marines properly into companies and platoons. Some of his men were just coming up from their launches when Dawson received a third urgent command from Breese. "Bring up the marines at once," Breese ordered, "or [you'll] be late." Dawson gave up trying to organize his force and obeyed. He and his marines jogged on past the sailors toward the front, but he was frustrated: he felt he had not been given enough time to get his men ready.[20]

Breese finally got the sailors formed into their three divisions, lined up in three waves on the beach. With the sailors facing him, revolvers holstered and cutlasses at their sides, he read them Admiral Porter's boarding orders. "No move is to be made forward until the army charges," he read. "Then the navy is to assault the sea or southeast face of the work, going over with cutlasses drawn and revolvers in hand. The marines will follow after, and when they gain the edge of the parapet they will lie flat and pick off the enemy in the works. The sailors will charge at once on the field pieces in the fort and kill the gunners. The mouths of the bombproofs must be secured at once, and no quarter given if the enemy fire from them after we enter the fort."

The white sand beach was bright and clean-looking under the cheerful winter sun. A few yards from the massed seamen, sea oats topping a row of sand dunes bent gently with the breeze. Seashells of various shapes and hues lay unnoticed above the high-tide line. In the blue sky nearby, seagulls dipped and soared and cried. The fleet's artillery boomed away in the distance, but in many ways it was like countless other days on this North Carolina beach, and Breese had to speak loud enough to be heard over the breaking surf.

"Remember," he continued, "the sailors when they start to board are to go with a rush, and get up as fast as they can. Officers are directed not to leave their companies under any circumstances, and every company is to be kept together. If, when our men get into the fort, the enemy commences firing on Fort Fisher from the Mound, every three men will seize a prisoner, pitch him over the walls, and get behind the fort for protection, or into the bombproofs.[21]

"The fleet captain will take charge of the landing party," Breese concluded, "and all the commands will report to him." The orders read, Breese put Lieutenant Commander Parker in temporary command of the naval brigade and hiked across the beach and into the woods toward the army's position, hoping to confer with General Terry. Behind him, the sailors remained in line, awaiting orders to advance, while the Federal fleet intensified its bombardment in preparation for the joint assault. "From the constant noise and jar of the firing, and the screaming of the flying shells, the volumes of gunpowder smoke, the movement of troops on the shore, it was evident that for better or worse, the mettle of Fort Fisher was to be put to a genuine test," recalled a Federal officer present at the scene. "But, though silent and sullen, the Rebel flag still fluttered [above the fort], and the walls loomed huge and formidable through the smoke-clouds."[22]

◆

By two o'clock the troops of Ames's division were massed in the edge of the woods, about a half-mile north of Fort Fisher's landface. Their fixed bayonets glinted in the sunlight filtering through the timber, and their unfurled regimental flags stood out in bright contrast to the drab foliage around them. The pickets of Curtis's brigade had edged the advance line of rifle pits to within about 250 yards of the fort. Colonel Ames moved through the ranks of troops, giving orders and directing their disposition. General Terry, who had been communicating with Admiral Porter with the signal flags, moved forward and joined some of his officers in the large abandoned Confederate earthwork about 500 yards north of the fort. He would direct the assault from this position. In the distance, on the far side of the Cape Fear River, Terry could see a Confederate steamer moving steadily downstream, its decks packed with Rebel troops. Obviously, they were reinforcements going to the fort. The Federal officers watched the troopship with little comment. One of them, Colonel Comstock, estimated to himself that there were some 300 Rebels aboard the ship—and this was the second troopship seen that afternoon. Comstock thought the reinforcements were an ominous sign. He wondered if perhaps the pending assault on the fort should be scrubbed, as the first one had been. Should he mention his doubts to General Terry? No, he decided, this time he would keep his thoughts to himself. Terry did the same. Watching the enemy reinforcements disappear downriver, however, he had the same doubts as Comstock. Should he cancel the assault and go to a prolonged siege? The doubts lasted but a moment—Terry had come too far, accomplished too much, to call it off now. The fort would be assaulted as planned.[23]

♦

Atop the walls of Fort Fisher, Colonel Lamb could see the Yankee troops massing in the distance. The woods obscured most of the army's maneuvering, but he could see their skirmish line advancing in fits and starts near the river and he could see the movement of a lot of enemy troops in the edge of the woods. Up the beach, he could clearly see the Federal naval brigade assembling in the distance. From his position atop the Pulpit, Lamb watched the dark body of enemy troops form itself and move forward until it stopped just out of rifle range from the fort. Studying the enemy movement closer to the fort, he could easily see the Yankee skirmishers—sailors and marines, it appeared—shoveling up spadefuls of sand into makeshift breastworks as they edged their skirmish line forward on the beach side of the peninsula.[24]

The Yankee skirmishers would have been obvious targets for the fort's landface artillery, but the guns were now destroyed. Lamb directed the two sally-port field pieces to open fire on the enemy soldiers, and ordered the two field pieces defending the riverside gate to stand by for action. The artillerists manned their guns and discharged grapeshot and canister across the open plain toward the Yankees. To discourage the Yankee skirmishers digging in near the beach, he ordered the Mound Battery's two heavy artillery pieces turned to fire up the beach, opened fire with the surviving landface Columbiad and put sharpshooters on the landface wall to unleash a harassing rifle fire. At the moment it was all he could do, and the fire did seem to restrict the Yankee skirmishers somewhat—but it was a costly act. It provoked a hail of concentrated naval fire, further depleting the fort's already thin garrison.[25]

From the enemy troop movements, Whiting and Lamb could see the Yankees were preparing for an assault, and it looked like the main attack would come down the beach, aiming for the fort's Northeast Bastion. Lamb and Whiting were surprised no enemy warships had tried to run the bar. Now it was low tide, which would prevent the warships from getting through the two shallow river entrances at least until the night high tide. The imminent danger to the fort was the ground assault, which appeared ready to begin, judging by the Yankee troops assembled up the beach.[26]

Whiting and Lamb had expected the assault since morning, and, faced with such an immediate threat, Whiting had ignored General Bragg's summons to Wilmington headquarters. Instead, Whiting had dispatched a message across the river to the telegraph operator at Battery Lamb, again urging Bragg to attack the Federal rear. Again,

Bragg ignored the plea. In fact, with the fort's telegraph line severed by the bombardment, confusion seemed to mark communications between the fort and Bragg's headquarters in Wilmington and at Sugar Loaf. Bragg seemed to think the fort artillery was undamaged, although Lamb had dispatched reports about the destruction. As the Federal assault appeared increasingly imminent, Whiting continued to press Bragg to attack. "Is Fort Fisher to be besieged, or you to attack?" he demanded. "Should like to know."[27]

◆

Bragg continued to remain silent about his plans, but he was clearly decisive about General Whiting's role. He suspected Whiting was drinking heavily, was perhaps even intoxicated. He was offended by the tone and phrasing of the dispatches Whiting was sending from Fort Fisher, and he was angered that Whiting had ignored the recall to headquarters. "My mind was now made up as to his condition and I felt the safety of the fort required his prompt relief," Bragg later confided to a relative. Accordingly, at one o'clock in the afternoon, Bragg had ordered Whiting out of Fort Fisher. He was to be replaced by Brigadier General Alfred H. Colquitt, who was ordered downriver to take command of the fort, effective that night. The order was not directed to Colonel Lamb, even though he officially commanded the fort. Bragg apparently considered Whiting, as Lamb's superior officer, to be Fort Fisher's commander, even though Whiting had declined Lamb's offer to relinquish command. With one order, Bragg would deal with Whiting and Lamb, removing the former and making the latter a subordinate. It was not Lamb, however, that Bragg sought to reprimand—it was Whiting. Whiting was the one who was pushing Bragg to attack the Federals, pleading and demanding in one telegraph after another. He would be replaced by an officer of Bragg's choosing and this time Bragg's order to Whiting was undeniably clear: "Colquitt assigned to immediate command of Fort Fisher. Will go there to-night. General Bragg directs you to report in person at these headquarters this evening, for conference and instructions."[28]

◆

Bragg's order was a hard blow for both Whiting and Lamb, delivered at the worst possible moment. Just up the beach, a superior enemy force was preparing to launch the assault Lamb and Whiting had feared for more than two years—and at practically the very moment of attack, they were being removed from command. To Whiting, the order was undoubtedly final confirmation of the opinion he had formed about Braxton Bragg: the commanding general was an incompetent imbecile who was afraid to attack the enemy.[29]

For Lamb, the order was demoralizing. It was devastating news to come at such a critical time. General Whiting was "a gifted, brilliant and courageous hero whose men loved him," Lamb believed, and his removal would likely demoralize the garrison at the worst possible moment. General Colquitt, a volunteer officer from Georgia, was a seasoned combat veteran with a distinguished record as a brigade commander. But Fort Fisher's garrison knew nothing about him and, as far as Lamb was concerned, Colquitt was but a mere "Georgia militia general" in comparison to General Whiting. To Lamb, Bragg's order was a disaster.[30]

It would not take effect until nighttime, however, and the danger now looming over the fort allowed no time for further reflection. The Yankees would be coming soon. When the assault came, the Federal fleet would have to cease fire to avoid hitting its own troops. At that moment, Lamb would rush his soldiers to the landface wall to make their defense. He would leave the seaface lightly manned, using most of his garrison to defend the landface. About 500 riflemen would be concentrated along the eastern end of the landface and on the Northeast Bastion, where he expected the main Federal assault to strike. Some 250 other troops would be used to defend the western, riverside end of the fort's landface. Major James Reilly would command the lesser force, which would be aided by the two field pieces stationed at the riverside entrance to the fort and by the minefield of buried torpedoes—if the bombardment had not severed the ignition wires. Aware of what seemed to be hordes of Yankees ready to assault, the troop dispositions looked desperately thin to Lamb. Then he received some good news: Hagood's South Carolinians, Bragg's promised reinforcements, had finally arrived.[31]

◆

It had not been an easy voyage for the men from the Palmetto State—and their delay was not simply because their ships had run aground. The stranded steamers had floated free during Saturday night's high tide. The main problem lay with the transport crews: they were so afraid of the Federal naval bombardment that they had refused to land the troops. Shortly after they were spotted on the river by General Terry and Colonel Comstock, the troopships were also sighted by the Federal fleet, which had then shifted some of its fire to the river. As the enemy shells splashed into the Cape Fear, two of the steamers retreated, fleeing across the river to Smithville. A single transport landed its troops—and only because some of the

South Carolinians on board trained their loaded weapons on the ship's crew and forced the vessel to go on to Battery Buchanan. At gunpoint, the steamer's crew landed the South Carolina soldiers, then quickly retreated. Two-thirds of the promised reinforcements did not make it into the fort, including the brigade's commander, Colonel Robert Graham. Of the 1,000 troops dispatched by Bragg, no more than 350 actually landed at Fort Fisher.[32]

Those who did land were hustled into Battery Buchanan's bomb-proof, where they were issued a scanty ration of worm-infested hard-tack. Then, about two o'clock Sunday afternoon, they were ordered to move double-quick up to the fort's landface during the height of the naval bombardment. These were combat veterans—the 25th South Carolina Infantry and detachments of the 21st and 11th South Carolina Infantry—and they had endured heavy bombardments or bloody fighting at places like Fort Sumter, Cold Harbor and Peters-burg. But none had ever experienced such a hellish fire as this. They were ordered to move fast, single file and spread out, staying close to the seaface wall for as much protection as possible. Despite the precautions, it was a harrowing experience.[33]

Captain James F. Izlar of the Twenty-fifth South Carolina was one who led the way. "It was terrible, appalling," he recalled. "Shot hissed and shell bursted in every direction." For more than a mile they had to withstand the exploding shells and spinning iron, and behind them they left a trail of dead and wounded. "The whole of this distance was covered and swept by the guns of the enemy," Izlar remembered. "The scene was enough to terrify the stoutest heart." Private William Greer of the Twenty-fifth South Carolina was knocked flat by an exploding shell, stunned and buried by a geyser of sand with nothing but one foot exposed. A fellow soldier assumed Greer was dead, but grabbed his foot anyway and hauled him out of his live burial—surprised to find him living and unhurt.[34]

The dash across the fort thoroughly terrorized the South Carolini-ans. Many ducked into the seaface bombproofs along the way and, once safely inside, refused to come out again. The force was dis-persed, thinned by casualties and demoralized. Their senior officer, Captain James Carson, was among the wounded. He and part of the force remained on the seaface near the Northeast Bastion. Except for stragglers scattered through the seaface bombproofs, Captain Izlar had the rest of the force with him—and he could account for barely 100 troops.[35]

Colonel Lamb was dismayed to discover what had become of the long-awaited reinforcements, but he had no time to worry about it. As he hurried back to the Pulpit, one of his lookouts yelled to him,

"Colonel, the enemy are about to charge." Up the beach, the dark mass of enemy troops appeared to be advancing in an assault formation. Whiting was nearby. Lamb turned to him, and asked him to once more call for help from General Bragg. Quickly, Whiting scrawled a desperate message and sent it by courier to the signal corpsmen at Battery Buchanan. They would flag it across the river to Battery Lamb, where it would be sent by telegraph to Bragg. "The enemy are about to assault; they outnumber us heavily," Whiting wrote. "Enemy on the beach in front of us in very heavy force, not more than 700 yards from us. Nearly all land guns disabled. Attack! Attack! It is all I can say, and all you can do."[36]

The frantic message sent, Whiting headed for the Northeast Bastion. Lamb ran to the landface, into the sally port and down through the tunnel under the traverses, ordering the troops inside the bombproofs to prepare to man the parapets when the bombardment ceased. He issued orders sending more sharpshooters to the landface wall—with specific instructions to pick off the Yankee officers leading the assault. The fort electrician was told to allow the enemy's first wave to cross the minefield before exploding the underground torpedoes. Lamb hoped that the explosions would shatter and demoralize the enemy support troops, while the first wave would be taken down by rifle volleys from the fort. Those orders issued, he hurried back toward his Pulpit headquarters. He was still yards away when he heard it—a shrill, spine-tingling wail, almost a screech—the unmistakable, unnerving sound of more than sixty ships' steam whistles. It obscured all other sound—the exploding enemy shells, the rifle fire of the skirmish lines, the shouts of all those around him—and Lamb knew instantly what it meant. It was the signal for the Yankee assault to begin.[37]

◆

Events were unfolding rapidly for Randolph Breese. It had been time-consuming to organize the naval brigade; the marines were slower getting ashore and up to the front than he had expected; and he was still unsure exactly when the army was going to make its assault. His trek across the peninsula and through the army's lines had not resolved the problem of coordinated timing. The assaults were still scheduled to occur at three o'clock, and although he had managed to get the naval brigade formed and the battle plan fixed well before the deadline, complications still remained. The forward entrenchments were not ready and apparently would not be ready in time, so the sailors could not advance under cover as close to the fort as planned. Now that they saw the intended route of assault,

Breese and other officers felt it was far too exposed, far too un-protected for a long charge. Furthermore, his organization of the naval brigade had drawn criticism from the army. "Going into action as your men are now formed, you will get fearfully punished," an army officer had advised.[38]

He consulted with his division commanders and made some last-minute adjustments: the assault route would be moved to the left flank, closer to the ocean, so the sailors would gain some protection from the sloping beach. The naval brigade was ordered forward, along the water's edge, to a point about a half-mile from the fort, where they would halt and take cover under the crest of the beach. There they would await orders to charge. Meanwhile, Breese sent couriers hurrying to the front with orders for Lieutenant Preston and Captain Dawson, instructing them to move. There was "splendid cover" at water's edge, they were told, and they should relocate to the left flank and dig new entrenchments and rifle pits there.[39]

Led by Acting Master's Mate Joseph Simms, Preston's seamen had already dug deep entrenchments for the sailors to occupy prior to their assault. Farther to the front, Dawson's marines were advancing their skirmish line toward the fort—all under harassing enemy fire. "We were under a galling fire from a hateful gun mounted upon a field carriage at the fort's sally port, as well as musketry along the land face," Simms recalled. "Together with musketry, canister, and grape fired by the enemy in front of us, and fragments of bursting shell fired by our ships at the rear and left of us, intrenching near the face of Fort Fisher was not a very pleasant job." As ordered, Preston's naval detail climbed out of their trenches and double-quicked to the left, where they began shoveling new entrenchments.[40]

When the order to relocate reached the marine force at the front, it surprised Dawson. He had been pushing his skirmishers forward steadily since they arrived at the front and now his forward line was only 150 yards from the fort. That meant the sailors would have cover fire most of the way to their objective, but moving down to water's edge meant the marines would have to dig new rifle pits and they would not have time to get as close to the fort. Studying the new route of assault, Dawson figured that at best he could advance new rifle pits along the revised route to within no more than 600 yards of the fort—meaning the sailors would have to make the final 600 yards of their charge without cover fire. Could there be some mistake about the new order? No, he was reassured, the order came from Breese himself. Obediently, Dawson promptly recalled his skirmish-ers, hustled them over to a point near water's edge and began shovel-ing a new skirmish line for his marines.[41]

Minutes later, before Dawson had time to dig new rifle pits or even get his men deployed, the full 1,600-man naval brigade arrived near his newly emerging advance line and lay down under the crest of the beach in preparation for the assault. There had been no time for the naval detachment to dig new entrenchments along the assault route, nor were the marines yet in a position to provide adequate cover fire. To Dawson, it was all happening too fast. He peered over the long sandy plain toward the river and saw no sign of the army advance. He knew Admiral Porter had ordered the naval assault to begin only after the army was on Fort Fisher's western wall, yet the naval brigade appeared on the verge of making its charge. The sailors had been moved forward; they were now under sporadic fire from the fort and stray fire from the fleet, and they appeared restless and ready to go. It was obvious to Dawson that the naval assault would be launched momentarily, yet his marines were not yet properly deployed in their new positions.[42]

As the deadline neared, the naval brigade began to draw more enemy fire, perhaps because the sailors had already ignored one of Admiral Porter's orders. Presumably to avoid attracting hostile fire, he had pointedly ordered all flags to remain furled until the sailors were atop the fort walls. Now, however, as they lay in the sand under the crest of the beach, colorbearers from various ships unfurled their flags overhead and let the banners flutter defiantly within sight of the fort.[43]

Lying there on the beach, waiting to go into combat, they composed a diverse group. It was a strictly volunteer force. Even those detailed to the task had been given the option of withdrawing, so they were all there by choice. Among them were officers like Lieutenant Commander William Cushing, the daredevil who had sunk the *Albemarle* and sounded New Inlet in broad daylight; Acting Ensign Robert Wiley, a popular young officer from the USS *Montgomery;* and Lieutenant R. H. Lamson, commander of the USS *Gettysburg,* who had left his ship to lead a seventy-man detail from his vessel. But most were not officers; most were men whose names would never appear on an official report unless cited for exceptional valor or listed as casualties. Many had left safe shipboard duties to sample the kind of wartime excitement that normally excluded them. Charles Norman of the USS *Powhatan* was a carpenter's mate. Robert Harlow of the USS *Montgomery* was a second-class fireman. James McDonald was a musician aboard the USS *Vanderbilt.* John Barber was captain of the hold aboard the USS *Iosco.* His shipmate, Thomas Berry, was a ship's cook. Thomas Connolly was quartermaster on the USS *Ticonderoga.* William Cain of the USS *Shenandoah* was a coal heaver. William Scott of the USS *Sassacus* was a sail-maker's mate. The youngest was probably the *Powhatan*'s H. N. Barrow, a third-class boy, age unknown. The oldest may have been Boatswain's Mate Henry Harrison of the *Shenandoah,* age forty. One sailor, Landsman Henry Snow of the USS *Pequot,* had once been a Confederate soldier. Now uniformed in blue, he prepared to assault his former comrades-in-arms, knowing that if captured and identi-fied, he would surely be executed. Some, like Lieutenant Samuel Preston, had been among the first to volunteer. Others, like Robley Evans of the *Powhatan,* had cast lots for the privilege of joining the storming party. Going ashore was an afterthought for the *Vander-bilt*'s Corporal Thomas Cosgrove, a replacement for a sailor who dropped out. Cosgrove's best friend, a former soldier, had tried un-successfully to talk him out of going, but Cosgrove thought he would be exposed to little danger. Others in the naval brigade agreed with him.[44]

Three o'clock finally came—and passed—with no sign of move-ment from the army. Then it was 3:10. And 3:15. And 3:20. Finally, at 3:25, there seemed to be movement among the troops visible across the peninsula. General Terry's signal corpsmen had finally flagged the fleet. Almost immediately, the *Malvern* hoisted signal "2211"—the order to cease fire. For Breese, it was time to go: he had decided not to wait for the army to reach Fort Fisher's walls. Offi-cially, he kept his reasons to himself. Perhaps he chose not to wait any longer because the assault was almost a half-hour late. Maybe he was carried away in the excitement and confusion of the moment. Or perhaps he viewed this assault as the much smaller naval landing party had viewed the "assault" on Battery Anderson during the first battle—as a rivalrous race between army and navy. For whatever his reasons, Lieutenant Commander Breese did not wait on the army to take the lead. Turning to the 1,600 seamen and officers lying on the beach, he shouted the order—"Charge!"[45]

They were on their feet instantly, cheering wildly and racing for-ward down the beach toward the distant fort. Immediately, Daw-son's marines were swept forward in the surge, cheering as they joined the charge, forgetting their orders to remain in line and pro-vide cover fire. Dawson was startled: he was sure Breese had launched the assault too soon—no Federal soldiers had scaled the fort's walls or appeared to have even begun their assault. He shouted for his marines to remain in line, to stay back, to get down and provide cover fire—but most ignored his commands amid the wild cheering.[46]

The blue-clad mob bounded forward under unfurled flags, revolvers and cutlasses ready. Almost simultaneously, the *Malvern* discharged two long, shrill blasts from its steam whistles, igniting a mass wail from the ships of the fleet—the signal to assault Fort Fisher. The shrill clamor of expelled steam rolled across the ocean and the peninsula like an audible cloud, and the thunderous bombardment of the fort landface immediately ceased. Admiral Porter had anchored the *Malvern* opposite the naval brigade, and as the seamen started forward, he ordered his flagship to get under way, paralleling their route offshore. Aboard the other warships, crewmen scaled the riggings and crowded the rails to watch their shipmates charging down the beach toward the Rebel fort. "We almost held our breath as they charged," reported a shipboard eyewitness. "The noise of the guns, whistles, cheers and yells of the sailors and marines was terrific," recalled another, "and made the most exciting and indescribable event."[47]

◆

When the long, shrill chorus of steam whistles ceased and the bombardment ended, Confederate Point was strangely quiet for a moment. Then the engaged warships resumed their fire, now pounding the fort's lower seaface, far away from the landface—the target of the Federal assault. Immediately, Fort Fisher's garrison poured forth from the bombproofs and joined the scattered sharpshooters and gun crews already manning the landface. As Lamb had ordered, the 500 troops he had selected were hurriedly placed on the fort wall on and around the Northeast Bastion, the fort's center and the area he was sure would be the target of the main Federal assault. Among them were the sharpshooters assigned the task of picking off the Yankee officers. Turning to one of his aides, Captain Charles Blocker, Lamb ordered the officer to get the available South Carolinians over to the western landface wall in a hurry. They could reinforce the troops defending that part of the fort and—with help from the cannon at the gate and the buried torpedoes—it was hoped that they would be able to hold off any secondary assault by the enemy against the fort's river side.[48]

The two sally-port artillery pieces were already discharging canister toward the distant, advancing Federal force, and so was the lone Columbiad still in working order on the landface. With his troops in position behind the sandbagged parapet, rifles at the ready, Lamb ordered the soldiers to hold their fire. The sharpshooters and cannoneers would continue to fire at selected targets, but Lamb wanted his main force held in reserve, prepared to fire in volleys upon his command.[49]

The sailors and marines had numerical superiority: Fort Fisher's entire garrison amounted to fewer men. However, the pistols and cutlasses issued to the naval brigade would be no match for Confederate rifles until the seamen scaled the fort wall. A scattering of marines had stayed on line as planned, instead of joining the assault, and now they worked their carbines as fast as possible, trying to provide cover fire for the charging seamen. Porter had been determined that his "Webfoots" would participate in the land assault, even though most had exhibited dismal marksmanship in target practice, and now they were assaulting the great fort armed with weapons that were worthless until they were almost face to face with the enemy. And to reach that enemy, they had to move approximately 1,200 yards across open terrain, exposed to hostile fire from an elevated, fortified position. They still had stretching before them some 600 yards—half the distance to the fort—when Lamb's Confederates were in place behind the fort parapet, weapons loaded and waiting.[50]

Lieutenant Commander Breese had to run hard to stay at the head of the assault column as the sailors raced each other to lead the charge. The three divisions Breese had so carefully formed quickly merged into one large mass of running men. At first, the charging sailors acted like they were still on a lark, as if they were merely engaging in an off-duty athletic contest. Lieutenant Commander Parker, trying to stay at the head of the second division, had come ashore in a knee-length officer's overcoat, and as he ran, the cape of the coat whipped wildly behind him, giving him the appearance of a madly flying bat. Stirred by the sight, the sailors around him burst into raucous laughter.[51]

Moments later, the first man went down. It was Seaman James Flannigan, the young sailor from the *Powhatan* who had shared his certainty of pending death with Robley Evans the night before. Now Flannigan was down in the sand, shot through the chest by an enemy sharpshooter. Evans was in the pack a few steps back, and dropped to his knees beside the fallen man. "Are you badly hurt?" he asked anxiously. Flannigan said nothing, smiled slightly and died. Evans ran on. So did Acting Ensign Francis Sands of the USS *Gettysburg*, who was running shoulder to shoulder between two seamen when both were struck down by Rebel fire. Sands continued running, wondering why neither bullet had hit him.[52]

Seaman Auzella Savage held the ship's flag from the USS *Santiago de Cuba* above him as he raced toward the fort. Suddenly, a round from the fort severed the flagstaff and knocked the ship's flag into the sand. Savage stopped long enough to retrieve the fallen colors, then resumed the assault—carrying the banner by its short, splintered flagstaff. Another sailor went down, shrieking "I'm dying! I'm dying!" as he fell. A shipmate stooped over the writhing man and ripped open his shirt, revealing nothing more than a red streak where a spent bullet had grazed the seaman's chest. Embarrassed but reassured, he rejoined the charge.[53]

At the head of the assaulting column, leading the detail from the *Malvern,* Lieutenant Benjamin H. Porter raced toward the fort with the admiral's flag. He was nineteen years old. In the navy since age fourteen, Porter was a combat veteran, cited for bravery and daring under fire. Like Samuel Preston, his close friend, Porter had spent a year as a prisoner of war, and in fact he and Preston had spent time together in the same South Carolina prison. Upon his exchange he had been placed on Admiral Porter's staff, recently succeeding Cushing as commanding officer of the *Malvern.* Serious and businesslike despite a schoolboy face, he had added discipline to the *Malvern*'s crew, often choosing extra duty over courting jaunts to the homes of Norfolk's eligible young ladies. Off-duty in the *Malvern*'s wardroom, however, he often put aside his professional demeanor to swap tales and sing sailor ballads with Preston, Cushing and other young officers. Porter was a striking figure—tall, erect, handsome—and his height and gold-braided officer's uniform made him a conspicuous target at the head of the naval brigade. Holding the admiral's flag aloft as he led the charge made him an even more tempting target, and he attracted persistent fire from the fort's marksmen. Yet, as sailors began to fall, Porter ran on, unscathed.[54]

◆

High above the beach in the Northeast Bastion, Colonel Lamb watched intently as the dark mass of enemy troops surged forward, heading for the angle of the fort as he had expected. The sally-port field pieces, the lone landface Columbiad and the two guns in the Mound Battery spat grapeshot and canister at the approaching horde as fast as the gun crews could work their guns, and the sharpshooters on the landface wall fired, reloaded and fired again—but the Yankees kept coming. The fort electrician had orders to explode the underground torpedoes as soon as the first Federals reached the fort wall, but now Lamb could see their attack route would carry the Yankees alongside the surf and away from the fort minefield. Despite all his elaborate preparations, the torpedoes would be useless. The advancing enemy column was much larger than the 500-man force defending the Northeast Bastion—Lamb could easily see that now—but without artillery and the torpedoes, the Yankees would have to be repelled by the soldiers on the fort wall.[55]

Those soldiers, uniformed in gray and butternut, could also see that they were far outnumbered by the enemy now bearing down on them. Peering over the sandbagged parapet, undoubtedly tense and dry-mouthed, they obeyed their colonel's order and held their fire, rifles loaded, half-cocked and fitted with percussion caps. As the tension increased, General Whiting suddenly climbed over the sandbags and stood atop the parapet of the Northeast Bastion, silhouetted against the smoke-streaked afternoon sky. He shouted words of encouragement to the defenders waiting in line around him, then brazenly turned to face the approaching attack. It was a daring act, a dangerous and calculated gesture designed to reassure his nervous soldiers—and it worked. A wave of renewed determination gripped the tense riflemen and steadied the Confederate line.[56]

By then the naval column was less than 300 yards away, heading for the point near water's edge where the palisades ended. There, at low tide, a narrow opening existed between the end of the fence and the surf—the easiest way for a large force to reach the fort. Lamb readied his troops for their first volley, and as they cocked their rifles a collective, metallic rattle sputtered along the parapet. Hold your fire, they were urged, hold your fire. The first volley had to hit the enemy with maximum effect. They were now only about 250 yards away, a compact mass of blue uniforms—Yankee sailors and marines. The fort parapet bristled with rifles, each now carefully trained on the rapidly approaching enemy. Still Lamb waited. On they came, unchecked by the grapeshot and canister, their ranks full despite the best efforts of the fort sharpshooters. At less than 200 yards, the mass became personal, composed of individuals, men with faces, officers with gold braid. They were running full speed, revolvers out and ready, flags flapping wildly above them, officers out in front. There were many of them and they made a large target. In moments, if unchecked, they would be surging around the palisades, scaling the fort walls, pouring over the parapet and grappling with the garrison. Finally, with the first wave less than 150 yards away, in easy rifle range, Colonel Lamb shouted a command and the fort parapet exploded in smoke and flame and noise.[57]

◆

The volley flattened the officers and sailors in front. "The whole mass of men went down like a row of falling bricks," recalled a survivor, "in a second every man was flat on his stomach." Stunned by the effect of the volley, the other seamen immediately dropped to the beach and the assault lurched to a halt. Some were dead, killed instantly by the gunfire. Others lay moaning in the sand. Dazed and uncertain, the survivors lay on their stomachs as a thick white cloud of rifle smoke drifted off the fort parapet and onto the beach. For a long moment the men in blue did not move, then the officers were up—Breese, Parker, Cushman, Selfridge and others—waving their swords and shouting for the seamen to rise and charge. Obediently, the men scrambled to their feet and resumed the assault, charging over the bodies of their dead and wounded companions.[58]

◆

As the seamen rose and rushed forward again, the front ranks of Confederates on the fort wall handed their discharged rifles to troops behind them—reloaders—and in exchange were handed freshly loaded weapons. On command, the front line fired again, discharging another awful volley into the closely packed column of seamen below them. The sailors had covered barely 50 yards more when the second volley ripped into their ranks. Again, the entire assault force went down. Now there were many dead and wounded lying in the sand.[59]

◆

Again the officers were up quickly, shouting commands, urging the men onward. Again the seamen pulled themselves to their feet, their numbers now thinned and bloodied. Over the bodies of the dead, through the smoke and the groans and the cries, they again stumbled forward and resumed their run toward the fort wall. Breese and the divisional commanders were still alive, running hard to stay at the head of the column, which had now lost all formation and was going forward as a single dense mass of men. Urging the seamen on, the officers pushed forward, competing for positions at the front, leaving the sailors and marines to follow as the assault resumed.[60]

There were no more volleys. Now Lamb's Confederates fired as rapidly as possible, unleashing a deadly, sustained fire as each rifleman repeatedly swapped discharged weapons for reloaded ones, firing again and again. Many aimed at the naval officers, distinguished by their uniforms and caps. Smoke rolled off the parapet in a thick haze, and the noise of the gunfire rose in a harsh, loud roar, pierced by cries and moans and the chilling thud of lead striking flesh. "[It was] a perfect hail of lead, with men dropping in every direction," recalled a survivor. "The officers were pulling down their caps over their eyes, for it was almost impossible to look at the deadly flashing blue line of the parapet," he recalled. "I have been in a great number of battles," reported Seaman William Cobb, "but I never saw men fall so fast in my life. . . . There was a shower of canister [that came] through the ranks where I was running up the beach and out of about twenty that stood within eight paces of me, there was but four of us that came out. . . ."[61]

Somehow Lieutenant Porter had made it to the front unhurt. Faster men like his friend Preston had overtaken him, but Porter had kept well ahead of the mass of blue-clad seamen, racing toward the fort with the admiral's flag in hand. He headed for the end of the palisades, intending to take his flag and his men straight up the fort's sodded wall and over the parapet. He was only 50 yards from the big fence when a Confederate bullet struck him square in the chest, transfixing his body and killing him instantly. He fell lifeless in the sand with the admiral's flag beside him.[62]

Several paces ahead, Lieutenant Preston continued sprinting toward the fort, unaware of his friend's death. After overseeing construction of the forward skirmish lines, Preston could have remained in line with no obligation to join the assault. Instead, he had taken a position out in front. Back in his quarters aboard the *Malvern,* he had left a note requesting burial at his alma mater, the U.S. Naval Academy, just in case he fell at Fort Fisher. Seconds after Porter was shot dead, Preston pitched face-first into the sand, struck in the left groin by an enemy round. The bullet severed the femoral artery and apparently knocked him senseless. A sailor stooped over Preston's fallen form, trying to help, but he too was hit, and collapsed lifelessly on top of the young officer, who was quickly bleeding to death. Another seaman pulled the dead man off and Preston managed to roll onto his back, but then he was still. Lieutenant R. H. Lamson, one of the officers who had helped Preston explode the powder boat back in December, fell a few steps away with a bullet in the shoulder. After crudely bandaging his wound, Lamson tried to crawl over to his friend, but was waved away by another wounded man, who yelled that Preston was already dead. Together, Preston and Porter had endured enemy prisons and courted the young ladies in port; now they lay near each other in death. Lieutenant Lamson stared across the beach at Preston's still body, and was moved to tears.[63]

So intense, so violent was the gunfire now coming from the fort that it stunned the assaulting force, pelting the seamen as if it were a deadly, driving, gale-force hailstorm. A half-century later, survivors would describe the torrent of lead as "withering showers" and "hellish fire," which raked the mass of men in blue, tearing great gaps in their ranks. The seamen were now less than 50 yards from the fort, near water's edge and heading for the opening between the surf and the palisades. Seconds now seemed like minutes. They were so close they could hear the Rebels yelling above them. Atop the fort parapet, they could see a Confederate officer clapping his hands and shouting to his men, "Get up and shoot the Yankees!" Stunned by the murderous fire, most of the officers and men leading the assault force wavered, then stopped. Almost immediately, the main part of the naval column charged into the terrible rain of fire—and stopped. Then those bringing up the rear came under the deadly deluge—and *they* stopped. For one long and terrible moment, the whole force halted, hesitated and stood as if paralyzed under the awful, fiery storm. "The rush of the sailors was over," recalled one who was there. "They were packed like sheep in a pen, while the enemy were crowding the ramparts not forty yards away, and shooting into them as fast as they could fire. There was nothing to reply with but *pistols.*"[64]

Amid this violent chaos, the sailors began to lie down on the beach, desperately seeking cover where there was none. Dead and wounded were everywhere. Among the many killed were Robert Harlow, the fireman from the *Montgomery,* and John Barber, who had left his safe duties as captain of the hold on the *Iosco.* Dead too was Corporal Thomas Cosgrove of the *Vanderbilt,* who had gone ashore expecting a lark. Third Class Boy H. N. Barrow was wounded in his left thigh. Charles Norman, the carpenter's mate, also had a leg wound. Wounded too were William Scott, the sailmaker's mate; Musician James McDonald; Coalheaver William Cain; Thomas Berry, the ship's cook; and many others. Funneled into one large compact mass near water's edge, the naval column was now an unavoidable target, flayed horribly by the storm of lead pouring forth from Fort Fisher's walls. Determination and discipline dissolved in seconds under such conditions. "The shrieks and groans, mingling with the fiendish rattling around us, together with the whistling bullets and the bursting shells over us were enough to cause one to feel he was in [hell]," recalled Acting Master's Mate Joseph Simms.[65]

Some of the officers stayed on their feet. Breese and Parker were still alive. So were Selfridge and Cushman. Waving their swords and yelling commands above the racket of battle, they tried to rouse the men once more, to get them up and charging forward again. But most could take no more. Fewer than 200 struggled to their feet, but instead of charging around the palisades toward the Northeast Bastion, they broke to the right and scrambled for cover behind the palisades. The rest of the assault force lay immobile on the beach, despite all commands and pleas. Confused and indecisive, most of the officers also retreated to the protection of the palisades, huddling behind the fence with their men while enemy bullets thudded into the thick timbers. Even the famous daredevil, Lieutenant William Cushing, had taken cover.[66]

Not Lieutenant Commander Parker. He ran on to the opening

between the palisades and the surf, paused beside the end timbers
of the fence and shouted for the seamen to follow him. Only a handful obeyed—maybe no more than fourteen in all. Acting Ensign
George Wood of the USS *Chippewa* charged past Parker and around
the palisades, heading for the fort's sloping wall. He was followed by
shipmates John Wilson, Richard Gallagher and William McGill, who
carried the *Chippewa*'s flag. The men sprinted toward the towering
Northeast Bastion, but paused in confusion when they realized the
rest of the assault force was not following. Winded from the long run,
Ensign Wood hesitated for a moment, then, as bullets whizzed
around him, he darted back through the shattered fence, followed by
his shipmates.[67]

A marine from Parker's ship, Private Henry Thompson, charged
on, accompanied by Acting Master's Mate Joseph Simms and Acting
Master's Mate Arthur Aldrich of the USS *Tuscarora*. They were so
close to the sloping walls of the Northeast Bastion that the Confederate riflemen on top had to mount the parapet to get a clear shot at
them. Bullets hit the sand all around them. An enemy round
whipped through Simms's cap, and nearby, he saw a sailor take a
bullet through the chest. The round knocked the man off his feet and
left him sprawled in the sand. Thompson, Aldrich and Simms hesitated, then turned and made for the palisade. Only Thompson
reached it unhurt. Aldrich was seriously wounded, but managed to
stay on his feet. "I'm shot," he yelled, then staggered through the
fence and collapsed. Simms was hit in the right thigh, the bullet
deflecting off the bone and coming out near his hip. He fell, tried to
rise, fell again and tried to crawl to the safety of the palisade. Parker
too had retreated back outside the fence. "Lie down, Simms, lie
down!" he yelled. "There are two holes in you." Simms obeyed, and
lay still several yards inside the palisades.[68]

Meanwhile, Acting Ensign Robley Evans had tried to lead the
Powhatan's detail through a shattered section of the fence, but only
Landsman Archibald Campbell had followed him. Inside the palisade, Evans looked at the high earthen walls towering over him and
realized he faced a steeper climb that he had expected. Undaunted,
he charged ahead, even though he had already suffered two flesh
wounds in the charge. At eighteen, Evans felt indestructible. The son
of a slave-owning Virginia physician, he had gone West as a youth,
lived with the Shoshone Indians and been shot twice by arrows. A
graduate of the U.S. Naval Academy, he had chosen to go to war
against his native South, even though he had a brother in the Confederate army. He was plucky, headstrong and daring—and he intended

to scale Fort Fisher's walls and pitch into the enemy with his cutlass and Colt.

As he approached the fort's battered earthen wall, however, he realized one of the Confederates on the parapet above had singled him out as a target. A second later he was shot again, knocked flat by a bullet through his right knee. At the same time, Landsman Campbell fell into the sand a few feet away, shot through the lungs. As Evans tried to bandage his wounded knee with a handkerchief, another bullet knocked up a spray of sand nearby. Looking up, he could see the Confederate riflemen on the parapet above, and one was definitely aiming right at him. Another round plowed into the sand inches away, and he could hear the Rebel soldier curse aloud. Twice more he fired at Evans, missing, then fired a round that hit the young seaman's right foot, painfully taking away a toe.

Furious, Evans rolled onto his stomach, shouted a curse at his assailant and fired his Navy Colt at the man's midsection. The round went high and struck the soldier in the throat. He dropped his rifle and tumbled off the parapet, landing limply near Evans, who could see the man was dead. Landsman Campbell, lying mortally wounded nearby, called out, "Mr. Evans, let me crawl over and give that ——— another shot." Before Evans could reply, Campbell died. Moments later, one of the *Powhatan*'s marines, a private named Wasmuth, darted through a gap in the palisade, grabbed Evans under the arms and dragged him to a large crater made by an exploding naval shell. Then, from crater to crater he dragged Evans toward the protection of the palisade, ignoring Evans's pleas to leave him and take cover. "The bullet has not been made that will kill me," he said. They made it as far as a shell crater near the fence before Wasmuth was hit. Evans heard a peculiar thud, then looked up to see his marine rescuer turning round and round, holding a neck wound from which blood was spurting in a steady stream. Wasmuth staggered down to the edge of the surf and fell into the shallow water, where he died. Weak from shock and loss of blood, Evans peered sadly over the edge of the crater at Wasmuth's body, amazed by the dead man's unselfish act.[69]

Acting Ensign George Davis from the USS *Wabash* had also continued the charge, passing around the big fence and heading toward the fort walls. He was followed by two of his shipmates, Seaman Albert Burton and Ordinary Seaman Louis Shepard. The three endured the hail of fire for only seconds, however, before they dashed back outside and took cover behind the palisade. A few of those who made it inside the palisade courageously tried to scale Fort Fisher's walls, but only one was reported to have reached the top.[70]

His name was James Tallentine. He was a native Englishman who had joined the U.S. Navy almost three years earlier in Baltimore. In his mid-twenties, he was a short man—only five-foot-two—and he looked decidedly British, with blue eyes, brown hair and a light complexion. He had served aboard the USS *Fort Jackson* before joining the *Tacony*'s crew, and he had just three weeks to go before his enlistment expired. With so little time left in the service, he hardly could have been blamed for avoiding hazardous duty. But that was not Tallentine's way. As a quarter gunner on the *Tacony*, he was known as a man who would obey orders—"ever foremost in his duties," according to his commanding officer—and he had already demonstrated his coolness under fire. Two months earlier, he and four other seamen had braved enemy fire to spike a Confederate battery near Plymouth, North Carolina. Now, when others who had passed through the palisade were dead, wounded or seeking cover, Tallentine kept going.[71]

Perhaps, in the single-minded fixation of combat, he did not realize the others were no longer with him, or perhaps he was simply determined to assault the enemy fort regardless of the cost. Whatever his motivation, he apparently scaled the fort's steep earthen wall alone, all others now driven back, killed or wounded. Up, up, he went, a solitary figure in blue, climbing toward a parapet swarming with enemy troops—troops who were unleashing a torrent of deadly fire. Still he climbed. Still he was not shot. It was an incredible act, witnessed by but a few amid the turmoil of this battle. Perhaps the fort's defenders held their fire, awed by this act, or perhaps Tallentine's climb was simply one of the oddities of war. However it happened, Quarter Gunner James Tallentine made it to the top—to the crest of the great fort, to the sandbagged parapet, crowded with Colonel Lamb's desperate, determined Confederates. Then he fell, shot by some unknown defender amid the clamor of battle, and he toppled over the parapet into the ranks of the enemy.[72]

Tallentine's dramatic, futile climb was the climax of the naval assault. The charge was spent. The main body of seamen remained pinned down on the beach, raked by the deadly fire spewing forth from Fort Fisher's walls. The sailors huddling behind the palisade were in comparative safety for the moment, but they too were pinned down by the hailstorm of lead. Despite its awful losses, however, the naval brigade outnumbered the Confederates defending the walls above. There still remained an opportunity for victory if the charge could be renewed, some of the officers believed. The assault could still succeed, they believed, if the seamen could only bear the horrendous fire a few dozen more yards and go over the walls of the fort as planned.[73]

Even that might be preferable to the deadly plight they now endured. The rattle of gunfire was mixed with shouts and moans, and muffled the roar of the ocean. Near the water, dazed sailors saw the bodies of their shipmates rolled back and forth by the incoming surf. Incapacitated by wounds in both legs and unable to crawl from the surf where he had fallen, Landsman Edward Lindsay was pulled seaward by the undertow until he drowned. Some wounded dragged themselves to shell craters, leaving trails of blood in the sand. Others lay where they had fallen. One man called for his mother. "Dead and wounded men were lying about in ghastly piles," a survivor would later recall. "The scene on the beach was a pitiful one—dead and wounded officers and men as far as one could see. As a rule, they lay quiet on the sand and took their punishment like the brave lads they were, but occasionally . . . a sound wave would drift along, 'Water, water, water!' " Ignoring the deadly fire, Assistant Surgeons William Longshaw and John Blackmer moved from man to man, toting instruments and tourniquets, but there were more casualties than they could treat. Both doctors were shot to death as they tended to the wounded, Longshaw falling dead upon the body of a mortally wounded marine he was tending.[74]

Most of the officers had raced to be at the head of the charge, leaving their commands behind. Now, twenty-one of them were dead or wounded, and most of the surviving officers were crouched behind the palisades—still separated from their commands. In the absence of their officers, the hundreds of sailors lying on the beach were left confused and indecisive. Resuming the assault seemed unthinkable to many under such withering fire, yet they could not survive lying on their stomachs on an open beach in such a deadly hail. "It would have been impossible for men made of tougher material than flesh to have withstood that firing," reported one who had endured it. "Neither would the palisades afford shelter for more than were already under them." Probably no more than ten minutes had passed since the assault had floundered, certainly no more than twenty, but under such a murderous fire minutes seemed like hours. "Something must be done and speedily," a survivor recollected. "Flesh and blood could not long endure being killed in this slaughter-pen. . . ." Frightened, leaderless and confused, the seamen began to panic.[75]

In desperation, some of the sailors lying near the palisades began shouting for an officer to lead them in a renewed charge against the fort. Acting Master's Mate Abraham Louch, the executive officer of the USS *Mackinaw,* lay a few feet away beneath the palisade. No one else responded to the sailors' pleas, so Louch jumped up, drew his sword and shouted for the men to rise and follow him. Instead, the sailors stared blankly at him and remained frozen in the sand, immobilized by the withering fire coming from the fort. Louch frantically turned to the other officers for support, but none responded. Realizing he stood alone, he lay down again—then was painfully struck by a spent bullet. He did not try to rally the seamen again.[76]

At about the same time, Lieutenant Commander Cushman rose from his position near the end of the palisades and sprinted along the fence toward the fort until he reached the point where Parker and some of the other officers had huddled. There they held a brief, frantic discussion, trying to decide what to do now that the charge had stalled. Cushman was afraid the seamen were about to break— something had to be done. Parker wanted to resume the assault and was willing to lead it. Others agreed. But Breese was in command, not Parker. Cushman could see Breese farther up the palisade, but he was too far away to include in the discussion, and anybody going to him would have to wade through a mass of sailors crowded along the fence. There wasn't time to get Breese's approval, Cushman believed. The other officers agreed: Parker was the senior officer in the group, *he* should lead them off the beach and renew the charge. Parker was willing. He arose and shouted for the bewildered seamen to follow him around the end of the palisade and against the walls of the fort. Immediately, several dozen sailors got to their feet and followed Parker and the other officers, who were now charging along the fence toward the water, heading toward the end of the palisades.[77]

Seeing the movement down the palisades where the sailors were beginning to rally, Lieutenant Commander Breese stood up and waded into the blue carpet of seamen sprawled on the beach around him. "Rise, men, and charge!" he shouted, but hardly anyone moved. Bullets buzzed by his face, but he ignored the fire and pushed his way through the thick, crowded ranks of seamen, sword in hand, shouting repeatedly, "Rise, men, and charge!" In the rear, some men arose, but began to drift back up the beach—away from the fort. Seeing the stragglers begin to retreat, Breese shouted toward the rear of the column, trying to stop the straggling. "Charge!" he yelled. "Charge! Don't retreat!"[78]

Down the palisades toward the surf, more sailors were rising and some turned around to watch Breese, straining to hear his commands above the racket of battle. "What did he say?" some of the men shouted in confusion. "What did he say? Is it to retreat?"

"Retreat!" someone shouted, and a dozen voices echoed the word—"Retreat! Retreat!"

Approaching the end of the palisades, Parker and the other officers looked back at the commotion behind them, and were horrified to see their attempt to rally the seamen dissolve in a wave of panic. In the rear, clusters of men began to rise up off the beach and fall back in confusion. Some ran. Then a frenzied chorus swept through the ranks: "Retreat! Retreat!" Suddenly, the suppressed panic erupted: beginning in the rear like a rapidly rolling wave, the sailors and marines rose, turned their backs to the fort and fled, terrified, back up the beach in a frantic stampede.[79]

The officers had raced each other to the front and now none was in the rear to stop the retreat. "Cowards!" one officer shouted angrily at the backs of the stampeding sailors. Others cursed the retreating mob. Some joined the rout. One of the officers nearest the rear, Lieutenant Commander Selfridge, shouted for the men to come back, but even the seamen of his ship ignored him. Captain Dawson tried to get his marines to stop and provide cover fire for the retreat, but few obeyed him. Waving his sword aloft, Lieutenant Commander Breese did everything he knew how to do to stop the wild rout, but nothing worked. Eventually, he gave up and coolly followed the retreating mob at a walk, still ignoring the bullets that buzzed past. In the frantic dash to the rear, men who had competed with each other to lead the assault minutes earlier now raced each other back up the beach. Parker and the other officers could do nothing. "I could have cried when the bluejackets retreated," reported Lieutenant John Bartlett. "I shouted and waved my sword for the sailors to come back, but no, off they went down the beach."[80]

It was an inglorious moment for the navy and marines. They had come as if on a lark, confident they would dislodge the Rebels and conquer Fort Fisher with ease—as predicted by Admiral Porter's blustering boasts. "You need not be surprised to hear that the web-footers have gone into the fort," he had privately bragged. "I will try it anyhow, and show the soldiers how to do it." Instead, Porter's naval brigade had been shattered, bloodied and repulsed in an embarrassing rout. So thoroughly terrorized were the "webfooters" in their flight that they abandoned their casualties in the face of the enemy. Lying dead or wounded on the beach behind the retreating sailors and marines were more than 300 of their shipmates. And on Fort Fisher's parapet, Colonel Lamb's Confederates stood up and cheered wildly at the backs of the fleeing seamen.[81]

10

"The Air Seems Darkened with Death"

WILLIAM LAMB WAS ECSTATIC. THE YANKEES WERE FLEE-ing back up the beach in disarray. Their assault force had been met, shattered and sent reeling in a retreat, in a wild rout, in a mad and frantic scramble to escape the fire unleashed by Fort Fisher's defenders. Thrilled, Lamb's Confederates climbed up on the fort parapet with General Whiting and cheered and yelled and whooped in victory. "Come aboard!" they shouted in glee at the mass of blue-clad seamen, now racing away in the distance. "Come aboard!" For Lamb, it was a supreme moment of triumph. But amid the celebration, something was wrong. Something was happening to the left, down the landface, toward the river. Through the haze of battle smoke, Lamb could see movement on the far end of the land-face: men were clambering over the batteries nearest the river, and atop the landface wall he could see flags, held high above the swirl of activity. They were not his flags—not the fort's, not Confederate— and they did not belong there. They were guidons and regimental standards, Yankee battle flags. Lamb stared at the banners atop his fort in stunned disbelief. So did his exultant soldiers. Then the cheering stopped. Enemy battle flags were atop the parapet—the Yankees were inside Fort Fisher.[1]

◆

The Federal flags waving above the fort's riverside batteries were also visible to General Terry, and to him, the sight was reassuring. It meant his troops were inside the fort and had a foothold. Watching the action unfold from the unfinished Confederate earthwork where he had made his command post, about 500 yards from the western end of the landface, Terry could see the army's attack route much better than Colonel Lamb could. And from Terry's viewpoint, the army assault had begun smoothly, precisely according to plan.[2]

◆

By two o'clock the troops were in place, ready to form for the assault. They waited in the edge of the woods, among the stands of pine and scrub oak. Skies were a clear winter blue and the temperature had risen to a comfortable 50 degrees. A slight breeze blew from the south, carrying the aroma of pine resin through the ranks of soldiers sprawled at ease among the trees. "They were chatting and laughing indifferently," noted an observer, "behaving as troops before a battle always do behave, as far as my observation goes—that is, doing anything except indulging in the heroics of a grand moment or the prayers of an awful one. Passing down still nearer [the front], I reached a low line of rifle-pits where were more soldiers, still busy with cards or luncheon, and indifferent to the coming moment."[3]

Unlike Fort Fisher's garrison, these men of the Army of the James were veterans. They had seen and survived hard fighting before on numerous battlefields and they knew what now lay ahead. "Rough-looking, with frowsy clothing and disheveled hair and beards, after long and hard experience on the transports, these soldiers had their arms clean and bright and cartridge boxes filled with forty rounds," reported one present. "They aligned and dressed in line of battle as coolly and precisely as if on parade. Probably not a man was among them who had not been 'in' a dozen times before. There was but little fuss about it, and no noise of either bugling or verbal commands."[4]

As planned, Ames's division would make the assault. The First Brigade—Curtis's brigade—would lead the charge, followed by the Second Brigade under Colonel Galusha Pennypacker and the Third Brigade, commanded by Colonel Louis Bell. Abbott's brigade would stand by in reserve, going in if needed. The black soldiers of Paine's division would hold the Federal rear line against Hoke's Confederates and would not be put into action on the front unless it was absolutely necessary. The assault would be made according to a plan developed by Colonel Curtis, who had outlined it for General Terry earlier in the day. Instead of charging the fort in a single column as the naval brigade would do, Curtis proposed moving his brigade as close to the fort as possible, sheltered by heavy cover fire from a large detachment of sharpshooters. Then, upon command, they would charge the fort in a long line, angling toward the riverside or western end of the fort landface. This way, Curtis believed, the troops would present much less of a target.[5]

General Terry liked the plan and approved it. "With your brigade on parapet, I feel certain of success," Terry had told Curtis. The young colonel was complimented by the general's words, but they did not alleviate a concern that had developed within him. Despite all his criticism of General Butler for not attacking Fort Fisher at Christmas, and despite all his boasts of how easily the fort could have been taken, Curtis now had doubts of his own. He shared them privately with Colonel Comstock, who had considered the fort difficult to take on the first expedition and still felt the same. In a matter of minutes, Curtis would be leading the assault he had talked of since Christmas, and now that the moment had finally arrived, he wondered if Fort Fisher really could be captured. Yet, despite his secret worries, Curtis remained personally fearless—his troops would assault the fort and he would lead them.[6]

General Ames apparently had other ideas. He had failed to talk General Terry out of naming Curtis to lead the charge, but apparently had not given up his attempts to deny Curtis the place of glory. A wiry New Englander from Rockport, Maine, Ames was a strong-willed man and not one to easily put aside an affront. Slim, smooth-faced and boyish-looking with a French-style mustache and goatee, he was twenty-nine years old and, despite his rank, was actually five months younger than Curtis. Unlike Curtis, however, he was a professional soldier. Seriously wounded at First Manassas just ten weeks after graduating from West Point, he had ordered his men to prop him up on an artillery caisson and had continued to exercise command until he collapsed. He recovered from his wound, returned to the front and afterwards saw action in almost every major battle in the Eastern theater: Malvern Hill, Antietam, Fredericksburg, Chancellorsville, Gettysburg, Cold Harbor, Petersburg. Promoted to brigadier general at age twenty-seven, he had come to Fort Fisher with a string of brevet honors, a division command and a reputation for "peculiarities." Perhaps he had earned too many honors too soon. Perhaps others were jealous of his youthful accomplishments. Perhaps he simply had a quarrelsome personality. Whatever it was about Adelbert Ames, even a mild-mannered officer like Terry considered him somewhat difficult to get along with, and Ames apparently no longer cared about getting along with Curtis. Ames was still incensed that Curtis, a junior officer, had sailed for Fort Fisher without him. He was only following orders, Curtis insisted, noting that when the brigade's troopship, the *Atlantic,* departed at 4 A.M. Ames was more than ten hours late. The general had spent the night ashore somewhere, unaware of the sailing schedule. His staff had not been notified either, they said, a claim that Curtis disputed. Ames never explained his whereabouts—an "unauthorized absence," Curtis called it—and although he and Curtis had been poker partners on the first expedition, Ames had continued to hold a grudge. Now, with the assault ready to begin, he prepared to put his aide-de-camp, Captain Albert G. Lawrence, at the head of Curtis's brigade.[7]

At exactly two o'clock, a force of 100 sharpshooters was sent forward. Sixty troops had been detached from one of the Third Brigade's regiments, the Thirteenth Indiana, because the troops were armed with Spencer repeating rifles. They joined a detail of 40 volunteers from Curtis's brigade and, led by Lieutenant Colonel Samuel M. Zent of the Thirteenth Indiana, the combined force was charged with laying down a heavy cover fire in preparation for the assault. They were to fire on the Confederates when they manned the fort's walls and had special orders to pick off the Rebel gunners before they could fire their artillery.[8]

As the 100-man detachment appeared from the tree line, the Confederates defending the western landface rushed from their bombproofs to man the fort parapets. Lieutenant Colonel Zent took the sharpshooters forward at a run, halting on a line about 175 yards from the fort. Half the force had been issued spades and they quickly threw up a line of rifle pits, trained their Spencers on the fort and delivered a deadly fire. "The men went forward gallantly, the enemy instantly opening fire upon them and knocking over several of them," reported a Federal officer. "The remainder soon got into their assigned position. . . . Their fire joined with the tremendous broadsides of the navy, which were at this time appalling beyond description, soon drove the garrison to their bombproofs again. . . ."[9]

With the sharpshooters now out in front, it was time for Ames to put his division into assault formation. Curtis had carefully explained the plan of assault to his officers and had instructed them to pass the information down the chain of command, until each man in the ranks understood where to go and what to do. Now, at about two-thirty, the order went out to form up and prepare to go forward. "When the order came to 'fall in,' then I knew that desperate work was in store," a New York lieutenant later confided to his wife. "As I looked down the line I knew that very many of the brave boys who formed must fall. It was a most solemn moment. The very air seemed oppressive. A silence such as I never before witnessed seemed to rest on all, but it was not fear. Men were thinking of the loved ones far away."[10]

It was past three o'clock by the time the troops were formed and ready to go forward—the assault was late. Terry directed the preliminary movements himself: Curtis's brigade was moved forward out of the woods double-quick to a line of battle about 400 yards from the fort, where the troops lay down and hastily threw up crude breastworks with anything at hand—bayonets, tin plates and cups, pocketknives and sword blades. Almost immediately, Confederate troops manned the fort parapets and opened fire, and the sally-port field artillery began to pepper the Federals with grapeshot and canister. Curtis waited until the naval bombardment drove the Rebels back to their bombproofs, then he sent his brigade forward again, one regiment at a time. Again, they quickly threw up makeshift breastworks on a line just behind the sharpshooters, about 200 yards from the fort. The Second Brigade, led by Colonel Pennypacker, then advanced to the line vacated by Curtis's brigade, and in the rear, Colonel Bell prepared to lead the Third Brigade forward in the same maneuver. Each time the Federals raced forward, the fort's troops would brave the bombardment long enough to deliver a harassing fire, then would retire to their bombproofs until another Federal advance was made.[11]

The Army of the James now began to take casualties. In Curtis's brigade, Lieutenant Frank Lay of the 117th New York lay near one of his privates when a grapeshot round struck the man in the head, killing him instantly. Earlier, the soldier had been talking about his wife and three-year-old daughter. Even the Third Brigade was now drawing fire: as Colonel Bell's troops waded waist-deep through an icy cold swamp 600 yards north of the fort, several officers and men fell from the fort's fire. Still, the troops moved forward into position without hesitation.[12]

While Terry issued orders and directed the troop movements, General Ames and his staff stood quietly by, looking almost bored, according to one of Terry's aides. "I remember that Ames and his staff during all the preliminary movements stood idly looking on," recalled Captain George F. Towle, "like persons who had no personal interest in what was going on." Ames's aides remembered it differently: "General Ames gave a most minute and careful supervision to every detail of these preliminary maneuvers," recalled Captain Henry C. Lockwood, "not hesitating to go himself to direct the troops into proper positions and to correct and establish the lines of attack, although at each time he and his staff showed themselves on this plateau of sand they became targets for the sharpshooters stationed on the parapet. . . ."[13]

Finally, the troops were ready. General Terry noted the time. It was 3:25. Then he issued the order everyone had been waiting for: signal the fleet to change the direction of its fire. Seconds later, a huge signal flag was waving back and forth above the command-post earthwork, easily visible to Admiral Porter on the *Malvern.* Then Terry suddenly seemed aware of Ames's presence. "General Ames," he said, "your division is all ready to make the assault."[14]

Ames immediately turned to Captain Lawrence, who was eager to lead the charge, and instructed him to join Curtis's brigade and give the colonel the order to go. A dark-headed young man with striking good looks, Lawrence was among the clique of young officers that made up General Ames's staff. It was a close knit, carefree group, fond of partying together and visiting the theater at leave-time. Aboard the transport en route to Fort Fisher, they had occupied themselves in day-long poker games and were sometimes joined by the general. Like the others, Lawrence was intensely loyal to Ames, and now the youthful captain undoubtedly planned to carry out the general's wishes. Lawrence delivered the order to Curtis, but said nothing about leading the assault. Instead, he simply asked if he could join the charge. Ames and Curtis had avoided personal contact because of their feud, and Curtis believed that Terry had given him independent command, excluding him from Ames' authority. He was apparently suspicious of Lawrence's request, but he agreed anyway—on one condition. Lawrence could accompany the First Brigade, Curtis said, but only "if he would not interfere with its movements." Lawrence made no protest and Curtis told him to join the brigade on the far right, near the river road, and report to Lieutenant Colonel Francis X. Meyer of the 117th New York. Obediently, Lawrence hurried across the plain and joined the line of troops near the river.[15]

Now it was time to go. Curtis sent the word up and down the line—charge at a run when the colonel waves his hat. The soldiers of the First Brigade waited, lying on their stomachs along a line stretching from the river to a point roughly opposite the fort's land-face sally port. Fifty yards ahead, the sharpshooters worked the loading levers on their Spencers, firing rapidly at the fort parapets. Interspersed among the riflemen of the First Brigade were "pioneer troops"—volunteers equipped with axes and battering rams—who would head up the assault. They were assigned the dangerous task of chopping holes in the palisades or knocking down the timbers to open the way for the troops behind them. Now they gripped their axes, waiting for the command to go. At the wave of the hat, every-one would rush forward—no cheering allowed—and angle for the riverside end of the fort. The route would funnel many of the troops over and around the bridge, down the river road and through the gate into the fort. Others would pass through openings in the pali-sade, but all were aiming for the fort's riverside battery—the princi-pal point of attack. Only a few long minutes had passed since the signal flag waved back and forth above Terry's command post. Sud-denly, the shrill whistles of the fleet sounded with a blast—the same sound that alarmed Colonel Lamb and excited the sailors charging down the beach. Then Colonel Curtis was on his feet and the hat was held high, waving for all to see.[16]

◆

Inside Fort Fisher, at the riverside end of the landface, Captain Kinchen Braddy also heard the steam whistles and knew what they meant. It was bad news: he did not like the way things were going. The twenty-six-year-old officer commanded Second Company C of the Thirty-sixth North Carolina and was charged with defending the westernmost battery on the fort's landface. The garrison knew it as "Shepherd's Battery," and it mounted two heavy artillery pieces, or at least it had before the bombardment. The battery was crucial to the defense of the fort: it overlooked Fort Fisher's riverside entrance, where the Wilmington road entered the fort through the palisades gate. If not stopped, an enemy assault entering the fort along the Wilmington road would pass between Shepherd's Battery and the river, flanking the landface and putting the enemy immediately in-side the fort. The battery's two guns had been knocked out by the bombardment; Braddy's only artillery support now consisted of two field pieces charged with defending the riverside gate. One, a Parrott field piece, had been placed on the very edge of the river where the palisades ended and was trained on the wooden bridge leading to the fort. The other, a twelve-pounder Napoleon, had been placed behind a wall of sandbags blocking the gate, and was aimed menacingly up the Wilmington road.[17]

Braddy had been in Wilmington on court-martial duty when the Federal fleet had reappeared, and he had returned to the fort on the same steamer that had brought General Whiting. The day before, Colonel Lamb had sent Braddy and half his company to defend Shepherd's Battery and the riverside gate. More than twenty-four hours had passed since he had received those orders, and in that time Braddy had not talked to a single senior officer. He had no idea how the other troops were deployed or what duties the garrison's other officers had been assigned. Lamb had placed Major James Reilly in command of the fort landface, but Braddy had not heard from the major and someone said he was waiting out the bombardment in a nearby bombproof. So were others. Lieutenant Charles Latham, whose gun crews manned the two field pieces defending the palisades gate, had asked Braddy for permission to take his men into the safety of the bombproofs. Latham and his troops were detached from another company, Adams's battery, which manned the other field pieces down the landface at the sally port, and they understandably preferred the safety of the bombproofs to the awful hail of enemy iron. Braddy had agreed—the bombardment was deadly and he would need every soldier—but Latham was told to be ready to man his guns at a moment's notice. The blue-clad troops had been moving forward in fits and starts in the distance, and several times some of Braddy's troops had braved the bombardment to fire on the enemy troops as they advanced.[18]

Now the Yankees were coming, and when Braddy looked across the open plain toward the enemy lines, he knew which way they were coming—right for him. Already, many of the 250 Confederates assigned to defend the western landface were rushing to the fort parapets. Braddy immediately ordered Lieutenant Latham to man his two field pieces. Those guns were crucial: they were his only artillery and they would have to do good work. Soon the Yankees would come tearing down the Wilmington road, crossing the bridge that spanned the edge of the marsh and heading for the fort gate. If everything worked as planned, the underground torpedoes would claim many of them, and planks had been pulled from the bridge flooring to slow them down, but a lot would depend on Latham's guns. A few well-placed blasts of grapeshot at a crowded bridge could be vital to the fort's defense. But where *was* Lieutenant Latham? Where were his gun crews? He had not followed orders—the guns were not being manned. Latham and his men were not coming out of the bombproofs.[19]

◆

"Forward!"

Curtis yelled the command from the middle of the Federal line, waving his hat back and forth to launch the assault. Then he was running toward the fort, a guidon in one hand, his saber in the other. The soldiers of the First Brigade rose as one and followed him. They had been commanded not to cheer, to save their breath for the charge, but they ignored that order and collectively emitted a loud Yankee hurrah as they headed toward the enemy fort. A volley of gunfire immediately erupted from the western half of the fort land-face, but most of the charging Federals were not yet erect and the volley passed over their heads. "The very air seems darkened with death-dealing missiles," recalled a participant. "I could feel the wind of the balls as they flew by."[20]

As planned, the troops went forward in a single, long, thin line and "obliqued" or angled toward the right, aiming for the riverside end of the landface, where the Wilmington road entered the fort. As they advanced at a run, the fire from the fort increased in volume and accuracy. The Army of the James was composed of veterans, and these troops—men of the 3rd, 112th, 117th and 142nd New York—had experienced heavier fire in other battles; but never, thought some, had they encountered such a deadly accurate fire. "It was not a blind fire whistling and humming overhead," reported a survivor. "The number of stricken men, increasing from moment to moment, showed how well the [Confederates] on the ramparts could aim. Caps and clothing were pierced, swords and scabbards were hit, belts and canteen straps were cut."[21]

Among the first struck down in the assault was Colonel John F. Smith, commanding officer of the 112th New York. Popular and respected in the regiment, he stood up when the order to charge was given and waved his men on, shouting encouragement and issuing orders cheerfully, as if the men were rushing forward into some sort of collegiate sporting event. Several paces toward the fort he fell, mortally wounded. He lay bloodied in the sand with shot and shell striking all around. Despite the hail of gunfire, some of his soldiers stopped, hastily dug a shallow entrenchment in the sand and lay their bleeding colonel in the little ditch until they could return for him.[22]

Lieutenant Frank Lay of the 117th New York raced forward with a private on one side and a major on the other. Both were shot down, but Lay kept going. Oddly, he realized later, he did not experience even a tinge of fear. "My whole soul was wrapped up in the idea of taking that fort," he later told his wife. Less fortunate was Private Paul Horvath, a young Hungarian immigrant who had reenlisted in time to make the Fort Fisher Expedition. Horvath had served with distinction as a sergeant and had been promoted to lieutenant upon reenlistment, but his paperwork had not caught up with him. Under the circumstances, he could have dodged combat, but instead he had gone into the battle as a private. He was near the head of the assault when he went down, killed instantly. In his pocket, awaiting confirmation, was his lieutenant's commission.[23]

In seconds, the first Federal troops reached the riverside marsh spanned by the bridge. They plunged waist-deep into the icy backwater, splashing and struggling across to higher ground. Others crowded onto the bridge, stepping hastily from beam to beam and rushing forward despite the structure's missing planks. The soldiers of the First Brigade had charged forward as a single long line, but now, as they converged on the western end of the fort landface, the line became a crowded mob, an easy target for the Confederates manning the parapets. "The garrison lined the ramparts," reported an observer, "and poured tremendous volleys into the advancing column . . . yet on they rushed until further advance was impossible unless the stockade could be removed or a passage forced through the gate." Even with the gaps blown in it by the naval fire, the fort palisade was a formidable structure, and when the men of the First Brigade reached that obstacle they hesitated, and for a moment the army assault appeared as if it might be checked.[24]

But leading the assault were the axmen—the pioneers—and the sharpshooters of the advance skirmish line, who had joined the charge as it came forward. Firing round after round from their Spencer repeaters, the sharpshooters delivered a fierce cover fire toward the fort parapet, and the pioneers attacked the big fence like lumberjacks. The thud of axes striking wood joined the cacophony of battle, as the pioneers widened gaps in the palisades and chopped open passageways for the assault force. Conspicuous with his ax was Private Zachariah Neahr of the 142nd New York. He reached the palisade ahead of almost everyone else and with surprising speed chopped open a passageway that perfectly accommodated a large group of the assault force.[25]

The first man through the fence, however, was not one of Curtis's New Yorkers nor an Indiana sharpshooter. It was Captain Lawrence, General Ames's aide-de-camp. When the charge began, Lawrence had sprinted for the front and had outdistanced the other troops. He was indeed the first man to the palisades—he had gotten there ahead of Curtis. He slipped through a jagged opening in the fence, then as the troops behind him reached the palisades and hesitated, he looked back and spotted a colorbearer on the other side of the fence. The captain reached through the palisades for the man's guidon and the soldier obediently handed it over. Lawrence intended to take the banner to the top, to scale the towering wall of the fort's westernmost battery and to be the first man on the enemy parapet. He was reaching back through the hole in the fence, his hand on the flagstaff, when a shell burst beside him. The blast took off his left arm and wounded him in the neck and right arm. Captain Lawrence's charge was over: it was a mortal wound. He would live long enough to dictate a letter to his father, and to demonstrate impressive pluckiness in the face of death. When one of his poker buddies stooped over him, Lawrence held up his gory stump and wisecracked, "Isn't this a devil of a bob-tailed flush?"[26]

The assault force lost formation at the palisades, but the soldiers did not stop. One after another and in small groups they slipped through the openings in the palisades and rushed to a "ditch"—a shallow depression where sand had been removed to build the fort landface. Located at the foot of the fort's high earthen wall, the depression provided some safety for the assault force. There, in a blind spot out of view of the fort's riflemen, the troops leading the assault found momentary relief from the Confederate fire. Quickly, the area between the palisade and the sloping walls of the fort's riverside battery filled with men in blue uniforms. For one long moment they paused as if to catch their breath, then men began cheering—*go on, go on, up the walls.* Curtis was inside the palisade, in the lead, and he pushed on. So did others, and amid a new chorus of hurrahs the front rank began swarming up the battered, grassy slope, led by Curtis and several standard-bearers. "It was an exciting moment," remembered a veteran. "Regimental pride—nothing shows a soldier's spirit more strongly—animated the broken mass of men in the rough clamor up the slope; and a rush of color-bearers led the way, in the ambition to be the first on the parapet."[27]

◆

It was Shepherd's Battery they were scaling, the fort's riverside battery, the intended target of the army assault, and it was defended by Lieutenant Braddy's thin detail of Confederates. Lieutenant Latham and his gun crews still had not come out of the bombproof—except for one man, a corporal whose name Braddy did not know. Fearlessly, the solitary gunner went to his post, manning one of the guns protecting the sandbagged gate. The palisade fence momentarily slowed the enemy charge, but the Yankees were coming fast. Where was the line of buried torpedoes—the acclaimed minefield, the secret weapon—which was supposed to shatter the enemy assault? Braddy could not know, nor did he have time to even think about it, but at a point down the landface, the fort electrician was trying unsuccessfully to detonate the underground explosives. Nothing happened—no explosions, no slaughter of troops, no shock and shattering of the enemy assault force. The naval bombardment had severed the underground ignition lines connecting the minefield to the electrician's detonation device. The mines were useless. Captain Braddy's men would have to meet the Federal onslaught alone.[28]

At a glance, Braddy could see that his skeletal force was overwhelmingly outnumbered. Lamb and Whiting were elsewhere, commanding the defense. He had no idea where Major Reilly was, nor had he heard from any other superior. Part of his force refused to come out of the bombproofs. The torpedoes had not been exploded and the Yankee army was racing right for him. Even the advantage of defense had been accidentally compromised: a few of Braddy's riflemen were firing from the palisades near the gate or from the battery's parapet, but most had taken positions behind the sandbagged wall of the first gun chamber—instead of atop the traverses straddling the gun chamber. There they would have had a wider, clearer field of fire, but from the gun chamber they would be unable to see the enemy soldiers when they reached the foot of the high, sloping earthen wall. The front line of Federal troops would be out of sight until they appeared over the crest of the wall. Then they would be over the top, face to face and hand to hand. The culminating moment of contact came when Curtis's New Yorkers scrambled over the rim of the battery. First to appear were the Federal guidons, moving upwards above the parapet, followed by a line of blue hats and kepis, then a row of faces—some bearded, others shaven—and then a line of torsos, uniformed in blue, crossed by black leather belts adorned with shining brass eagle emblems—a host of men with guns and fixed bayonets. And then Braddy's riflemen cut loose a volley into the faces.[29]

◆

"A fierce outburst of musketry greeted the first heads that rose above the level of the fort," remembered one of the Federal soldiers, "and at least one flag and its bearer rolled down the slope into the ditch. But the fort wall once gained, the assaulters were as much protected by it as the garrison, and so our men made some sort of foothold on the slope, and delivered over the parapet as fierce a fire as they received. They were thus burning powder close in each other's faces."[30]

The men of Curtis's brigade took their losses and kept coming. Beneath the regimental flag of the 117th New York, they continued up, scrambling over the dead and wounded, climbing the fort's grassy slopes. Among the first up the wall was twenty-nine-year-old Sergeant Edward K. Wightman of the Third New York. Tall, bewhiskered and athletic, the son of a former Connecticut state senator, Wightman had been a journalist—the holder of bachelor's and master's degrees—and easily could have avoided military duty. Instead he had volunteered, serving first as a Zouave in the Ninth New York Volunteers—the famed Hawkins Zouaves—and later in the

Third New York. He would have felt disgraceful, he had told his mother, "living peacefully and selfishly at home, while the land is rent by faction and threatened with ruin by violence." He had survived murderous fire at Fredericksburg and had seen action at Charleston, Richmond and Petersburg. A model soldier known for his dependability, temperance and quiet popularity among the troops, he had dodged promotion to lieutenant because of a disdain for officers, and blamed "Old Butler" for the failure of the Christmas expedition. Now he boldly led his regiment through the palisade and up the sloping walls of Shepherd's Battery, amid the gunfire, shouts and curses of battle. "Our family is very fortunate, indeed, to have preserved thus far its circle unbroken," he had written home in his last letter. ". . . I long to join you and resume my place in your midst." Rifle in hand, he charged up the traverse, leading the way for the men of the Third New York. Near the top he looked back, shouted for the others to follow and took a round through his right arm and into his chest. His legs buckled, and Sergeant Wightman—journalist-turned-soldier—collapsed and died among the many dead and wounded now littering the riverside battery.[31]

◆

Nearby, fighting on the other side, was Private Robert Harvey of the Bladen Artillery, officially known as Second Company I of the Thirty-sixth North Carolina. Harvey was nineteen years old and had volunteered for Confederate service even though he was the surviving male member of an old and distinguished family from nearby Bladen County. Known as "Bob" to his fellow soldiers, he had enlisted for twelve months, but had wound up serving more than four years—most of it at Fort Fisher. His company had returned to the fort less than two weeks before, after doing battle with Sherman's troops near Savannah. Now, he was fighting to defend his own state, his own post, and he climbed to the top of the battery's parapet to get a good shot at the Yankees. The act was typical of the teenaged soldier, cited by Colonel Lamb as "a recklessly brave boy." Accompanied by another soldier, he climbed to the top of the grassy parapet and opened fire on the Yankees. Moments later, both were shot down. Young Bob Harvey's family line would end on the walls of Fort Fisher. Like Wightman's, his wound was mortal.[32]

At the palisade gate, the lone corporal left to service Lieutenant Latham's two field pieces managed to fire at least one round before he was killed in action. Some of Curtis's troops tried to force their way through the sandbagged gate, firing at the Confederates on the other side of the palisades. Then, about thirty of Braddy's men reached the guns—dispatched by Braddy from his already thin force in the battery's gun chamber. They fired their weapons point-blank at the Federals trying to breach the palisades gate, and struggled to reload and fire the two artillery pieces. One after another, members of the detachment fell dead or wounded. When their numbers were perilously low, they were reinforced by troops from the First North Carolina Heavy Artillery, shifted from their post on the landface wall. Four of them fell manning the Napoleon at the gate, but not before they discharged a well-placed round of canister which momentarily cleared the Wilmington road of Federals. They also managed to fire an explosive round from the riverside Parrott. The shell hit the little bridge when it was crowded with Curtis's New Yorkers. It was a deadly shot, almost wrecking the bridge in an explosion of flame, smoke and splinters, and it left a terrible harvest of dead and wounded. For a long moment afterwards, the Northern officers had difficulty getting their troops to cross the bridge: the men were afraid that the underground torpedoes they had heard about were now exploding. The First North Carolina suffered casualties too—almost thirty dead and wounded in minutes—but somehow they held the gate. Atop the battery, however, Braddy's Confederates were taking a pounding.[33]

◆

In the scramble up the battery's steep wall, Colonel Curtis saw that the battery's riverside parapet was practically undefended. If his men could take that prominence, Curtis realized, they could direct a deadly fire down into the Confederates massed in the gun chamber below. He led the way to the top, and his troops soon killed or drove away the few defenders there. The guidon of the 117th New York went up atop the parapet, and Curtis's New Yorkers began to fire down into the gun chamber from an elevated position. "Burrowing for a foothold, [we] fired steadily over the bank, [and] the character of the battle changed from the wild, dashing assault to a steady, deliberate attack," recalled a Federal survivor. The struggle for Shepherd's Battery was confused, chaotic, closeup fighting, with both sides blasting away at each other from only a few feet apart.[34]

◆

For more than twenty minutes the outnumbered Confederates had held their own, fighting ferociously, making the Federals pay heavily for every foot of turf they occupied, but Braddy had no men to replace those who were falling. He could see that the odds were against him—gradually, his men were giving way. Not only were the

Yankees pouring a killing fire into his troops from the parapet above, they were also edging toward the first traverse, and once atop it, they would have the battery's defenders in a deadly crossfire. Braddy dispatched a messenger to Colonel Lamb with an urgent summons for reinforcements. When he heard nothing, he sent another man, but neither returned. Nor did any reinforcements appear. Where *was* Colonel Lamb? Or General Whiting? Or Major Reilly? Braddy knew nothing of the assault by the Federal sailors—the fort's officers, he decided, were simply out of place. His situation was now critical: his position was on the verge of being overrun—he *had* to have some help. Beside him another man went down, shot almost point-blank by a Federal officer. Finally, Braddy decided, he would go himself. Above the tumult of battle, he yelled to the men around him to try to hold their own, that he was going for help. Taking several soldiers with him, he left the battery and hurried toward the distant Northeast Bastion, where he hoped to find Colonel Lamb. He had gone only a few yards when he rounded a traverse and was met by a blast of rifle fire. It was a band of the South Carolinians, who had mistaken Braddy's little group for the Yankees. The volley felled men on both sides of Braddy, but he was unhurt. It was a deadly mistake—the reinforcements were killing their own men—but there was no time to deal with it now. He ran on toward the seaface, searching desperately for Colonel Lamb or someone who could come to the aid of his men.[35]

◆

From his command post north of the fort, General Terry could see the fighting on the landface. Curtis's troops were swarming over the first battery, but they appeared stalled at the gate, and the rear of the brigade had meshed into a blue-clad mass just outside the palisades. Shoulder to shoulder, men were still wading through the edge of the marsh, crowding the bridge and squeezing through the gaps in the fence. It was like a mob scene, but in a moment, they would all be inside the palisades: it was time for reinforcements.[36]

"Put in Pennypacker's brigade," Terry ordered Ames, who immediately gave the command. When Curtis's brigade had rushed cheering toward the fort, the troops of the Second Brigade—Pennypacker's brigade—had immediately moved forward and occupied the line of entrenchments Curtis's men had vacated. Now, they rose from the forward line and charged the fort, led by Colonel Galusha Pennypacker, age twenty. Darkly handsome, with a boyish face and an ever-ready grin, Pennypacker was Terry's youngest colonel, and was said to be the youngest brigade commander in the army. He was too young to vote, but he was a natural leader and a veteran combat officer, who carried the scars of thirteen wounds on his young body. His grandfather had fought in the Revolution, his father in the Mexican War, and his childhood home in Pennsylvania had been George Washington's winter headquarters. Orphaned as a child, he was raised by relatives—prominent Quaker abolitionists—who operated a station on the "Underground Railroad." In 1861, he volunteered for service at age sixteen. At seventeen he was major of the Ninety-seventh Pennsylvania and was promoted to colonel shortly after his twentieth birthday. He had seen men fight and die at Fort Wagner, Drewry's Bluff, Cold Harbor, Petersburg and elsewhere, and he was no stranger to leading men into the deadly turmoil of combat. Three of his battle wounds had been life threatening. He was treated as an equal by older officers, and was known for his integrity, fairness and cheerful disposition. He was also a favorite of General Terry's. As Pennypacker's brigade trotted past Terry's command post on the way to the front, Terry came out, draped his arm around Pennypacker's shoulders and, fatherlike, spoke words of encouragement to the young colonel.[37]

Now Pennypacker was up and calling his troops forward, and the Second Brigade charged the fort, advancing double-quick in a long, extended line like Curtis's brigade before them. There was less cheering now; the men were intent on plunging into the storm of smoke, flame, fighting and death that lay before them. The fury of battle came to them quickly: as they arose and charged forward, angling for the fort's riverside entrance, they were raked immediately by gunfire and canister. It was a "murderous fire," recalled a veteran years later. The gunfire came from the fort parapet, now manned by more defenders than when the First Brigade went forward, and the canister came from the field pieces in the fort sally port.[38]

◆

The sally-port artillery was manned by Adams's battery—Second Company G of the Thirty-sixth North Carolina—and commanded by Captain Zachariah T. Adams. When the bombardment ended, the field pieces had been run out of the safety of the sally port to the earthwork battery just outside the fort's landface wall. From their slightly elevated position, Adams's gun crews had a clear field of fire up and down the length of the landface. They had run out the guns in time to hurl some grape and canister toward the advancing naval brigade, but the sailors' assault route made them a distant target. The army's assault force was a much easier one, especially the Federal troops on the army's left flank near the sally port. Captain Adams had his guns charged and ready when the men of Pennypacker's brigade scrambled to their feet and charged forward across the open plain.[39]

◆

Closest to sally-port artillery position were the troops of the Forty-seventh New York, who held the left flank of the Federal line. The assault route carried them directly past Adams's battery, and when they rose to their feet and started forward, Zachariah Adams's gun crews opened fire. Leading the Forty-seventh into battle was the regimental color guard—a detail of troops allowed the honor of carrying the regiment's flags into combat—and the blast of canister from Adams's artillery flattened the entire detail. The Forty-seventh's commander, Colonel Joseph McDonald, coolly kept the regiment moving and the men would not leave their flags down, but none of the color guard got up. All were dead.[40]

General Ames had watched the First Brigade make the charge from the command post, but as Pennypacker's brigade went in, he intended to go also. Turning to his staff, he said formally, "Gentlemen, we will now go forward." Besides Captain Lawrence, now lying mortally wounded at the palisades, there were five other young captains on Ames's staff. Among them was Captain Richard W. Dawson. At twenty-three, Dawson could have been a lawyer. He had graduated from college with that intention, but had joined the army instead. He was a Pennsylvanian, one of ten children, and he had already seen a lot of war—at Yorktown, Williamsburg, Fair Oaks, Battery Wagner, Petersburg, Deep Bottom and the first Fort Fisher Expedition. He had made a good soldier, but had retained his interest in law, spending part of his time aboard ship off Fort Fisher reading a book entitled *Mysteries of the Crimes of London.* Dawson, Lawrence and Captain Birney Keeler had enjoyed some good times together and now, together, they were going into battle.[41]

As they left the relative safety of General Terry's earthwork command post, Dawson and Keeler could not yet have known that their friend Lawrence was shot down and dying. But they undoubtedly recognized the deadly accuracy of the rifle fire coming from the fort. Such a large group of staff officers made an inviting target, and enemy bullets began buzzing past. Ames realized the danger immediately. "We had better separate somewhat from each other," he warned his staff, but the words were barely said when Dawson and Keeler went down, both struck by enemy rounds. Keeler would eventually recover, but Dawson would never practice law nor read another book—his was a death wound.[42]

Ames joined the charge; others would have to tend to his fallen staff officers. All along the line the Rebel fire took a deadly toll. Besides the 47th New York, Pennypacker's brigade was composed of the 48th New York and the 76th, 97th and 203rd Pennsylvania Infantry—and within the next few violent minutes, each regiment would be severely bloodied. It began with the officers: Lieutenant Colonel William B. Coan, commanding the 48th New York, was shot down while forming his troops. Colonel John S. Littell, commanding the 76th Pennsylvania, also went down before reaching the fort, falling wounded at the head of his regiment. Lieutenant John Wainwright, leading the 300-man force of the 97th Pennsylvania, was hit in the shoulder during the charge, but kept going. Despite the casualties, Pennypacker's brigade rushed onward and quickly overtook the rear of Curtis's brigade, struggling to cross the swampy marsh near the river. "In the crash and uproar of the battle, and the enthusiasm of the advance, the men shouldered their way forward with little regard to the regimental formation," recalled a Federal veteran. "The result was a crowd of men pouring through the log obstacles into the ditch, cheering and impetuous, but with no longer any visible military formation." Momentarily, the troops of Pennypacker's brigade bunched against the rear of Curtis's brigade, then they broke to the right, flowed around Curtis's men, pushed across the bridge and waded the marsh heading for the fort's riverside gate.[43]

◆

At the gate, many of the Confederate artillerymen had fallen around their guns, and the handful of survivors could do nothing to stop this new wave of blue uniforms, pushing and crowding across the bridge and through the edge of the marsh toward the fort gate. The cannoneers managed to fire their field pieces again, and more Yankees fell on the bridge and on the sandy road, but there were others, many others, to take their places and they kept coming. The men of Pennypacker's brigade came hurtling into the chaos like a powerful blue flood, knocking down the sandbags and surging through the gate, spilling through the shattered palisades, flowing around the riverside end of the tall fence and flanking the thin Confederate force manning the riverside artillery. The Confederates had fought hard to hold off the Federal assault, but now numbers overcame them and the men at the gate were shot down, falling on top of and beside the bodies of those who had manned the guns before them.[44]

Pennypacker's troops also charged up the sloping wall of Shepherd's Battery, surging around the gun chamber and carrying the men of Curtis's brigade with them. The guidons and regimental flags of the 203rd and 97th Pennsylvania now joined the banner of the 117th New York held aloft above the blue mob thronging the traverses. Near the top of the parapet, the colorbearer of the 97th, Corporal William McCarty, fell shot through a knee, and Colonel Pennypacker took the flag. Steps away, Colonel John W. Moore, the twenty-five-year-old commander of the 203rd Pennsylvania, climbed the landface wall with his regiment's flag in hand. He was a veteran of three years of combat with the Army of the Potomac and he carried his battle standard fearlessly. Seeing Moore nearby, Pennypacker yelled to him above the clamor of battle. "Moore," he shouted, holding up McCarty's banner, "I want you to take notice that this is the flag of my old regiment." Moore may have been forming a reply, perhaps planning to race Pennypacker to the top, but instead he toppled over, a bullet through his heart.[45]

Soon both Federal brigades were atop the riverside battery, intermingling now, and they unleashed a wilting crossfire into the Confederate defenders the gun chamber below. Moments later, they spilled into the gun chamber, led by Colonel Curtis, who carried a guidon in one hand and a saber in the other. It was hand to hand now, soldiers firing point-blank into each other's faces. Some of Braddy's Confederates were trying to fire one of the battery's disabled heavy artillery pieces, which was pointing into the mass of Federals swarming over the parapet. The cannoneers were overpowered just as they rammed home the charge, leaving the rammer poking out of the big gun's muzzle, but the gunner managed to stick a friction primer into the cannon's breech vent and was trying desperately to fire the gun. Curtis yelled at the man to surrender, and when he did not, the colonel struck him down with a saber blow.[46]

The battery's defenders were being overwhelmed. Corporal Henry Clay McQueen of the First North Carolina saw twelve men of his company killed in the desperate fighting. "A comrade next to me on the traverse was shot in his brains and killed," McQueen recalled. "His brains splattered in my face." Another round shot off McQueen's hat, then he fell, wounded in the leg. Others were falling, and the survivors were slowly being driven out of the gun chamber and off the traverses. Then, having overrun the gate defenders, Pennypacker's troops swarmed around the battery from the rear. Shepherd's Battery was surrounded. The Confederates were cut off, and while some managed to escape up the landface or through the bombproof passageways, most now dropped their weapons and surrendered, watching helplessly as their battery was quickly cloaked with Yankees.[47]

Cheering wildly, the Federals pushed on, quickly seizing the second gun chamber. Then they clambered to the top of the adjacent traverse, and pushed on to another gun emplacement. Pennypacker led the way, still holding aloft the flag of the Ninety-seventh Pennsylvania. He was the first man to scale the third traverse—and there the battle ended for the twenty-year-old colonel. He had just reached the top and was planting his regimental flag on the traverse when he was shot down. It was a severe wound. The bullet entered his right hip near the joint and came out his lower back, barely missing his spine and doing serious damage to bones and nerves. His soldiers got him on a blanket and hustled him to the rear, convinced he would not recover this time. Headed in the same direction by then, over the battered bridge and up the Wilmington road, were more than a hundred Confederate prisoners—the former defenders of Shepherd's Battery—who had been captured at a pivotal moment by Pennypacker's brigade. Somehow Pennypacker remained conscious. He was a bloody mess, and as this was his fourteenth wound, he had become somewhat of an expert on these things: this time he was sure the wound was mortal. But he had seen enemy troops surrendering and he was consoled by the belief that the fort was won. As he was being carried to the rear, he was met by one of Terry's staff officers, who expressed "deep sympathy" for Pennypacker's condition. "I know I cannot live with such a wound," Pennypacker told the officer, "but I want you to tell the general that when I fell the two leading flags on those ramparts were those of the 97th and 203rd Pennsylvania, two of my regiments." Moments later, General Terry appeared beside Pennypacker's litter, a look of sorrow on his face. Pennypacker looked up at Terry and managed to speak: "We have the fort, General." "I know it," Terry immediately replied, then Pennypacker was hurried away to the Federal field hospital. Terry sounded confident when he spoke of victory to Pennypacker and he was not just trying to console a young man who appeared near death. The army did have a foothold and a good one, but Terry also knew the battle for Fort Fisher was far from over.[48]

◆

Up the peninsula at Sugar Loaf, General Robert F. Hoke ordered two brigades of his division forward to attack the Federal rear. Hoke had received Whiting's plea for help and had forwarded it to Bragg. At four o'clock, despite his fear of the Federal fleet, Bragg had finally issued the command Whiting and Lamb had so urgently requested: Hoke was ordered to assault the enemy's rear line. He was ready, and his troops promptly advanced in battle formation, their line stretching across the peninsula. Brigadier General Colquitt and his brigade of Georgians were being held in reserve, and Hagood's brigade of South Carolinians was already downriver, so Hoke's assault force was composed entirely of North Carolinians—the soldiers of Kirkland's and Clingman's brigades. These were experienced combat troops, men who had fought the Army of the James before, and they were ready to fight.[49]

Captain Charles Elliott of Kirkland's brigade felt confident as he moved his troops through the thick underbrush toward the Yankee line. Elliott was a competent, zealous officer—not absent a single day in his wartime service—and he was looking forward to pitching into the enemy. He thought the order to attack was way overdue, that more should have been done to aid his fellow North Carolinians in the fort. Now at last they were going forward, and he expected the assault to smash the Yankee rear and plunge the Federals into confusion. In the woods south of Hoke's advance was Abbott's brigade of white troops on the ocean side of the Federal line, and Paine's Division of U.S. Colored Troops on the river side. Like many of his counterparts in the Northern army, Captain Elliott did not have much regard for the fighting ability of black soldiers. He expected his troops to easily overrun the troops defending the Federal rear.[50]

When they encountered the enemy picket lines in the woods, Hoke's Confederates opened fire. The pickets on the ocean side of the Federal line—Abbott's white troops—immediately folded up, and Hoke's soldiers occupied their vacated rifle pits. On the river side, however, Paine's black soldiers held firm, and a brisk exchange of small arms fire erupted. Then the Federal warships opened fire, sending shells hurtling into the thickets of pine and scrub oak occupied by Hoke's men. It was a formidable display of power, but once Hoke's troops moved in close to do battle with the Federals, the fleet would have to restrict its fire to avoid hitting its own troops. Captain Elliott and the men around him were now entrenched in rifle pits occupied by the enemy only minutes before, and at any second they expected to receive the order to charge.[51]

Instead, they were recalled: General Bragg had canceled the attack. Elliott and other officers were surprised by the order—they were certain they could defeat the Yankees. Reluctantly, however, they obeyed, and the two brigades withdrew through the woods back to their former positions. General Hoke had led the advance in person, and when he emerged from the woods with two bullet holes in his uniform, his narrow escape seemed to confirm Bragg's worst fears. The Federal fleet would destroy his force, Bragg believed, and his troops were too outnumbered to overcome the enemy anyway. It was useless to attack the Federals, he concluded. Besides, had he not already reinforced Fort Fisher with Hagood's South Carolinians? Why risk slaughtering Hoke's troops when they might be needed to defend Wilmington? He was confident, he claimed, that Fort Fisher would be "perfectly safe."[52]

◆

The citizens of Wilmington did not share Bragg's optimism. For three days, they had heard the distant thunder of the naval bombardment, and many feared Fort Fisher would fall this time. On Sunday morning, a large congregation assembled for the worship service at St. James Episcopal Church, but the worshipers found it difficult to concentrate amid the sounds of battle. Another distraction was the large number of female worshipers already dressed in mourning for friends and relatives killed in earlier engagements. The gloomy apparel, the worried expressions of the worshipers and the constant rumble of the bombardment created a mood of anxiety and dismay among the congregation.

"The thunder of the guns, distinctly audible and shaking the atmosphere like jelly, had been irregular until the Litany was read," recalled a worshiper. "Then from the beginning of that solemn service to its conclusion, almost simultaneously the responses of the congregation and the roar of the broadsides united. 'From battle and murder, and from sudden death,' read the minister. 'Good Lord, deliver us,' prayed the congregation, and, simultaneously 'Boom— boom—boom' answered the guns. The situation was almost intolerable."[53]

◆

Downriver from Wilmington, a handful of citizens had a front-row seat for the battle. Local residents and refugees lined the western bank of the Cape Fear River and watched the battle from a safe distance. Among them was Mrs. T. C. Davis. Her husband, Sergeant Thaddeus C. Davis of the Fortieth North Carolina, was one of Fort Fisher's defenders, and she watched the battle nervously. "At times my imagination would tell me that my anxious eyes were resting upon him in the little group of heroic defenders that we could see distinctly," she recalled. "The next instant a monster shell would explode in their midst, enveloping everything in smoke and dust. At such moments I would feel as if my heart would burst. . . . When the smoke would lift, we could see distinctly the lines engaged often in hand-to-hand fighting; but O! we could see so distinctly that the thin, gray line was growing thinner, and that the dark, heavy masses were growing heavier."[54]

Daisy Lamb was back at the spot she had occupied during the first battle, again studying the fort through binoculars. After crossing the Cape Fear River in the early morning darkness, she and the children had been welcomed as emergency guests at the home of Mrs. Enoch Robbins, a prominent local widow. Throughout the battle, Daisy had kept her vigil on the riverbank, anxiously watching the deadly inferno that had engulfed her "Will" and his fort. For the rest of his life, twelve-year-old John Robbins would remember how "this very beautiful lady" stood transfixed at river's edge, straining through her binoculars for a glimpse of her husband. At that moment, in the smoke-shrouded fort across the river, Daisy Lamb's husband and men of both armies were fighting for their lives.[55]

11

"Our Men Began to Waver"

ENERAL WHITING SHOUTED AN ORDER TO THE SOLDIERS
crowded around him on the wall of Northeast Bastion: *Pull
down those flags and drive the enemy from the works!* Whiting and
Lamb had discovered the Federal flags atop the riverside batteries
at the same moment, and now Whiting instinctively ordered a
counterattack. The shattered naval brigade was still retreating up
the beach when he led the defenders off the wall of the Northeast
Bastion and toward the distant traverses, now swarming with Federal troops. Admiral Porter's disastrous naval assault was an uninten-
tional decoy: it had drawn Whiting's and Lamb's attention—and
most of the fort's defenders—away from the target of the main Federal assault. Now, they realized, the enemy had to be forced from the
fort or all would be lost.[1]

In the battery just west of the Northeast Bastion, where the fort's
surviving landface gun was mounted, Major William Saunders could
also see the Federal flags on the distant traverses and the enemy
troops pouring across the plain toward the fort gate. As Fort Fisher's
chief of artillery, Saunders had little left to work with on the landface,
but he immediately ordered the battery's gun crew to swivel the

heavy Columbiad around and open fire on the enemy. While the gun crew went to work, Saunders led the rest of his troops out of the gun chamber, off the wall and down to join the counterattack. Captain Izlar of the Twenty-fifth South Carolina was also there with a detachment of the South Carolinians, bringing Whiting's force to about 500 troops.[2]

With Whiting in the lead, they raced down the landface, swarmed over the parapet and slammed into the Federals at the fourth gun chamber. There was little room for either side to maneuver. Men fired their rifles point-blank into the faces of their opponents, then plunged into a brutal, hand-to-hand fight—swinging rifles like clubs, grappling with each other, struggling, falling, wrestling in death grips with one another, killing up close any way they could. "It was a soldier's fight now," recalled a Confederate survivor. "As a man would fall, another sprang up to take his place, our officers loading and firing with us . . . a hand-to-hand fight." The Confederates were outnumbered, but in the frenzied, closeup fighting, numbers did not immediately matter, and slowly, with awful slaughter, Whiting and his desperate troops drove the Federals out of the fourth gun chamber.[3]

The fighting spilled over onto the parapet and up the third traverse, where Pennypacker had fallen moments before. Bodies were everywhere. The living trampled on the dead and wounded, stumbling over the bodies, jabbing, swinging, firing, as more casualties fell beneath the struggling mass of men. "You would constantly see them, by two's and three's, fall off [the traverse] and roll to the bottom," remembered a Northern officer, "there weltering in their blood and gore. . . ." The Federal color guards were forced back with the other Northern troops and the regimental flags went back down the third traverse.[4]

At the head of this wild-fighting force of Confederates, some Federal soldiers saw a Confederate general. It was Whiting, wading into the violent chaos at the head of his troops. Atop the traverse he grabbed for one of the Federal flags—and was instantly confronted by a score of Northern soldiers determined to protect their banner. "Surrender!" they yelled at him. "Go to hell, you Yankee bastards!" he shouted back. They fired and Whiting fell, hit twice and severely wounded in the right thigh. Some of his men saw him go down. They reached him before he was hit again and dragged him down off the parapet and out of the fight.[5]

One who rushed to Whiting's side was Captain Braddy, whose frantic search for reinforcements had brought him to the area of the third traverse just as Whiting went down. He ran to the general, who admitted he was seriously wounded. Even so, Braddy spilled out his story. "Everything [is] confusion," he blurted out above the racket of battle, and reported his near escape from the fire of Hagood's troops. "The South Carolinians [are] killing more of our men than the Yankees," he reported. "Captain," Whiting urged him, "for God's sake, try and stop it." Then he was borne away to the Pulpit Battery's field hospital, so Surgeon Spiers Singleton could tend to his wound. Braddy tried to recruit some reinforcements to return with him to Shepherd's Battery, but no one paid him any attention—just yards away up on the third traverse was battle enough for anyone. Braddy gave up and ran back toward the men he had left at the riverside battery, only to learn his post had been overrun by the Yankees.[6]

Colonel Lamb, meanwhile, was outside the fort, conducting a one-man reconnaisance. While Whiting mounted the counterattack, Lamb had hurried through the tunnel leading to the landface sally port. From there, outside the walls of the fort, he hoped he could determine the enemy positions. He scaled the sally-port earthwork and ran to the palisades, ducking behind one of the shattered timbers. He could clearly see the desperate fighting when Whiting's counterattack reached the third traverse—and he could also see Federal troops pouring into the western side of the fort. While he studied the enemy deployments, trying to formulate the best defense, Lamb was spotted by two U.S. Marines who had remained at the front when the naval brigade had retreated. They had played dead, lying unmoving in the sand near the Northeast Bastion, until they saw Lamb come out and expose himself within easy range. A high-ranking Confederate officer was too good a target to resist, and one of the marines sat up to take a shot at Lamb. Before he could fire, however, he was shot dead by an alert sharpshooter on the fort parapet. Unaware of his close call, Lamb made sure Captain Adams's gun crews were firing on the Yankees, then hurried back into the fort.[7]

There, Lamb could see disaster unfolding. Whiting's counterattack had pushed the Federals out of the fourth gun chamber, but had stalled in a bitter hand-to-hand struggle for the third traverse. General Whiting had been wounded and evacuated to the Pulpit hospital, Lamb learned, and he could see enemy troops surging around Shepherd's Battery and taking position in the rear of the landface. He rounded up every available soldier, sent them to a line of light earthworks behind the landface and ordered them to pour fire into the Federal troops massing behind Shepherd's Battery. Moments later, Lamb's hastily assembled force of riflemen unleashed a fierce fire at the blue-clad soldiers from relatively close range, stemming the flood of enemy troops flanking the landface.[8]

While Lamb was getting the troops in place, his aide, Captain Charles Blocker, ducked in behind the earthworks with a disastrous report: many of the South Carolina troops refused to leave the safety of the bombproofs, he told Lamb. Despite threats and pleas from their officers, they refused to come out and fight. Moreover, the underground torpedoes had failed to explode, apparently because the ignition wires had been severed by the Federal bombardment. The Yankees had sent two columns of troops against the fort, Blocker explained, and they had gotten into the fort at Shepherd's Battery while most of the garrison was occupied with the defense of the Northeast Bastion. Adding to the dilemma, Battery Buchanan's gun crews were now firing on the landface, presumably in an attempt to repulse the enemy, and the battery's fire was killing Confederate and Federal alike.[9]

Battery Buchanan's gun crews were firing with a serious handicap—their officers were drunk. When Federal flags were sighted atop the western landface, Captain Robert T. Chapman, the battery's commander, had mustered his troops, announced that the fort was lost and ordered them to their boats for an evacuation. To board, the surprised seamen had to wade waist-deep in the chilly waters of the Cape Fear River—then, after they were soaked, their intoxicated officers had recalled them with orders to man their guns. Now, wet to the waist, the naval gunners were lobbing shells toward the fort, and their fire was dangerously wild.[10]

Lamb was dismayed by Blocker's report, but he still believed Fort Fisher could be saved. It would be dark in a little over an hour. If the Yankees could be held off until then, he told Blocker, they could be driven from the fort. He dispatched the captain with a telegram for Bragg, urging him to attack. If Bragg would just attack and distract the Yankees, Lamb believed, the enemy could be repelled from the fort. Off Blocker ran, to send the message on its time-consuming, circuitous route: down to Battery Buchanan, across the river by signal, up to Wilmington by telegraph, then down to Sugar Loaf for a reaction. It would take some time for Lamb's desperate plea to reach Bragg, and then what? Lamb knew his time was running out—but he was determined to save his fort.[11]

Lieutenant Braddy appeared with a report—finally, he had found Colonel Lamb. The enemy had overrun his position, he announced, and his men had been captured. "What should we do?" he implored. "Get me some men," Lamb ordered. "I want to drive those Yankees out of the fort." Braddy disappeared, hurrying to round up squads of men to add to the force Lamb had assembled in the rear earthworks behind the landface.[12]

Lamb rallied the troops around him, and they responded by pouring an effective fire into the Federal troops massed at the foot of Shepherd's Battery and those moving to support the hand-to-hand struggle for the third traverse. There the Confederates were holding their own in the bloody brawl, even without Whiting, and the Federal battle standards had disappeared from the fort wall. The flags were also down among the mass of Federal troops spread out around the base of Shepherd's Battery. The tide of battle seemed to be turning. Lamb grew hopeful: if his men could drive the Yankees off the wall by nightfall, and if after dark Bragg attacked, then maybe. . . .[13]

Suddenly, accompanied by an unnerving screech, a storm of artillery shells came hurtling out of the sky, falling into the fort and exploding among Lamb's hard-pressed troops. These weren't stray rounds from Battery Buchanan—they fell in profusion, knocking up great geysers of sand, bursting in smoke and flame and deadly chunks of iron. Instantly, Lamb knew what was happening: the Federal fleet had renewed the landface bombardment. The lethal hail of artillery shells fell with incredible precision, walking along the landface wall, clearing it of Confederate defenders, edging up to within yards of the Federal infantry fighting on the third traverse. The Confederates on the wall fled to the bombproofs, leaving behind only the men struggling hand to hand with the Federals on the third traverse—men so close to the enemy they were spared the barrage. The shells rolled down the landface wall and exploded among the Confederates even as they scrambled down off the wall and out of the gun chambers. For the first time too, the landface sally port took a pounding, forcing Captain Adams to withdraw his two field pieces into the sally-port tunnel. But even there, Adams's men were not safe: artillery shells rolled off the nearby wall and exploded just inside the tunnel, giving the gun crews no place to hide. In moments, most of Adams's men were dead or wounded, and the landface was almost empty of defenders, leaving the Confederates on the contested third traverse to battle alone. To their rear, at the earthworks behind the landface, Lamb and his force hunkered down beneath the awful bombardment and looked toward the riverside gate: something was happening among the Federals massed behind Shepherd's Battery.[14]

◆

Colonel Louis Bell waited impatiently for the order to lead his brigade against Fort Fisher. He had moved the Third Brigade—Bell's brigade—to the earthworks vacated earlier by Curtis's and Pennypacker's brigades. Now, as Curtis's and Pennypacker's troops swarmed over the western end of the fort landface and battled with the Rebels, Bell was ready to go into action. In his hand he held a discarded ramrod and in his uniform pocket he carried a small white seashell.[15]

He had picked up the ramrod on the advance to the front, using it as a walking stick as he moved his six-foot-two-inch frame over the sandy plain in long, athletic strides. He *was* a natural athlete—gifted at fencing, swimming, horseback riding and a variety of other sports—and at age twenty-seven, he was in superb physical condition. He was a large-built man, muscular, with a drooping mustache and a shock of curly brown hair protruding from beneath his officer's hat. He gloried in the soldier's life, although by profession he was a lawyer, not a soldier. After graduation from Brown University, he had become a practicing attorney at age twenty, then justice of the police court, and later county solicitor. It was natural for people to think of him following in the footsteps of his father, former New Hampshire governor Samuel Bell, two-term senator and intimate friend of Daniel Webster. But there had been no time for a political career; the war had come.[16]

In 1861, Bell was made captain of the First New Hampshire Volunteers, then lieutenant colonel of the Fourth New Hampshire and finally he was promoted to colonel and brigade commander. He was among the first to defend the nation's capital in the summer of 1861; then had come duty in South Carolina, Florida and Virginia—and combat at Port Royal, near Charleston, at Drewry's Bluff, Cold Harbor and Petersburg. He had learned from study as well as duty, hauling a library of military works around with him, immersing himself in cavalry tactics, engineering details and infantry maneuvers. He was naturally inquisitive, always observing, testing and experimenting.[17]

Even here at Fort Fisher, his personal studies enabled him to look around and classify the local foliage. The seashell he now carried in his pocket he had plucked from the beach soon after coming ashore, thinking it would be a novelty for his four-year-old daughter, Marian. She and six-week-old Louis Junior, whom he had never seen, were his primary preoccupation next to his wife, Mollie. A preacher's daughter, she was a cheerful, pretty young woman of curled brown hair and blue eyes. She and their daughter had joined him at Beaufort, that sea island corner of South Carolina secured by Northern forces early in the war. Those had been heady days, odd for war, days of picnics, strolls along the beach, soldier serenades—a reunion of married life for a brief and happy time. And then it was over, ended by a transfer to more perilous duties. Now Bell knew he was facing mortal danger again. He had already suffered two slight wounds and some bullet-riddled garments, so he understood the deadly potential that lay before him now as he waited to take his troops into action against Fort Fisher. "If I die, do not forget, my own precious wife, that I die in defense of our country," he had written his wife. "Teach our children, darling Mollie, that liberty and freedom are first freedom for all, and that for it we are bound to lay down our lives."[18]

In the Federal command post, General Terry received a dispatch from General Ames, now inside the fort. The Federal advance was stalled, the troops inside needed help. Send in the Third Brigade and he could take the fort, Ames reported. Even with the help of the fleet, whose fire the army was directing through signals, Terry realized he was in danger of losing his foothold—it was time to put in Bell's brigade. Turning to Captain George F. Towle, Terry ordered the Third Brigade forward. Towle immediately left the command post and hurried across the plain to give Bell the order. Bell was out in front of his brigade, standing on a rise of ground, trying to observe the action in the fort. He had left Colonel Alonzo Alden of the 169th New York in command, with instructions to bring up the brigade when signaled. Towle reached Bell and gave him Terry's order, and Bell signaled Alden to advance. The troops of the Third Brigade then moved forward double-quick, angling to the right toward the bridge and the gate in the same route of assault as the two brigades before them. Bell ran forward, hurrying to reach the head of his brigade before the troops reached the bridge, so he could lead them into the fort.[19]

A brisk fire erupted from Confederates on the landface who saw Bell's brigade making its charge. In a moment, Bell's men would be across the bridge and rushing through the gate that Pennypacker's troops had already breached. Some of Pennypacker's men had replaced the missing planking on the bridge, so charging across it now would be easier. Bell caught up with his men, taking his position at the head of the brigade. "How well the brigade is coming on under so severe a fire," he told one of his officers, as they raced toward the fort. Then they were at the bridge, the mob of blue-uniformed soldiers funneling themselves into a narrow column to cross the little span. Bell led the assault, conspicuous by his height and his position at the head of the column.[20]

He was shot just as he reached the bridge. The bullet came from atop the fort wall, angling downward, entering the left chest, transfixing the torso and exiting from the lower back. The blow knocked Bell flat. "My arm is broken," he managed to say to his aide, Lieutenant Hugh Sanford, but the lieutenant had heard the hideous thud of the bullet when it hit and he knew it was a body wound. He quickly examined Bell and found the bullet holes in his uniform, already bloody. Some of Bell's men saw their colonel was down and stopped, but the torrent of feet rushed by, thumping over the bridge—Colonel Alden was taking the brigade forward into the fort as he should. "Lift me up a little, if you please," Bell said, and hands grabbed him gently, carrying him back the way he had come, away from the fort and out of range. In the rear, Dr. David Dearborn, the Fourth New Hampshire's regimental surgeon, hurried to Bell's prostrate form, now blood-soaked, and quickly began cutting away the uniform to reach the wound. One look and he knew. "Is the wound mortal?" Bell asked calmly, as if inquiring about a plant species or a legal brief. "I am fearful it is, Colonel," Dearborn replied. "Well," Bell commented in the same calm voice, "I thought as much myself." By now Bell's men were inside the fort, heading up and across the fort parapet, and their battle flags were visible atop the fort wall. Someone told Bell and he managed to raise himself a little, saying, "I want to see *my* colors on the parapet." He saw a flag, looked at the distant banner for an instant, then dropped back to the ground. As the litter bearers prepared to carry him farther to the rear, pale and dying, he spoke again. "I am satisfied," he said, and was borne away.[21]

Bell's brigade was composed of four regiments—the 169th New York, the 115th New York, the 4th New Hampshire and the remnants of the 13th Indiana. Leading the assault was the 169th New York, which had been posted on the right, closest to the riverside entrance to the fort. When Bell went down and Colonel Alden assumed command of the brigade, he passed command of the 169th New York to Lieutenant Colonel James A. Colvin and, accompanied by Alden, Colvin led the regiment into the fort at the head of the brigade. The New Yorkers charged through the gate, past the two Confederate field pieces, now unmanned and silent, and into the mass of troops from Curtis's and Pennypacker's brigades, who were deployed at the foot of Shepherd's Battery, trading fire with Colonel Lamb's nearby Rebels.[22]

Other troops from Bell's brigade quickly scaled the fort's western slopes, now cleared of resistance, and joined the fight at the third traverse. Sergeant Peter Kreck, the colorbearer from the 115th New York, planted his regiment's flag on the first traverse. So did the colorbearer from the 13th Indiana, after which the two raced each other along the fort wall toward the third traverse, planting their flags on one traverse after another. Then Kreck was wounded and had to give up the competition. Lieutenant Erastus Mosher conducted his own odd race: he had been hit in the leg by a spent bullet two days earlier, but had insisted on joining the assault, and now hopped about in the chaos using a cane.[23]

◆

From his position behind the fort's rear earthworks, Colonel Lamb realized the new activity among the enemy troops near Shepherd's Battery meant the Federals had been reinforced. It appeared that an entire new column of Yankees had entered the fort. For the moment his troops seemed to be holding them at bay—they appeared surprised by the brisk fire from Lamb's position and were deploying cautiously—but it was clear that his little force was greatly outnumbered. Shells from Battery Buchanan were now falling among the Federals, adding to their hesitancy, but Lamb knew his men could be overwhelmed at any moment, especially if the naval bombardment shifted off the landface wall and came their way. He had to have reinforcements and artillery support from somewhere. Ordering his men to hold their ground at all costs, he left the earthwork, and ran across the fort's interior to the seaface. There, he ran down the rear of the seaface, ordering all artillery turned to fire at the Yankees and collecting every available soldier he could find. Only four heavy artillery pieces—two Columbiads and the two guns in the Mound Battery—could be turned around far enough for use against the Federals, but those immediately opened fire, carefully placing their rounds over Lamb's troops. Lamb managed to round up more than a hundred soldiers from the seaface and hurriedly brought them back to the earthworks behind the landface, increasing his firepower.[24]

He could see the struggle for the third traverse still under way, still a bloody, closeup fight. The troops Lamb had assembled behind the breastworks now delivered a deadly fire at any Northern troops appearing on the landface parapet, forcing the Federals to stay on the front of the landface. The fire restricted their movements and prevented them from flanking the rest of the landface like they had done at Shepherd's Battery. The Confederates were holding their ground in the struggle for the third traverse, even though the bombardment had cleared the rest of the landface of defenders. Stalled at the third traverse, the Federal forces now appeared indecisive, perhaps even demoralized by the garrison's stubborn resistance. Many of them lay in a shoulder-to-shoulder mass in a depression behind Shepherd's Battery. Now was the time to counterattack, Lamb believed. Maybe, just maybe, he could hit the Yankees hard enough and hurt them badly enough to drive them out of the fort the way the enemy assault force had been repelled from the Northeast Bastion.[25]

He left his troops again, and ran back up the landface to a bomb-proof occupied by some of the South Carolinians. He implored them to come out and help save the fort, to join him in a counterattack against the Yankees. They promised they would join the battle, but when Lamb left, they were still in the bombproof. Lamb ran on, up to the landface tunnel, where he ordered Captain Adams to run out his field artillery and fire on the enemy from the sally port. The battery had taken so many casualties from the naval fire that Adams was not sure he could properly man his guns. Then find some volunteers, Lamb ordered him, and hurried on from bombproof to bombproof, begging the ill and wounded to join the battle and repel the Yankees. Join him for one more counterattack, he urged everyone he encountered—one last, major attempt to dislodge the Yankees and save the fort. He grabbed a courier and sent him running to Battery Buchanan with a request for any reinforcements the navy could spare and a notice to Captain Chapman to hold his fire when he saw Lamb and his troops make their charge.[26]

Then he hurried back to the rear earthworks to prepare his troops for the counterattack. He desperately hoped it would be enough to break the enemy's will, to spur a retreat from the fort. As he ran back down the landface, he suddenly became aware of the appearance of his fort and he was shocked by what he saw. The landface artillery pieces stood unmanned and battered into various shapes by the enemy bombardment. Wooden carriages were shattered and splintered; the enormous iron gun tubes were broken in half or lay immobile beside their battered carriages. The landface was battered and pockmarked by huge shell craters, and everywhere, it seemed, lay the dead of his garrison. In the gun chambers, on the parapet, draped over the guns, sprawled on the floor of the fort, the dead lay all around, some half-buried in the sand by the naval shells that killed them. Never had Lamb seen such carnage, nor could he ever have imagined such death and destruction at his post. It was horrible beyond words.[27]

Back at his position behind the earthworks, he found the Federals were now less than a hundred yards away, but their advance appeared to have been blunted for the moment. Had any reply come from General Bragg—any indication of support? No, there was nothing. If Fort Fisher was to be saved, all appeared to depend on Lamb. It was almost five o'clock, about a half-hour to dark. If the Yankees were repelled now, it would be nighttime before they could recover and then they could not unleash the naval fire without endangering their own troops. By morning the fort surely could be reinforced enough to withstand another attack. Lamb moved along the line of troops he had assembled, telling them to prepare for a bayonet charge and asking if they would follow him. Yes sir, officers and men alike assured him, they would follow. He went back down the line, preparing the men to rush the Yankees on his command. The troops were ready, bayonets fixed, bracing to rise and charge over their earthworks into the face of the enemy. Lamb drew his saber.

It had all come down to this—two and a half years as Fort Fisher's commander, all the work, all the plans, all the building and arming, all the nighttime vigils for blockade runners, all the worries about troops and ammunition and rations, all that went into defending the great fort in the first battle, all the lives lost in the past three days, and the fate of Wilmington, and maybe the survival of the Confederacy—so much now depended on what he was about to do, so much depended on this counterattack he would command. Most of these men had never made a bayonet charge. Maybe none of them had. But they had fought as hard as men could fight this day and now they were ready to follow him. He had never led a bayonet charge, but that fact meant nothing to him now—he would lead this one. And now it was time.[28]

"Charge bayonets!" he shouted and sprang upon the breastwork. "Forward! Double-quick, march!" he yelled, holding his saber aloft. The officers and men were already up, starting over the earthworks. They were met immediately by a heavy volley of gunfire, discharged from countless Federal rifles less than a hundred yards away. The Federals were lying flat, shooting upwards, and most of the volley went high. Some rounds went true, however, and one hit William Lamb.[29]

It was a serious wound. He was struck full in the left hip. The bullet went through his greatcoat, taking some of the red flannel lining with it, through his uniform, picking up gray wool fibers, and struck his hipbone a mighty blow. The bone fractured, issuing fragments, and Lamb was instantly knocked to his knees. Collapsing into the sand beside him was one of his officers, Lieutenant Daniel R. Perry, hit and dying. Everyone saw Lamb go down. The troops hesitated, unsure, then dropped back behind the earthwork. A soldier lifted Lamb and moved him out of the line of fire. The senior officer present was Captain Daniel Munn, from Company B of the Thirty-sixth North Carolina, one of Lamb's longtime hands. He was by Lamb's side immediately. Take command of the men and keep the Yankees in check, Lamb told Munn. Just as soon as he could get his wound bandaged, Lamb assured him, he would be back to resume command.[30]

Before he had even reached the hospital, however, Lamb knew he would not return to the battle. The wound was too bad—he was already weak from loss of blood. He joined Whiting in the hospital bombproof beneath the Pulpit Battery. Major Saunders was there also. He had been slightly wounded during the naval assault and had collapsed during the counterattack Whiting had led against the Federals on the landface. Placed on a litter near Whiting, Lamb summoned his adjutant, Lieutenant John Kelly, and sent him off to find Major Reilly, now the senior officer available to take command of Fort Fisher's beleaguered garrison.[31]

Laid side by side in the Pulpit hospital, Lamb and Whiting discussed the grim conditions of the battle despite the pain of their wounds. They would keep fighting—they agreed on that—and they would try once again to summon aid from General Bragg. Whiting dispatched a terse message, downplaying his wound and pleading for help. "The enemy are assaulting us by land and sea," he reported. "Their infantry outnumber us. Can't you help us?" Off went another courier, starting the plea on its route to Bragg. Meanwhile, the defense of Fort Fisher would be taken up by Major Reilly.[32]

James Reilly had been in the military almost all his life, and at forty-two, he had seen a lot of soldiering. Back in his native Ireland, he had run away from home to join the British army at age sixteen. Two years later, he was ready for greater adventure and immigrated to America, deserting his regiment, some said, by disguising himself in women's clothing. In the United States, like many young Irishmen, he joined the U.S. Army. He served in the Mexican War, hunted Indians in the West and, ironically, was in charge of Smithville's Fort Johnston in early 1861, when a band of armed civilians demanded that he surrender the fort. Reilly was sympathetic to the South, but he was also duty-minded: he surrendered, but he insisted the secessionists sign a receipt for the fort's ordnance. Later, as a Confederate captain, he commanded what became known as Reilly's battery and served with the Army of Northern Virginia in most of its campaigns through Gettysburg, where he distinguished himself in action. Then he had been posted back to the Cape Fear in late 1863, as a major of artillery in the Tenth North Carolina. Now, due to a fluke, he was Fort Fisher's ranking officer; although ill, Lamb's second-in-command, Major James Stevenson, had mounted the fort wall during the battle—and had been blown off the parapet and injured by an exploding Federal shell. Lamb had put Reilly in charge of the landface, and the Yankees had gotten in. Lamb held Reilly responsible for that crucial event, and Captain Braddy believed Reilly had sought the safety of the bombproofs when he should have been directing his troops. Still, Lamb believed Reilly was capable of making a good defense, and he *was* the fort's senior officer. Now he became Fort Fisher's commander and the job of repelling the Yankees belonged to him.[33]

From wherever he had been, Reilly soon appeared at the Pulpit hospital, accepted command of the fort from Lamb and Whiting, and promised he would keep fighting "as long as a man or a shot was left." Then he hurried away to battle the Yankees. The naval fire, which had driven so many defenders from the landface, suddenly slackened to allow Terry's troops to advance. Immediately, more Confederates left the bombproofs and joined the struggle for the third traverse, where they continued to hold off the Federals. Meanwhile, Reilly tried to reassemble the force Lamb had put together at the rear earthworks, but many men had either joined the battle on the land-face or had retreated to the bombproofs. Munn and Braddy had managed to hold together about 150 men, and Reilly withdrew the force to an earthwork near the huge main magazine. There he re-grouped and prepared for a counterattack. When his force was orga-nized and ready, he called one of Captain Izlar's South Carolinians to his side—a colorbearer, holding up one of the battle-worn stan-dards of Hagood's brigade. Then, with the colors flapping overhead, Reilly took his men forward against the Yankees massed in the rear of Shepherd's Battery. "As soon as the enemy observed our object, they opened a very destructive fire on our advancing column," Reilly later reported. "Under such a fire our men began to waver and fall back. . . ." The colorbearer was shot dead and Reilly's troops were dispersed in confusion. The major again withdrew to his position near the main magazine. He had taken heavy casualties and many of the survivors had retreated to nearby bombproofs. When he reas-sembled his force this time, Reilly counted fewer than 60 men.[34]

◆

On the third traverse, Colonel Curtis and the Federals were having difficulty climbing over their dead and wounded. Curtis was ready to make a charge to the fourth traverse, but the Federal casualties lay so thick on the parapet that it was hard for him and his men to advance. Once inside the fort, Curtis and the Federals found them-selves fighting what amounted to two battles—one on the landface parapets and another in the fort interior behind the landface. Even after Curtis's Brigade had been joined by Pennypacker's and Bell's men, the Federal advance had bogged down, hampered by a stiff

Confederate fire coming from the rear of the landface and by a stubborn resistance on the third traverse. After Pennypacker's brigade arrived, the western end of the landface was overrun fairly quickly, although at a costly loss of life. Then the Confederates had counterattacked, pushing Curtis's and Pennypacker's men back to the third traverse. There, the struggle became an awful, prolonged affair of violent give-and-take over a few bloody feet on the big mound's crest. The Federals were taking heavy losses—especially among officers. Colonel Moore was dead. Pennypacker had been carried off, bloody and presumed dying. Colonel Bell had not even made it into the fort. Captain John F. Thomas of the 117th New York had been shot dead on the third traverse. Lieutenant Colonel Francis Meyer of the 117th had been wounded, and a host of other officers were now casualties. Curtis did not know exactly what was happening to the Federal troops massed in a human heap on the sandy floor of the fort's interior, but he and the Northern troops atop the third traverse had to break through the Rebel defense.[35]

They made a rush over the top and the Confederates gave way, falling back past the gun chamber to the fourth traverse. There, Curtis thought, the fighting was even worse. Dead and wounded cluttered the Federal side of the traverse. The living clambered over the bodies to discharge their weapons over the crest of the hill into the faces of the Confederates on the other side, who were fighting just as desperately. Man after man went down until the parapet was cloaked with a carpet of blue bodies. More men rushed in from the front of the landface where they were massed—men of the First, Second and Third brigades, New Yorkers, Pennsylvanians, soldiers from New Hampshire and Indiana—all the brigades and regiments were now mixed together. The dead and wounded were dragged out of the way and new men took their places. Many of them in turn were shot down, then dragged aside, and replaced by others while the bloody fight continued.[36]

"A soldier was shot in the head by a rifle-ball; there was no outcry—simply a spurt of blood and all was over," recalled a survivor of the struggle:

> An agonizing clamor [came] from wounded men, who were writhing in the sand, beseeching, in heart-rending accents, those near them to end their suffering. The dead certainly, and perhaps the wounded, [did not] count for much on [this] battlefield. A color-bearer had fallen, and though choked by blood and sand, he murmured, "I am gone. Take the flag." An officer who had been shot through the heart retained nearly an erect position—he seemed to

be leaning against a gun carriage. Some lay face downward, with their faces in the sand, and others who had been near each other when a shell exploded had fallen in a confused mass, forming a mingled heap of broken limbs and mangled bodies.[37]

Finally, the Federals went over the top of the fourth traverse. The Confederates fell back again and the fighting became a struggle for control of the fifth traverse. Curtis seemed to be everywhere, moving through the battle at the head of his troops, giving orders and issuing commands amid the violent confusion. Many officers had been killed or wounded, but Curtis remained unscathed. Some soldiers marveled at what appeared to be his charmed life. After his troops swarmed over the fourth traverse, Curtis grabbed a courier and dictated a message for General Terry. The messenger was a sailor, Acting Master's Mate Silas Kempton of the *Santiago de Cuba*. Kempton and a handful of other seamen had been at work on the naval brigade's advance rifle pits close to the army's extreme left line, and had decided to make the assault with the soldiers. Now they were the only sailors in the fort, and Curtis had detailed Kempton as a courier. Go to Terry, Curtis told Kempton, and tell him to signal for the naval fire to come closer and help clear out the Rebels. Kempton headed for the rear and Curtis went forward to join the troops fighting for the fifth traverse.[38]

Soon afterwards, the naval fire increased and moved slowly westward along the landface. It caused greater slaughter among the Confederates there, but it also had an unexpectedly deadly effect on some of Curtis's troops. One shell fell wide of the mark and exploded among Curtis's front line atop the fifth traverse. When the smoke cleared, only four men were left. Afraid that the Rebels would counterattack before more troops could come forward, Curtis scrambled up the traverse, grabbed the rifles dropped by the dead and wounded and began firing them, one after another, until reinforcements secured the front line. More and more troops arrived, until the blue-clad soldiers were thronging their side of the fifth traverse, pouring a devastating fire into the thinning ranks of the Confederates fighting to hold on to the other side. "It was a noble sight to see our troops hanging on to the side of the fort like so many leeches sticking to an afflicted man," reported a Federal officer. "Men unable to stand and fire their pieces handed up the guns of their dead and helpless comrades," recalled another, "and reloaded them again and again, exhibiting a frenzied zeal and unselfish devotion that seemingly nothing but death could chill." Several times Curtis received loaded weapons from wounded soldiers, turned and fired, then handed the guns back for reloading—only to find the soldiers were dead.[39]

Then they had the fifth traverse. They pushed on, and quickly overran two more with bloody hand-to-hand fighting, the men raising their rifles above their heads to fire over the crest of each traverse. "Such fighting was never seen before, I believe," recalled a Federal officer. "It surpassed all that I had ever seen or thought that men were capable of doing. There they fought, from parapet to parapet, through traverse and bombproof, outside and in, the Navy in the meantime throwing shells just ahead of our soldiers. We could see them advance by the glorious old Stars and Stripes, which our people planted upon each successive parapet as they took them."[40]

Fort Fisher's defenders fought hard, making the Federal soldiers pay dearly in blood and lives for each foot of the landface they captured. "When the Rebels were driven out of one traverse, they would rally behind the next," reported one Federal witness to the struggle. "We could plainly see them cautiously crawl up the sides of the mound with our soldiers doing the same thing on the other side, and when near the top, they would bring their muskets into position, and the one who could fire first generally had the best of it. It was throughout a hand-to-hand, or rather a musket-to-musket, encounter, and the enemy contested every inch of ground." Never had he seen such bitter close-quarter fighting, recalled one Federal officer, a seasoned combat veteran. "The method by which we succeeded in dislodging [the Rebels] from one traverse after another was to crawl near the crest of the traverse, then quickly elevating the guns above our heads with both hands, fire at random down the slope on the opposite side. . . . Even then some of my men were shot through their hands."[41]

Now Curtis and the Federal troops were near the sally port, where Adams's battery was posted. Captain Adams and his gun crews had been doing deadly work against the Yankees, despite the casualties inflicted on the cannoneers by the naval fire. Lieutenant William Ketcham of the Thirteenth Indiana was close enough to see Adams's two brass Napoleon field pieces mounted in the sally port. He had seen their murderous effect on his fellow soldiers and he wanted to put the guns out of commission. Finding his regimental commander, Lieutenant Colonel Samuel Zent, he asked for permission to lead a detail of troops on an assault against the sally port. "That is just the thing," Zent responded. "Pick up a dozen men and go at it." Ketcham organized a detail from the Thirteenth Indiana—all armed with Spencer repeating rifles—and led them double-quick along the front of the landface toward the sally port. Forty feet away from the guns, Ketcham saw Adams's gun crews rush out of the sally-port tunnel to man their battery. When they spotted Ketcham and his squad, the Confederates darted back into the bombproofed tunnel. Ketcham turned to urge his men forward, and was shocked to find he was all alone—the others had abandoned the charge and had taken cover. Ketcham saw a huge shell crater nearby and he promptly dived into it. Moments later he heard conversation and peered over the rim of the big hole, expecting to see that his squad had reappeared. Instead, he saw men in gray uniforms loading the guns just a few yards away. He checked his Spencer and was alarmed to find it clogged with sand, and unserviceable. Realizing he was in a serious predicament, he fished a tin cup and a big spoon out of his haversack and began digging furiously, burrowing himself down deep into the shell crater and out of sight.[42]

While Curtis and his men battled from traverse to traverse, Lieutenant Colonel Jonas Lyman of the 203rd Pennsylvania was trying to advance with the large force of troops stalled inside the fort. After flooding through the riverside gate and surrounding Shepherd's Battery, they had been stymied by the heavy fire that Lamb and his hastily assembled force had unleashed from behind the rear earthwork. Their momentum stalled, principal officers dead or wounded, this force had lost its organization and had become little more than a huge, blue-uniformed mob, sprawled on the fort's sandy interior behind Shepherd's Battery. They had not lost their will to fight, they outnumbered the Rebel force facing them and their return fire had abruptly deflected both Lamb's and Reilly's counterattacks. Lyman knew, however, that they had to break out of their defensive position and help sweep the Confederates off the landface. Finally, after an agonizingly long stalemate, the Rebel fire slackened and the Confederates manning the rear earthwork appeared to be withdrawing.[43]

Lyman got the Federals on their feet and ordered them forward. They advanced steadily, paralleling Curtis's progress along the landface wall. When opposite the seventh traverse, which Curtis's men were then trying to capture, they established a new forward line, throwing up breastworks with tin plates, shovels and anything else they could find. With an interior line secure, Lyman then took part of the force and led a charge up and over the contested traverse. The Confederate defenders fell back in retreat, giving the Federals one more traverse, but Lyman was shot dead in the charge. Even so, his advance had allowed the Federals to move close enough to almost flank the sally-port tunnel and the Confederates inside.[44]

Meanwhile, Lieutenant Ketcham had cleaned the sand out of his Spencer repeater and had used the fast-firing weapon to keep the

Confederate gun crews away from the sally-port field pieces. When the Federal troops on the traverses finally neared the sally port, members of his detail joined him in the shell crater. He convinced them to resume their assault on the sally port and they charged forward. When they reached the unmanned field pieces opposite the sally-port tunnel, they emptied their fully loaded weapons into the tunnel's dark entrance, yelling for the "Johnnies" to come out and surrender. A moment later, a Johnny Reb appeared in the tunnel entrance, giving up the fight. He was quickly followed by another, and another—until Ketcham and his squad had seventeen Confederate prisioners on their hands.[45]

Inside the bombproofed tunnel were the survivors of Adams's battery and soldiers of Melvin's company—Second Company I of the Thirty-sixth North Carolina. Commanded by Captain John T. Melvin, they had helped fight Sherman's army near Savannah and had returned to Fort Fisher just in time for the second battle. After hours of brutal combat, their sally-port position was now on the verge of being overrun. On one side of the tunnel, they could see the Yankees inside the fort, throwing up a line of rifle pits just yards away; above them, the enemy had already captured almost half the fort landface; and from the other side of the tunnel, they were being flailed with a fusillade of rifle fire. Escape was still possible through the connecting bombproofs, but Captain Melvin apparently considered further resistance hopeless: on the interior side of the sally-port tunnel, a white flag protruded from the tunnel entrance and began waving back and forth.[46]

Major Reilly saw the white flag from his position near the main magazine. As far as he could tell, the Yankees had not reached the sally-port tunnel, so what could it mean? Who was surrendering? The officers with him urged him to cease fire—maybe some of the Yankees were giving up. Reilly ordered his men to stop firing, pulled out a white handkerchief, gave it to Captain Braddy and told him to go find out what was going on. Braddy stuck the handkerchief on the point of his sword, took another officer with him and headed for the sally-port tunnel. He had not gone far when the Confederates posted to the sally port emerged from the tunnel carrying their white flag, but instead of heading toward him, they began jogging toward the enemy. Braddy looked to his left and was shocked to see hundreds of Yankees getting to their feet and moving forward. He wheeled and raced back toward his position, yelling for Reilly to open fire. Reilly gave the order even before Braddy reached the cover of the earthwork, and the thin Confederate line belched forth a carefully aimed volley which sent the Federals diving back behind their line of rifle pits. Reilly and his men could not understand why their fellow soldiers in the sally-port tunnel were giving up, and they were incensed by the surrender.[47]

Atop the fort wall, Colonel Curtis could now plainly see the Confederate gun crew working the lone surviving Columbiad on the landface wall. Ever since Curtis had led the assault on the western end of the landface, two long and bloody hours before, that gun had been doing deadly work against any Federal troops within range. Hoping to put the big Columbiad out of commission, he ordered sharpshooters to man the crest of the newly captured traverse and try to pick off the distant Confederate cannoneers. Soon the gun was silenced. With that done and the sally-port field pieces captured, Curtis realized he could advance his troops along the front of the landface without having to worry about enemy artillery fire. Why not charge along the landface, he reasoned, flank the Rebels on the remaining traverses and seize the huge battery at the angle where the landface met the fort's seaface? That would almost certainly end the Rebel resistance on the landface and might even be enough to end the battle. Curtis grabbed a soldier from the 117th New York and sent him hurrying back to the west end of the fort to bring up more men. A few minutes later, the courier returned with a report that surprised Curtis: General Ames said no more troops could be sent forward; instead, spades would be sent up so Curtis and the troops could entrench for the night.[48]

General Ames was worried. The Federals now held approximately half the fort's landface and had established a line of rifle pits inside the fort; but from Ames's perspective, back near the riverside gate, the situation did not look too promising. More than ten of his principal officers were believed to be dead or dying, more than forty others were wounded. More than half the members of his staff had been shot down. Casualties were also heavy among the troops, and the survivors were in a disorganized state with brigades, regiments and companies all intermingled. For Ames, it had been a very confusing battle almost from the beginning. Following Pennypacker's brigade into the fort, he had seen the Confederates at the gate quickly overwhelmed and, thinking the fort had fallen, he had begun waving a white handkerchief and yelling for his troops to cease fire—until a volley from Lamb's Confederates changed his mind. Then had come the hard-fought struggle for the traverses and even now, two hours after the assault was launched, the Federal drive seemed to be slowing down again. Furthermore, he believed, the troops were exhausted, and more reinforcements were needed—that was what he reported to Terry. After Bell's brigade had come in and the Rebels had still continued to resist, he had taken a pencil and scribbled a dispatch to Terry, stating he "would be compelled to withdraw if not reinforced." Now the sun was disappearing behind the tree line across the river, and before long it would be dark. It was time to entrench and be reinforced, Ames believed: the battle could be renewed in the morning.[49]

The idea was nonsense to Curtis. He had no intention of entrenching for the night. For two of the longest hours of his life, he and his men had fought their way along the landface wall, traverse by traverse, with a great loss of life and blood—and now was the time to strike the Rebels with a death blow. Go back to General Ames, he told his orderly, explain what needs to be done and request more troops for the assault. Curtis turned back to the battle—the Confederates were still stubbornly defending the next traverse—but the orderly returned in just a few minutes. He had orders from General Ames, he reported: the men were exhausted, the general said, and no further advance would be attempted until reinforcements arrived in the morning. The troops at the gate were already entrenching. Curtis should hold his ground if possible and entrench—spades were on their way up from the rear.[50]

Curtis ignored the order. Go back again, he told the orderly, find some subordinate officers and tell them to round up more troops and come forward for an assault. Off the orderly ran once more. A few minutes later he was back—without troops. Instead, he carried an armload of spades. General Ames had sent the shovels, he told Curtis, and the general had repeated his orders: Curtis was to hold his ground and entrench for the night. Curtis was enraged. He grabbed the spades from the startled orderly, stomped up to the crest of the traverse where the battle was raging and threw the shovels over the top of the big mound toward the Confederates below, yelling to the enemy that he would be back soon and would fall on them just like those spades.[51]

Convinced Ames was going to try to shut down the offense for the night, Curtis summoned Acting Master's Mate Kempton, who had delivered the earlier dispatch to Terry. Report to Terry again, Curtis told Kempton, and tell him Curtis believes the fort could be taken with more men and "a bold push." The colonel next turned to Captain David B. Magill of the 117th New York, ordering him to put together all the troops he could find and take the next traverse. Curtis then headed back to the western end of the landface to round up more troops himself—he would not wait on Ames or General Terry.[52]

Back at the gate, Curtis found the troops entrenching—and he encountered General Ames. It was the first time the two officers had spoken since coming ashore. "I have two or three times sent you word to fortify your position and hold it until reinforcements can be sent to aid us," Ames told Curtis above the roar of battle. "The men are exhausted, and I will not order them to go forward." Curtis protested: they almost had a complete victory now, and if they did not push on, the enemy would probably land reinforcements during the night. Ames repeated his orders, but Curtis refused to obey, confident he had been given independent command by General Terry. No, he told Ames emphatically, Fort Fisher must be taken now or it could not be taken at all. He was going to make his assault, Curtis vowed, even if he had to do it with no more than fifty men. Ames said nothing else, and Curtis set about rounding up officers and men for the assault, finding plenty of volunteers. He left some junior officers to assemble the troops, and hurried back to the front to plan his attack.[53]

On the landface, the Federals had pushed the fort's defenders farther back in Curtis's absence, and now were hugging their side of the ninth traverse, trying to catch their breath. Curtis, apparently still worked up from his confrontation with Ames, barged into the action in a surly mood and accosted Lieutenant Colonel Zent, who was the senior officer now present. "Why in hell [are you] not advancing?" Curtis barked. At the moment, the Confederate fire coming over the traverse was especially heavy. "Keep down," Zent replied to Curtis evenly, "or you will find out why we don't advance." Curtis ignored the advice, stretching his six-foot-four frame to peer over the traverse, trying to study the route of assault he was planning. At that instant a shell exploded just above the traverse, knocking him flat. He landed limp and unmoving. The men around him rushed to his side. He was still alive, but his face was a bloody wreck. He had been struck by two shell fragments. One had destroyed his left eye, the other had ripped open his face, tearing away part of the left frontal bone. He was hustled unconscious to the rear, carried unaware over the row of traverses he had fought so hard to capture, past the troops entrenching near the gate, over the battered bridge he had charged across two hours earlier and on to the Federal field hospital in the rear. Somehow he was still alive, but for Colonel Newton Martin Curtis, the battle was over.[54]

◆

Back at his command post, General Terry was beginning to doubt whether his army could take Fort Fisher. It was almost dark now and his troops had been engaged in bitter fighting for more than two hours. Across the peninsula, Admiral Porter's naval brigade had been routed. After capturing half the landface, the army was now stalled and no longer advancing. Colonel Curtis, who had been the driving force on the landface, had been borne to the rear, seriously injured; and Pennypacker and Bell appeared mortally wounded—which meant the three brigade commanders Terry had sent into the fort were now out of commission. Casualties among the troops were heavy. He had sent three brigades into the fort—more than 3,000 men—and still it had not fallen. The troops were tired and disorganized. There were even reports that the men were running low on ammunition. Everything seemed confused. If the Confederates were reinforced, or if they just managed to launch a serious counterattack, his troops might be routed and driven from the fort like the naval brigade. Ames wanted more reinforcements and was reportedly considering entrenching for the night. Curtis had wanted to make "a bold push" against the enemy. It was a crucial moment for Terry: What should he do?[55]

He turned to Colonel Comstock for advice and Comstock had a definite opinion: Bring up Abbott's brigade and throw it into the fort against the Rebels. Bring up Paine's troops too—risk everything. Forget about the threat from Hoke; throw Abbott's and Paine's men into the fort. Overwhelm the Rebels and finish the job. Comstock's advice had played a vital part in General Butler's decision to withdraw during the Christmas battle; now, for this position, Comstock was even more emphatic—he was certain Fort Fisher would fall if Terry moved quickly and forcefully.[56]

When the naval brigade was repulsed, Terry had sent Captain Towle over to find the naval commander with a request that the defeated force of sailors and marines be sent to the rear to reinforce Abbott's and Paine's defensive line. Towle had been unable to find Lieutenant Commander Breese, who was still huddled behind the palisade, but he had found Cushing, who had agreed to Terry's request. Now Terry summoned Towle again, gave him General Ames' penciled plea for reinforcements and told him to go back to Cushing, show him Ames's request and impress upon Cushing the importance of getting all available hands into the army's rear defensive line. Terry had made up his mind: he would follow Comstock's advice and send in Abbott's brigade.[57]

Towle hustled across the open, sandy plain with Ames's note in his hand. He had not gone far when he began to draw sporadic fire from Confederate sharpshooters atop the landface wall. The bullets were coming close. Towle figured the Rebels could see the note he was carrying, recognized him as a messenger and were trying to shoot him down to disrupt communications. Defiantly, Towle held up the note and shook it at the distant walls of the fort as he hurried toward the beach. There he found that the sailors and marines had been rounded up and taken to the Federal rear line as promised. Meanwhile, Terry sent an order to Abbott, commanding him to move into the fort. To Comstock, who had so confidently advised his superior, Abbott's brigade seemed to take a long time to arrive. Finally Colonel Abbott was in the command post, receiving his orders from Terry. His troops were fresh, Abbott was told, while the Rebels were no doubt exhausted. Go in, he was ordered, and finish the work. Abbott left, and his brigade moved forward—the fourth Federal brigade to rush into the fort this day.[58]

Now Ames would be reinforced. Now the battle would resume anew. Now they would drive the Rebels and take the fort. Those were Terry's and Comstock's expectations. By now the sun had disappeared in a western glow and the sky was darkening. Terry and Comstock waited, expecting to hear the roar of the battle suddenly increase as Abbott's troops added their firepower to the struggle. Nothing changed. They began to feel uneasy. What was wrong now? Comstock turned to Terry and urged him to put in the men of Paine's division—the U.S. Colored Troops. Hoke had tested their lines earlier and had withdrawn. Even if he attacked again, it would be too late to save the fort, Comstock advised. "Bring up a whole colored brigade," he urged, "even if Hoke captures everything in our rear." Terry agreed, and ordered General Paine to send forward "one of the strongest regiments in his division." Paine promptly obeyed, dispatching the Twenty-seventh U.S. Colored Troops, commanded by Colonel Albert M. Blackman, and for the first time since Terry's forces had established their lines, black soldiers moved toward the front.[59]

◆

In the command post a while later, Terry and Comstock grew increasingly impatient. Blackman's regiment had reached the fort and Abbott's brigade had been inside a long time, but there was still no indication the battle had been renewed, no sign of a Federal advance. Finally, Terry decided to see for himself. Accompanied by Comstock, he headed for the fort, crossing the ground over which his troops had rushed, passing over the bridge where Bell had fallen, entering the riverside gate Pennypacker's men had breached. There he encountered utter confusion. Troops were milling around, brigades and regiments intermixed, soldiers were shoveling entrenchments and no attempt to advance was being made. Instead of rushing

Abbott's brigade full scale against the Confederates defending the landface, Ames had put part of the brigade to work digging entrenchments, had placed one regiment in his rear on a picket line and had ordered the U.S. Colored Troops back outside the fort to dig a line of entrenchments in the rear. A single regiment—the Third New Hampshire—had been sent forward on the landface wall to the front, but instead of joining the troops already there in an assault, they had been ordered to relieve those in front. The battle had continued there, and the troops now were fresh, but Terry's plan for a final, combined assault had not been implemented and now it was dark.[60]

Ames advised Terry to entrench and hold on until daylight, but Terry disagreed. Echoing Curtis's argument, he expressed concern that the Confederates would probably heavily reinforce the garrison and might be able to retake the fort. He considered bringing up the rest of Paine's troops to relieve Ames's division, but Comstock weighed in with another persuasive argument: Forget about bringing up more troops; something should be done immediately, and Abbott's entire brigade was on hand and fresh. Why not organize the brigade into squads of 100 men each and throw them one after another at the next traverse? If one squad took heavy losses, it would be reinforced immediately. That way they could keep up the pressure on an exhausted enemy, advancing until the entire landface was taken—and then turn to the seaface. Terry agreed and ordered it done. It took a while to reorganize the scattered regiments of Abbott's brigade, but within the hour they were moving forward in squads against the battle-weary Confederates on the landface.[61]

◆

Captain William H. Trickey and the troops of the Third New Hampshire had been fighting for the ninth traverse since they had relieved the exhausted troops of Ames's division. It was the same bloody, close-quarter fighting that had marked the struggle for traverse after traverse on the landface. "The bursting of shell, the rattling of musketry, shouts of the men, groans of the wounded, all went to make up a perfect pandemonium," remembered one soldier. Now it was dark, however, and that added a peculiar dimension to the bitter struggle. The naval fire was less precise at night and now accidentally killed scores of Federal soldiers, until army signal corpsmen got the navy to shift its fire to the fort seaface. The flash of exploding shells and the flare of rifle fire lit the struggle with a bizarre, sporadic light, as the squads of Abbott's brigade joined the landface fight.[62]

"Here it was a soldiers' fight," reported a Federal survivor. "The men would wait until there were enough together for a charge, then some officer would form them into line, and they would rush up a traverse and over. When they came against the enemy it was cold steel or the butt of a gun. At other places the contending forces would blaze away in the darkness. They would throw themselves on the ground and then come alternately crawling or running for position. Hoarse voices were shouting orders, and from the huge round traverses, that looked like great sea-billows toppling over to engulf all before them, shadowy forms of friend and foe were seen in confused masses. . . . The outlines of the work could now and then be seen by the flash of exploding shells or blaze of musketry, but indistinct as the creation of some hideous dream."[63]

◆

The Confederates facing Abbott's fresh troops now had little hope. They had been fighting for hours, engaged in the most brutal sort of combat. They were surely exhausted, were clearly outnumbered and were now low on ammunition. Yet they kept fighting, holding off scores of well-trained, better-equipped combat veterans from the Army of the James. From his position near the main magazine, Major Reilly and his diminished band of troops poured as much supporting fire into the enemy ranks as they could muster—but the brunt of the fighting, the primary defense of the fort, was waged by these men on the landface traverses. Since General Whiting was shot down hours earlier, they had fought without the immediate presence and leadership of a high-ranking officer. All afternoon and far into the night, they had stubbornly resisted the Federal advance, making the enemy pay a terrible price for every traverse, for each foot of gory sod. Had a seasoned officer organized a counterattack after Curtis had fallen, when the Federal advance was stalled, they might have driven the enemy from the fort. But no counterattack had been mounted then—it had remained a soldiers' fight. The Confederates defending the landface had given ground grudgingly, but their ranks had been worn away as the bloody hours passed, and now the bodies of their dead and wounded littered the gun chambers and traverses they had so stubbornly yielded. Chaplain Luther McKinnon, the post preacher, had led a search for ammunition among the dead and wounded, carrying the paper cartridges from man to man in a blanket. But now even that supply of ammunition was unavailable. Then, led by the men of the Third New Hampshire, Abbott's troops overwhelmed the jaded Confederates, overran the ninth traverse and quickly carried two more. The Confederates rallied again on the next traverse and again managed to stall the Federal advance, but coming up along the landface from the rear were two more regiments of Abbott's troops—the Seventh New Hampshire and the Sixth Connecticut—ready to do battle.[64]

Inside the Confederate field hospital under the Pulpit Battery, Whiting and Lamb tried to judge the course of the contest outside by the racket of battle. What little hope they had clung to had begun to fade just before sundown, when Major Reilly had burst into the hospital with a disheartening report: one of the garrison officers had raised a white flag, let the Yankees into the sally port and surrendered what looked like a large portion of the garrison. After Reilly rushed back to the battle, General Whiting had ordered Colonel Saunders to hurry down to Battery Buchanan and bring up the rest of Hagood's brigade—which Whiting was sure by then had arrived. Saunders had hurried away despite his wound and had not returned, which was a bad sign. Now—sometime after eight o'clock—Lieutenant John Kelly, Lamb's aide, returned to the hospital, waded past the dead and wounded and delivered more bad news: the troops were almost out of ammunition with no more to be found, he reported, the Yankees had now taken almost all the landface and the fort's defenders could not be expected to hold out much longer. More fighting, he said, would be a useless waste of life. Should they surrender?[65]

No—Lamb refused to do it. As long as he lived, he would not surrender the fort, he told the aide. Whiting agreed: *Do not surrender.* Even now, Lamb hoped for a rescue. Surely Bragg would not desert them—surely Hoke's men would attack at any moment. Reinforcements could arrive at any second and turn the tide. General Lee had sent word that if the fort fell and the South lost its last port, he could not keep his army in the field. It was his duty, Lamb believed, to keep fighting—he would not surrender. Kelly was sent back with orders to keep the defense going as long as possible, to hold on until Bragg rescued them and saved the fort. After the aide had left, Whiting spoke to Lamb: "Lamb, when you die," he said, "I will assume command and I will not surrender the fort."[66]

◆

Outside, the troops of the Seventh New Hampshire and the Sixth Connecticut were advancing double-quick inside the fort, hurrying alongside the landface wall in the darkness. At the third traverse, they turned and quickly ascended the steps into the nearest gun chamber, scaled the chamber wall, continued down the outside slope and moved in force between the palisades and the fort wall—heading toward the Northeast Bastion. They were under orders from Colonel Abbott, issued from General Ames, passed down from Gen-

eral Terry, and, ironically, they were following the plan Colonel
Curtis had been trying to execute when he was wounded. It was
happening more than three hours later, and the troops belonged to
Abbott instead of Curtis, but it was Colonel Curtis's assault, finally
under way.[67]

Lieutenant Colonel Augustus W. Rollins commanded the Seventh
New Hampshire Infantry. He led his troops along the landface,
flanked the three traverses still held by the Confederates, then
stopped below the Northeast Bastion long enough to organize his
regiment into two wings. By now, the Rebel gunfire seemed to be
dying out, and only sporadic small arms fire could be heard in the
night—the fort's defenders were out of ammunition. Using his left
wing as support, and reinforced by the Sixth Connecticut, Rollins
took his right wing charging up the fort wall, turned back toward the
river and quickly captured the remaining three traverses from the
ocean side. Then he sent the New Hampshire and Connecticut
troops clambering up the slopes of the Northeast Bastion, seizing the
prize that had eluded Admiral Porter's sailors and marines. All Confederate resistance now collapsed and the bloody struggle for the
landface ended. Surrounded by a great host of blue-uniformed soldiers, the exhausted landface defenders finally gave up, dropped
their weapons and surrendered to Rollins and his troops. Atop the
Northeast Bastion, Corporal Eric Peterson of the Seventh New
Hampshire confronted a Confederate field officer who was carrying
a battle flag. Peterson took the officer prisoner, but Lieutenant Colonel Daniel Klein of the Sixth Connecticut pulled rank and confiscated the flag. The Confederate fire ceased and an odd silence replaced the tumult of battle. For the first time that day, Terry's
soldiers could hear the nearby surf breaking on the beach. It was
almost ten o'clock. Finally, after more than six hours of hard fighting,
despite the repulse of Admiral Porter's naval force and a bloody
harvest of dead and wounded, despite moments when Terry's troops
seemed on the verge of failing—despite all that—the fort's tough,
stubborn defense had collapsed and Terry's army now occupied Fort
Fisher from the river to the ocean.[68]

From his position near the main magazine, Major Reilly had seen
the enemy soldiers swarm over the last landface traverses and
scale the Northeast Bastion. The Federals soon would be moving
against the handful of soldiers under his immediate command, seizing the Pulpit hospital and storming the seaface batteries. Already he
had ordered General Whiting and Colonel Lamb evacuated to Battery Buchanan, a mission performed by Captain Alfred C. Van Benthuysen, a wounded Confederate officer who had left Battery Bu-

chanan to join the troops at the fort. There was no protest Lamb could make when the litter bearers came for him—his fort had fallen and he could only hope that it could be retaken. The battle's final flurry of gunfire was under way when he and Whiting were hastily carried from the hospital bombproof, and enemy rounds were striking the sand all around the retreating party. The shower of bullets reminded the wounded Lamb of a hailstorm. Then it was strangely quiet, the fighting had ended, and the two officers were being borne over the open plain toward Battery Buchanan, following Major Reilly's preplanned escape route.[69]

Reilly had a contingency plan. That afternoon he had sent Captain Adams down to Battery Buchanan with a message for Captain Chapman, the battery's commander: if the fort fell, Reilly and all the troops he could muster would retreat to Battery Buchanan and make a stand there, so Chapman should remain at his post. "Very well," Chapman had told Adams, who reported the response to Reilly, apparently unaware of the drunkenness at the battery. Reilly figured when he reached Battery Buchanan he could reform the garrison troops, turn the battery's heavy artillery on the Federals if they pursued and, he hoped, hold off the enemy until reinforced by Bragg. Then perhaps the fort could be retaken. If that plan failed, then the troops at least could be evacuated by a flotilla of small boats moored at the battery. Reilly counted heads: he had only thirty-two men now. He tried to cover Van Benthuysen's retreat as long as possible, then calmly formed his troops into a column of fours, and set out on the mile-and-a-half march down the peninsula to Battery Buchanan.[70]

It was a moonlit night and the visibility was good. When he came into sight of Battery Buchanan, Reilly halted his small column. He gave orders to check the rear to see if the enemy was in pursuit, and sent Captain Oliver H. Powell forward to notify Captain Chapman of their approach, so the battery's gun crews would hold their fire. No Federals were in sight in the rear and Captain Powell soon returned—but the report he brought left Reilly in a state of shock: Battery Buchanan had been abandoned. Its guns were spiked and useless, the gun crews were gone and so were all the battery's boats. Captain Chapman and his naval force had abandoned their post and had taken all means of transportation with them. Several hundred survivors of the fort's garrison were there, milling around, but with no ammunition many of them had thrown away their arms and were now incapable of making a defense. The members of Fort Fisher's garrison who had escaped capture, along with the fort's surviving officers—Whiting, Lamb, Reilly and others—were now stranded with no means of escape, left to face the Yankees.[71]

For Colonel Lamb, it was the final blow. Typical of his optimistic nature, he had held on to every hope throughout the battle, but now all hope was gone. He and the others had been abandoned, left to their fate by General Bragg, whose reinforcements had never arrived and whose diversionary attack on the enemy rear had never occurred. Now, they had been left to die or be shipped to some Yankee prison camp thanks to Captain Chapman of the Confederate navy.[72]

Unknown to Lamb and the others stranded at Battery Buchanan, the fort's chief of artillery, Major William Saunders, was also responsible for their plight. At dusk, Saunders had gone to Battery Buchanan as Whiting had ordered, hoping to bring up the rest of Hagood's South Carolinians, but the reinforcements had not arrived. After waiting more than three hours at the battery, Saunders had hiked back up to the fort to report the bad news to Whiting. He arrived at the fort just as the Federals overran the final traverses and the North-east Bastion. Certain all was lost, he had hurried back to Battery Buchanan to report what he had seen. The Yankees had the fort and were probably heading toward Battery Buchanan right now, he had told Chapman. Who was left to defend the post? Most of the naval detachment had been sent into the fort as reinforcements. The few men left at the battery should be withdrawn immediately, Saunders believed. It was all Chapman needed to hear: some of his men had already been evacuated across the river, beginning at dark, and Chapman was ready to go. So was Saunders. He dispatched a final message across the river to General Hebert at Smithville: "The fort will be surrendered. We can get no help." That done, the major joined Chapman and the rest of the naval detachment in the battery's flotilla of launches and headed across the river. Behind them, they left the battery's four heavy artillery pieces spiked to discourage the Federals from using them. As they pulled away from the shore, Lamb, Whiting, Reilly and the others were just minutes away, heading toward the battery in the darkness.[73]

◆

Meanwhile, back inside the fort, the Federals were swarming over the Northeast Bastion and the Pulpit Battery in a mopping-up operation, rousting Confederates out of the bombproofs and rounding up prisoners. Captain Daniel Munn and a squad of about fifteen men from the Thirty-sixth North Carolina managed to escape the roundup and headed south toward Battery Buchanan. They had not surrendered, but they had given up—outside the fort they threw away their weapons and cartridge boxes. As he led the men down the darkened peninsula, Munn realized his was probably the last organized Confederate force to evacuate the fort. Another officer in the Thirty-sixth, Lieutenant Henry Benton, meanwhile retreated with a handful of men into the fort's main magazine. The big bombproof's entrance was soon surrounded by Federal troops. "Come out of there, Johnny Rebs, or we'll shoot into you," they called. Thirteen thousand pounds of highly explosive black powder were stored in the magazine bombproof. "Shoot and be damned to you, and we'll all go to hell together," Lieutenant Benton yelled back. No one fired, but Benton knew it was all over. Moments later, he and the others filed out under the guns of their captors. The lieutenant's defiant taunt was apparently the last act of Confederate resistance at Fort Fisher.[74]

Suddenly, the men of Terry's army realized the battle was over. All resistance had ended. Every enemy soldier in sight was now a prisoner, and the rest of the Rebels were reported fleeing down the peninsula away from the victorious Federals. "They have surrendered," men began to shout. The word raced through the Federal ranks: they had done it—Fort Fisher was theirs. Wild, triumphant cheering erupted among the troops. "Victory! And we proclaimed it too," reported a Federal soldier, "till sea and shore, and the tall, solemn pines echoed back wilder and heartier cheering than had ever before disturbed a midnight at Federal Point." Men whooped and jumped and danced crazily around with each other atop the blood-soaked traverses. Others were moved to tears. "My very heart went up in thanksgiving," reported Lieutenant Frank Lay of the 117th New York, who realized he was the only officer in his regiment not dead or wounded. "Never did I feel as I felt then," he wrote his wife. "Men grasped each other's hands and wept only as brave men can in the hour of victory."[75]

◆

The cheering carried over the Atlantic and reached the fleet. Aboard the *Malvern*, Admiral Porter sat in his stateroom smoking his pipe. He felt ill. That afternoon he had stood on the bridge of his flagship and watched his seamen turn their backs to the enemy and retreat in a wild rout. He had freely boasted that his naval assault would teach the army a thing or two about storming a fort; instead, it had ended in a humiliating repulse. Later that evening, Lieutenant Commander Cushing had come aboard the *Malvern* with a firsthand report about the naval brigade, and it was bad, very bad: almost 400 of the 2,000 volunteers were dead or wounded—a shocking casualty rate. Sam Preston and Benjamin Porter were dead. So were Surgeon

Longshaw, Ensign Wiley and a long list of seamen. A host of officers were wounded too—Cushman, Simms, Louch, Evans and others. It was a sickening report and certainly nothing like the glory Porter had expected. Bad as he felt, however, he would not sleep until he heard the result of the army assault. A victory would undoubtedly make the navy's losses more tolerable, but another defeat . . . ?[76]

In the *Malvern*'s wardroom, the ship's junior officers were talking in hushed voices about their friends who had died on the beach that day. Ensign John Grattan and Lieutenant William Clemens, the army signal officer assigned to the admiral's flagship, were among the group exchanging maudlin comments. Just as the ship's bell sounded ten o'clock, Lieutenant Clemens was summoned to the bridge to read an army signal on shore. Peering into the darkness, Clemens could see the signal torch blinking in the distance—from atop the walls of Fort Fisher. Letter by letter, it spelled out a message: "THE FORT IS OUR—." Before the last letter was signaled, raucous cheers erupted aboard the warships. Ensign Grattan, the admiral's aide, would always remember what happened next.[77]

"In a moment, the meaning of the signal was conveyed to the Admiral," Grattan reported. "He jumped on deck, and called all hands aft to the quarter deck. Every man and boy was soon around him, and in a loud, thrilling voice he directed them to give three cheers for the capture of Fort Fisher. The Admiral never before gave an order which was as heartily obeyed. Everyone appeared to be wild with joy, all discipline was relaxed and the cheers of the officers and sailors could be heard far and wide over the smooth water. Loud cheering could be heard in the fort and lights began to flash in all directions." Overcome by the events of the day, Porter had to be assisted to his stateroom.[78]

The fleet immediately ceased firing on the fort seaface, and signal rockets of various colors were launched from the warships, decorating the night sky above Fort Fisher like a gala Fourth of July celebration. Ensign Robley Evans, now evacuated from the beach, was lying on the deck of the USS *Nereus* with other wounded seamen when the missiles began streaking through the night. "There was a great burst of rockets and blue lights and the men manning the rigging cheered as the guns roared with saluting charges," he recalled. "Long after I was comfortably swung in the wardroom I could hear the fleet rejoicing over the downfall of the great rebel stronghold." Behind the earthworks of the army's rear line, Seaman William Cobb saw the rockets streaming across the sky and felt good—he had survived the disastrous naval assault and, despite the outcome, he felt like he had contributed to the fort's capture. "It done me more good to see it,"

he wrote home. "Such another noise you never heard, of men hur-
rahing, steam whistles screaming. Rockets, the air was alive with
rockets of all colors." The men of the Army of the James were also
impressed with the navy's triumphant display. "At once the southern
sky seemed full of rockets and many colored lights," recalled one
soldier, "and as the showers of red, white and blue stars fell into the
sea, we knew that the navy was proclaiming *Victory!*"[79]

◆

Inside Fort Fisher, Colonel Comstock watched the fireworks with
mixed feelings. He was moved by the cheers—they were "rousing &
beautiful"—but he knew the victory had been bought at an awful
price. "What our feelings were in the moonlight," he confided to his
diary. "We looked on the huge mounds & hollows, the disabled guns
& the dead men scattered thickly around & knew how great the
work was we had done & how terrible the hurrah we had passed. . . ."
Others were also sobered by the carnage around them. "The fort had
been ploughed by our shells until everything looked like a heap of
destruction," Chaplain Henry Turner wrote in his journal. "Dead
bodies were lying in desperate confusion in every direction. In some
places they were lying in piles and heaps. Several rebels had been
utterly buried by our shells. Guns of the largest caliber had been
broken to pieces and their carriages swept from under them. The
wounded were groaning and begging for assistance." Federal casualties littered the fort too. As he was marched over the traverses and
toward the rear under guard, Lieutenant Henry Benton, now a prisoner of war, had to pick his way around the bodies of the fallen
Northern troops. "The ground on the outside was red with blood,"
he remembered, "and [the] dead were lying scattered about."[80]

   When the cheering finally ended and the last rocket flare faded
into the darkness, all the Confederate prisoners were herded together and escorted up the beach to the rear by troops of the Third
New Hampshire. Meanwhile, following General Terry's orders, Colonel Abbott re-formed the Seventh New Hampshire and the Sixth
Connecticut and led a sweep down the fort seaface, supported by the
Twenty-seventh U.S. Colored Troops. Leaving General Ames behind
in charge of the troops in the fort, Terry and Comstock followed
Abbott's advance down the seaface. Abbott took the force alongside
the seaface wall, rounding up a handful of prisoners along the way,
and quickly concluded that the seaface batteries had been abandoned. Even so, when his troops neared the towering Mound Battery, he formed them into a line of battle and advanced cautiously
on the sixty-foot-high structure. It too had been abandoned, appar-

ently hurriedly: atop the famous battery the garrison flag was still flying in the darkness. When Federal troops scaled the Mound, Captain J. Homer Edgerly of the Seventh New Hampshire hauled down the flag and gave it to Colonel Abbott, who in turn presented it to General Terry as a trophy. Meanwhile, a couple of Confederate stragglers had been rounded up, and when interrogated amid a host of blue uniforms, they pointed the Federals south: there, about a mile away in the darkness, was Battery Buchanan, and it was to there that the rest of the garrison had fled. Abbott re-formed the three regiments and moved on down the peninsula. About a mile from Battery Buchanan, he detailed ten soldiers armed with Spencers as skirmishers, sent them about 100 yards out in front of the main force, then resumed the advance.[81]

◆

By now, Battery Buchanan was crowded with hundreds of Fort Fisher's soldiers, stranded beside the Cape Fear River with no means of escape. No one appeared in command and all discipline had vanished. The troops milled around aimlessly or stood huddled in despondent-looking groups. Except for the squad Reilly had brought with him, hardly anyone was armed. Some men appeared drunk. One officer had found a horse somewhere and rode away from the crowd and up the peninsula, watching for the approach of the enemy. Most, however, simply waited, apparently resigned to whatever happened next. Major Reilly knew the Yankees would be there soon, and when they came into range he figured they would immediately open fire. His disorganized, demoralized troops would not stand a chance. Even if they somehow found more ammunition, making a defense would be impossible now that the men had discarded their rifles. It was all over, he concluded. They had no choice but to surrender. He summoned Captain Van Benthuysen and Whiting's aide, Major James Hill, and both concurred: they would go meet the Yankees away from the battery and they would surrender the remnant of the garrison. The three officers left the confusion at the battery and walked back toward the fort in the darkness. About three hundred yards away they stopped and waited, but only briefly. A few minutes later they saw movement in the distance—armed men heading their way. Reilly fished his handkerchief out of his pocket, stuck it on the tip of his saber and waited for the Yankees.[82]

◆

Back at Battery Buchanan, Colonel Lamb and General Whiting lay on their litters at the foot of the battery's high sodded walls. They too knew surrender was now unavoidable. They had lost, the enemy had won. The distant cheering and the dramatic display of fireworks was final confirmation. Both blamed General Bragg. He had given up before the battle had even begun, they believed, and he had coolly abandoned the fort and all its men to the enemy. Whiting had come into the battle believing the fort and its garrison would be sacrificed, and now all that he feared had come to pass. Fort Fisher was lost. Wilmington was lost. What would Lee's army do now that the lifeline was cut? What would happen to the dream of an independent South? There was nothing they could do now, in their pain and misery, except lie there amid the gloom and confusion of defeat, and wait.[83]

A figure stood over Lamb's litter. Lamb looked up—and came face to face with General Colquitt of Hoke's division. Under orders from Bragg, Colquitt had come downriver from Sugar Loaf in a rowboat, sent to take command of Fort Fisher. After canceling Hoke's assault on the Federal rear that afternoon, Bragg had made no other serious attempt to attack the enemy. Nor had he insisted that the rest of Hagood's brigade be put into the fort. Only when the pleas for help coming from the fort began to exhibit an increasing tone of anxiety did he try to hurry Hagood's brigade across the river to reinforce the fort. By then it was too late; there were more delays with the troop-ships, and reports that the fort had fallen were beginning to arrive. The news had alarmed Wilmington's anxious citizens, especially the editor of the *Wilmington Journal,* who had apparently camped at army headquarters, but Bragg had sent word for everyone to calm down—he was confident that the reports were false. Even when he had received the word from Major Saunders and the naval officers who had evacuated Battery Buchanan, Bragg would not believe the fort had fallen, nor did he prepare any of his 6,000-man force for an attempt to retake the fort if the reports proved true. Instead, he would wait for word from General Colquitt, who had been dis-patched in his rowboat to relieve General Whiting.[84]

The civilian oarsmen who had brought Colquitt and three of his aides down the Cape Fear had refused to land at Fort Fisher and instead had put ashore at a point about 500 yards north of Battery Buchanan. Almost as soon as they had landed, they had encountered stragglers, who all said the same thing: Fort Fisher had fallen and the Yankees would probably show up at any moment. Captain Munn and his squad of men had then appeared, identifying themselves as being the last troops from the fort, and acting for a moment as if they might seize Colquitt's boat. Farther downstream near the battery, the gen-eral and his party had been hailed by the officer on horseback who had assured them the fort had "gone up." Leaving his staff to guard the boat, Colquitt had then hiked down to the battery to find Lamb and Whiting.[85]

The general and his aides were shocked at what they saw: "[The] men were without guns, without accouterments, some of them without hats, and all in a very bad state of demoralization," they would report to Bragg. "The beach was crowded with a disorganized, demoralized rabble, and it was with the utmost difficulty that we prevented them from taking our boat." The "rabble" Colquitt and his staff saw crowding the riverbank had been through a horrendous three-day ordeal and some of the bitterest fighting of the war—and now, finally overwhelmed, many wanted desperately to get away. But not Colonel Lamb; he still wanted to fight. When he saw Colquitt, hope was kindled again: a fresh brigade might retake the fort. Had Colquitt brought reinforcements? Even now, Lamb urged, if Bragg would just attack . . . but it was not to be. Colquitt quickly doused the brief flame of hope—he had brought no brigade. There would be no reprieve, Lamb knew that for certain now, and for the rest of his life he would affirm Whiting's prediction: "Lamb, my boy," Whiting had said, "I have come to share your fate. You and your garrison are to be sacrificed."[86]

Colquitt could see General Whiting lying nearby, but he had not spoken to him yet or relieved him of whatever command he now exercised. First Colquitt had to get the story from Lamb. He inquired about Lamb's wound and Lamb downplayed its severity, figuring the report might find its way to Daisy. Then he outlined the events of the day for Colquitt, relating hurriedly how they had routed the enemy on one side of the fort, only to have the other side overwhelmed, how Whiting and he had been shot, how they had seemed on the verge of retaking what had been lost, how it had all seemed to fall apart after he was wounded. Someone suggested that Colquitt evacuate the colonel, but Lamb would not hear of it—he would not abandon his men. However, General Whiting was also badly wounded, Lamb noted, and *he* was a volunteer in the fort. Would Colquitt take General Whiting to safety? But Colquitt was not listening now. One of his men was there, frantically urging him to leave—the Yankees were coming, the man said—and then Colquitt was gone with no further comment, leaving Lamb and Whiting behind.[87]

◆

Meanwhile, holding his handkerchief aloft on his saber, Major Reilly confronted the first Federal soldiers who appeared in the moonlight—but the troops he met in surrender were not part of Abbott's force. Instead, it was a volunteer force commanded by General

Terry's aide-de-camp, Captain Charles H. Graves. As Abbott and his three regiments had begun their probe along the seaface, Graves had assembled a small force of willing troops and had led them down the peninsula alongside the river, hoping to prevent the defeated Confederates from escaping until Abbott's larger force arrived. Graves had reached the enemy first as he had hoped, but there was no worry about escape: to his surprise, he had encountered a Confederate major who said he wanted to surrender Fort Fisher's garrison.[88]

Graves knew Abbott's troops would soon reach Battery Buchanan, and he was afraid they might open fire on the Rebels. So he took Reilly and one of the officers and hurried across the sandy plain in search of Abbott and his force. Moments later, they encountered Abbott's advance skirmishers and the colonel's assistant adjutant general, Captain E. Lewis Moore. Reilly solemnly presented his saber to Captain Moore, who received it courteously. It was the closest thing to a surrender ceremony at Fort Fisher that night, but there was nothing ceremonial about it. Standing in the moonlight amid a host of enemies, Major Reilly glumly announced defeat and quietly handed over the saber he carried. Moore kept it as a souvenir. However, someone thought General Terry should be the one to accept the fort's surrender, so the men in gray had to announce surrender again when the general came up.[89]

◆

Near Battery Buchanan, Abbott re-formed his force in two lines: the troops of Abbott's brigade advanced toward one side of the battery and the men of the Twenty-seventh U.S. Colored Troops moved forward toward the other. On the riverbank where General Colquitt's boat waited, the general's staff was getting nervous. Soon after Colquitt had gone in search of Whiting and Lamb, a drunken Confederate marine had shown an acute interest in the party's boat, at one point leveling a cocked rifle at Colquitt's aide-de-camp. Now there was an even greater threat—fifty yards away Yankee skirmishers had appeared in the moonlight. They halted and seemed to be reconnoitering. In a moment they would no doubt start forward again. Some of Colquitt's staff began to envision themselves in a Northern prison, and then the general finally returned. Hurriedly, they climbed into the boat and the oarsmen began rowing frantically into the darkness, heading across the wide river toward the opposite shore. Seconds later, as they pulled away, a line of blue-uniformed soldiers strode by just twenty yards away with weapons ready, moving confidently toward Battery Buchanan in a battle line.[90]

It was the Twenty-seventh U.S. Colored Troops, led by Colonel

Albert Blackman. Largely unused throughout the battle, except for clearing the advance of brush and holding down the rear line, now the black soldiers of the Twenty-seventh were present at the end. "As we came into close proximity to the battery, we could dimly discern men on top of it," recalled Lieutenant Albert G. Jones. "As soon as they saw us, they disappeared. We continued to advance, and as we neared the wharf leading out into the Cape Fear River, we could hear the sound of oars. . . . We did not try to stop them, but continued on our way, and suddenly came into the presence of the enemy." Several hundred Confederates, the remnant of Fort Fisher's garrison, stood mutely clustered beside the river, waiting calmly to see what would become of them. Jones confronted an officer and demanded surrender. On the other side of the battery, Colonel Abbott arrived with the rest of the troops—and he too demanded surrender.[91]

In the years to come, no fewer than six Federal officers would claim to have received Fort Fisher's surrender. According to the claims, various Confederate officers surrendered the fort, including Whiting, Lamb, Reilly, Major James Hill, who was Whiting's aide, and Lieutenant George Parker, who was Lamb's aide. General Ames would credit his aide-de-camp, Captain Henry C. Lockwood, with being first to accept the surrender. After the war, the captain would claim that Ames had placed him in command of Colonel Abbott and his troops, that he had gotten to Battery Buchanan before anyone else, had personally accepted the fort's surrender from Whiting and Lamb and had tried unsuccessfully to obtain their swords. His story would gain credibility by being published in postwar journals, but General Terry's staff officers would strongly denounce it. "That fellow Lockwood . . . deliberately lied," Captain George Towle would assert. General Terry's brother and trusted aide, Captain Adrian Terry, would concur: "Lockwood . . . is a liar," he later confided to friends. All the conflicting claims were "nonsense," Captain Towle would declare. "The fort never surrendered to anybody. It was taken by Gen. Terry by force of arms after a long and desperate resistance which did honor to both sides."[92]

The man who probably had the most legitimate claim to receiving the fort's surrender—General Terry—officially made no such assertion. Yet it was Terry to whom Whiting, the highest-ranking Confederate officer present, tendered Fort Fisher's surrender. The act occurred when Terry and his staff reached Battery Buchanan, following Abbott's troops. Both Comstock and Adrian Terry recorded the event. By Colonel Comstock's reckoning it was after midnight. Terry had now been up for more than twenty-one hours, and the trek down the peninsula through the deep sand had been long and tiring. Even so, Terry unquestionably felt elated: he had done it. He had won. He had taken Fort Fisher. With the indispensable help of Admiral Porter's armada, the New Haven law clerk-turned-soldier had captured the mighty fortress, the most powerful coastal fortification in the Southern Confederacy. He had done what General Butler had been unable to accomplish. The reputation of the Army of the James had been restored, even enhanced. Much was still to be done—he knew that well enough. Wilmington still awaited capture, and it would take a full-scale campaign to push upriver and occupy the city. But he had plenty of time for that now—Wilmington was out of business. With Fort Fisher now in Federal control, blockade running at Wilmington was ended forever. Wilmington was sealed. The Confederacy's last major port was closed to traffic. No more foreign weapons and equipment and foodstuffs would be flooding into Lee's army through Wilmington. The lifeline of the Confederacy had been severed.[93]

Terry and his staff followed Abbott's route around the huge battery and encountered the remnant of the fort's garrison—the men who had fought them so desperately for more than six hours. Now the battle-worn Johnny Rebs stood by the river, unarmed and despondent. Adrian Terry thought they looked "utterly cast down and helpless." The general and his staff kept walking, and then, at the foot of the battery's towering earthen walls, they saw the two men whose giant fort had proven almost invincible—General Whiting and Colonel Lamb—now lying wounded on hospital litters.[94]

Seeing Terry's staff, Whiting asked for the commanding officer. A man stepped forward, a tall, serious-faced, tired-looking officer with a dark beard and mustache, attired in a Federal general's uniform. Standing over Whiting's prone form, he identified himself: Alfred Terry, major general, United States Army. Whiting looked up at the man whose army he had been unable to repulse and spoke the words that once had seemed unthinkable: "I surrender, sir, to you the forces under my command, I care not what becomes of myself." Terry responded respectfully, offering his personal assurances. Whiting and Lamb would be treated kindly—and so would the soldiers of their command.[95]

And then it was over. The Battle of Fort Fisher had ended. Terry turned away: other things were on his mind, details requiring his attention, the things necessary to secure his victory. Lamb and Whiting lay quietly among their enemies, sorrowful, but grateful for honorable treatment, waiting now to begin the prisoner routine that would take them North. The war would go on for an indefinite time and no one could predict with certainty what the outcome would be—even with this terrible blow to the South—but for Lamb and Whiting, all the fighting was over.[96]

◆

Colonel Comstock accompanied Terry as the victorious general issued orders for troop deployments, handling of the prisoners and other mopping-up exercises. Then, astride two captured horses someone had found, Comstock and Terry rode back through the fort to the rear, where Terry would busy himself writing a victory dispatch to Grant. Fixed firmly in Colonel Comstock's memory, as he guided his mount past the now silent hills and valleys of the fort's landface, was the climactic moment when the victory was consummated—when General Terry met General Whiting in the final act that ended the great and violent drama of Fort Fisher. In his diary for that unforgettable day, Comstock would record his relief and gratitude for the outcome of the awful struggle: "All praise to the all merciful God for his favor today."[97]

12

"Wilmington Is Closed"

ALIGHT DRIZZLE FELL ON CONFEDERATE POINT MONDAY
morning. It dimmed the dawn, dampened the pines on the
upper point, soaked the peninsula's sandy beach and lay like dew on
the faces of the dead. Gone were the blue skies and high temperatures of the previous days, replaced by morning clouds and a damp
chill. However, on this day—January 16, 1865—more than the
weather had changed on Confederate Point. From this day forward,
the peninsula would again bear the name Federal Point, and inside
Fort Fisher, dawn revealed dramatically different conditions. Gone
were the defenders uniformed in butternut and gray, replaced now
by the men in blue of General Terry's army. The fort's daily ritual
of garrison duty had permanently ended, and the Confederate national flag no longer flew above the fort walls. Instead, atop the high,
sandbagged parapet of the Mound Battery, the Federal Stars and
Stripes stirred gently in the morning breeze.[1]

Fort Fisher's seaface wall was deserted; its long, bumpy line of gun
batteries was unmanned for the first time since construction. The
fort's landface wall was also unmanned, and there a scene of grisly
horror greeted the new dawn. "Such a sight my eyes never beheld,"

a Northern sailor wrote home. "Dead lay in all directions and positions. It was a horrid sight to look at, some mangled terrible. The beach for 1,000 acres is covered with shot and broken shell. . . . Some [of the fort's guns] were broke off in the middle, some at the muzzle, some dismounted, and O, the earth was plowed up. Bodies lay mangled, the Horror of War is to be seen at every hand." A *New York Tribune* correspondent who entered the fort that morning found himself "breakfasting on horrors." Examining the line of landface batteries where Sunday's bloodiest fighting had occurred, he was shocked at the number of Federal and Confederate bodies strewn over the traverses and around the battered and broken artillery. "Among these are entangled Rebel dead in almost every shape and position," he reported, "some standing on their feet and others on their heads, all glaring and grinning. . . ."[2]

Ensign John Grattan, Porter's aide, went ashore and followed the route of the naval brigade, finding it hard to climb the Northeast Bastion even in the absence of heavy fire. "With some difficulty we managed to ascend the steep side of the fort nearest the sea," he recalled, "and stood upon the parapet from which a clear and uninterrupted view could be obtained of the interior and exterior of the immense earthworks. All around us in every conceivable attitude lay the dead and mangled bodies of both Rebel and Union soldiers." In one seaface battery, Grattan discovered all the guns dismounted and surrounded by the dismembered bodies of the battery's gunners. Atop the Mound Battery, he later recalled, one of the battery's heavy artillery pieces "was splattered with the blood and brains of a Rebel gunner."[3]

Sergeant Christian Fleetwood of the Fourth U.S. Colored Troops had won the Congressional Medal of Honor for action near Richmond a few months earlier, but even he, a hardened combat veteran, was appalled by what he saw inside Fort Fisher. "Scarcely a square foot of ground without some fragment or unexploded shell," he wrote home. "Heavy guns bursted, others knocked to pieces as though made of pipe clay, heavy gun carriages knocked to splinters and dead bodies of rebels lying as they fell with wounds horrible enough to sicken the beholder. Some with half of their heads off, others cut in two, disemboweled and every possible horrible wound that could be inflicted. Oh this terrible war!"[4]

Sailor James Cleer of the USS *Maratanza* was so unnerved by what he saw in the fort that he welcomed a drink of captured whiskey. "I never saw such a sight in all my life," he wrote his parents. "There was soldiers and sailors laying around me dead, some with arms and legs and heads off. I [found] a demijohn of whiskey. I filled a quart bottle with the whiskey, took a drink of it and I tell you it did not come amiss. I never wanted it more in my life than I did then."[5]

Exhausted from Sunday's fighting, many of the troops were sleeping late. After marching their prisoners up the beach, most Federal soldiers had gratefully dropped to sleep wherever possible. "In the uncertain light of the early dawn our exhausted men could be seen, with here and there one of the enemy of whom no notice had been taken, lying on the sand wrapped in their blankets where they had lain down in the night," remembered a Federal officer. "[They lay] just where they found themselves after the fight, whether they had joined their own regiments or not. They did not stir, but lay like corpses with their bronzed faces rigid in the slumber of sheer exhaustion." Some troops had been moved back outside the fort, others encamped inside. The men of the 169th New York, the 115th New York and the 4th New Hampshire had bivouacked on and around the fort's huge main magazine.[6]

A few men were up early and stirring, visiting makeshift latrines and building campfires for their morning coffee. Others were plundering. Looting had begun during the night and now continued in the early morning light. Soldiers, sailors and marines went from bombproof to bombproof, searching for anything of value and picking up souvenirs. One man found a Confederate pistol. Another carried away the fort logbook. Some found the medicinal whiskey in the hospital bombproof and now were drunk. "The soldiers were ransacking every nook and corner in search of trophies and other memorials, such as tobacco, segars, clothes and pistols," reported an officer. "I got quite a bundle of rebel checks," boasted a sailor from the *Britannia* to the folks back home. "I will send you some reb letters that I got. I got a gun and a cartridge box and a piece of wire that led to the torpedoes that they were going to blow us sky high with. . . ." For some, it was a looting spree. "I went a ransacking," reported another seaman. "Sometimes I would have a load and then I would throw it away and pick up something else. . . ." An attitude of carelessness affected officers and troops alike. At Shepherd's Battery, quiet now and littered with dead, a handful of junior officers were examining the two field pieces that had guarded the riverside gate. A lanyard hung limply from one of the guns—just as its Confederate gunner had left it. One of the officers flippantly jerked the cord and the cannon discharged its last round, narrowly missing a group of soldiers.[7]

Lieutenant Colonel Zent of the Thirteenth Indiana was up early Tuesday morning. After the last of the garrison had surrendered, General Ames had ordered Zent to post guards at all the bombproofs.

Now, at first light, he wanted to inspect the guard detail. He left his encampment near the Mound Battery and walked through the deep sand to the fort's main magazine. On the eastern base of the huge mound the troops of the 169th New York lay on the ground, wrapped in their blankets and still sleeping soundly. Zent could see their arms stacked on top of the sodded magazine. The regiment's adjutant was just awakening and offered to go with Zent on his rounds. The two walked around the main magazine and over to the landface, where they began going from guard to guard. Weary from combat when he had posted the guards the night before, Zent had failed to put a sentry at the entrance to the main magazine. The giant man-made cavern was now open to looters, and although it contained no valuables, just 13,000 pounds of black powder, men had been wandering in and out of it. Even if he had posted a guard at the magazine's entrance, however, Zent might not have deterred looters: guards at other bombproofs had allowed troops to rummage around inside despite orders. Even so, the lieutenant colonel from Indiana had made a deadly error.[8]

While Zent was making his rounds, Lieutenant George Quimby of the Fourth New Hampshire was making a personal tour of the fort. At the main magazine he noticed a group of soldiers standing around the entrance, examining a pile of debris. "Have you got it all out?" one man called to someone just inside. "I have—perhaps not," a voice replied, "they've got a light in there now." Quimby stopped long enough to ask what was inside. "Boxes of powder," someone called out. The lieutenant resumed his morning walk, but not before ordering the soldiers to put out that light—it could be dangerous.[9]

At 7:30, the main magazine exploded. It was a volcanic blast. Sand, timbers and bodies shot skyward in a giant geyser of smoke and debris. An immensely powerful shock wave flattened everyone nearby, and tons of falling sand buried and suffocated some who survived the blast. Many of the troops encamped around the magazine died in their sleep. "The entire structure, with a dull heavy sound that shook the surrounding country, went up into the air like an immense water-spout, with timbers, debris, and human forms flying against the sky," recalled an observer. "The earth was seen flying in great banks towards the very heavens," reported another, "and the debris were spreading like monster wings, and the shafts of vengeance seemed to be flying from the mouth of an awful crater to the summit of the angry elements. . . ."[10]

The 117th New York's regimental surgeon, Dr. J. A. Mowris, had just entered the fort to search for the dead of his regiment when the magazine blew up. The explosion knocked him flat, then buried him with falling sand. "I felt myself as an atom amid the crash of the worlds," he later recalled.

> Then came a distressing sense of suffocation with a clear conviction that my immediate death was inevitable. There was not only the extinguishment of every glimmer of hope, but a certainty that I could not survive this commotion, or be rescued from the jaws of death. I felt the grave rudely closing round me, and realized the horrors of being buried alive. Then followed the pangs of severing earthly ties. Then a temporary lull in the descent of the debris. Instinctively I thrust out a hand—as the hand gained the external air—extended hope. Again I was depressed and overwhelmed by a fresh fall of sand and rubbish, another agony of suspense, another struggle for life and I gained the atmosphere.[11]

Colonel Zent and the adjutant from the 169th New York had worked their way to the sally-port tunnel when the magazine exploded. Moments before, they had seen some marines enter the magazine and Zent then had realized that he had failed to post a guard there. He sent the adjutant to investigate while he stopped to give orders to the sally-port sentry—and then the magazine exploded. Standing just inside the sally-port tunnel, Zent was protected and survived the blast, but the guard he was addressing and the 169th's adjutant were killed instantly.[12]

An official army board of inquiry would blame the explosion on "soldiers, sailors, and marines [who] were running about with lights in the fort, entering bombproofs with these lights, intoxicated and discharging fire-arms." Zent, however, would blame himself. Three decades later, he would still be haunted by the tragedy. "Oh would to God," he would confide, "that I could obliterate from my memory the horror that was enacted. . . . Thirty years have elapsed since then, yet I can not think of it without a pang of sorrow and regret that is at times almost unendurable."[13]

The rank and file of Terry's army were not so inclined, however; instead, they blamed the defeated Confederates. The troops knew about the buried field of torpedoes outside the fort and were inflamed by a report that an officer had discovered a detonation wire leading to the magazine. "Many were for killing all the rebel prisoners, while others were for blowing them up," reported an officer. From the army's field hospital, General Whiting sent assurances that the Confederates were innocent and that the suspicious wire was nothing but a telegraph line. His claims would be confirmed by the board of inquiry, but the rumors of sabotage would continue among Federal veterans for years to come.[14]

There would never be an exact count of the casualties caused by the explosion. General Terry reported 130 dead, injured and missing. Other officers set the number at more than 200. The *New York Tribune* reporter assigned to the expedition—most likely correspondent Elias Smith—was at the fort when the explosion occurred, and he reported 265 dead and wounded among the three regiments encamped around the magazine. The explosion was ironically similar to the one Butler and Porter had planned: it leveled part of the fort and killed many of the troops inside while they slept; however, the circumstances and the victims of the blast were far different than what the admiral and the general had intended. All day Monday and Tuesday, burial details cleared the wreckage of the blast and removed the bodies of Federal troops. "Visited Fort Fisher and saw large fatigue parties removing the sand and debris caused by the explosion," wrote a Northern soldier. "One of the traverses was completely filled with sand. Some of the bodies were quite warm."[15]

The dead from the explosion were added to the bodies killed in battle. The precise number of Federal dead and wounded at Fort Fisher would never be known. Federal casualty reports conflicted— even General Terry recorded different figures—and Confederate casualties were no more than good guesswork. Depending which sources were consulted, students of the Fort Fisher Campaign would conclude that as few as 670 or as many as 955 Federal troops were killed, wounded and missing in the second expedition. Adding the army's casualties from the first battle and the magazine explosion to the toll from the second battle's fighting would produce a total ranging from 814 to 1,234 dead, wounded and missing. The navy's final casualty reports were precise: 393 seamen and marines were killed or wounded during the second battle, with most casualties inflicted during the naval assault. With the 83 casualties recorded in the Christmas bombardment, Admiral Porter had incurred 476 dead and wounded in the campaign. Total Federal casualties for both battles would range from 1,290 to 1,710, meaning the capture of Fort Fisher may have cost the Federals almost one man for every Confederate defender inside the fort.[16]

Confederate dead and wounded during the second battle were estimated at about 500, more than 25 percent of the 1,900 troops Lamb reported present for the battle. Adding the dead and wounded from the Christmas battle would raise the numbers to approximately 600 Confederate dead and wounded. If figures included the estimated 250 Junior Reserves captured during the first battle, the prisoners taken from Kirkland's brigade during the Christmas expedition and the estimated 1,400 to 1,500 garrison troops surrendered in the second battle, the total Confederate casualties in the Fort

Fisher Campaign would amount to approximately 2,300 dead, wounded and captured. Combined Federal and Confederate casualties in the Battles of Fort Fisher would then total approximately 3,600 to 4,000 dead, wounded and captured.[17]

On paper, the casualties would appear as impersonal statistics, but to the Reverend Henry M. Turner, the chaplain of Paine's First U.S. Colored Troops, the dead and wounded were unforgettably real. Turner presided over the burial of many of the Federal dead and ministered to the wounded of both sides. "It fell my lot to bury with religious ceremony many of our noble dead," he recorded in his diary. "I did [so] with a sensation not felt in any previous instance since I have been connected with the army. It would be impossible to describe what I witnessed among the wounded. But one thing I must mention as fact. I found twice the number of rebels calling upon God for mercy to what I found among our own wounded soldiers. . . . the prayers that went up from the rebel wounded completely bought off my prejudice, and I rendered them every comfort in my power. . . ." The Federal dead were temporarily buried on the open plain about 250 feet north of the landface palisades. The Confederate dead may have been buried there also, or perhaps at the post cemetery. Later, the remains of the battle dead were reinterred in a national cemetery established in Wilmington.[18]

◆

Early Monday morning, the *Malvern* signaled all warships to transfer their wounded to the *Santiago de Cuba*, which would take them to Norfolk for treatment. The warships were also ordered to hoist their colors at half-mast if they had dead aboard. "I shall never forget the sight that greeted me when I was carried on deck to be put into the boat [for transfer to the *Santiago de Cuba*]," recalled Ensign Robley Evans. "The fleet lay just in the position in which it had fought the day before, and it seemed to me that every ship had her flag at half-mast lazily flapping in the drizzling rain." Aboard the fleet flagship, the bodies of Flag Captain Benjamin Porter and Lieutenant Samuel Preston lay in a makeshift morgue, awaiting shipment North for burial. Ensign John Grattan took a last look at his dead friends, remembering all the nights ashore they had spent courting Norfolk's young ladies. "The gallant flag captain was in full uniform, his coat glittering with gold lace," Grattan recalled. "A bullet wound was discovered in his breast. A calm, peaceful smile played around his mouth, but Preston wore a look of agony as his suffering must have been terrible."[19]

By late 1864 Wilmington was the only major seaport in the Confederacy still open to receive the imported munitions and supplies vital to Lee's army at the Virginia front. As the South's surviving seaport, Wilmington had become almost as important as Richmond. *(Leslie's Illustrated)*

In the years before the war, Wilmington had prospered as a pleasant, moderately busy port and North Carolina's largest city. The war had brought dramatic changes to the seaport, and visitors to wartime Wilmington were reminded of San Francisco at the peak of the gold rush. *(Leslie's Illustrated)*

Sleek, fast blockade runners like the British-built *Dee* kept the Confederate lifeline open
by running the Federal blockade into Wilmington with cargoes of war matériel and
consumer goods. After six successful trips, the *Dee* was forced aground by Federal
warships near Fort Fisher, but other ships replaced her and blockade-running continued
to flourish at Wilmington. *(USAMHI)*

Known as "the Gibraltar of the South," Fort Fisher overlooked North Carolina's
Cape Fear River on one side and the Atlantic Ocean on the other. The sprawling,
powerful fortification protected blockade runners using the port of Wilmington.
This wartime illustration depicts key landmarks at Fort Fisher: (1) the Mound
Battery, (2) Fort Fisher seaface, (3) Battery Buchanan, (4) post barracks site, (5)
Cape Fear River, (6) site of Federal advance line, (7) approximate site of powder
boat explosion, (8) Federal fleet, (9) Fort Fisher landface, (10) Federal landing site.
(Leslie's Illustrated)

Confederate Army headquarters for the Cape Fear region were located in Wilmington's DeRossett house. Here, Gen. Braxton Bragg outlined the defensive plans that convinced Gen. W. H. C. Whiting that Fort Fisher would be "sacrificed" to the enemy.
(North Carolina Department of Archives and History)

Fort Fisher's landface and seaface intersected at the Northeast Bastion, rising above the fort's interior plain in the center of this photograph. Colonel Lamb's combat headquarters were atop the crescent-shaped Pulpit Battery on the far right, and the fort's main magazine stood in the foreground. *(USAMHI)*

Fort Fisher's Northeast Bastion looms over the beach behind a formidable log palisade. Confederates atop the fort walls poured deadly fire into the ranks of the Federal sailors and marines, who had to charge across this open beach to reach the fort. *(USAMHI)*

Fort Fisher's Pulpit Battery basks in the sun of a winter afternoon. During the battle, the Pulpit bombproof served as the fort's field hospital. *(USAMHI)*

The fort seaface ran parallel to the ocean in a bumpy, fortified line of traverses and gun chambers. Unexploded ordnance from the naval bombardment lies scattered around the sandy plain in this post-battle photograph. *(USAMHI)*

Fort Fisher's celebrated 150-pounder Armstrong cannon was well maintained by the fort's artillerists, but when battle finally came, the huge artillery piece was rendered ineffective by a lack of ammunition. *(USAMHI)*

A wartime engineering marvel, Fort Fisher's Mound Battery towered sixty feet above New Inlet, the preferred entrance to the Cape Fear River. The Confederate national flag flew atop the Mound flagstaff, which was shattered in battle and later repaired. *(USAMHI)*

Completed just weeks before the Federal attack and manned by Confederate sailors and marines, Battery Buchanan overlooked the Cape Fear River and protected Fort Fisher's rear. When Federal troops assaulted the fort, the battery's guns struck down friend and foe alike. *(Library of Congress)*

The landface batteries closest to the Cape Fear River were the scene of bitter hand-to-hand fighting. The Federal army assault was aimed at Shepherd's Battery, pictured here on the far left with the fort flagpole in the rear. Once inside the palisade gate, Federal troops regrouped on the plain in the foreground. *(USAMHI)*

Dismounted cannon litter the rear of Shepherd's Battery following the battle. Capt. Kinchen Braddy of the Thirty-sixth North Carolina was left to defend the crucial position with a thin force of troops. Braddy placed his men at the riverside gate *(far left)*, and behind the walls of the sandbagged gun chamber. When the Federal troops attacked, they would have to be beaten back by Braddy and his skeleton force. *(USAMHI)*

Fort Fisher's first three batteries resemble a line of bumpy hills on the river side of the fort landface. Three brigades of Federal troops charged across the foreground to assault Shepherd's Battery on the far right. *(USAMHI)*

Beneath the high sodded wall of Shepherd's Battery, a Federal soldier stands guard beside the entrance to the battery's bombproof. During the battle, some of fort's garrison took shelter in the bombproof and refused to come out and fight when the Federal troops assaulted the position. *(USAMHI)*

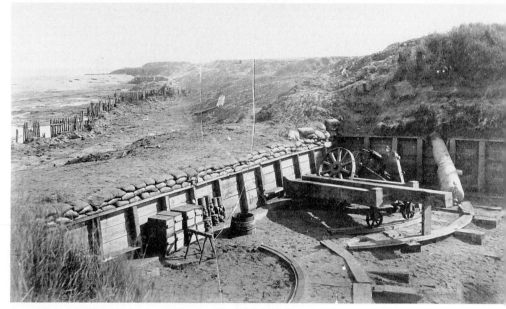

The fort's battered landface stretches toward the Atlantic in this photograph, taken from the second landface battery following the battle. The Federal naval bombardment pounded the fort and dismantled the landface artillery, but left some of the Confederate artillery stacked uselessly against the gun chamber walls. *(USAMHI)*

Midway down the fort landface, the sally-port gun battery interrupts the log palisade, now riddled with gaps following the navy's pounding. Despite the naval bombardment, the field pieces at the sally-port battery did bloody work among the Federal attackers. *(USAMHI)*

Admiral Porter assembled his fleet at Hampton Roads, Virginia, prior to departure for Fort Fisher. Soon after these warships were photographed, they helped unleash the greatest bombardment of the war. *(U.S. Navy Historical Center)*

The USS *New Ironsides* had survived repeated Confederate attempts to sink her and had revolutionized naval warfare as one of the first ironclad warships used in battle. At 12:15 P.M. on December 24, 1864, the *New Ironsides* was granted the honor of firing the first shot against Fort Fisher. *(USAMHI)*

The 3,000-ton USS *Minnesota* went into action at Fort Fisher with forty-eight guns and a crew of 540. When the campaign ended, almost 10 percent of her crew would be casualties. *(USAMHI)*

The USS *Canonicus* was one of four ironclad monitors used against Fort Fisher. En route her decks leaked a foot of water, and in battle her bolts were knocked loose by Confederate fire, but the *Canonicus* used her two guns to drop 441 rounds on the fort during the battles. *(USAMHI)*

The USS *Louisiana* was a decrepit, flat-bottom navy relic, but when packed with 200 tons of highly explosive black powder, the ship became a floating bomb. Her final mission: destroy Fort Fisher. *(Harper's Weekly)*

Unlike the Federal soldiers and sailors forced to endure the voyage to Fort Fisher below decks, the expedition's commanders enjoyed opulent quarters. General Butler's stateroom aboard the transport *Ben De Ford*, pictured here, boasted wall-to-wall carpet and plush furniture. *(USAMHI)*

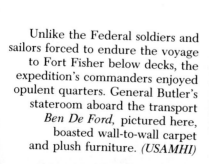

Sailors aboard the USS *Wabash* pose around a 10-inch Dahlgren pivot gun, which would be brought to bear against Fort Fisher. Almost 500 seamen like these from the North Atlantic Blockading Squadron would become casualties during the battle. *(USAMHI)*

Well-armed, well-equipped, and well-fed, troops from the Army of the James stand behind stacked weapons inside Fort Fisher's Pulpit Battery. "They aligned and dressed in line of battle as coolly and precisely as if on parade," noted an observer. *(USAMHI)*

Black soldiers like these from the U.S. XXV Corps had proved themselves in numerous hard-fought contests by late 1864, but the U.S. Colored Troops accompanying the Fort Fisher expedition were used mainly to clear brush and hold down the Federal rear. By the climax of the battle, however, they would be sorely needed at the front. *(Library of Congress)*

Fort Fisher was defended by an undermanned, inexperienced garrison; but when it came time to fight, Colonel Lamb's Confederates proved themselves equal to the task. "If the yankees ever get this place," predicted one of the defenders, "they will never get us all alive." Here, in this enlarged photograph, what appears to be a group of Fort Fisher's Confederates poses on the side of a seaface traverse. *(USAMHI)*

A half century after the fighting ended, well-attired tourists pose atop the weathered ruins of Fort Fisher's Northeast Bastion. Within a few decades of this photograph, most of the great fort would fall into the ocean.
(New Hanover County Public Library)

On the beach near Fort Fisher, an army officer walked the route taken by the Naval Brigade and picked up two United States flags from where they had fallen. In one of the Federal camps, the troops of the Ninety-seventh Pennsylvania counted the bullet holes in their regimental flag, the banner held by Colonel Pennypacker when he was shot down. When they tallied the tears, they figured the flag must have been pierced by more than a hundred bullets. Up the beach from the fort, where the fort's dejected garrison waited under heavy guard, Captain James Izlar of the Twenty-fifth South Carolina carefully examined the blanket roll he had worn throughout the battle. He found it riddled with bullet holes.[20]

◆

Separated into 150-man groups, the Confederate prisoners had spent a soggy, cold night on the beach. Daybreak brought some relief: at least they were alive and the bloody fighting had ended. "After the battle was over, seeing so many of our comrades alive and able for duty, was a cause of deep gratitude to Almighty God," noted one captive Confederate. Good treatment and Yankee rations also improved their lot. Unable to cook for days because of the naval bombardment, they eagerly consumed the Federal hardtack. "They appreciated those Union rations," remembered a Pennsylvania officer, "for those of the Confederacy in January 1865 were poor in quality and meager in quantity . . . composed mostly of coarse corn and not an ounce of sugar or coffee. It was almost pathetic to see how those iron-sided veterans took to the Union coffee. As they drank it, they were heard to say, 'This is the first we've tasted since early in 1862.' Those men had marched, toiled and fought during the last year of the war on rations which might have caused a mutiny had they been served to the Union army . . . and there was not a man among the victors who did not thereby get an access of admiration for the gallant men whom the fortune of war had made our prisoners."[21]

As they questioned their prisoners, some of the Federal troops were surprised to learn that they had faced some of the South Carolinians at Battery Wagner in 1863. Hours before, these men had desperately fought each other to the death; now they joked and swapped stories. At least one Confederate, Private William H. Haigh of the Thirty-sixth North Carolina, was given money by a Northern officer, although the precious cash was later stolen by a less charitable Federal. "As to which was right and which was wrong, the question was not discussed after the battle was over," a Yankee officer observed. "It had been discussed on the deadly parapet and over the bloody traverses. Our brave foemen believed they were right; we on our part felt sure the Union ought to win, but rough veterans, as both victors and vanquished were, each was careful of the other's personal feelings. The traditions of the Southern gentlemen even there cropped out, while we, on our part out of pure respect and kindly feeling, emulated their conduct. But all were real soldiers and always the bravest are the gentlest." Later, the captured garrison was moved back down the peninsula to Battery Buchanan, where they waited for the troopships that would take them to the North and imprisonment. Recalled one captive Confederate: "I was cold, sad and restless."[22]

◆

At four o'clock Monday afternoon, the steamer *S. R. Spaulding* appeared from the south, bearing U.S. Secretary of War Edwin M. Stanton. It was a surprise visit, but Admiral Porter reacted quickly. He ordered the secretary greeted with an artillery salute from the *Malvern,* and soon the portly, bespectacled Stanton with his bucktail goatee was aboard, enthusiastically congratulating Porter on the fall of Fort Fisher. Stanton was returning from a visit with Sherman in Savannah, made more for his health than official business, he said, and he was delighted to find Fort Fisher in Federal hands. When he spotted the U.S. flag atop the fort, he said, he was "almost overwhelmed" by surprise. General Terry was summoned from shore and arrived aboard the *Malvern* with his own salute to Stanton, presenting the secretary with the Confederate flag hauled down from the Mound Battery.[23]

Stanton heaped praise on Terry and Porter, listened intently to their reports of the battle, then dispensed the favors of war to the victors. Terry won two stars, a promotion from brigadier to major general of volunteers, and was made a brigadier general in the regular army. Comstock and Abbott were made brevet brigadiers. Ames was brevetted major general. Captains Terry and Graves, General Terry's aides, were promoted to major. Colonel Pennypacker would rise to brigadier general. When informed of Colonel Curtis's actions in the army assault, Stanton put his pen to a legal-size scrap of paper and dashed off an on-the-spot promotion to brigadier general "for gallant services in the capture of Fort Fisher." Back aboard the *Spaulding,* Stanton also drafted a statement publicly congratulating Terry and his troops for their victory. "The combined operations of the squadron under command of Rear-Admiral Porter and your forces deserve and will receive the thanks of the nation," Stanton wrote, "and will be held in admiration throughout the world as proof of the naval and military prowess of the United States." Stanton then continued north to Fort Monroe, carrying detailed reports of the Federal victory.[24]

He was not first with the word, however; both Porter and Terry had promptly dispatched ships back to Hampton Roads with their initial reports of the victory. Porter sent the USS *Vanderbilt,* and Terry dispatched the transport *Atlantic.* A desire to be first with the news produced another army-navy race, and this time the army won. The *Atlantic* arrived at Fort Monroe shortly after nine o'clock Tuesday morning, allowing the ship's commander, Edward T. Nichols, to be the first to announce the fall of Fort Fisher to the world—and to a chagrined U.S. secretary of the navy. Welles piled public praise on Admiral Porter, but privately he wanted to know why naval authorities had to learn of the victory from the army. How could Porter and his entire fleet get beaten in a race with an army transport? Porter was embarrassed and infuriated. He had issued orders dispatching the *Atlantic* with the official news no more than ten minutes after learning of the fort's capture, and had gone to bed that night confident that the navy would have the honor of breaking the news to the nation. Upon arising Monday morning, he had been almost panicstricken when he discovered the *Vanderbilt* still lying offshore from Fort Fisher. "Proceed without delay," he had signaled. "Wait for nothing." Finally, the vessel had gotten under way, heading northward at full speed, but had been unable to overtake the army's *Atlantic.* The *Vanderbilt*'s commander, Captain Charles W. Pickering, officially explained his delay—crew members from the assault party had to be rounded up on shore—and noted that he had never been censured in forty-three years of service with the navy. Even so, Pickering soon found himself and his vessel transferred to another squadron.[25]

◆

The news of Fort Fisher's fall prompted a national celebration in the North. At his City Point headquarters, near Fort Monroe, Grant ordered the troops to fire a series of one-hundred-gun salutes in honor of Terry's "great triumph." Cheer after cheer rolled through the camps of the Federal armies threatening Petersburg and Richmond, and Federal pickets yelled the news across the lines to their Confederate counterparts. A joint resolution was passed by the U.S. Congress, issuing the official "Thanks of Congress" to Terry and Porter. Assistant Secretary of the Navy Gustavus Fox sent Grant official congratulations, and Major General George Meade, commander of the Army of the Potomac, tendered enthusiastic praise to Grant "in honor of the brilliant and glorious capture of Fort Fisher, which I deem to be one of the most important events which could have occurred at this time. . . ."[26]

President Lincoln was overjoyed. The victory was the primary topic of the president's Tuesday cabinet meeting. Secretary of State William Seward joked with Welles that the navy now had nothing else to do. Postmaster General William Dennison told the group he'd like to have a couple of leftover warships—fast ones—for mail delivery. Lincoln was unusually cheerful, reporting that some politicians were now telling him he could do anything he wished without political liability. In most cases, he laughed, those offering such advice wanted something done under the table. Navy Secretary Welles shared Lincoln's satisfaction about Fort Fisher. "The congratulations and hearty cheer of the people over the victory at Fort Fisher are most gratifying," he noted in his diary. Surely, he mused, the fall of Fort Fisher and the end of blockade running would speed the collapse of the Confederacy. "How soon [the Southerners] will possess the sense and judgment to seek and have peace is a problem," he mused. "Perhaps there must be a more thorough breakdown of the whole framework of society, a greater degradation, and a more effectual wiping out of the family and sectional pride in order to eradicate the aristocratic folly which has brought the present calamities upon themselves and the country."[27]

"Fort Fisher was the strongest fort in the South," proclaimed the *New York Tribune*. "Now for the first time is a really formidable earthwork carried by a direct assault, and in a military view, therefore, the storming of Fort Fisher is probably entitled to be reckoned the most brilliant, as it surely is the most remarkable, victory of the war. . . . The practical value of this success is two-fold. The port of Wilmington is closed absolutely against blockade-running. . . ." *Harper's Weekly* echoed the *Tribune*'s editorial: "The assault made on the 15th and the five hours' fight hand to hand with the garrison of the fort is not surpassed in the annals of warfare. . . . This success is of first importance. The capture of Fort Fisher does not mean alone the taking of 75 guns and several hundred prisoners. It involves a loss to the rebels of their principal port. . . ."[28]

The newspapers were right—the capture of Fort Fisher sealed Wilmington and shut down the Confederacy's last major port. The U.S. Navy's stranglehold on the South was now complete. Even the troops in the field understood the significance of the Federal victory. "To hold our ground is to cut off the main artery of the Confederacy and that is done," observed one of Terry's sergeants. "This celebrated vein of supplies is effectively stopped off. . . . The blockade is now effectual."[29]

◆

The impact of the loss on the Confederacy was equally obvious to Southerners, including soldiers in the field. "I am sorry to inform you that Fort Fisher is gone," wrote a North Carolinian from Sugar Loaf. "It is a sad blow to lose Fort Fisher. . . ." Among the first to learn of the fort's fate was General Braxton Bragg. Although Bragg initially refused to believe the fort had fallen, a firsthand account by General Colquitt left no room for doubt. At one o'clock Monday morning, when he telegraphed the news to Lee and Davis, Bragg expressed shock. "I am mortified at having to report the unexpected capture of Fort Fisher . . . ," he reported. By daylight, President Davis was urging Bragg to counterattack. "The intelligence is sad as it is unexpected," the president wired. "Can you retake the fort?" Bragg would not hear of it—not even from his friend the president. He remained consistent in his thinking, using the same argument that had kept him from attacking in response to the earlier pleas from Lamb and Whiting. "The enemy's enormous fleet alone would destroy us in such an attempt were we unopposed by the land force," he replied to Davis.[30]

In his official report later that week, Bragg praised "the courage and devotion of Lamb and Whiting" and offered no explanation for the fall of the fort. "Without better information than is now possessed," he wrote, "no opinion should be hazarded as to how this misfortune was brought about." He was less charitable in a lengthy letter written to his brother the same day. "The responsibility is all mine, of course, and I shall bear it as resolutely as possible," he assured his kin. Then he proceeded to blame a host of others for the loss: he suggested that Fort Fisher had fallen because Whiting was drunk; because the fort's garrison was composed of amateurs; because the cavalry had let the Yankees slip past; because the high-life atmosphere of blockade running had made the fort's defenders unfit for service. "Blockade running has cured itself," he wrote. "I knew its demoralizing influences, and even before I came here, had urged the President to remove these officers and troops, replacing them by veterans." Things might have turned out differently, he suggested, if he had been put in charge sooner. "The defense of the fort ought to have been successful against *this* attack," he wrote, "but it had to fall eventually—the expedition brought against it was able to reduce it in spite of all I could do."[31]

His brother might have absolved Bragg of all blame, but the *Wilmington Journal* did not. "There is no doubt but that there is strong excitement against Gen. Bragg," wrote editor James Fulton in the paper's January 17 edition. "There can be no doubt either, that Gen. Bragg has attached to him the prestige of bad luck. Unfortunately he always has that prestige. Permanent luck means permanent bad management, somewhere. A man with this prestige ought not to have been sent here. . . . Our port ought not to have fallen."[32]

Others were saying the same—and not just the Southern press. President Davis's political critics saw the loss of the Confederacy's last major port as another example of poor leadership. Some Confederate congressmen even called for the president's resignation. The increased political pressure was too much for Confederate Secretary of War James A. Seddon, and he resigned. Typically, Davis withstood this new storm of criticism and remained in office; although soon afterwards the Congress did create the post of general in chief, which Davis filled with Robert E. Lee. Vice President Alexander Stephens considered the fall of Fort Fisher equal to the loss of Vicksburg or Atlanta. "The fall of this fort was one of the greatest disasters which had befallen our Cause from the beginning of the war . . . ," he wrote. The Davis administration searched in vain for a port to replace Wilmington. Galveston was too far away to be practical. So was the Florida coast. Georgetown, South Carolina, located between Charleston and Wilmington, seemed like a possibility—but in February, the U.S. Navy steamed into Winyah Bay and captured the small port without opposition. Nothing could replace Wilmington and Wilmington was useless without Fort Fisher. Significant supplies of foreign arms, goods and foodstuffs no longer rolled up the railways from Wilmington to Lee's army in Virginia; the lifeline of the Confederacy had been severed and there was no effective substitute. Lee's overburdened troops now found life in the lines even harder. With the enemy poised in force on the Cape Fear River and how threatening their homes, soldiers from Lee's North Carolina regiments began dropping from the ranks at a disastrous rate. By late February, Lee would send an ominous report to Richmond: "Hundreds of men are deserting nightly. . . ." With the fall of Fort Fisher, pressure mounted for Davis to negotiate a peace settlement.[33]

A little more than two weeks after the fort's capture, a three-man peace commission reluctantly appointed by President Davis journeyed to Hampton Roads to discuss a proposed peace settlement with U.S. officials. The commission was headed by Vice President Stephens and included Senator R. M. T. Hunter, the president pro tem of the Confederate Senate, and Assistant Secretary of War John A. Campbell, who was a former U.S. Supreme Court justice. At the last moment, President Lincoln left Washington and joined Secretary of State William Seward at the conference, which was held aboard the Federal transport *River Queen* on February 3, 1865. The meeting failed to produce a settlement. Lincoln offered amnesty to Confederate leaders and indicated slave owners might receive some Federal compensation for their freed slaves, but he rejected the suggestion of an armistice. Instead, he insisted the Southern states surrender, return to the Union and comply with some form of compensated emancipation. Lincoln was unyielding on the question of an armistice—the South *had* to surrender and rejoin the Union. The peace conference was a failure. Lincoln was no longer interested in negotiating a peace settlement, Davis said, and instead now insisted on a "humiliating surrender." The Confederate president attributed Lincoln's change in attitude to the fall of Fort Fisher: the loss of the Confederacy's last major port and the resulting isolation of the South had convinced Lincoln that the death of the Confederacy was only a matter of time. Because of Fort Fisher, Davis believed, Abraham Lincoln was no longer willing to make a deal.[34]

Fort Fisher's capture also affected other crucial negotiations. Confederate Congressman Duncan F. Kenner, a major slaveholder and a wartime proponent of emancipation, had been dispatched to Europe by the Davis administration to win an agreement from France and Great Britain: the Confederacy would emancipate its slaves if either nation would officially recognize the sovereignty of the Confederate States. Kenner was in Wilmington preparing to take passage on a European-bound blockade runner when Fort Fisher fell. His mission was delayed while he searched for another way out of the Confederacy. Finally, he slipped through Federal lines and traveled in disguise to New York City, where he managed to secure space on a transatlantic voyage. By the time he reached Europe, however, he found French and British officials uninterested in his proposal. As demonstrated by Sherman's March, the Confederacy was too weak even to defend its heartland, and now had lost its last real seaport. Neither France nor Britain was now prepared to offer formal recognition of the Confederacy—even with emancipation. At home and abroad, the fall of Fort Fisher was viewed by many as the final nail in the Confederate coffin. Under guard at Fort Fisher, Private William Haigh of the Thirty-sixth North Carolina fingered a roll of Confederate currency and contemplated its worthlessness. "[Now] it is only kept in memoriam of a dead treasury and a fast-dying nation," he told a friend.[35]

◆

At 1:30 A.M. on Tuesday, January 17, General Terry's troops were startled by the sound of another huge explosion. This one came from across the river and it was followed by more explosions: General Bragg had ordered Fort Caswell and supporting defensive works abandoned and blown up. He did not have adequate transportation to move all the heavy artillery from Fort Caswell, Bragg reported to Richmond, so he had ordered the guns disabled and the fort's magazine blown up. The works on Smith's Island were abandoned and destroyed, and so were the works at Fort Johnston and Fort Lamb. Smithville was evacuated and left to the Yankees, and the Confederates retreated upriver to Fort Anderson, which was across the river from his line at Sugar Loaf.[36]

The once-powerful Cape Fear defense system, which had seemed impregnable for most of the war, was now largely nonexistent. Bragg vowed to defend Wilmington, but the *Wilmington Journal* was not alone in its lack of confidence in the general's ability to do so. "The people in Wilmington seem to think the enemy can take possession whenever they are ready," observed one of Bragg's soldiers. "They have no confidence in Genl. Bragg, and in fact the army has little." Confided another: "Bragg has had bad luck wherever he has been and always will. He is too fond of retreating or too fearful of being taken by the enemy." Major Benjamin Sloan, the young aide who had mournfully watched General Whiting head downriver for battle, could not help but wonder what would have happened if Bragg had allowed Whiting to command Hoke's division in defense of Confederate Point. "If on the night that Fisher fell, Whiting could only have been on the outside in command [of] the troops that stood idly by," Sloan later speculated, "a very different story would now be history."[37]

On the morning of January 18, Lieutenant Commander William B. Cushing and a naval landing party from the USS *Monticello* raised the Federal flag over the abandoned ruins of Fort Caswell. Later that day, Admiral Porter moved warships through New Inlet and into the Cape Fear with surprising ease. General Terry deployed troops to occupy the abandoned Confederate defensive works, then awaited the reinforcements he believed were necessary to take Wilmington. By now there was no shortage of Federal reinforcements, and about a month after the capture of Fort Fisher, General John M. Schofield arrived with the U.S. XXIII Corps from Tennessee. Arriving too was Lieutenant General Grant, who viewed the once-formidable walls of Fort Fisher, now his prize of war, and counseled with Terry, Porter and Schofield aboard the *Malvern*. It was agreed that Schofield, who outranked Terry, would command the campaign to take Wilmington, then would drive upcountry to Goldsboro to meet and resupply Sherman's victorious army.[38]

The combined Federal force consisted of approximately 12,000 troops. After an unsuccessful attempt to advance up the peninsula, Schofield launched a drive up the west side of the Cape Fear toward Wilmington. Supported by the guns of Porter's warships, a division of Federal troops under General Jacob D. Cox led the advance. Their first target was Fort Anderson, a large and well-fortified earthen fortification which was defended by troops under General Johnson C. Hagood, now back with Hoke's division. The Federal forces moved aggressively through the swamps and woods to surround the fort, and in the early morning darkness of February 19, Hagood and his troops abandoned the work and retired upriver toward Wilmington. Across the river, Hoke and his troops also abandoned Sugar Loaf and retreated up the peninsula. Now it was just a matter of time. The Confederates fought a series of delaying actions, but it was now obvious to many that Wilmington was destined to fall.[39]

On the night of February 21, with Federal forces poised on the edge of the city, General Bragg made the decision to abandon Wilmington. He ordered Hoke and Hagood to pull their troops from the city's defensive lines and begin a retreat northward. Military supplies, naval stores, tobacco, cotton, even ships at dock were set afire to prevent capture by the enemy. The CSS *Chickamauga* was taken upriver and scuttled, and the railroad bridge across the Northeast River was destroyed. "At 1 AM an officer came around and turned us out and ordered us to pack up and take everything we wished to carry with us and not to make any noise," reported one of Wilmington's defenders. "It was bitter cold and I thought that my feet would freeze. Started and marched through the city of Wilmington, not a word spoken for the Yankees were very close to us. . . ."[40]

By daylight on Wednesday, February 22, a pall of smoke hovered over the city. It was Washington's birthday, but there was no holiday spirit in Wilmington. The residents of the port city, defiant throughout four years of war, now awaited the coming of the enemy. Businesses were closed and the once-bustling docks were deserted. The city was unnaturally quiet. Some people had fled, but most waited anxiously behind closed doors. Here and there, small groups of glum-faced citizens stood nervously on the street, waiting for the inevitable. Braxton Bragg with his legacy of bad luck was gone, leaving Wilmington undefended, and soon the Yankees would be in the city. "I think this has been one of the saddest days of my life," wrote one Wilmingtonian in his diary. "I never had such a hard thing to do as leave all my old friends and home where my childhood's days were spent. I procured a horse . . . and rode over the town for the last time." Wrote another: "I am completely heartbroken, can't eat, or sleep. God have mercy on me, I feel that it will kill me."[41]

Wilmington Mayor John Dawson and a group of men were standing at curbside on the morning of February 22 when a squad of
cavalry appeared on Wilmington's Market Street. These were not
Bragg's men—their uniforms were blue. They galloped up to Dawson and his party and an officer among them politely asked the
whereabouts of the city's mayor. "I am the man," said Dawson, stepping forward. "General Terry would meet the mayor and the commissioners at the City Hall in five minutes," the officer announced.
Mayor Dawson rounded up whatever city officials could be found and
waited at city hall for General Terry, who had earned the honor of
accepting Wilmington's surrender. Five minutes passed, then ten,
then fifteen. From time to time, Federal horse soldiers clattered back
and forth, herding captured Confederate stragglers along the street.
A half-hour went by. Then, faintly, Dawson and the others heard
martial music in the distance. It grew louder and closer. Down at the
intersection of Front and Market streets, a wide column of well-
equipped, blue-clad troops appeared with their battle standards flying overhead and their officers out in front on horseback. They halted
and their officers spurred their horses forward, heading for city hall.[42]

"We entered Wilmington about 10 o'clock A.M. without opposition, passing through the heavy fortifications," reported a New
Hampshire soldier.

> We entered the city with colors flying and music from the drum
> corps, and General Terry and staff rode at the head of the column.
> . . . The sights we saw that day are seen but once in a lifetime, and
> then only by a few. One little Union flag particularly, a genuine stars
> and stripes, was seen timidly fluttering from the second-story win-
> dow of a house, and was lustily cheered by the troops. . . . The
> unbounded joy of the colored people could only be appreciated by
> being seen. It was expressed according to their different tempera-
> ments; some by sitting on the ground, rocking to and fro, lustily
> shouting, "Bress de Lord! Bress de Lord! We knowed you's comin'!
> We knowed Massa Linkum's sojers would come!" Others were
> shouting and singing, dancing and hugging each other, and showing
> the gladness of their hearts.[43]

General Terry and his staff officers galloped up the street to city
hall and dismounted. Wilmington would be occupied by Federal
forces and placed under the command of General Joseph Hawley, a
native North Carolinian and one of Terry's best friends, but Terry
had no intention of seeing Wilmington put to the torch as Sherman
had done to Atlanta, Columbia and numerous smaller cities. Wil-

mington, with its shady streets, towering steeples and graceful mansions, would be spared. "Is this the mayor?" Terry asked Dawson upon dismounting. "It is," Dawson replied. Terry then respectfully removed his hat and offered his hand. Dawson took off his hat too, and formally shook Terry's hand, undoubtedly relieved that the man who now controlled his city appeared to be quite different from the house burner Sherman. In fact, Mayor Dawson and General Terry—the conquered and the conqueror—treated each other so cordially they might have been mistaken for old friends. Side by side, they climbed the steps to city hall, where they would conduct the official surrender of Wilmington.[44]

Epilogue

The surrender of Wilmington to Federal forces was the final act in the wartime saga of Fort Fisher. In little more than six weeks, in a similar ceremony, Robert E. Lee would surrender his depleted army, signaling the collapse of the Confederacy and the death of Southern independence. Already, the dramatic struggle for Fort Fisher was only a memory. The dead were buried and the survivors faced new duties, new challenges, new lives. Nevertheless, the chaotic, bloody drama at Fort Fisher would forever affect the men who fought there.

WILLIAM HENRY CHASE WHITING was imprisoned at Fort Columbus on Governor's Island in New York harbor. Beginning the day after the fall of Fort Fisher, the captured Confederates were shipped in groups North to prison camps. The garrison's enlisted men were imprisoned at Point Lookout, Elmira and Fort Delaware. Some officers were also sent to Fort Delaware, but an ice-clogged river caused a detour to Fort Columbus, where many of the officers remained imprisoned. The voyage north was cold and punishing for some of the men. Private William Haigh was among a group of 600 prisoners who left Battery Buchanan on January 18, bound for Point Lookout aboard the transport *North Point.* "Memory sometimes sickens me with a retrospective view of that motley medley of men, almost stifled and crushed to death," he wrote from prison. "Cooped up in that 'cattle transport' (for such it literally was) midst the darkness of night, the hatches down, men writhing in agony, many blaspheming, cursing and quarrelling, it made one feel that he was next door neighbor to the damned spirits of the infernal regions. Morning after morning came, but still endless waste of waters, tossed and heaving with a winter's storm." Another captive Confederate echoed Haigh's misery in a diary entry: "Were it not for the abiding faith I have in God and the belief that He will do what is best for those who trust in Him," he wrote, "I could not bear this weary confinement, this sad separation from home and those I love."[1]

In prison, Haigh found conditions were not much better than aboard ship. "Never as long as memory lasts will I forget that night of nights, the 22nd of Jan. 1865," he wrote. "Cold, cheerless, raining, sleeting, snowing & blustering—the ground partly frozen and partly slush, we were put into that old rickety tent without fire or fuel to pass the night on the damp frozen ground, with no covering but a blanket & nothing to protect us from the ground. It was the acme of human patience to remain quiet and contented—but that we had to do—*for we had nowhere else to go.*"[2]

The officers had it better at Fort Columbus, but imprisonment was still an ordeal. They arrived in New York harbor at 11 o'clock on the evening on January 25. After processing, they were imprisoned on January 27. Captain James Izlar of the Twenty-fifth South Carolina had never seen New York City and was impressed with his first view of its skyline—until he remembered he was a prisoner of war. The hard reality of prison was soon evident. "My thoughts were busy with home and loved ones far away," he penned in his journal. "O God, bless, console and comfort the wife Thou has given me, and our darling little ones. Keep them safe from harm and reunite us soon again."[3]

General Whiting was still suffering from the serious wound in his thigh. The week-long voyage from Fort Fisher had left him too weak even to turn over in bed, and he was attended by Surgeon Spiers Singleton, who had been sent North with the rest of the fort's captives. One of Singleton's first acts in prison was to endorse a request dictated by Whiting to prison authorities, asking to be allowed to remain indefinitely in the prison hospital. "At present, I am completely helpless and unable to turn in bed," Whiting reported. "I have been seven days on a transport ship in heavy weather and really

must rest." Permission was granted, Whiting remained hospitalized
and his wound began to heal.[4]

Despite his wound, Whiting had found the strength to call for an
official investigation of General Bragg's behavior during the battle.
Three days after the fort fell, while still in the Federal field hospital
at Fort Fisher, Whiting had dictated an official after-action report to
General Lee. In it, he blamed Bragg for the fort's capture. "I think
that the result might have been avoided, and Fort Fisher still held,
if the commanding general had have done his duty," Whiting asserted. "I charge him with this loss; with neglect of duty in this, that
he either refused or neglected to carry out every suggestion made
to him in official communications by me for the disposition of the
troops, and especially that he, failing to appreciate the lesson to be
derived from [the] previous attempt by Butler, instead of keeping his
troops in the position to attack the enemy on his appearance, he
moves them twenty miles from the point of landing in spite of repeated warnings. . . . I charge him further with making no effort
whatsoever to create a diversion in favor of the beleaguered garrison
during three days' battle. . . ."[5]

Unable to get his charges against Bragg delivered to Confederate
authorities, Whiting included them in another dispatch drafted in
the prison hospital at Fort Columbus on February 19. Again, he
called for an official investigation of Bragg's actions during the battle.
"I demand, in justice to the country, to the army, and to myself," he
charged, "that the course [of action] of this officer be investigated."
It was too late for that. The Confederacy was on the verge of disinte-
gration. Whiting's two reports would eventually find their way into
the official record of the battle, but Confederate officials had no more
time for such duties, even had sentiment for such an investigation
gained popular support.[6]

Whiting's wound healed, although he remained in the prison hospital in a weakened condition. On February 28, he felt well enough
to answer a long questionnaire about the battle. Oddly, it was sent
to him by General Butler, who was seeking information for inclusion
into the record of the first Fort Fisher expedition then being compiled by the Joint Committee on the Conduct of the War. Whiting
agreed with Butler's decision to withdraw his troops, and took the
opportunity to go on record with his criticism of General Bragg. "[It]
is a matter of grave charge against General Bragg that the whole
[Federal] force was not captured on the 26th of December," Whiting
reported. "Neither attack was practicable in the presence of the
supporting force, provided that [it] had been under a competent
officer. The first landing ought assuredly to have been captured en-

tirely; and as for the second, although deriving much greater advantages from the different mode of attack by the fleet, and though pressed with great vigor, it is due to the supineness of the Confederate general that it was not destroyed in the act of assault."[7]

In early March, many of the officers captured at Fort Fisher were removed from Fort Columbus and transported south to City Point, Virginia, where they were freed in one of the war's final prisoner exchanges. Captain Izlar went, and so did Captain Charles Blocker, Lieutenant George Parker and others of the Thirty-sixth North Carolina. Surgeon Spiers Singleton went with them. He had taken personal charge of General Whiting after he was shot, but the general's wound was healed now and Singleton had a chance to be free. His two assistant surgeons, Powhatan Bledsoe and Charles Gregory, were freed also. Maybe Singleton had second thoughts about leaving the general, but Whiting was recovering under a surgeon's care at the Fort Columbus hospital, and as a high-ranking officer, he had access to the best of care at the post.[8]

On Friday, March 10, 1865, Whiting died. His death was unexpected and surprised friend and foe alike. The official cause of death cited by hospital officials was the common killer of prison—diarrhea—produced, no doubt, by a crippling round of dysentery. Generations of historians would incorrectly report Whiting to have been mortally wounded at Fort Fisher. His wound had certainly placed him in prison and had left him in a weakened condition, but when death came for Chase Whiting, it came in a form unpleasantly familiar to the soldiers in the ranks. Uncounted numbers of Fort Fisher's former garrison had been carried away by the deadly disease while in prison, and now General Whiting died the soldier's death.[9]

At the end, he knew what was coming and he met it gracefully. All the bitterness and frustration seemed to disappear and for the first time in years, Whiting seemed to be at peace. "I have seldom stood by a death-bed where there was so gratifying a manifestation of humble Christian faith," reported the prison chaplain, who had certainly seen death many times. "I asked him if he would like to see some of the [Northern] religious papers. He said, 'No, that they were so bitter in their tone, he preferred the Bible alone; that was enough for him.' He partook of the holy communion, at his own request, in private, on the Sunday afternoon before his death. . . . That was very sudden to all here, but it was a Christian's death, the death of a trustful, hopeful soul."[10]

Whiting's brother lived in New York; his mother and two sisters lived in Connecticut; and on March 11, his funeral was held in New York City's Trinity Episcopal Church. Whiting's rosewood, silver-mounted coffin was borne down the aisle at Trinity by several Federal officers and Confederate General William Beall, the New York–based liaison for Confederate prisoners. "On the coffin lid were laid beautiful floral offerings of natural camellias in the shape of a cross and a heart," reported the *New York Daily News.* "The face of the deceased was of the handsomest and most manly character." At the conclusion of the service, Whiting's coffin was carried from the church, through a large crowd of curious New Yorkers, and was placed in a waiting hearse for transportation to Brooklyn's Greenwood Cemetery. Thirty-five years later, in January of 1900, Whiting's remains would be reinterred at Oakdale Cemetery in Wilmington, where his widow resided, and in the city he had considered home.[11]

To the very end, Whiting held Braxton Bragg accountable for the fall of Fort Fisher and the loss of Wilmington. After Whiting died, the Federal surgeon attending him discovered an unfinished letter Whiting had been writing when he became mortally ill. Preserved by the doctor, the letter finally reached its intended recipient, Blanton Duncan, who had been a prominent Kentucky Confederate. In his private correspondence, written from what became his deathbed, Whiting was even more critical of Bragg. "That I am here and that Wilmington and Fort Fisher are gone," Whiting confided, "is due wholly and solely to the incompetency, the imbecility and the pusillanimity of Braxton Bragg, who was sent here to spy upon and supersede me about two weeks before the attack. He could have taken every one of the enemy, but he was afraid." Fifteen years later, Duncan would release the letter to the press, and finally, in death, Whiting himself would deliver the public censure he believed Braxton Bragg so justly deserved.[12]

BRAXTON BRAGG received no official reprimand for his exercise of command during the Battles of Fort Fisher. After evacuating Wilmington, he and the forces under his command joined General Joseph E. Johnston's Army of Tennessee in the futile attempt to halt Sherman's march through North Carolina. Bragg commanded a division at the Battle of Bentonville in March of 1865, then returned to Richmond as a military advisor to President Davis. He was with Davis on his retreat south after the evacuation of the capital and was captured by Federal troops in Georgia. After the war, Bragg served as Alabama's commissioner of public works for a while, then moved to Galveston, where he became chief engineer for the Gulf, Colorado, and Sante Fe Railway Company. His primary postwar achievement was his selection of the site for the first railway bridge connecting

Galveston Island with the mainland. On September 27, 1876, while walking with a friend in downtown Galveston, Bragg suffered a heart attack and fell dead in the street.[13]

Legions of historians would debate Bragg's military abilities and many would give him poor marks. "Bragg displayed talent as an organizer and strategist, qualities negated by serious defects of personality and intellect," observed one scholar in a typical analysis. "The story of his military operations is a dismal one of blunders, wasted opportunities, useless slaughters, and ultimate disaster." Ironically, Braxton Bragg's name would be far more familiar to future generations of Americans than Lamb's, Whiting's, Terry's, Butler's or Porter's. Long after Bragg's death, the Federal government would bestow his name on one of the nation's most prominent military posts, Fort Bragg in North Carolina.[14]

ALFRED H. TERRY was hailed throughout the North as "the hero of Fort Fisher." His image decorated the front page of *Harper's Weekly,* his biography appeared in newspapers across the land and he received effusive praise from editorial writers who probably had never heard of him a month earlier. "Alfred H. Terry, brevet major-general United States Volunteers, is the hero of this new success," gushed the *New York Tribune.* "He . . . has won in a single day a national fame and a professional military renown not inferior to the proudest." Amid the public acclaim, the official thanks of Congress and the commendation of the president, some army officers even spoke of Terry as a possible presidential candidate.[15]

Through it all, Terry remained typically modest. "I am heartily sick and ashamed of the wretched stuff the newspapers have been saying about me," he confided to a friend while still at Fort Fisher. "I feel like playing ostrich and sticking my head in the sand, of which there is plenty around here. I tried to do my duty and, favored by the most remarkable weather and God's good providence, I succeeded, and that is all." Despite his embarrassment at all the attention, Terry was pleased by his jump to major general of volunteers and especially by the promotion to brigadier general in the regular army. A regular army commission as brigadier meant he would keep his general's star when the war ended, and it made him one of the rare volunteer officers to end the war as a general in the regulars.[16]

Terry planned to leave the army, however, and return to a law practice in New Haven. Had it not been for Secretary of War Edwin Stanton, he might have spent the rest of his life in Connecticut courthouses, or perhaps in a political career. Stanton insisted that

Terry remain in uniform. He summoned the newly made hero to Washington and appealed to his sense of duty, urging him to accept command of the Department of Virginia and help restore Federal control in the South. Although he was prepared to resume his law career and was being promoted by some as a candidate for governor, Terry reluctantly submitted to Stanton's prodding and remained in the army.[17]

In 1866, he was transferred west to command the Department of the Dakota. Other commands followed, and in 1886, he was promoted to major general as commander of the Division of the Missouri with headquarters in Chicago. He was the first volunteer officer from the Civil War to attain that rank, but it was not that achievement, or even his victory at Fort Fisher, that earned him the most attention from historians. Instead, it was the action of a subordinate—Lieutenant Colonel George Armstrong Custer. In June of 1876, while on an expedition commanded by Terry, Custer and his immediate command were wiped out by a superior force of Sioux and Cheyenne at the Battle of the Little Big Horn. Typically, Terry refrained from public criticism of Custer, even though some of Custer's friends tried to blame Terry for the disaster.[18]

The controversy did not prevent his rise to major general, and he remained in the army for another twelve years, spending most of the time protecting railroad construction in the Dakotas and Montana. While serving at Chicago headquarters, he contracted Bright's Disease, and in 1888 he retired to New Haven. There, still a bachelor, he established a residence with two of his sisters and refused all pleas to enter politics. His illness worsened, and at 4 A.M., Tuesday, December 16, 1890, Alfred H. Terry died at age sixty-three. His funeral, held at New Haven's United Church on the Green, was modest and unmarked by ceremony, except for the firing of a thirteen-gun salute. In Washington, the secretary of war publicly noted Terry's death, and in New Haven, bells tolled in his honor. Elsewhere around the United States, however, his passing received little attention compared to the public adulation that had followed the capture of Fort Fisher. The *New York Times,* which had trumpeted the victory on its front pages twenty-five years earlier, buried Terry's obituary five pages deep and spent the day's headline reporting the misconduct of a Syracuse alderman.[19]

DAVID DIXON PORTER was the only naval officer of the war to receive the thanks of Congress on three occasions. The victory at Fort Fisher obscured the disastrous ground assault by Porter's naval brigade, and the admiral managed to put the best possible face on the debacle by blaming it on the Marine Corps. He was lauded by the press for his cooperation with the army, but in private his attitude was hardly cooperative. "I shall bless the day when I am clear of these soldiers and on my native element again co-operating with no one but myself," he groused to a friend. He reserved his harshest criticism for Grant, whom he privately accused of trying to rob the navy's glory at Fort Fisher. "He wants magnanimity, like most officers of the army, and is so avaricious as regards fame that he will never, if he can help it, do justice to our department," he griped to Navy Secretary Welles in a confidential letter. "His course proves to me that he would sacrifice his best friend rather than let any odium fall upon Lieutenant-General Grant. He will take to himself all the credit of this move now that it is successful, when he deserves all the blame for the first failure to take the place."[20]

Porter's career was also boosted by the victory. As he had long desired, he now rivaled his foster brother Farragut in national prominence. In March, he joined Lincoln, Grant and Sherman for an end-of-the-war conference at City Point—a measure of his new status. That month he also journeyed to Washington to testify before the Joint Committee on the Conduct of War. Committee members had already sailed south to conduct a preliminary interview with him on the *Malvern,* and he was sure they had left with a positive impression. "They will go back thinking I am the cleverest fellow they ever saw," he had predicted to Assistant Navy Secretary Fox. "I don't wear a long feather, big boots and spurs, and have a long sword jingling after me, which I know is very impressive, but I keep a good larder and some good champagne, which is always a passport to a sensible man's heart." In his testimony before the committee in Washington, Porter gave a fairly accurate account of the navy's role in the first expedition against Fort Fisher, although he shaded events in the navy's favor and exaggerated at times. "There was not a blade of grass or a piece of stick in that fort that was not burned up," he said at one point.[21]

At war's end, Porter was appointed superintendent of the U.S. Naval Academy. His four-year administration upgraded the academy and earned him praise among navy professionals. In 1866, he was made vice-admiral, but Farragut, still a step ahead, was promoted to full admiral. Not until Farragut's death in 1870 did Porter attain the stature he sought. By then he was "advisor" to the secretary of the navy, and soon afterwards he became full admiral and the highest-ranking officer in the U.S. Navy. Instead of glory, however, he encountered twenty years of career frustration. He chafed in the bureaucracy, made powerful enemies and was forced to spend much of his time on obligatory tours of navy yards and warships. His intemperate remarks following the capture of Fort Fisher came back to haunt him during the Grant administration, when a political rival discovered Porter's critical 1865 letter to Welles and presented it to President Grant. After reading Porter's bitter comments, including the admiral's statement that Grant "would sacrifice his best friend," Grant summoned Porter to the White House and informed him that their relationship thereafter would be strictly official.[22]

As he had vowed, Porter wrote his share of the history of the war. He produced a ponderous narrative of the naval war and a fairly interesting, gossipy book of anecdotes. He also wrote poetry and novels, although the former went unpublished and reviewers thought the latter should have too. His last years were spent in Washington, in a residence at 1718 H Street. He remained unchanged in habit and temperament. In the summer of 1890, while vacationing at Newport, Rhode Island, the seventy-nine-year-old retired admiral insisted on performing strenuous exercises despite repeated warnings from his doctor. During the regimen, Porter was stricken with a heart ailment and collapsed. He was later moved to his Washington home, where he lingered for more than six months. His mind came and went, and he was forced to sleep propped up on a sofa. Friends and former military colleagues called, but the doctors offered no hope. His old friend Sherman came by in late January, less than two months after Terry's death, found Porter napping and left him a note. "I will be the next one and perhaps I may go before Porter does," Sherman half-joked as he was leaving. He was wrong: Sherman died three weeks later at his home in New York City. A day earlier Porter had preceded him, dying in his sleep at 8:15 A.M., February 13, 1891.[23]

President Benjamin Harrison ordered flags flown at half-mast on all Federal buildings and closed the Executive Department's offices the day of Porter's funeral. Signal guns were fired at navy yards throughout the nation, and naval vessels around the globe lowered their colors. Amid pomp and pageantry, Admiral David D. Porter was buried in Arlington National Cemetery at one of the cemetery's most prominent points. The prime location of the gravesite was no accident—Porter had selected it himself.[24]

BENJAMIN F. BUTLER remained flamboyant and controversial. He waded into the hearings by the Joint Committee on the Conduct of the War with his customary cockiness and ingenuity. The Federal victory at Fort Fisher was made public the day Butler began his testimony—a development some considered a death blow to Butler's case. As usual, the opposition underestimated the eccentric, brilliant Butler. He delivered a well-crafted defense and repaired the damage caused by Terry's victory by producing supporting testimony from a surprise source—the late Confederate General W. H. C. Whiting. When all the political smoke settled, the Joint Committee exonerated Ben Butler. "In conclusion," stated the findings, "your committee would say, from all the testimony before them, that the determination of General Butler not to assault the fort seems to have been fully justified by all the facts and circumstances then known or afterwards ascertained." Butler had won again.[25]

He returned to Massachusetts and for the next twenty years pursued a predictably unorthodox and controversial political career. He switched from the Democratic party to become a Radical Republican. Later he joined the National Greenback party. Then he rejoined the Democrats. Still later he was nominated for office by the short-lived Anti-Monopoly party. Eventually he again became a Democrat. Butler switched political parties, noted one observer, "somewhere nearly as frequently as a snake does its skin." Elected to Congress as a Radical Republican in 1866, he held the seat for a decade until he was swept out in the Democratic tidal wave that ended Reconstruction. He continued his persistent quest for the Massachusetts governor's office, running and losing repeatedly. Finally he was elected on his seventh try, in 1882. He served a single controversial term in which he seemed to offend almost everyone. Even Harvard University, which routinely awarded an honorary degree to the state's governor, broke with tradition during Butler's term and withheld the honor. In 1883, he lost his bid for reelection, but ran for president a year later with two nominations—one from the Anti-Monopoly party and another from the Greenbackers. He had offended much of the electorate, but with the support of labor and the nation's black voters, his unsuccessful race for the White House drew more than 175,000 votes.[26]

Political foes never tired of twitting him as "Spoons Butler," but he knew how to deflect the blows. At one political rally, a heckler posted overhead in a tree dangled a collection of spoons on a line in front of Butler's face while he was speaking. Butler paused until the laughter subsided, then quipped, "These are some of the spoons that I did not get at New Orleans." As good-natured applause erupted, he resumed his speech. Throughout his postwar career, he continued to practice law, shuttling between homes in Lowell and Washington, where he frequently appeared in major cases before the U.S. Supreme Court.[27]

By the late 1880s, his personal wealth was estimated at $7 million. He invested in a ranch in Colorado and another huge spread in New Mexico, and he was president of a Western gold mine. Yachting remained a hobby, and he gloried in his ownership of the famous yacht *America*. In later years, he became a familiar, odd-looking figure in Washington courtrooms. He took to wearing a broad-brimmed hat, and he always came to court equipped with the same lunch—a sandwich and a bottle of beer. As he aged, his girth increased and he shuffled more than he walked. However, he could still leave an audience or a jury spellbound, and during court recess he was usually surrounded by an appreciative crowd eager to hear more of Butler's famous tall tales.[28]

He remained popular with many veterans of the Army of the James. At veterans' rallies like those sponsored by the GAR, he was routinely applauded, and once stood bareheaded in a downpour to pay tribute to his former troops at a veterans' march. He remained active and in good health until the end of his life, but in early January of 1893, he caught a cold and was taken ill while traveling by train from New York to Washington. The cold was followed by pneumonia, then heart failure, and Ben Butler died at his Washington home on January 11, 1893.[29]

His obituary was printed in newspapers throughout the United States and as far away as South Africa. "He was always bobbing up in the most unexpected places and appearing in the most surprising characters," editorialized the *New York Times*, "always fighting with somebody with great vigor and vindictiveness, and neither giving nor expecting quarter, while his fighting seemed for the most part to be undertaken for its own sake. . . . He was a very spiteful politician, but his spite was almost unfailingly amusing, except to its immediate object, and for twenty years he was the leading low comedian of American politics." In a speech delivered a year before he died, Butler had suggested his own epitaph. "When you bear me to that little inclosure on the other side of the river, which I hope will be my last resting place," he had said, "I pray you will put over me for my epitaph: here lies the General who saved the lives of his soldiers at Big Bethel and Fort Fisher and who never commanded the Army of the Potomac." Even in death, Butler wanted to have the last laugh.[30]

CYRUS B. COMSTOCK received little public praise for his role at Fort Fisher, but General Terry reportedly gave Comstock credit for the fort's capture. Late on the night of January 16, Terry came to Comstock's tent after meeting with Secretary of War Stanton and handed Comstock a document. It was his promotion to brevet brigadier general in the regular army. "I was perfectly overpowered," Comstock confided in his diary. "Gen. Terry told [Stanton] that the capture of Ft. Fisher was due to me, more than to any one man. . . . I doubt if Terry would have assaulted if I had not urged it so strongly & think when we went into the fort that Ames & Abbott would have been allowed to intrench til morning & much of the garrison would have escaped if I had not urged that Abbott should go on. But . . . Terry has been only too generous & flattering—the responsibility was all his."[31]

When the war ended, Comstock chose to remain in the army. He became a principal aide to the general in chief in Washington, and after Grant was elected president in 1868, Comstock was a frequent guest at the White House. As an army engineer he directed various projects on the Great Lakes, on the Mississippi, in the West and at numerous American harbors. He was promoted to lieutenant colonel in 1881, and was named to the National Academy of Sciences in 1884. Despite those achievements, his postwar life was affected by personal tragedy. He married Elizabeth Blair, daughter of Postmaster General Montgomery Blair, but after three years of marriage his wife and an infant daughter died from childbirth complications. He was also present for Grant's last days, as the former general in chief and president succumbed to throat cancer. He helped plan Grant's funeral in August of that year, and marched near the head of the funeral procession. He finally received his full promotion to brigadier general several years after he retired from duty. On May 29, 1910, Comstock died of arteriosclerosis at his home in New York City, and was buried at West Point. He received little credit publicly for the capture of Fort Fisher, but forever affixed to the official U.S. Army map of the historic fort would be the name Cyrus B. Comstock.[32]

JAMES REILLY, the last commander of Fort Fisher, spent four months at Fort Delaware as a prisoner of war. In May of 1865, he took the oath of allegiance to the Federal government and was released. He returned to the Wilmington area, where he spent the postwar years as a farmer. He became a celebrity in Wilmington, acclaimed for his role at Fort Fisher. Active in reunions of the battle's survivors, he was always eager to tour the ruins of the old fort with a wartime comrade or a former foe, and he named one of his numerous children Katherine Whiting Reilly, in honor of General Whiting and his wife.

In 1894, he died on his farm near Wilmington, in the midst of family and friends. The year before his death, he received a unique Fort Fisher souvenir from Captain E. Lewis Moore, the Federal officer who had received Reilly's saber near Battery Buchanan the night the fort fell. Moore, retired from the army and living in Massachusetts, made inquiries through Southern publications until he located Reilly. Then he sent the old Confederate a present—the saber Reilly had surrendered almost thirty years earlier.[33]

KINCHEN J. BRADDY, the Confederate captain who commanded Shepherd's Battery, was imprisoned with most of the garrison's surviving officers at Fort Columbus. He was freed in the City Point prisoner exchange in March of 1865, and eventually he returned to North Carolina, where he settled near Fayetteville. Years later, when Colonel Lamb and others began publishing memoirs of the battle, Braddy felt the thin force he had commanded at the riverside gate was unfairly slighted for its inability to resist an overwhelming enemy force. "Seems I have been made the scapegoat of others," he confided to Texas judge Zechariah Fulmore, who was also a Fort Fisher veteran. In a private letter to the judge in 1901, Braddy told his whole story, reporting how Lieutenant Latham and his men refused to leave the safety of the bombproofs when the Yankees were attacking, and how Braddy and his men were overpowered by the assaulting enemy columns. Someone saved the letter, and eventually, long after Captain Braddy was in the grave, his candid account of the battle was preserved for the record at the North Carolina Department of Archives and History.[34]

ALFRED H. COLQUITT, the officer Bragg sent to replace General Whiting, made it safely back from Battery Buchanan to Bragg's headquarters, avoiding the imprisonment that killed Whiting. After the war, Colquitt returned to Georgia, where he farmed, practiced law and eventually entered politics. In 1876, he was elected governor, and six years later he was elected U.S. senator—a post he held until his death in 1894.[35]

K. RANDOLPH BREESE, the admiral's aide who commanded the disastrous naval assault, was rewarded by Admiral Porter with a recommendation for promotion to commander. With his new rank, Breese accompanied Porter to the U.S. Naval Academy, where he served as assistant superintendent. He held postwar commands ashore and afloat and made captain in 1874. Four years later he was awarded command of the USS *Pensacola,* the flagship of the navy's Pacific squadron. There his rise in rank ended. He fell ill aboard his flagship in 1880, and had to return home on sick leave. He never recovered, and died at age fifty the following year—more than a decade before the admiral who had been his career-long mentor and promoter.[36]

ROBLEY EVANS, the eighteen-year-old ensign shot up so badly in the naval assault, eventually became a rear admiral. Hospitalized at Hampton Roads after the battle, he used his Navy Colt to keep surgeons from amputating his battered legs. When the navy discharged him as an invalid, he formally appealed to Congress and won reinstatement. Known as "Fighting Bob" Evans, he rose steadily in rank, became an expert on steel ship construction and played a major role in the government's decision to build a postwar navy of steel ships. In 1891, as commander of the steel warship *Yorktown,* he won national acclaim for holding off the entire Chilean navy with one vessel during an international incident off the coast of South America. Promoted to captain in time for the Spanish-American War, Evans and his warship, the *Iowa,* helped destroy the Spanish fleet at the Battle of Santiago. In 1901, he was commissioned rear admiral, and a year later he was given command of the navy's Asiatic fleet. In 1907, when President Theodore Roosevelt decided to send the fleet on a saber-rattling cruise around the globe, he chose Evans as the expedition's commander in chief. Before the cruise ended, however, Evans became ill and had to retire from active duty. He authored a two-volume memoir—*A Sailor's Log* and *An Admiral's Log*—and in retirement was famous throughout the country. "Fighting Bob" Evans died on January 3, 1912, and was buried with honors in Arlington National Cemetery.[37]

WILLIAM B. CUSHING, the navy daredevil who sounded New Inlet under fire, remained in the service after the war, married a hometown girl and was promoted to commander. On voyages throughout the world, he discovered he was internationally famous as "Albemarle" Cushing. Ironically, after all his narrow escapes in action, he almost drowned in a sailing accident on an icy hometown lake. Following the mishap, his health deteriorated and eventually he suffered a mental and physical breakdown. On December 8, 1874, William "Albemarle" Cushing died in Washington's Government Hospital for the Insane.[38]

JOSEPH C. ABBOTT, the Federal officer who commanded Abbott's brigade, apparently liked what he saw when Wilmington was occupied by Federal forces. After the war, he left his native New Hampshire and moved south to Wilmington. He established a Republican newspaper, the *Wilmington Post,* engaged in the local lumbering industry and was active in Reconstruction politics. He won a seat in the state legislature and was elected to a term in the U.S. Senate, but was viewed by many North Carolinians as just another carpetbagger politician. He died in Wilmington in 1881, at age fifty-six.[39]

FRANK VIZETELLY, the *London Illustrated News* correspondent at Fort Fisher, apparently was sent North to prison for a while along with the fort's Confederate captives. On March 18, 1865, the *London Illustrated News* carried an insider's story about prison life in New York Harbor, filed by "an Englishman who has . . . lately undergone a detention in one of the Federal prisons." Appearing in the same issue was Vizetelly's dramatic on-the-scene illustration of the Battle of Fort Fisher. After the war, Vizetelly continued to court danger as a war correspondent, and in 1883 he disappeared in a massacre of British troops in the Sudan.[40]

EDWARD K. WIGHTMAN, journalist-turned-sergeant of the Third New York, was buried with other Federal dead just north of the fort palisade. His elderly father, New York attorney Stillman K. Wightman, made a remarkable journey to Fort Fisher and recovered Wightman's body. Thus, Sergeant Wightman, killed on the sloping walls of Fort Fisher, was buried in his family's New York cemetery plot. As his father stood beside Wightman's grave at Fort Fisher, the thoughts he later recorded could have been spoken by countless bereaved parents throughout the North and South: "All his life came up before me, and how beloved he was by his parents and brothers and sisters, and what an interest we felt and manifested in his welfare and happiness—and there I stood alone and mourned and wept."[41]

GALUSHA PENNYPACKER, the youthful commander of Pennypacker's brigade, lay wounded in the Federal field hospital at Fort Fisher the day after the battle, when General Terry appeared and read him an order from Secretary of War Stanton. "Sir," Terry read. "You are hereby informed that for gallant services in the capture of Fort Fisher, the President of the United States has appointed you provisionally Brigadier General of Volunteers. . . ." At age twenty, Pennypacker became the youngest general in the United States Army. He would also receive the Congressional Medal of Honor. He survived his wound, although he was hospitalized for ten months and would walk with a limp for the rest of his life. When discharged from the hospital, he returned to his home in West Chester, Pennsylvania as a national hero—"the boy general," newspapers called him. Declared totally disabled by army surgeons, he initially decided to leave the service at war's end. Then he changed his mind and spent the next seventeen years in the army as a regimental commander, first in Reconstruction duty in Tennessee, then in frontier service in the West.

Patient and tactful in the exercise of his duties, he was one of the few Reconstruction commanders to win the widespread affection and respect of postwar Southerners. Throughout his postwar service, he was plagued with health problems from his Fort Fisher wound, and in 1883, he finally took a disability retirement. A lifelong bachelor, he rejected invitations to run for governor of Pennsylvania and instead spent his last years in quiet, solitary retirement in Philadelphia. In 1896, he eagerly responded to queries about Fort Fisher from another veteran of the campaign and closed his letter with the farewell of a lonely man. "I wish you well," he wrote, "do not entirely forget me." On October 1, 1916, more than a half-century after charging up the fort's traverses with flag in hand, Galusha Pennypacker, "the boy general," died of complications from the wound he received at Fort Fisher.[42]

LOUIS BELL, commander of Bell's brigade, was carried to the rear after he was shot down on the bridge outside Fort Fisher's landface. He died the next day, murmuring his wife's name until the end. He was posthumously brevetted brigadier general and his body was sent home to New Hampshire. His son, Louis Junior, six weeks old and never seen by his father, was baptized beside Bell's coffin, then the colonel was buried in a snow-covered hometown churchyard. Bell's widow, Mollie, died four months later of a heart attack.

Young Louis Junior, raised by his grandmother, grew up to become a nationally renowned physicist.[43]

ADELBERT AMES married General Butler's daughter Blanche. Wedlock tied him to the controversial Butler, and he also became embroiled in the sometimes seamy politics of Reconstruction—first as provisional governor of Mississippi then, in 1870, as a U.S. senator elected by the state's "carpetbag legislature." He was elected governor by popular vote in 1873, but his term of office was marked by repeated controversy, political and racial violence, and even a full-fledged riot at Vicksburg. Many Mississippi Democrats saw Ames as the epitome of corrupt Reconstruction rule; Ames viewed the state's Democrats as lawless, rebellious and unreconstructed. His political career came to a stormy end in 1876, when Mississippi's Democrats regained control of the state legislature and began impeachment proceedings against the governor. Certain of conviction, Ames cut a deal: the impeachment charges were withdrawn and he in turn resigned, becoming the last Northern governor to yield control of a Southern state.[44]

The political controversies marred his military fame. Forsaking politics, he moved to New York City, then retired to a large estate near Lowell, Massachusetts. He and his wife had six children, and his oldest son, Butler Ames, became a West Point cadet. The general lived a quiet life in Massachusetts and avoided further controversy until 1897. In February of that year, he traveled to New York City to address an influential veterans' group, the New York Commandery of the Military Order of the Loyal Legion, composed of Federal officers who had served in the war. His topic was the capture of Fort Fisher. What happened next put Fort Fisher in the headlines again—thirty-two years after the battle.[45]

The Loyal Legion's biannual meeting was held at Delmonico's restaurant in New York. After dinner, the tables were moved, the chairs were rearranged in rows and Legion members settled back to hear another recollection of the war. Among those present was General Ames's old adversary, Newton M. Curtis, now a member of Congress from New York. Ames was introduced by the commandery's president, General Horace Porter, and then began reading a fifty-minute speech. His remarks caused a near riot among the aging officers.[46]

The time had come "to right a wrong," Ames proclaimed. "Truth has been outraged—truth [has been] overslow in the pursuit of false-hood," he declared. He then recited his view of the Battle of Fort

Fisher, absolving his father-in-law, Ben Butler, of all blame for the failure of the first expedition. As for the second, successful expedition, Ames gave little credit for the victory to Terry—dead now for six years—and much credit to himself. In Ames's version of the battle, Terry was a mere spectator who wanted to halt the advance and entrench, while Ames led the assault, pushing, driving, taking the battle to the enemy. "I commanded all the troops engaged," Ames proclaimed, "from the first act, when my aide, Captain A. G. Lawrence, led the first brigade into the fort, to the last act, when the garrison surrendered to my aide, Captain H. C. Lockwood."[47]

Ames also reopened the old feud with Curtis, who in 1891 had been awarded the Medal of Honor for being "the first man to pass through the stockade" at Fort Fisher. Perhaps it was jealousy over the medal that prompted Ames to renew the feud, although in 1894, he too had received the Medal of Honor for gallantry at First Manassas. "[Curtis] fired off some guns dropped by killed and wounded soldiers," Ames told a reporter, "that and nothing more did he do to justify the award of a medal." In his speech, Ames publicly belittled Curtis's role in the battle, telling the startled veterans that if Curtis and his troops "had pressed as rapidly to the front as they did to the rear" the fort might have fallen with fewer Federal casualties. Twice during the speech, Curtis angrily rose from his seat but was restrained by others. Finally, Ames finished and sat down at the head table. No one applauded. No one spoke. Then Curtis jumped to his feet and demanded to be heard. The room errupted in applause and cheers. "Curtis! Curtis!" men shouted. "Answer him, Curtis. He didn't put down the Rebellion by himself."[48]

The crowd quieted as Curtis spoke from the floor, refuting Ames's account. He did not respond to Ames directly—three decades later the two still refused to address each other—but instead he referred to Ames in the third person. "Why does that person wait thirty-two years to tell the story of Fort Fisher?" he asked angrily, working himself into a rage. "Why does he wait until General Terry is dead, and then attempt to rob him of one of the grandest achievements of the war? Why does he wait?" Then, flush-faced and glaring angrily with his remaining eye, Curtis stretched out his arm, pointed an accusing finger toward Ames and thundered, "That craven-hearted coward!" His words ignited a howl from the veterans, and now Ames jumped to his feet and had to be restrained. Finally, order was restored among the old soldiers, who then passed a motion censuring Ames and calling for a formal report on the battle from Curtis.[49]

Three months later, Curtis presented his account of the Battles of Fort Fisher to another Loyal Legion assembly at Delmonico's, which was packed with almost 500 Legion members and guests eager to hear Curtis's rebuttal. This time he was calm, and delivered a thoroughly researched, generally balanced and almost scholarly history of the Fort Fisher Campaign. He gave Ames credit as a division commander who "bore himself with coolness and courage," but he made it clear that at the height of the battle Ames wanted to entrench, not fight. "Had General Ames been killed," Curtis speculated, "the battle would have gone on much the same as it did." Credit for the victory at Fort Fisher, he told the crowd, properly belonged to General Alfred H. Terry.[50]

The conflict among the aging warriors was eclipsed a year later by real warfare—the Spanish-American War. At age sixty-three, Ames accepted a command as brigadier general, although he got no closer to the fighting than a training camp in South Carolina. Even as an elderly commander he remained cocky, confident that the Spanish leaders in Cuba were quaking at the thought of facing General Adelbert Ames. "The regulars under me are constantly rejoicing that they have me as commander," he wrote Blanche from camp in 1898. "I know that my old status of Civil War times has not been changed as to the generals of this war. Phil Read told me that the generals at Santiago 'respected and feared me.' "[51]

Curtis may have had the last word with the Military Order of the Loyal Legion, but Ames outlived all the Fort Fisher principals— Northern and Southern—and perhaps everyone else connected with the battle. He was the last surviving full-rank general from either side of the war and lived until 1933. He eventually moved to Daytona Beach, Florida, where he spent his last years playing golf with retired oilman John D. Rockefeller. At about 10 o'clock on the evening of April 13, 1933, Adelbert Ames died quietly of old age at his home in Ormond, Florida. He was ninety-seven, and had become a living anachronism. The day his obituary appeared in the *New York Times*, Coca-Cola, General Motors and AT&T were listed on the New York Stock Exchange; the Soviet Union had a British citizen on trial for espionage; President Franklin Roosevelt was pushing for legislation to protect home mortgages; Nazi Propaganda Minister Joseph Goebbels was promoting a crackdown on Jewish educators; and World War II was but six years away. Amid such twentieth-century events, or even on a Florida golf course, words and deeds at a North Carolina fort in 1865 must have seemed far, far away.[52]

NEWTON MARTIN CURTIS was so badly wounded at Fort Fisher that his men believed him dead. They roughly dragged him off the field, tearing his uniform and cutting his back. Even after he was found alive and was treated, chances for his survival were viewed as so slim that a shipping coffin was ordered for his body. He lost an eye, but he fooled everyone and recovered from his wound. He chose not to remain in the army, however, despite his promotion to brigadier general. Back in home in Ogdensburg, he became one of New York's most prominent figures, first as a customs official, then as a U.S. Treasury agent, a state legislator and a three-term member of Congress. In the New York State Assembly and later in the U.S. Congress, he pushed reforms for the mentally ill and elimination of capital punishment. He lectured frequently on both issues, and on the history of the Civil War. Throughout his postwar life, he was active in Northern veterans' groups, serving as state commander of the GAR and participating in numerous reunions. In 1906, after his retirement from Congress, he chronicled the war's first two years in a history entitled *From Bull Run to Chancellorsville.*[53]

His wife Emeline died in 1888, and he never remarried. He spent his last years in New York City, serving as inspector general of the National Soldiers' Home and working on a survey of American history. By New Year's of 1910, he had written about half the manuscript, which he called "The Making and Welding of the Nation." On Saturday, January 8, 1910, he carried copies of the unfinished book to friends around the city. "I want you to read it," he told them. "I might not be able to finish it." That afternoon, near his home at 20 Irving Place, Curtis collapsed in the street, struck down this time by what appeared to be a ruptured brain aneurysm. Bystanders carried him into the nearby offices of Consolidated Gas Company and summoned a physician, but the seventy-four-year-old general was dead when the doctor arrived. Twenty-three years later, upon the death of Adelbert Ames, the *New York Times* would devote seven paragraphs to Ames's Reconstruction controversies, but would cite his role at Fort Fisher in a single sentence. In reporting Curtis's death in 1910, however, the *Times* obituary gave no less than fifty-four lines of type to Curtis' exploits in the battle. The story was topped by a headline Curtis would have relished: it identified him as "the Hero of Fort Fisher."[54]

WILLIAM LAMB became a three-term mayor of Norfolk. It was perhaps the highlight of his postwar life, which was marked as much by hardship as by success. After the fall of Fort Fisher, he was put aboard the USS *California* to be transported North with the other captives as a prisoner of war. En route, however, Lieutenant James

Parker, one of the Federal naval officers Lamb had tried his best to slay, learned Lamb's home was in Norfolk and arranged for him to be put ashore at nearby Fort Monroe. While the other officers and troops from Fort Fisher continued the voyage to New York and prison, Lamb was hospitalized in the U.S. Army's Chesapeake Hospital. Parker's intervention might have saved Lamb's life; at the very least it meant he was hospitalized where he could be aided by family, instead of spending months in a distant prison.[55]

Daisy Lamb had no idea what had become of her husband. The day after Fort Fisher was captured, she persuaded Confederate authorities to let her try to reach him through the enemy lines. Escorted by General Hoke's adjutant general, who held up a flag of truce, she approached the Federal rear line and was halted by pickets from the U.S. Colored Troops. A Federal officer came forward, and she made her case to him—but without success. She apparently did learn Lamb was alive, although wounded, but she was not allowed to go to him nor was she told what would become of him. Unable to obtain any more information, she took the children and went to Wilmington, then back home to her parents in Providence, Rhode Island. Finally, somehow, word came that Lamb was hospitalized as a prisoner of war at Fort Monroe.[56]

She was determined to reach him and this time, coming with her father from Rhode Island, she succeeded. "My precious wife arrived today with Pa from Providence," Lamb wrote in his diary on March 22. "I am better." Afterwards, with Daisy occupying a nearby room, Lamb's situation steadily improved. On the night of April 9, he was awakened by a middle-of-the-night celebration by Fort Monroe's Federal troops—drum rolls, blaring bands and the whooping of drunken soldiers signaled Lee's surrender. Lamb knew the war was over. Two weeks later, he took the oath of allegiance to the U.S. Constitution, "deeming further resistance useless & wrong & believing a life in prison could do no one good & that it would result in my death." On May 1, he left the hospital as a free man and went North with Daisy to her family home in Rhode Island. In the fall, a team of surgeons operated on his hip and removed the Yankee Minié ball that had struck him down at Fort Fisher. Gratefully, Lamb gave the big bullet to one of the physicians as a souvenir. He gradually recovered from the wound, although he would be on crutches for seven years to come, and returned home to Norfolk.[57]

There he became an agent for some of the British shipping lines he had grown to know so well during the war, but conditions in the shattered South frustrated his hopes of prosperity. He suppressed his interest in politics to concentrate on business affairs and his attempts to aid his hometown. He became head of the Norfolk Board of Trade and president of Norfolk's First National Bank, but the bank failed and Lamb was left with $20,000 in debts.[58]

His political fortunes were brighter. He was chosen as a delegate to the Democratic National Convention in 1875, and enjoyed the support of local Republicans as well. In 1880, a Democratic-Republican coalition elected him to his first term as mayor of Norfolk, enabling him to hold the post once held by his father and grandfather. Gradually, as he struggled to improve conditions in his city, Lamb came to view the Republican party as more supportive of the free enterprise system, and in 1882, he joined the Republican ranks he had attacked in his prewar newspaper editorials. He declined a fourth term as mayor, but remained active in party politics, serving as a delegate to the 1888 Republican National Convention. Eventually, however, Lamb became disillusioned with both parties. He concentrated instead on other forms of public service, promoting a local orphanage, boosting development of Phi Beta Kappa, serving on William and Mary's board of visitors and—despite his personal financial problems—donating thousands to aging and destitute Confederate veterans.[59]

Amid the often harsh life of the postwar South, memories of the historic struggle at Fort Fisher seemed to become increasingly important to Lamb. In 1875, he spearheaded a reunion of Fort Fisher survivors in Wilmington. The veterans formed the Fort Fisher Confederate Survivors Association, planned more reunions and urged Lamb to write a history of the fort's defense. He did, first for newspapers and magazines, then for *Century Magazine*'s immensely popular four-volume work, *Battles and Leaders of the Civil War,* which was published in 1888.[60]

The same year, at the Republican National Convention, Lamb was introduced to General Newton Martin Curtis, and the former enemies became intimate friends. Lamb, who referred to Curtis as "my friend the enemy," was a favored guest at Curtis's home in Ogdensburg, and Curtis joined Lamb for reunions and visits to Fort Fisher. On one trip in the 1890s, Lamb and Curtis walked together through the long-deserted ruins of the fort. The overgrown, windswept batteries were quiet now, but the two old soldiers could still see the chaos and violence that covered the once-bloodied ground some thirty years before. Curtis walked over the assault route, noted where he and his troops had scaled the wall at Shepherd's Battery and pointed out where he had fallen wounded. Lamb explained how the fort was defended, pointed out the spot where Whiting fell at the head of his counterattack and identified the spot where he too was shot. At one point during the visit, Lamb and Curtis ventured out in the Cape Fear in a small boat with a local fisherman and a reporter from the *Wilmington Messenger.* While trying to put ashore, the oarsman grounded the boat in knee-deep water. Curtis took off his shoes, rolled up his trouser legs and waded ashore, but Lamb had been in frail health and was worried about getting wet. Still robust in his sixites, Curtis offered to carry Lamb ashore on his back. Instead, the newspaper reporter did so, and afterwards realized what a story he had missed: had he not intervened, he could have witnessed the Federal officer who led the assault on Fort Fisher going ashore three decades later with the fort's Confederate commander on his back.[61]

Through the ups and downs of the depression-ridden postwar years, Daisy remained the center of Lamb's attention, and the two appeared to enjoy a generally happy home life. Daisy gave Lamb eleven children, six of whom did not live beyond infancy. Maria, Dick, Willie, Madge and Henry Whiting—who was named for General Whiting—all reached adulthood. At age fifty-four, Daisy contracted pneumonia, and on March 30, 1892, she died. "The world is absolutely a different place," Lamb wrote in his diary soon afterwards. "I seem to have no settled plans for the future; for everything I did or planned was for her pleasure or comfort, or with a view to contributing to it in the future."[62]

Lamb never remarried. He plunged into more public service, more veterans' activities and new business deals, but without Daisy life was even harder. More business ventures failed, investment partners died and the South's economic climate remained bleak. In his seventies, Lamb tried again to establish another business, but failed and for a while was almost penniless. Despite the financial setbacks, he remained a respected figure in the South, and, even in old age, he remained generally optimistic and resourceful. To make ends meet, he sold the family home in late 1906, and moved into an apartment with one of his daughters. About a year later, he was appointed auditor in a court case at a retainer of $100 a month— more than enough to provide financial relief in the South of his day. He had suffered his share of hard blows, but he nevertheless considered himself blessed by God. "I should be very ungrateful if I did not acknowledge that a kind Providence has given me more success than I deserved," he told a magazine interviewer near the end of his life.[63]

In February of 1909, at age seventy-three, a sprained ankle sent him to bed. He had been fighting a cold for several weeks, and with the sprain, his frail health seemed to wither. On March 4, after keeping a personal diary day after day for more than half a century, he logged his last entry—"Stormy with snow." He hung on to life for a few more weeks, but at six o'clock on the morning of Tuesday, March 23, 1909, he died. Many histories of the war would ignore William Lamb—the Confederacy collapsed before his promotion to general was confirmed—but to a generation of Southerners, *he* was "the Hero of Fort Fisher." He had selected Daisy's gravesite in Norfolk's Elmwood Cemetery, and he was buried there beside her. For seventeen years, the spot had lain waiting.[64]

FORT FISHER after the war became an odd and impressive curiosity—a deserted, monster fortification swept by winds and worn by time. One of the first tourists to visit there was journalist Whitelaw Reid, who viewed the fort on a Southern tour at war's end. "The ground was covered with showers of musket balls," he wrote. "Behind every traverse could be found little heaps of English-made cartridges, which the Rebel sharpshooters had laid out for the convenience of rapid firing. . . . Fragments of shells lay everywhere over the works. Behind them were great heaps of shells, bayonets, broken muskets and other fragments of iron, which were being dug out and collected to be sold for old iron."[65]

The veterans came, relived the old memories of those violent hours and left. Slowly the Atlantic winds wore down the fort's towering outline. The bombproofs caved in and thickets of undergrowth began to take over the parapets and the plain. As the years passed and the veterans aged, memories of the war mellowed and the Federal government began to convert former battlefields into national parks. In 1907, Wilmington hosted a reunion of Fort Fisher veterans, including old warriors from the North. More than fifty Federal survivors of the battle attended, joining twice as many old Confederates for celebration and speeches in Wilmington. Led by Colonel Lamb, they sang "Dixie" and "The Star-Spangled Banner," and went downriver to visit Fort Fisher. There they relived the battle, recalled their exploits and remembered the names and faces of the dead. It was a memorable, emotional experience and it produced a campaign to have Fort Fisher preserved as a national battlefield park.[66]

A bill requesting $40,000 to purchase and preserve the fort was introduced in Congress, pushed by Northern and Southern veterans of the battles. On January 16, 1909, as a snowstorm blanketed Washington, a handful of old soldiers from the Fort Fisher Survivors Association appeared before the House Committee on Military Affairs and testified in support of the legislation. Joining them was former Lieutenant Commander James Parker, now a seventy-eight-year-old retired admiralty lawyer from New Jersey. "I think it was one of the decisive battles," Parker told the politicians. "There were only a few of the battles which, in my judgment, were decisive—Vicksburg, Chattanooga, Lookout Mountain, Gettysburg, Petersburg, Appomattox, and last but not least, Fort Fisher."[67]

Despite assurances from the politicians, the bill died in committee. Maybe there were too many requests for battlefield funding. Maybe the snowstorm was to blame—it had kept Colonel Lamb and a majority of the committee from attending the hearing. The old veterans tried again the next year, but without success. By then Colonel Lamb was dead. So was General Curtis, and so were other influential veterans. The campaign to make Fort Fisher a national park died, and with it died the best hope of preserving the old fort.[68]

The massive, sprawling ruin became a remote oddity, a destination for picnics, campouts and day-long treks by history buffs. And then it began to fall into the sea. In 1881, the U.S. Army Corps of Engineers had closed New Inlet in an attempt to improve navigation of the Cape Fear River. Damming the inlet caused a dramatic shift in the shoreline, and the beach off Fort Fisher began to erode rapidly into the ocean. After more than 400 feet of beach was lost, the erosion stopped and the process began to gradually reverse itself, although the ocean was now much closer to the fort's towering walls. Then in 1928, as beach resorts began to arise along the Carolina coasts, the New Hanover County Board of Commissioners established a mining operation on the beach off Fort Fisher. Tons of natural "coquina rock" were dredged up and hauled away to build a road that would improve access to the fort from Kure Beach, a nearby beachside community undergoing commercial development. The shelf of coquina was a natural sea wall, and when it was removed, the ocean began to devour Fort Fisher's beachfront at an alarming rate.[69]

By the mid-1930s, the Northeast Bastion, where Lamb and Whiting had repelled Porter's naval brigade, had disappeared into the Atlantic and still the ocean was slowly driving inward. Various groups of concerned Wilmingtonians beseeched the state and federal governments for help, but with little result. "The North Carolina coast is gradually sinking and the eventual submergence of Fort Fisher is inevitable," one expert told a citizen's group in 1931. "Kiss it goodbye and save your money is my advice." Fort Fisher did receive some government attention in the first half of the twentieth century, but much of the official activity simply damaged the site even more. During World War II, Federal Point was reactivated as a small military post and the federal government bulldozed part of the fort's landface wall to build an airstrip. Most of Battery Buchanan was razed for building material and modern ammunition bunkers were constructed along what was left of Fort Fisher's seaface wall.[70]

Private citizens continued to push for preservation of the fort's ruins. The county had acquired a small tract of land south of the fort landface, and on it the United Daughters of the Confederacy erected an impressive monument. In 1958, as the Civil War centennial approached, the state of North Carolina did what the federal government had failed to do a half-century earlier and acquired what was left of the old fort. Fort Fisher was designated a state historic site, a state-supported museum was constructed nearby and attempts began to preserve the riverside half of the fort landface. Expensive efforts were made to halt the beach erosion, but the Atlantic continued to gnaw away steadily at the site. By the centennial of the fort's capture, the ocean had accomplished what Ben Butler's powder boat and Admiral Porter's fleet had failed to do a hundred years earlier: most of Fort Fisher—the Confederate Goliath—had disappeared, washed into the sea.[71]

Appendix:
The Opposing Forces
at Fort Fisher

January 13–15, 1865

U.S. ARMY—Major General Alfred H. Terry

TWENTY-FOURTH ARMY CORPS

SECOND DIVISION

Brig. Gen. Adelbert Ames

First Brigade

Bvt. Brig. Gen. N. Martin Curtis
Maj. Ezra L. Walrath

3rd New York:
  Capt. James H. Reeves
  Lieut. Edwin A. Behan
112th New York, Col. John F. Smith
117th New York, Lieut. Col. Francis X. Meyer
142d New York, Lieut. Col. Albert M. Barney

Second Brigade

Col. Galusha Pennypacker
Maj. Oliver P. Harding
47th New York, Capt. Joseph M. McDonald
48th New York:
  Lieut. Col. William B. Coan
  Maj. Nere A. Elfwing
76th Pennsylvania:
  Col. John S. Littell
  Maj. Charles Knerr
97th Pennsylvania, Lieut. John Wainwright
203d Pennsylvania:
  Col. John W. Moore
  Lieut. Col. Jonas W. Lyman
  Maj. Oliver P. Harding
  Capt. Heber B. Essington

Third Brigade

Col. Louis Bell
Col. Alonzo Alden
13th Indiana, Lieut. Col. Samuel M. Zent
4th New Hampshire, Capt. John H. Roberts
115th New York, Lieut. Col. Nathan J. Johnson
169th New York:
  Col. Alonzo Alden
  Lieut. Col. James A. Colvin

Second Brigade, First Division (temporarily attached to Second Division)

Col. Joseph C. Abbot
6th Connecticut, Col. Alfred P. Rockwell
7th Connecticut:
  Capt. John Thompson
  Capt. William S. Marble
3d New Hampshire, Capt. William H. Trickey
7th New Hampshire, Lieut. Col. Augustus W. Rollins
16th New York Heavy Artillery (detachment), Maj. Frederick W. Prince

TWENTY-FIFTH ARMY CORPS

THIRD DIVISION

Brig. Gen. Charles J. Paine

Second Brigade

Col. John W. Ames
4th U. S. Colored Troops, Lieut. Col. George Rogers
6th U. S. Colored Troops, Maj. Augustus S. Boernstein
30th U. S. Colored Troops, Lieut. Col. Hiram A. Oakman
39th U. S. Colored Troops, Col. Ozora P. Stearns

Third Brigade

Col. Elias Wright
1st U. S. Colored Troops, Lieut. Col. Giles H. Rich
5th U. S. Colored Troops, Maj. William R. Brazie
10th U. S. Colored Troops, Lieut. Col. Edward H. Powell
27th U. S. Colored Troops, Bvt. Brig. Gen. Albert M. Blackman
37th U. S. Colored Troops, Col. Nathan Goff, Jr.

ARTILLERY

1st Connecticut Heavy, Companies B, G, and L, Capt. William G. Pride
New York Light, 16th Battery, Capt. Richard H. Lee
3d United States, Battery E, Lieut. John R. Myrick

ENGINEERS

15th New York, Companies A and I, Lieut. Keefe S. O'Keefe

January 13–15, 1865

CONFEDERATE ARMY—General Braxton Bragg (department commander)
Major General W. H. C. Whiting (district commander)

GARRISON OF FORT FISHER

Col. William Lamb
10th N.C. (1st Artillery, 2 companies)
  Maj. James Reilly
36th N.C. (2d Artillery, 10 companies)
  Maj. James M. Stevenson (ill)
  Capt. Daniel Munn
40th N.C. (4 companies)
1st N.C. Artillery Battalion (1 company)
  Capt. James L. McCormick

3d N.C. Artillery Battalion (1 company)
   Capt. John M. Sutton
13th N.C. Artillery Battalion (1 company)
   Capt. Z. T. Adams
Naval Detachment
   Capt. A.C. Van Benthuysen
Battery Buchanan
   Capt. R. F. Chapman, C.S.N.

HOKE'S DIVISION

Maj. Gen. Robert F. Hoke

Clingman's Brigade

8th N.C.
31st N.C.
57th N.C.
61st N.C.

Colquitt's Brigade

Brig. Gen. A. H. Colquitt

6th Ga.
19th Ga.
23d Ga.
27th Ga.
28th Ga.

Hagood's Brigade

11th S.C.
21st S.C.
25th S.C.
27th S.C.
7th S.C. Battalion

Kirkland's Brigade

17th N.C.
42d N.C.
50th N.C.
66th N.C.

Cavalry

Col. T. J. Lipscomb

2d S.C.

NAVAL FORCE AT FORT FISHER,
December 23–26, 1864, and January 13–16, 1865

NORTH ATLANTIC SQUADRON

Rear-Admiral David D. Porter, Commanding. Lieutenant Commander K. R. Breese, Fleet Captain. Lieut. M. W. Sanders, Signal Officer. Lieutenant S. W. Terry and Lieutenant S. W. Preston (k), Aides.

FIRST DIVISION, Commodore Henry K. Thatcher; SECOND DIVISION, Commodore Joseph Lanman; THIRD DIVISION, Commodore Jas. Findlay Schenck; FOURTH DIVISION, Commodore S. W. Godon; IRONCLAD DIVISION, Commodore Wm. Radford.

FLAGSHIP—*Malvern*, Lieut. William B. Cushing (1st attack); Lieut. B. H. Porter (k), (2nd attack).

IRONCLADS—*Canonicus*, Lieut. Comm. George E. Belknap. *Mahopac*, Lieut. Comm. E. E. Potter (1st attack); Lieut. Comm. A. W. Weaver (2nd attack). *Monadnock*, Comm. E. G. Parrott. *New Ironsides*, Commodore William Radford. *Saugus*, Comm. E. R. Colhoun.

SCREW FRIGATES—*Colorado*, Commodore H. K. Thatcher. *Minnesota*, Commodore Joseph Lamman. *Wabash*, Capt. M. Smith.

SIDE-WHEEL STEAMERS (1st class)—*Powhatan*, Commodore J. F. Schenck. *Susquehanna*, Commodore S. W. Godon.

SCREW SLOOPS—*Brooklyn*, Capt. James Alden. *Juniata*, Capt. W. R. Taylor (1st attack); Lieut. Comm. T. S. Phelps (2nd attack). *Mohican*, Comm. D. Ammen. *Shenandoah*, Capt. D. B. Ridgely. *Ticonderoga*, Capt. C. Steedman. *Tuscarora*, Comm. J. M. Frailey.

SCREW GUN-VESSELS—*Kansas*, Lieut. Comm. P. G. Watmough. *Maumee*, Lieut. Comm. R. Chandler. *Nyack*, Lieut. Comm. L. H. Newman. *Pequot*, Lieut. Comm. D. L. Braine. *Yantic*, Lieut. Comm. T. C. Harris.

SCREW GUNBOATS—*Chippewa*, Lieut. Comm. A. W. Weaver (1st attack); Lieut. Comm. E. E. Potter (2nd attack). *Huron*, Lieut. Comm. T. O. Selfridge. *Seneca*, Lieut. Comm. M. Sicard. *Unadilla*, Lieut. Comm. F. M. Ramsay.

DOUBLE-ENDERS—*Iosco*, Comm. John Guest. *Mackinaw*, Comm. J. C. Beaumont. *Maratanza*, Lieut. Comm. G. W. Young. *Osceola*, Comm. J. M. B. Clitz. *Pawtuxet*, Comm. J. H. Spotts. *Pontoosuc*, Lieut. Comm. Wm. G. Temple. *Sassacus*, Lieut. Comm. J. L. Davis. *Tacony*, Lieut. Comm. W. T. Truxtun.

MISCELLANEOUS VESSELS—*Fort Jackson*, Capt. B. F. Sands. *Monticello*, Act. V. Lieut. D. A. Campbell (1st attack); Lieut. W. B. Cushing (2nd attack). *Nereus*, Comm. J. C. Howell. *Quaker City*, Comm. W. F. Spicer. *Rhode Island*, Comm. S. D. Trenchard. *Santiago de Cuba*, Capt. O. S. Glisson. *Vanderbilt*, Capt. C. W. Pickering.

POWDER VESSEL—*Louisiana*, Com. A. C. Rhind (1st attack; blown up).

RESERVE—*A. D. Vance*, Lieut. Comm. J. H. Upshur. *Alabama*, Act. V. Lieut. Frank Smith (1st attack); Act. V. Lieut. A. R. Langthorne (2nd attack). *Britannia*, Act. V. Lieut. Samuel Huse (1st attack); Act. V. Lieut.

W. A. Sheldon (2nd attack). *Cherokee,* Act. V. Lieut. W. E. Denison. *Emma,* Act. V. Lieut. T. C. Dunn (1st attack); Act. V. Lieut. J. M. Williams (2nd attack). *Gettysburg,* Lieut. Comm. R. H. Lamson (w). *Governor Buckingham,* Act. V. Lieut. J. McDiarmid. *Howquah,* Act. V. Lieut. J. W. Balch. *Keystone State,* Comm. H. Rolando. *Lilian,* Act. V. Lieut. T. A. Harris. *Little Ada,* Acting Master S. P. Crafts. *Moccasin,* Act. Ens. James Brown. *Nansemond,* Act. Master J. H. Porter. *Tristram Shandy,* Act. Ens. Ben. Wood (1st attack); Act. V. Lieut. F. M. Green (2nd attack). *Wilderness,* Acting Master H. Arey.

At the second attack the fleet was composed of the same vessels, with the exception of the *Nyack, Keystone State,* and *Quaker City.* The following additions were also made to the fleet: *Montgomery,* Act. V. Lieut. T. C. Dunn; *R. R. Cuyler,* Comm. C. H. B. Caldwell; *Aries,* Act. V. Lieut. F. S. Wells; *Eolus,* Acting Master E. S. Keyser; *Fort Donelson,* Acting Master G. W. Frost; and *Republic,* Act. Ens. J. W. Bennett.

ARMY TRANSPORT VESSELS

McClellan (headquarters)
Atlantic
Varuna
Tonawanda
De Molay
Thames
Champion
Commodore DuPont
Montauk
Idaho
Euterpe
L. C. Livingston
Prometheus
General Lyon
California
Weybossett
North Point
Russia
Blackstone

Notes

1
"Black Smoke and Moon Nights"

1. William Lamb Diary, December 13, 1864, September 25, 1865, William Lamb Collection, Earl Greg Swem Library, The College of William and Mary; E. B. Long, *The Civil War Day By Day* (Garden City, N.Y.: Doubleday, 1971), p. 711; Gertrude Elizabeth Baker, "The Diary of William Lamb, August 18, 1859–May 21, 1860," master's thesis, The College of William and Mary, 1960, pp. vi–xxxviii.
2. Long, p. 711; Lamb Diary, December 16, 1864; Sarah Lamb to "My Own Dear Parents," January 9, 1865, Sarah Lamb Papers, William Lamb Collection, Earl Greg Swem Library, The College of William and Mary.
3. "Records and Letters of the Confederacy," Eleanor Ruth and Orre Knox Lamb Papers, Lower Cape Fear Historical Society; Lamb Diary, December 13, 1864; *The Atlas to Accompany the Official Records of the Union and Confederate Armies* (Washington, D.C.: U.S. Government Printing Office, 1891; cited hereinafter as *O.R. Atlas*), plate LXXV; John G. Barrett, *The Civil War in North Carolina* (Chapel Hill: University of North Carolina Press, 1963), p. 244.

4. J. W. Merrill, "The Fort Fisher and Wilmington Campaign: Letters from Rear Admiral David D. Porter," *North Carolina Historical Review*, vol. XXXV, no. 4, p. 461; Lamb Diary, December 16, 1864; *Wilmington Journal*, June 28, 1862; George E. Turner, *Victory Rode the Rails* (Indianapolis: Bobbs Merrill Co., 1953), p. 264.

5. Barrett, pp. 244–45; Richard Berringer et al., *Why the South Lost the Civil War* (Athens: University of Georgia Press, 1986), p. 159; T. E. Taylor, *Running the Blockade* (New York: Charles Scribner's Sons, 1896), p. 139.

6. Lamb Diary, December 16, 1864.

7. John McElroy, *Andersonville: A Story of Rebel Military Prisons* (Toledo: D. R. Locke, 1879); *Wilmington Journal*, November 20, 1862; James Sprunt, *Chronicles of the Cape Fear River, 1660–1916* (Raleigh: Edwards and Broughton Printing Co., 1916), p. 11; Robert Carse, *Blockade: The Civil War at Sea* (New York: Rinehart and Co., 1950), pp. 9–10; Malcolm Ross, *The Cape Fear* (New York: Holt, Rinehart and Winston, 1965), p. 223; Carse, p. 152.

8. Sprunt, *Chronicles*, p. 11; Whitelaw Reid, *After the War: A Tour of the Southern States, 1865–1866* (New York: Harper & Row, 1965), p. 49.

9. Andrew J. Howell, *The Book of Wilmington, 1730–1930* (Wilmington: n.p., 1930), pp. 120–21.

10. Ibid.

11. John Johns, "Wilmington During the Blockade," *Harper's New Monthly Magazine*, vol. XXXII, September 1866, pp. 498–99.

12. *Wilmington Journal*, January 1, 1861; Sprunt, *Chronicles*, p. 11; Lamb Diary, December 14, 1864.

13. Lamb Diary, December 14, 1864; Carse, p. 181; Barrett, p. 257.

14. *Official Records of the Union and Confederate Navies in the War of the Rebellion* (Washington, D.C.: U.S. Government Printing Office, 1880–1927; cited hereinafter as *O.R.N.*), series I, vol. VIII, p. 88; Ross, p. 223; *Wilmington Journal*, October 2, November 20, 1862; W. H. C. Whiting to S. Cooper, W. H. C. Whiting Papers, Compiled Service Records of Confederate General and Staff Officers and Non-Regimental Enlisted Men, National Archives; Howell, pp. 124–25; Henry Judson Beeker, "Wilmington During the Civil War," master's thesis, Duke University, 1941, pp. 1–10.

15. *Wilmington Journal*, October 9, November 20, 1862; *O.R.N.*, I, VIII, p. 88; Carse, p. 119; Mrs. C. P. Bolles to Col. F. A. Olds, "Reminiscences of Mrs. Bolles," Charles B. Bolles Papers, N.C. Department of Archives and History; Chris Fonvielle, Jr., "To Forge a Thunderbolt: The Wilmington Campaign, February, 1865," master's thesis, East Carolina University, 1987, pp. 19–20.

16. *O.R.N.*, I, IV, p. 692; *Wilmington Journal*, July 25, 1861.

17. Long, pp. 719–20; Barrett, p. 245; Mark Mayo Boatner III, *The Civil War Dictionary* (New York: David McKay & Co., 1959), p. 70.

18. Barrett, p. 252; *The War of the Rebellion: A Compilation of the Official*

Records of the Union and Confederate Armies (Washington, D.C.: U.S. Government Printing Office, 1880–1901; cited hereinafter as *O.R.*), series I, vol. XVIII, pp. 939–40; Bruce Catton, *The American Heritage Picture History of the Civil War* (New York: American Heritage Publishing Co., 1960), p. 199; *The Historical Times Illustrated Encyclopedia of the Civil War*, ed. Patricia L. Faust (New York: Harper & Row, 1986), p. 67; Boatner, p. 70; Beeker, p. 84; Berringer, pp. 60–61.

19. *Histories of the Several Regiments and Battalions from North Carolina in the Great War, 1861–65*, ed. Walter Clark (Goldsboro, N.C.: Nash Bros., 1901), vol. II, p. 631; "Fort Fisher Historic Site" (Raleigh: N.C. Department of Archives and History, 1962); Barrett, p. 247; John J. Almy, "Incidents of the Blockade," *War Papers Read Before the Military Order of the Loyal Legion, Commandery of the District of Columbia* (Washington, D.C.: Published by the Commandery, 1892), vol. IX, p. 3.

20. Sprunt, *Chronicles*, p. 19; *O.R.N.*, I, VIII, p. 82; *Wilmington Journal*, November 20, 1862; W. H. C. Whiting to S. Cooper, Whiting Papers, Compiled Service Records; Barrett, p. 247; Almy, p. 3; *Histories of Regiments and Battalions from North Carolina*, vol. II, p. 631; Carse, p. 125; *O.R.N.*, I, XI, p. 32.

21. *Historical Times Illustrated Encyclopedia*, p. 67; Francis Sands, "A Volunteer's Reminiscences of Life in the North Atlantic Blockading Squadron, 1861–1865," *War Papers Read Before the Military Order of the Loyal Legion, Commandery of the District of Columbia* (Washington, D.C.: Published by the Commandery, 1894), vol. XX, p. 6.

22. Francis Sands, pp. 6–8; Almy, p. 3.

23. Almy, p. 3.

24. Carse, p. 265; Benjamin Sands, *From Reefer to Rear Admiral* (New York: Frederick A. Stokes Co., 1899), p. 257; Barrett, p. 252; *O.R.N.*, I, XI, p. 5.

25. *O.R.N.*, I, VIII, p. 87; Barrett, p. 252; *Illustrated London News*, February 18, 1865; *O.R.*, I, XLII, pt. I, p. 990; Francis Bradlee, *Blockade Running During the Civil War* (Salem, Mass.: Essex Institute Press, 1959), p. 13; Sprunt, *Chronicles*, pp. 372, 376.

26. Barrett, p. 245; Johns, p. 501; Sprunt, *Chronicles*, pp. 372–76, 381; Beeker, p. 81.

27. Johns, p. 501; Sprunt, *Chronicles*, pp. 372–76, 381.

2

"They Will Never Get Us Alive"

1. *O.R.N.*, I, VIII, p. 259; *O.R.*, pt. II, p. 732; Barrett, pp. 245–47; Ross, p. 223; *Battles and Leaders of the Civil War*, ed. Robert U. Johnson and Clarence C. Buel (New York: The Century Company, 1884), vol. IV, pp. 642–43; Barrett, p. 266.

2. *O.R. Atlas,* plate LXXV; *Battles and Leaders,* vol. IV, pp. 642–43; *O.R.,* I, XLII, pt. II, p. 732.
3. *Battles and Leaders,* vol. IV, pp. 642–43; Barrett, p. 266; William Lamb, "The Battles of Fort Fisher," *Southern Historical Society Papers,* vol. XXI, pp. 259–60.
4. *Southern Historical Society Papers,* vol. XXI, p. 266.
5. "William Lamb," in *Men of Mark in Virginia,* ed. Lyon G. Tyler (Washington, D.C.: Men of Mark Publishing Co., 1906), pp. 190–92; Lamb Diary, September 7, 1857; William Lamb, "Autobiography of William Lamb," William Lamb Collection, Earl Greg Swem Library, The College of William and Mary; *Colonel William Lamb Day* (Wilmington: Carolina Printing Co., 1962), p. 1.
6. Baker, p. vi; "William Lamb," *Men of Mark in Virginia,* pp. 190–91.
7. "William Lamb," *Men of Mark in Virginia,* p. 190.
8. Ibid., pp. 191–92; Baker, pp. vii, 238.
9. Baker, pp. vii, viii, x.
10. Ibid., pp. vi–vii, 34; Sarah C. Lamb to "Cousin," December 3, 1859, Sarah C. Lamb Letters, William Lamb Collection, Earl Greg Swem Library, The College of William and Mary; Daisy to "My Dear Mother," July 12, 1864, ibid.
11. Baker, p. x.
12. Ibid.; William Lamb Papers, Compiled Service Records of Confederate General and Staff Officers and Non-Regimental Enlisted Men, National Archives.
13. Sarah Lamb to "Father and Mother," December 1, 1861, Sarah Lamb Letters.
14. William Lamb, "The Heroine of Confederate Point," *Southern Historical Society Papers,* vol. XX, pp. 301–2; Baker, p. 238.
15. "William Lamb," *Men of Mark in Virginia,* pp. 190–92; Baker, p. xi.
16. Lamb Papers, Compiled Service Records; William Lamb, *Colonel William Lamb's Story of Fort Fisher* (Carolina Beach, N.C.: Blockade Runner Museum, 1966), pp. 1–3; Samuel A. Ashe, "Fort Fisher," *Confederate Veteran,* vol. XL, p. 250.
17. Lamb, *Colonel Lamb's Story,* pp. 2–5; *O.R.,* I, XLVI, pt. I, p. 407.
18. *O.R. Atlas,* plate LXV; Lamb, *Colonel Lamb's Story,* pp. 2–5.
19. *O.R. Atlas,* plate LXV; *O.R.,* I, XLVI, pt. I, pp. 406–9; Lamb, *Colonel Lamb's Story,* pp. 2–5.
20. *O.R.,* I, XLVI, pt. I, pp. 406–9; Stanley South, "Excavation of the Ruin of the House of the Keeper of the Light and William Lamb's Headquarters at Fort Fisher State Historic Site," unpublished manuscript, Historic Sites Division, N.C. Department of Archives and History; *O.R. Atlas,* plate LXV.
21. *Battles and Leaders,* vol. IV, pp. 643–47; *O.R.N.,* I, XI, p. 529; Lamb, *Colonel Lamb's Story,* p. 4; Warren Ripley, *Artillery and Ammunition of the Civil War* (Charleston, S.C.: Battery Press, 1984), pp. 140–41; *O.R. Atlas,* plate LXXV.

22. *Battles and Leaders,* vol. IV, p. 647; Lamb, *Colonel Lamb's Story,* p. 4; *O.R.N.,* I, VIII, pp. 595, 812–13; *O.R.N.,* I, IX, p. 57; *O.R.N.,* I, XI, pp. 30, 529; *O.R.,* I, XLVI, pt. I, p. 409; *O.R. Atlas,* plate LXXV.

23. Lamb, *Colonel Lamb's Story,* pp. 3–4; *Battles and Leaders,* pp. 643, 654.

24. *O.R.,* I, XLVI, pt. II, p. 215; *O.R.,* I, XLVI, pt. I, p. 408; *Battles and Leaders,* p. 643; *O.R.,* I, XLVII, pt. III, pp. 1219–20.

25. *O.R.,* I, IX, p. 424; *O.R.,* I, XVIII, p. 865; *O.R.,* I, XXVII, pt. III, p. 1067; *O.R.,* I, XXXVI, pt. III, p. 893; Lamb, "Defense of Fort Fisher," p. 630; Louis H. Manarin, *North Carolina State Troops, 1861–1865: A Roster,* comp. (Raleigh: N.C. Department of Archives and History, 1966), vol. I, pp. 173–334; Johns, p. 503.

26. Robert Watson Diary, December 31, 1864, Manuscript Department, Cornell University; John B. McNeil to "Mollie," May 30, 1862, Mary Margaret McNeil Papers; Manuscript Department, William R. Perkins Library, Duke University.

27. "Cousin John to Cousin Mollie," March 31, 1863, Mary Margaret McNeil Papers; John B. McNeil to "Cousin," August 18, 1862, Mary Margaret McNeil Papers.

28. Watson Diary, December 31, 1864; John B. McNeil to "Cousin Mollie," May 30, 1862, Mary Margaret McNeil Papers; *O.R.N.,* I, VII, pp. 514, 518; *Wilmington Journal,* June 28, August 3, 1862; *O.R.,* I, XXXIII, pp. 307, 1028–29; *O.R.,* I, XLII, pt. III, pp. 1146–47; Lewis T. Moore, "The Heroine of Fort Fisher," *Confederate Veteran,* vol. XXXVII, no. 7 (July 1929), p. 258; *Hebe Skirmish Centennial Program* [Wilmington: Commercial Printing and Mailing Co., 1963], pp. 2–4; *Historical Times Illustrated Encyclopedia,* p. 324.

29. "M.L. to Miss Mollie," January 4, 1863, Mary Margaret McNeil Papers; J. A. McMillian to Mary Margaret McNeil, September 12, 1862, Mary Margaret McNeil Papers.

30. Thomas A. McNeil to "Father," November 4, 1862, Hector H. McNeil Papers, Manuscript Department, William R. Perkins Library, Duke University.

31. "D.E.B. to Mollie," July 6, 1862, Mary Margaret McNeil Papers.

32. T. J. Lane to Franklin McNeil, November 2, 1862, Hector H. McNeil Papers; "D.E.B. to Mollie," July 6, 1862, Mary Margaret McNeil Papers; Lamb, *Colonel Lamb's Story,* pp. 8–9; Lamb Diary, November 24, 1864.

33. A. D. McEwen to Eliza P. McEwen, July 18, 1862, Eliza S. McEwen Papers, Manuscript Department, William R. Perkins Library, Duke University; *The Uplift* (Concord, N.C.: Concord Presbytery of the Presbyterian Church, U.S.), vol. II, no. 2 (1910), pp. 1–2; T. J. Lane to Franklin McNeil, November 2, 1862, Hector H. McNeil Papers; Hugh McGoogan to Mary Margaret McNeil, September 8, 1862, Mary Margaret McNeil Papers.

34. Lamb Diary, November 19, 1864; Johns, p. 501.

35. "D.E.B. to Mollie," July 6, 1862, Mary Margaret McNeil Papers.
36. Lamb Diary, November 19, 1864; John B. McNeil to "Cousin Mollie," November 11, 1861, Mary Margaret McNeil Papers.
37. Daisy to "Mother," July 12, 1863, Sarah Lamb Letters; Lamb, "Heroine of Confederate Point," pp. 301–3.
38. Lamb, "Heroine of Confederate Point," pp. 301–3; Daisy to "Mother," June 30, 1863, Sarah Lamb Letters.
39. Lamb Diary, November 16–18, 1864; Lamb, "Heroine of Confederate Point," pp. 301–3; Johns, p. 499; Daisy to "Mother," May 25, 1863, Sarah Lamb Letters.
40. Lamb Diary, December 1, 12, 1864; Johns, p. 498.
41. Lamb, *Colonel Lamb's Story*, pp. 10–11.
42. Lamb Diary, November 9, 1864.
43. Don C. Seitz, *Braxton Bragg: General of the Confederacy* (Columbia, S.C.: State Co., 1924), p. 2; Ezra J. Warner, *Generals in Gray* (Baton Rouge: LSU Press, 1959), pp. 30–31; *Historical Times Illustrated Encyclopedia*, p. 75.
44. *Dictionary of American Biography*, ed. Allen Johnson and Dumas Malone (New York: Charles Scribner's Sons, 1928–1936), vol. I, pp. 585–87; *Historical Times Illustrated Encyclopedia*, p. 51.
45. Thomas L. Connelly, *Autumn of Glory* (Baton Rouge: LSU Press, 1971), pp. 70, 277–78; Sam R. Watkins, *Co. Aytch: A Side Show of the Big Show* (Jackson, Tenn.: McCowat-Mercer Press, 1952), p. 118; *Fighting for the Confederacy*, ed. Gary W. Gallagher (Chapel Hill: University of North Carolina Press, 1989), pp. 307–8; *Dictionary of American Biography*, vol. I, pp. 585–87.
46. Connelly, pp. 277–78; *Dictionary of American Biography*, vol. I, pp. 585–87; *O.R.*, I, XLII, pt. III, pp. 1149, 1163; *Fighting for the Confederacy*, pp. 307–8.
47. Barrett, p. 265; Johns, p. 502; Lamb, *Colonel Lamb's Story*, pp. 10–11.
48. Lamb, *Colonel Lamb's Story of Fort Fisher*, pp. 10–11. Lamb Diary, November 1, 8, 22, 1864; Louis Hebert Papers, Compiled Service Records of General and Staff Officers and Non-Regimental Enlisted Men, National Archives; Warner, *Generals in Gray*, pp. 130–31; W. Lamb to Captain Hardman, October 8, 1864, General Correspondence 1864–65, David D. Porter Papers, Manuscript Division, Library of Congress; Special Order No. 169, October 15, 1864, Fort Fisher Logbook, Military Collection—Civil War, N.C. Department of Archives and History.
49. Lamb, *Colonel Lamb's Story*, pp. 10–11; Lamb Diary, December 13–19, 1864.

3
"Something Must Be Done to Close Wilmington"

1. John W. Grattan, "Under the Blue Pennant or Notes of a Naval Officer," unpublished manuscript, John W. Grattan Papers, Manuscript Division, Library of Congress, p. 149.

2. Grattan, "Under the Blue Pennant," Grattan Papers; Deck Log, USS *Malvern*, December 13, 1864, National Archives; *O.R.N.*, I, XI, pp. xv–xviii; *Battles and Leaders*, vol. IV, p. 662.

3. *Battles and Leaders*, vol. IV, p. 662; *O.R.N.*, I, XI, p. xvi; *Dictionary of American Biography*, vol. VIII, pp. 86–88.

4. *Dictionary of American Biography*, vol. VIII, pp. 86–88; William N. Still, "Porter . . . Is the Best Man," *Civil War Times Illustrated*, vol. XVI, no. 2 (May 1977), pp. 46–47; *Civil War Times Illustrated*, vol. XVI, no. 2 (May 1977), pp. 46–47.

5. *Dictionary of American Biography*, vol. VIII, pp. 86–88; *Historical Times Illustrated Encyclopedia*, p. 594; Gideon Welles, *The Diary of Gideon Welles*, ed. Howard K. Beale (New York: W. W. Norton and Co., 1960), pp. 146–47.

6. *Dictionary of American Biography*, vol. VIII, pp. 86–88; *Civil War Naval Chronology* (Washington, D.C.: U.S. Government Printing Office, 1971), vol. II, pp. 21, 24, 32, 100.

7. *Dictionary of American Biography*, vol. VIII, pp. 86–88; Still, pp. 46–47; *O.R.N.*, I, XI, p. 266.

8. Deck Log, USS *Malvern*, December 13, 1864; Still, p. 47; James M. Merrill, p. 465.

9. James Merrill, p. 465; Charles Price and Claude Sturgill, "Shock and Assault in the First Battle of Fort Fisher," *North Carolina Historical Review*, vol. XLII (Winter 1970), p. 25.

10. Price and Sturgill, p. 25; *The Fort Fisher Expedition: Report of the Joint Committee on the Conduct of the War, 38th Congress Second Session* (Washington, D.C.: U.S. Government Printing Office, 1865), pp. 88–89.

11. *Fort Fisher Expedition*, pp. 88–89; *Welles Diary*, vol. II, pp. 127–55; *Historical Times Illustrated Encyclopedia*, pp. 254, 202, 230; Barrett, pp. 262–63.

12. Welles, *Diary*, vol. II, pp. 146–47.

13. *O.R.N.*, I, VIII, pp. 301, 420; *O.R.N.*, I, XLII, pt. II, p. 732; Ava L. Honeycutt, Jr., "Fort Fisher—Malakoff of the South," master's thesis, Duke University, 1963.

14. Price and Sturgill, p. 25; Barrett, p. 262; *Fort Fisher Expedition*, p. 1; Welles, *Diary*, vol. II, p. 127.

15. *Fort Fisher Expedition*, p. 1; Price and Sturgill, p. 25; Barrett, pp. 262–63; *Historical Times Illustrated Encyclopedia*, p. 301.

16. Ezra Warner, *Generals in Blue* (Baton Rouge: LSU Press, 1964), pp. 548–49; *Historical Times Illustrated Encyclopedia*, p. 301.

17. *O.R.*, I, XI, pp. 600, 971–73; Honeycutt, "Malakoff of the South," pp. 134–35; Boatner, pp. 168–69.

18. *Fort Fisher Expedition*, pp. i–6.

19. *Battles and Leaders*, vol. IV, p. 655.

20. *O.R.*, I, XLII, pt. I, pp. 970–72; Benjamin F. Butler, *Butler's Book* (Boston: A. M. Thayer and Co., 1892), p. 783; *Dictionary of American Biography*, vol. II, p. 359.

21. Robert S. Holzman, *Stormy Ben Butler* (New York: Macmillan Company, 1954), p. 133.

22. *Dictionary of American Biography*, vol. II, p. 358; Warner, *Generals in Blue*, p. 61; Holzman, p. 48; Howard P. Nash, Jr., *Stormy Petrel: The Life and Times of General Benjamin F. Butler, 1818–1893* (Rutherford, N.J.: Fairleigh Dickinson University Press, 1969), pp. 15, 29.

23. Holzman, pp. 4, 10, 43; Butler, p. 66.

24. *Dictionary of American Biography*, vol. II, pp. 358–59; Holzman, pp. 15–19.

25. Holzman, pp. 12–14.

26. Ibid., pp. 23–24; Butler, pp. 134–40.

27. Butler, pp. 140–45; *Dictionary of American Biography*, vol. II, p. 358; Richard J. Sommers, *Richmond Redeemed: The Siege at Petersburg* (Garden City: Doubleday, 1981), p. 20.

28. Sommers, p. 20; Holzman, pp. 39–40, 63; *Historical Times Illustrated Encyclopedia*, pp. 98–99; Dudley Taylor Cornish, *The Sable Arm: Black Troops in the Union Army, 1861–1865* (Lawrence: University Press of Kansas, 1987), pp. 59–63.

29. Shelby Foote, *The Civil War: A Narrative* (New York: Random House, 1958), vol. I, pp. 370, 533; Holzman, pp. 103–5; Peter Chaitin, *The Coastal War: Chesapeake Bay to Rio Grande* (Alexandria, Va.: Time-Life Books, 1984), pp. 76–77; Cornish, pp. 59–63.

30. *Dictionary of American Biography*, vol. II, pp. 358–59; *Historical Times Illustrated Encyclopedia*, pp. 98–99.

31. Holzman, p. 147; Butler, p. 775.

32. Butler, p. 775.

33. *O.R.N.*, I, XI, pp. 207–18; *Fort Fisher Expedition*, p. 51.

34. *O.R.N.*, I, XI, pp. 214, 217.

35. *O.R.N.*, I, XI, pp. 214–15; David D. Porter, *Incidents and Anecdotes of the Civil War* (New York: D. Appleton and Co., 1885), pp. 268–72; *Fort Fisher Expedition*, pp. 222–23.

36. E. Hepple Hall, "Reminiscences of the War: The Wilmington Expedition," *United States Service Magazine*, vol. IV (July 1865), p. 313; David Porter, *Incidents and Anecdotes*, pp. 268–72; *O.R.N.*, I, XI, p. 223.

37. *O.R.N.*, I, XI, pp. 254–60; *O.R.*, I, XLII, pt. I, pp. 988–90; Barrett, p. 264; Honeycutt, "Malakoff of the South," pp. 131–32.

38. Daniel Eldredge, *The Third New Hampshire, 1861–1865* (Boston: Stillings & Co., 1893), pp. 578–80; *O.R.*, I, XLII, pt. I, pp. 988–90; *Fort Fisher Expedition*, pp. 244–55.

39. *Fort Fisher Expedition*, pp. 244–255; Porter to Senator J. W. Grimes, January 4, 1865, South Atlantic Blockading Squadron Area File (M625, Roll 211), National Archives; James Merrill, pp. 464–65; Butler, pp. 1126–27.

40. Butler, p. 1101; *Fort Fisher Expedition*, pp. 73–74.

41. *Civil War Naval Chronology*, vol. IV, pp. 145–46; *O.R.*, I, XLII, pt. II, pp. 980–82; *Fort Fisher Expedition*, p. 69; Butler, p. 782.

42. *Fort Fisher Expedition*, p. 74.

43. Holzman, p. 65; David Porter, *Incidents and Anecdotes*, p. 262.

44. Porter, p. 262; James Merrill, pp. 469–71.

45. Butler, p. 1127; James Merrill, pp. 468–69; E. Wightman to "Bro.," December 11, 1864, Edward K. Wightman Papers, private collection of Dr. Henry B. Wightman, Ithaca, New York.

4

"There's a Fizzle"

1. *Fort Fisher Expedition*, pp. 69–74; E. Wightman to "Bro.," December 11, 1864, Wightman Papers; "Rocked in the Cradle of Consternation," ed. Edwin S. Redkey, *American Heritage*, vol. XXXI, no. 6 (Oct.–Nov. 1980), p. 74; Gerry to "Friend Albert," December 11, 1864, *Demolay* manuscript, author's collection.

2. E. Wightman to "Bro.," December 16, 1864, Wightman Papers; "Rocked in the Cradle of Consternation," p. 74.

3. *Fort Fisher Expedition*, pp. 16–17.

4. "Rocked in the Cradle of Consternation," p. 74; Christian A. Fleetwood Diary, December 16–17, 1864, Christian A. Fleetwood Papers, Manuscript Division, Library of Congress; Richard W. Dawson Journal, December 15–16, 1864, Richard W. Dawson Papers, Manuscript Department, William Perkins Library, Duke University; E. Wightman to "Bro.," December 16, 1864, Wightman Papers.

5. *Fort Fisher Expedition*, pp. 16–17; Fleetwood Diary, December 17, 1864.

6. *Fort Fisher Expedition*, pp. 18–19.

7. Ibid., pp. 18–21, 90.

8. Ibid., pp. 19–20; "Rocked in the Cradle of Consternation," p. 75.

9. Dawson Journal, December 19–23, 1864; E. Wightman to "Bro.," December 22, 1864, Wightman Papers; Fleetwood Diary, December 21, 1864; Howard Thomas, *Boys in Blue from the Adirondack Foothills* (Prospect, N.Y.: Prospect Books, 1960), p. 247.

10. *Fort Fisher Expedition*, pp. 20–21; Cutler J. Andrews, *The North Reports the Civil War* (Pittsburgh: University of Pittsburgh Press, 1955), pp. 614–15.

11. *Fort Fisher Expedition*, pp. 20–21.

12. Ibid., pp. 21, 90.

13. Ibid., pp. 21, 30; Cyrus B. Comstock, *The Diary of Cyrus B. Comstock,* ed. Merlin E. Sumner (Dayton: Morningside House, Indiana, 1987), p. 298.

14. Deck Log, USS *Malvern,* December 23, 1864; Price and Sturgill, pp. 34–35.

15. *O.R.N.,* I, vol. XI, pp. 222–27; W. F. Beyer and O. F. Keydel, *Deeds of Valor from Records in the Archives of the United States Government* (Detroit: Perrien-Keydel Co., 1907), vol. II, p. 81; *Civil War Naval Chronology,* vol. II, pp. 57, 71; ibid., vol. IV, p. 147; ibid., vol. V, p. 11; Price and Sturgill, pp. 34–35; *O.R.,* I, XLII, pt. I, p. 990.

16. Robley Evans, *A Sailor's Log: Recollections of Forty Years of Naval Life* (New York: D. Appleton and Company, 1908), pp. 77–78; Deck Log, USS *Malvern,* December 24, 1864; John W. Grattan Journal, December 24, 1864, John W. Grattan Papers, Manuscript Collection, Library of Congress.

17. Ibid.; Price and Sturgill, p. 35; *Fort Fisher Expedition,* p. 31; *O.R.N.,* I, XI, pp. 226–27; Andrews, p. 615.

18. "Story of the Powder Boat," *Galaxy Magazine,* vol. IX, January 1870, p. 88.

19. *O.R.,* I, XLII, pt. III, pp. 1297–99.

20. *Fort Fisher Expedition,* p. 31; Lamb Diary, December 24, 1864; *O.R.,* I, XLII, pt. III, p. 1301; Howe, p. 143.

21. Whiting Papers, Compiled Service Records; *O.R.,* I, XVIII, pp. 770, 773–75.

22. C. B. Denson, *An Address Delivered in Raleigh, N.C. on Memorial Day (May 10) 1895, Containing a Memoir of the Late Major General William Henry Chase Whiting of the Confederate Army* (Raleigh: Edwards & Broughton Co., 1895), pp. 10–11; Whiting Obituary, W. H. C. Whiting Papers, U.S. Army Military Academy Library, West Point.

23. Denson, pp. 10–12; Warner, *Generals in Gray,* p. 334; *Biographical Dictionary of the Confederacy,* ed. John L. Wakelyn (Westport, Conn.: Greenwood Press, 1977), pp. 435–36; *Wilmington Star,* Nov. 22, 1901.

24. Whiting Papers, Compiled Service Records; Sprunt, *Chronicles,* p. 281; Clyde Wilson, "W. H. C. Whiting," unpublished manuscript, history department, University of South Carolina; Warner, *Generals in Gray,* p. 334.

25. Warner, *Generals in Gray,* p. 334; Denson, p. 35.

26. Douglas Southall Freeman, *Lee's Lieutenants: A Study in Command* (New York: Charles Scribner's Sons, 1942), vol. I, pp. 119–20; Denson, p. 36.

27. Freeman, *Lee's Lieutenants,* vol. I, pp. 119–20, 143, 620–21; Denson, p. 36; Jefferson Davis, *The Rise and Fall of the Confederate Government* (Richmond: Garrett and Massie, 1938), p. 106.

28. Freeman, *Lee's Lieutenants,* vol. I, pp. 218, 620–21; Gustavus W. Smith, *Confederate War Papers* (New York: Atlantic Publishing and Engraving, 1884), pp. 328–29.

29. Freeman, *Lee's Lieutenants,* vol. I, pp. 620–21; ibid., vol. II, pp. 258–59; *O.R.,* I, XIX, pt. II, pp. 680–81; W. H. Whiting to Beauregard, October 17, 1862, Whiting Papers, Combined Service Records.

30. Whiting Papers, Compiled Service Records; *O.R.,* I, XVIII, p. 770.

31. John D. Taylor Papers, Manuscript Collection, N.C. Department of Archives and History; *O.R.,* I, XXIX, pt. II, pp. 670–71; *O.R.,* XXVII, pt. II, pp. 702–3; *O.R.,* I, XXVII, pt. III, p. 907; *O.R.,* I, XVII, pp. 775, 786–88.

32. *O.R.,* I, XLII, pt. II, pp. 1206–7; *O.R.,* I, XVIII, p. 1048; *O.R.,* I, XLII, pt. II, pp. 1241, 1253, 1300.

33. *O.R.,* I, XLII, pt. II, pp. 1295–96, 1299.

34. Ibid.

35. Freeman, *Lee's Lieutenants,* vol. III, pp. 474–75; *Historical Times Illustrated Encyclopedia,* pp. 838–39.

36. Edward P. Alexander, *Fighting for the Confederacy,* p. 394; Freeman, *Lee's Lieutenants,* vol. III, pp. 474–85.

37. *O.R.,* I, XLII, pt. III, pp. 1141–42, 1149.

38. *O.R.,* I, XLII, pt. III, p. 1160, 1171; *O.R.,* I, XLVI, pt. I, p. 442.

39. *O.R.,* I, XLII, pt. III, pp. 1171, 1201–2, 1225.

40. Lamb Diary, November 22, 1864; *O.R.,* I, XLII, pt. III, pp. 1171, 1201–2, 1225, 1233–34, 1260; Butler, pp. 779–880; *O.R.N.,* I, II, pp. 160–62.

41. *O.R.,* I, XLII, pt. III, pp. 1260, 1271, 1278–79; Lamb Diary, November 22, 1864; *Battles and Leaders,* vol. IV, p. 635.

42. *O.R.,* I, XLII, pt. III, pp. 1207–9, 1210–11, 1225, 1282–83; *Battles and Leaders,* vol. IV, p. 661.

43. Lamb Diary, December 24, 1864; Lamb, "Battles of Fort Fisher," p. 267.

44. Scarf, p. 422.

45. *O.R.,* I, XLII, pt. I, pp. 994, 1020–21; Lamb Diary, December 1864, Addenda.

46. *O.R.,* I, XLII, pt. II, pp. 1295–96, 1300; *O.R.,* I, XL, pt. II, p. 717; Lamb Diary, December 18, 1864; *O.R.,* I, XLII, pt. III, p. 1260.

5

"A Storm of Shot and Shell"

1. Grattan Journal, Grattan Papers, December 18, 1864.

2. *O.R.N.,* I, XI, pp. 254–60; Deck Log, USS *Malvern,* December 24, 1864; Grattan, "Under the Blue Pennant."

3. *Battles and Leaders,* vol. IV, p. 662; Joseph M. Simms, "Personal Experiences in the Volunteer Navy During the Civil War," *War Papers Read Before the Military Order of the Loyal Legion, Commandery of the District of Columbia* (Washington, D.C.: Published by the Commandery, 1903), pp. 9–10.

4. *O.R.N.*, I, XI, pp. 246–47; Deck Log, USS *Malvern*, December 24, 1864.
5. Lamb Diary, 1864, Addenda; Lamb, *Colonel Lamb's Story*, pp. 14–15.
6. *O.R.*, I, XLII, pt. I, p. 1101; Lamb, *Colonel Lamb's Story*, pp. 14–15.
7. Ibid.; Scarf, pp. 423–25; *North Carolina State Troops*, vol. I, p. 173.
8. Joe to "My Darling," December 21, 1864, Civil War Letters, Lower Cape Fear Historical Society; diagram of Fort Fisher, Grattan Journal, Grattan Papers, 1863.
9. *O.R.N.*, I, XI, p. 255; *Battles and Leaders*, vol. IV, p. 644.
10. *Battles and Leaders*, vol. IV, p. 246; Lamb, *Colonel Lamb's Story*, p. 15; Clarence Cary Report, Manuscript Division, Library of Congress, p. 24; William Lamb, "First Shot From Fort Fisher," William Lamb Papers, The College of William and Mary.
11. *O.R.N.*, I, XI, p. 647; Lamb, *Colonel Lamb's Story*, p. 15.
12. *Battles and Leaders*, vol. IV, p. 662; *O.R.*, I, XLII, pt. I, p. 1003; Clarence Cary Report, p. 25.
13. *Battles and Leaders*, vol. IV, p. 662; B. F. Blair to "Mother," December 27, 1864, B. F. Blair Papers, Civil War Miscellaneous Collection, Archives Division, U.S. Army Military History Institute.
14. Grattan Journal, Grattan Papers, December 24, 1864.
15. Lamb, *Colonel Lamb's Story*, pp. 14–15.
16. *O.R.*, I, XLII, pt. I, p. 1009.
17. Cary Report, p. 25; Scarf, p. 424.
18. Scarf, p. 424. *O.R.*, I, XLII, pt. I, p. 1003; *O.R.N.*, I, XI, p. 295; Hall, p. 316.
19. Evans, p. 81.
20. Ibid., p. 80.
21. *O.R.N.*, I, XI, pp. 359–60, 336.
22. Ibid., pp. 256–57, 330; Hall, p. 316.
23. *O.R.N.*, I, XI, pp. 246–47, 323; Grattan Journal, Grattan Papers, December 24, 1864; Hall, p. 316; *New York Times*, December 31, 1864.
24. *O.R.N.*, I, XI, pp. 319–20, 327–30, 331; Grattan Journal, Grattan Papers, December 24, 1864.
25. Lamb, *Colonel Lamb's Story*, pp. 14–15; *O.R.*, I, XLII, pt. I, pp. 1111–13.
26. Scarf, p. 424.
27. *O.R.*, I, XLII, pt. I, pp. 1002–4, 1006; Ashe, *History of North Carolina*, vol. II, p. 940; Christopher Bland Papers, Compiled Service Records of the 36th N.C. Artillery, National Archives.
28. *O.R.*, I, XLII, pt. I, pp. 997, 1000, 1006; *O.R.*, I, XLII, pt. III, pp. 1303, 1313.
29. *O.R.*, I, XLII, pt. I, pp. 1006, 1020–21; *O.R.*, I, XLII, pt. III, p. 1303; *North Carolina State Troops*, vol. I, pp. 30–31.
30. *O.R.*, I, XLII, pt. I, pp. 1020–21.
31. *Historical Times Illustrated Encyclopedia*, pp. 419–20; Warner, *Generals in Gray*, pp. 171–72; *O.R.*, I, XLII, pt. I, pp. 1020–21.
32. *O.R.*, I, XLII, pt. I, pp. 1020–21.

33. Ibid.; *Histories of Regiments and Battalions from North Carolina,* vol. IV, p. 539.

34. Deck Log, USS *Malvern,* December 24, 1864; Benson J. Lossing, "The First Attack on Fort Fisher," *The Annals of the War* (Philadelphia: Times Publishing Co., 1879), pp. 236–37; Lamb, *Colonel Lamb's Story,* p. 16.

35. *Fort Fisher Expedition,* pp. 89–90, 95–96; Butler, pp. 790–91; Comstock, *Diary,* p. 298.

36. Comstock, *Diary,* p. 298. *Fort Fisher Expedition,* p. 92; Butler, p. 796.

37. Comstock, *Diary,* p. 298; Butler, p. 808; *Fort Fisher Expedition,* pp. 75–77; *O.R.,* I, XLII, pt. I, p. 967.

38. Butler, p. 808; Comstock, *Diary,* p. 298.

39. Ibid.; Comstock to Grant, January 1, 1865, Cyrus B. Comstock Papers, Manuscript Division, Library of Congress.

40. *O.R.,* I, XLII, pt. III, p. 1303.

6

"The Enemy Has Landed"

1. Simms, p. 11.

2. *O.R.N.,* I, XI, pp. 332, 379; Benjamin Sands, p. 259; Deck Log, USS *Fort Jackson,* December 25–28, 1864.

3. Deck Log, USS *Malvern,* December 25, 1864; *O.R.,* I, XLII, pt. I, p. 967; Butler, pp. 790–92.

4. Joseph Scroggs Diary, December 25, 1864, Civil War Collection, Archives Department, U.S. Army Military History Institute.

5. "Rocked in the Cradle of Consternation," p. 76.

6. Edward Wightman to "Bro.," December 26, 1864, Wightman Papers.

7. Simms, p. 12.

8. Edward Wightman to "Bro.," December 26, 1864, Wightman Papers.

9. Lamb, *Colonel Lamb's Story,* pp. 16–18; *O.R.,* I, XLII, pt. I, pp. 1003–7; Grattan, "Under the Blue Pennant," Grattan Papers, p. 178.

10. *O.R.N.,* I, II, pp. 374–75.

11. J. R. Cromartie to "Sister," December 30, 1864, Junius Cromartie Papers, *Civil War Times Illustrated* Collection, Archives Division, U.S. Army Military History Institute; *O.R.,* I, XLII, pt. I, pp. 1015–16, 1018.

12. *O.R.,* I, XLII, pt. I, p. 1006.

13. Sarah C. Lamb to "My Own Dear Parents," January 9, 1865, Sarah Lamb Letters.

14. *O.R.,* I, XLII, pt. I, pp. 1023–25.

15. Ibid.

16. Ibid.

17. *O.R.,* I, XLII, pt. I, pp. 981, 1021; E. Wightman to "Bro.," December 23, 1864, Wightman Papers; *New York Times,* December 30, 1864;

O.R.N., I, XI, p. 333; H. C. Lockwood, "The Capture of Fort Fisher," *Atlantic Monthly,* vol. XXVII, May 1871, p. 630.

18. Lockwood, p. 360. Warner, *Generals in Blue,* pp. 106–7; *Dictionary of American Biography,* vol. II, p. 618.

19. *O.R.,* I, XLII, pt. I, pp. 674, 981–82; E. Wightman to "Bro.," December 23, 1864, Wightman Papers; Lossing, p. 239; *New York Tribune,* January 18, 1865.

20. *O.R.,* I, XLII, pt. I, pp. 981–82; Newton M. Curtis, "The Capture of Fort Fisher," in *Personal Recollection of the War of the Rebellion: Addresses Delivered Before the Military Order of the Loyal Legion of the United States, Commandery of Massachusetts,* ed. A. Noel Blakeman (New York: G. P. Putnam's Sons, 1907), pp. 29–32.

21. *O.R.N.,* I, XI, pp. 281, 332–33, 350.

22. Ibid., pp. 333, 350; Hall, p. 318.

23. *O.R.,* I, XLII, pt. I, pp. 981, 1021–22.

24. Ibid.; Curtis, "Capture of Fort Fisher," p. 30.

25. *O.R.N.,* I, XI, p. 258; Asa Betham Letter, December 25, 1864, Asa Betham Papers, Manuscript Division, Library of Congress.

26. *O.R.N.,* I, XI, pp. 193, 258; Ralph Roske and Charles Van Doren, *Lincoln's Commando: The Biography of Commander W. B. Cushing, USN* (New York: Harper & Brothers, 1957), pp. 38–39, 68, 88, 93; *Dictionary of American Biography,* vol. II, pp. 635–37.

27. *O.R.N.,* I, XI, pp. 309, 488, 737; Asa Betham Letter, December 25, 1864, Betham Papers; Scarf, p. 419.

28. *O.R.,* I, XLII, pt. I, p. 1028; *O.R.N.,* I, XI, pp. 374, 377; Scarf, p. 419.

29. *O.R.N.,* I, II, pp. 258, 334–35; *Civil War Naval Chronology,* vol. IV, p. 150; Scarf, p. 419.

30. *O.R.,* I, XLII, pt. I, pp. 994, 1019; *O.R.,* I, XLII, pt. I, p. 1022; Johns, p. 502.

31. *O.R.,* I, XLII, pt. I, pp. 674, 994; ibid., pt. III, pp. 1307–9.

32. Curtis, "Capture of Fort Fisher," p. 30; *O.R.,* I, XLII, pt. I, pp. 982–83, 986; G. Weitzel to "My Dear Comstock," January 1, 1865, Comstock Papers.

33. *O.R.,* I, XLII, pt. I, pp. 982–83, 986; Hall, p. 318; *Wilmington Journal,* January 7, 1865; *Battles and Leaders,* vol. IV, p. 646; Lamb, *Colonel Lamb's Story,* p. 18.

34. Hall, p. 318.

35. *O.R.,* I, XLII, pt. I, pp. 976–77, 1005.

36. Ibid., p. 976; Beyer and Keydel, p. 471.

37. *O.R.,* I, XLII, pt. I, pp. 976, 983; Dawson Journal, December 25, 1864.

38. *O.R.,* I, XLVI, pt. I, p. 403; *Battles and Leaders,* vol. IV, pp. 661–62; Comstock, *Diary,* p. 299.

39. *O.R.,* I, XLII, pt. I, p. 986; *Fort Fisher Expedition,* pp. 22–25.

40. *Fort Fisher Expedition,* pp. 22–25.

41. Ibid.; Dawson Journal, December 25, 1864; G. Weitzel to "My Dear Comstock," January 1, 1865, Comstock Papers.

42. Curtis, "Capture of Fort Fisher," p. 30; *O.R.*, XLII, pt. I, p. 983.

43. Curtis, "Capture of Fort Fisher," pp. 30–31; Col. Cyrus B. Comstock to Gen. Grant, January 1, 1865, Comstock Papers; Comstock, *Diary*, p. 299; *O.R.*, XLII, pt. I, pp. 983–86; Dawson Journal, December 25, 1864.

44. Dawson Journal, December 25, 1864; Howard Thomas, p. 248.

45. *Histories of Regiments and Battalions from North Carolina*, vol. IV, pp. 47–48, 590; *O.R.*, I, XLII, pt. I, pp. 1025–26.

46. *O.R.*, I, XLII, pt. I, pp. 983, 1025–26; *Wilmington Journal*, January 7, 1865; Howard Thomas, pp. 248–49.

47. *O.R.*, XLII, pt. I, pp. 980–82; Dawson Journal, December 25, 1864; Comstock, *Diary*, p. 299; C. B. Comstock to U. S. Grant, January 1, 1865, Comstock Papers; *New York Times*, May 30, 1910; Boatner, pp. 168–69.

48. Dawson Journal, December 25, 1864; Curtis, "Capture of Fort Fisher," pp. 30–31; *O.R.*, XLII, pt. I, p. 980–83.

49. Comstock, *Diary*, p. 299; *O.R.*, XLII, pt. I, p. 983; Curtis, "Capture of Fort Fisher," pp. 30–31; *O.R.N.*, I, II, p. 258.

50. *O.R.*, I, XLII, pt. I, pp. 995, 1005; *O.R.N.*, I, XI, p. 337; Scarf, p. 426; Curtis, "Capture of Fort Fisher," pp. 30–31; Cary Report, p. 28; Lamb, *Colonel Lamb's Story*, p. 19.

51. Lamb, *Colonel Lamb's Story*, p. 19; *O.R.*, XLII, pt. I, pp. 983, 1306–8; *Battles and Leaders*, vol. IV, pp. 642–47.

52. *O.R.*, I, XLII, pt. III, pp. 1306–8.

53. Curtis, "Capture of Fort Fisher," pp. 30–31; Lamb, *Colonel Lamb's Story*, p. 19.

54. Ibid.; *O.R.*, I, XLII, pt. I, pp. 980–84; E. Wightman to "Bro.," December 28, 1864, Wightman Papers.

55. E. Wightman to "Bro.," December 28, 1864, Wightman Papers; Curtis, "Capture of Fort Fisher," pp. 30–31; *Fort Fisher Expedition*, p. 25.

56. *Fort Fisher Expedition*, p. 25; *O.R.*, I, XLII, pt. I, p. 674; Curtis, "Capture of Fort Fisher," p. 30; E. Wightman to "Bro.," December 28, 1864, Wightman Papers.

57. *O.R.*, I, XLII, pt. III, pp. 995–96, 982, 1000, 1018, 1308, 1014–15; *O.R.N.*, I, XI, p. 377; Lamb, *Colonel Lamb's Story*, pp. 19–21; Lamb Diary, December 26, 1864.

58. *Fort Fisher Expedition*, p. 29; William L. Hyde, *History of the 112th New York Volunteers* (Fredonia, N.Y.: McKinstry & Co., 1865), p. 117; *O.R.*, I, XLII, pt. I, pp. 995–99; Lamb, *Colonel Lamb's Story*, p. 21.

59. *O.R.N.*, I, XI, p. 291.

60. Ibid.; E. Wightman to "Bro.," December 28, 1864, Wightman Papers.

61. *O.R.*, I, XLII, pt. I, pp. 966, 969, 983; *O.R.N.*, I, XI, pp. 250–51, 291; E. Wightman to "Bro.," December 28, 1864, Wightman Papers; Alonzo Alden to "Captain," December 31, 1864, Alonzo Alden Papers, Civil War Miscellaneous Collection, Archives Branch, U.S. Army Military History Institute.

62. Andrews, *The North Reports the Civil War*, p. 616; *O.R.*, I, XLII, pt.

I, p. 66; *O.R.N.*, I, XI, p. 264; D. Porter to W. T. Sherman, General Correspondence July–December 1864, David D. Porter Papers.

63. Lamb Diary, December 27–31, 1864; E. Wightman to "Bro.," December 28, 1864, Wightman Papers.
64. *O.R.*, I, XLII, pt. I, pp. 995, 999, 1006; "Memoranda," Lamb Diary, December 1864; David to "Miss Kate," January 1865, Catherine Buie Papers, Manuscript Collection, William R. Perkins Library, Duke University; Cary Report; *O.R.*, I, XLI, pt. II, p. 1056.
65. *O.R.*, I, XLI, pt. II, p. 1056; William Lamb Papers, Compiled Service Records; *O.R.*, I, XLII, pt. I, pp. 999, 1006.
66. *O.R.*, I, XLVI, pt. II, p. 105; Seitz, p. 27; *O.R.*, I, XLII, pt. I, pp. 993–97.
67. Lamb Diary, January 2, 1865; *North Carolina State Troops*, vol. II, pp. 174, 423; *The Uplift*, vol. II, no. 2, pp. 1–2; *Wilmington Journal*, January 7, 1865; Watson Diary, January 1, 1865; *O.R.*, I, XLVI, pt. II, pp. 1012–13.
68. Lamb Diary, January 2–4, 1865; *Wilmington Journal*, January 7, 1865.
69. Johns, pp. 502–3; *O.R.*, I, XLVI, pt. II, pp. 1015, 1021; Barrett, p. 271; *O.R.*, I, XLII, pt. I, pp. 993–97.
70. *O.R.*, I, XLVI, pt. II, pp. 1021, 1023; Johns, pp. 502–3.

7

"The Fort Will Soon Be Ours"

1. Deck Log, USS *Malvern*, January 12, 1865; Lamb, *Colonel Lamb's Story;* Watson Diary, January 13, 1865.
2. *O.R.N.*, I, II, pp. 254–64, 408; Butler, p. 1127; *Fort Fisher Expedition*, p. 27; D. Porter to Senator J. W. Grimes, January 4, 1865, South Atlantic Blockading Squadron Area File, National Archives.
3. Price and Sturgill, p. 39; Holzman, p. 151; T. Harry Williams, *Lincoln and His Generals* (New York: Alfred A. Knopf, 1952), p. 348; *O.R.*, I, XLVI, pt. II, pp. 29, 60.
4. Williams, p. 348; *Fort Fisher Expedition*, p. 52; *O.R.N.*, XI, pp. 388, 408.
5. Williams, pp. 347–48; *O.R.*, I, XLVI, pt. II, p. 29; Andrews, *The North Reports the Civil War*, p. 616.
6. "Rocked in the Cradle of Consternation," p. 79; J. W. Grattan to "Pa and Ma," January 4, 1865, Correspondence File, Grattan Papers; Capt. Solon A. Carter to "Emily," January 13, February 7, 1865, Solon Carter Papers, Archives Branch, U.S. Army Military History Institute; B. F. Blair to "Mother," December 27, 1864, Blair Papers.
7. *O.R.*, I, XLVI, pt. II, pp. 70–71; Holzman, p. 152.
8. Ibid.
9. D. Porter to W. T. Sherman, December 29, 1864, General Correspondence, David D. Porter Papers; *O.R.N.*, I, XI, pp. 388–89.
10. *O.R.N.*, I, XI, pp. 397–98.
11. William J. Finan, *Major General Alfred Howe Terry: Hero of Fort Fisher*

(Hartford: Connecticut Civil War Centennial Commission, 1965), pp. 4–5; Grattan, "Under the Blue Pennant," Grattan Papers; *New York Times,* December 17, 1890; *Dictionary of American Biography,* vol. IX, pp. 378–79.

12. *Historical Times Illustrated Encyclopedia,* pp. 748–49; *New York Times,* December 17, 1890; Finan, pp. 8, 15; *O.R.,* I, XLVI, pt. II, pp. 11, 46; Horace Porter, *Campaigning with Grant* (Secaucus, N.J.: Blue and Grey Press, 1984), pp. 368–69.

13. Horace Porter, p. 369; *O.R.,* I, XLVI, pt. II, p. 29.

14. Grattan Journal, January 1, 1865, Grattan Papers; Grattan, "Under the Blue Pennant," Grattan Papers, pp. 149–96; James Merrill, pp. 467–70.

15. Grattan, "Under the Blue Pennant," Grattan Papers, pp. 149–96; David D. Porter, *The Naval History of the Civil War* (Secaucus, N.J.: Castle Books, 1984), p. 711; "The Task Before Them," ed. Edward G. Longacre, *Civil War Times Illustrated,* vol. XXI, no. 10 (February 1983), p. 38; *O.R.,* I, XLVI, pt. II, p. 90.

16. *O.R.,* I, XLVI, pt. I, pp. 36, 165–67, 396; Henry Little, *The 7th Regiment of New Hampshire Volunteers in the War of the Rebellion* (Concord: n.p., 1986), pp. 355–57; *O.R.,* I, XLVI, pt. II, pp. 29, 69, 79.

17. Lockwood, p. 685; Grattan Journal, Grattan Papers, January 12, 1865; *Battles and Leaders,* vol. IV, p. 662; *O.R.,* XLVI, pt. I, pp. 403–5.

18. *O.R.,* XLVI, pt. I, pp. 403–5; *Historical Times Illustrated Encyclopedia,* pp. 181–82; Cornish, pp. 264–65, 281; T. Speed to "Bill," February 12, 1865, Thomas Speed Letters, Manuscript Collection, The Filson Club Historical Society.

19. *O.R.,* I, XLVI, pt. II, p. 46; Little, p. 354; Grattan, "Under the Blue Pennant," Grattan Papers, pp. 149–96; Deck Log, USS *New Ironsides,* January 12, 1865; "A Yankee Account of the Battles of Fort Fisher," *Our Living and Our Dead,* vol. I, September 1874–February 1875, pp. 315–25.

20. Lockwood, p. 685; "Task Before Them," p. 38; *O.R.,* I, XLVI, pt. I, p. 46; Deck Log, USS *Malvern,* January 12, 1865.

21. *Histories of Regiments and Battalions from North Carolina,* vol. II, p. 638; Lamb, "Heroine of Confederate Point," pp. 303–4; *Letters from the Colonel's Lady,* ed. Cornelius Thomas (Winnabow, N.C.: Charlestowne Preservation Trust, 1965), pp. 8–9.

22. *Histories of Regiments and Battalions from North Carolina,* vol. IV, p. 541; "Defense and Fall of Fort Fisher," *Southern Historical Society Papers,* vol. X (August–September, 1882), pp. 346–49; *O.R.,* I, XLVI, pt. II, pp. 1042–45; Johns, p. 503; unsigned letter from Ft. Holmes to "Kate," January 27, 1865, Buie Papers.

23. Deck Log, USS *Tacony,* January 13, 1865; "Task Before Them," p. 38; *New York Times,* January 18, 1865; Deck Log, USS *Malvern,* January 13, 1865.

24. *O.R.N.,* I, XI, pp. 424–27.

25. Deck Logs, USS *Brooklyn*, USS *New Ironsides*, USS *Malvern; O.R.N.*, I, XI, pp. 4–33, 461.

26. Lamb Diary, January 13, 1865; Lamb, *Colonel Lamb's Story*, pp. 22–23.

27. *O.R.N.*, I, XI, pp. 461–62; Deck Logs, USS *Mahopac*, USS *New Ironsides*.

28. Augustus Buel, *The Cannoneer* (Washington, D.C.: National Tribune, 1890), pp. 328–29.

29. "Task Before Them," p. 38; *O.R.*, I, XLVI, pt. II, p. 90; Lockwood, p. 685.

30. Deck Log, USS *Malvern*, January 13, 1865; "Task Before Them," p. 38; Leonard Thomas, *The Story of Fort Fisher* (Ocean City, N.J.: n.p., 1915), p. 6.

31. Leonard Thomas, p. 6; "A Yankee's Account," p. 318; Comstock, *Diary*, p. 301; Lockwood, p. 685.

32. Leonard Thomas, p. 7; *O.R.*, I, XLVI, pt. I, p. 396; Grattan Journal, Grattan Papers, January 13, 1865; Grattan, "Under the Blue Pennant," Grattan Papers, pp. 149–96.

33. Grattan, "Under the Blue Pennant," Grattan Papers, pp. 149–96; Grattan Journal, Grattan Papers, January 13, 1865; Little, p. 359.

34. Zera Tanner, "The Capture of Fort Fisher," *War Papers Read Before the Military Order of the Loyal Legion of the United States, Commandery of the District of Columbia* (Washington: Published by the Commandery, 1897), pp. 6–7; *New York Times*, January 18, 1865; Eldredge, pp. 616–17; Curtis, "Capture of Fort Fisher," p. 33.

35. *O.R.*, I, XLVI, pt. I, pp. 396–97.

36. Ibid., p. 432; *Histories of Regiments and Battalions from North Carolina*, vol. IV, p. 541.

37. Asa King Papers, Confederate Veterans' Talks, Lower Cape Fear Historical Society Archives.

38. Ibid.; "Task Before Them," p. 38; *O.R.*, I, XLVI, pt. I, p. 404.

39. King Papers.

40. *O.R.*, I, XLVI, pt. I, p. 396; Leonard Thomas, pp. 6–7.

41. "Task Before Them," pp. 38–39; *O.R.*, I, XLVI, pt. I, p. 410.

42. *O.R.*, I, XLVI, pt. I, pp. 440–42; Denson, pp. 45, 50.

43. *O.R.*, I, XLVI, pt. I, pp. 440–42; "Defense and Fall of Fort Fisher," p. 346; Denson, pp. 44–45, 50, 55.

44. Lamb, *Colonel Lamb's Story*, p. 23; Denson, pp. 44, 45, 50, 55; Johns, p. 497; Douglas Southall Freeman, *A Calendar of Confederate Papers* (Richmond: Whittet and Sheppersons, 1908), p. 299.

45. "Defense and Fall of Fort Fisher," pp. 365–66; Denson, pp. 44, 45, 50, 55.

46. *O.R.N.*, I, XI, p. 438; Deck Log, USS *New Ironsides*, January 13, 1865; Lamb, *Colonel Lamb's Story*, p. 23.

47. Lamb, *Colonel Lamb's Story*, p. 23; "Defense and Fall of Fort Fisher," pp. 365–66; Denson, pp. 44–55.

48. Lamb, *Colonel Lamb's Story*, p. 23.

49. James Alexander Montgomery Papers, Confederate Veterans' Talks, Lower Cape Fear Historical Society Archives; Watson Diary, January 13, 1865; R.P.C. to "My Dearest Cousin," January 24, 1865, Lybrook Collection, N.C. Department of Archives and History; *North Carolina State Troops,* vol. I, p. 214.

50. Denson, pp. 40, 50; *North Carolina State Troops,* vol. I, p. 257.

51. *O.R.,* I, XLVI, pt. II, pp. 1048–52.

52. Ibid.; *O.R.,* I, XLVI, pt. I, p. 432; "Defense and Fall of Fort Fisher," p. 346; Compiled Service Records, 2nd S.C. Cavalry, National Archives.

53. *O.R.N.,* I, XI, p. 438; Simms, p. 17; Deck Log, USS *Malvern,* January 13, 1865.

54. *O.R.,* I, XLVI, pt. I, p. 397; "Task Before Them," pp. 39–40; "A Yankee's Account," pp. 318–19.

55. *O.R.,* I, XLVI, pt. I, pp. 397, 418, 423; "Task Before Them," pp. 39–40; Christian Fleetwood to "Pop," January 21, 1865, Fleetwood Papers; "A Yankee's Account," pp. 318–19.

56. Lamb, *Colonel Lamb's Story,* p. 23.

8

"I Will Hold This Place"

1. *O.R.,* I, XLVI, pt. I, p. 432; "Defense and Fall of Fort Fisher," pp. 346–47.

2. Ibid.; Compiled Service Records, 2nd S.C. Cavalry, National Archives.

3. *O.R.,* I, XLVI, pt. I, p. 432; "Defense and Fall of Fort Fisher," pp. 346–47.

4. "Task Before Them," pp. 39–40; *O.R.,* I, XLVI, pt. I, p. 397; "A True History of the Army at Fort Fisher," ed. L. R. Hamersly, *The United Service: A Monthly Review of Military and Naval Affairs,* vol. X (Philadelphia: L. R. Hamersly & Co., 1893), p. 406.

5. *O.R.,* I, XLVI, pt. I, 396–97, 404; Eldredge, pp. 616–17; Tanner, pp. 6–7.

6. Deck Logs, USS *Malvern,* USS *New Ironsides,* January 14, 1865.

7. Deck Log, USS *New Ironsides,* January 14, 1865; Beyer and Keydel, vol. II, pp. 85–86.

8. Lamb, *Colonel Lamb's Story,* p. 23; *Battles and Leaders,* vol. IV, pp. 647–48, 661.

9. *O.R.,* I, XLVI, pt. II, pp. 1052–58; Lamb, *Colonel Lamb's Story,* p. 24.

10. *O.R.,* I, XLVI, pt. II, pp. 1052–58.

11. *O.R.,* I, XLVI, pt. I, p. 397; "True History of the Army," pp. 406–7; *Battles and Leaders,* vol. IV, p. 648; Deck Log, USS *Malvern,* January 14, 1865.

12. Deck Log, USS *Malvern,* January 14, 1865; *O.R.,* I, XLVI, pt. II, p. 1053; *Civil War Naval Chronology,* vol. VI, p. 211; "True History of the Army," p. 407.

13. *Battles and Leaders,* vol. IV, p. 648; "Defense and Fall of Fort Fisher," p. 352.
14. *O.R.,* I, XLVI, pt. II, p. 1056.
15. Ibid.
16. Ibid., pp. 1056–57; *O.R.,* I, XLVI, p. 1056; "Defense and Fall of Fort Fisher," pp. 346–49.
17. Curtis, "Capture of Fort Fisher," p. 34; *O.R.,* I, XLVI, pt. I, p. 397; Francis Lord, *The Civil War Collector's Encyclopedia* (Columbia, S.C.: Lord Americana and Research, 1975), vol. II, p. 53.
18. *O.R.,* I, XLVI, pt. I, pp. 397, 407; Curtis, "Capture of Fort Fisher," p. 34.
19. Ibid.
20. *O.R.,* I, XLVI, pt. I, pp. 397–98; Deck Log, USS *Malvern,* January 14, 1865; *O.R.N.,* I, XI, pp. 440–79; "Task Before Them," p. 40; Curtis, "Capture of Fort Fisher," p. 35.
21. "Task Before Them," p. 40; *O.R.,* I, XLVI, pt. I, pp. 397–98; *O.R.N.,* I, XI, pp. 438–39.
22. *O.R.N.,* I, XI, pp. 438–39; *O.R.,* I, XLVI, pt. I, pp. 397–98.
23. Ibid.; "Task Before Them," p. 40.
24. Solon Carter to "My Own Precious Wife," January 13, 1865, Carter Papers.
25. Evans, pp. 86–87.
26. Leonard Thomas, pp. 1, 8.
27. Lamb, "Battles of Fort Fisher," pp. 277–78; Deck Log, USS *Malvern,* January 14, 1865; Watson Diary, January 14, 1865; unsigned letter to "Kate," January 27, 1865, Buie Papers.
28. *Battles and Leaders,* vol. IV, p. 649; *North Carolina State Troops,* vol. I, p. 290.
29. *Battles and Leaders,* vol. IV, p. 649; Lamb, "Battles of Fort Fisher," p. 278.
30. *O.R.,* I, XLVI, pt. II, p. 1059; Johnson C. Hagood, *Memoirs of the War of Secession* (Columbia, S.C.: State Company, 1910), pp. 323–24; Boatner, p. 365.
31. Hagood, pp. 323–24.
32. Lamb, "Battles of Fort Fisher," pp. 278–79.

9

"Like Sheep in a Pen"

1. Deck Log, USS *Malvern,* January 15, 1865; *O.R.N.,* I, XI, p. 527.
2. Buel, p. 329; Leonard Thomas, p. 8.
3. *O.R.,* I, XLVI, pt. II, pp. 1061–62; *O.R.,* I, XLVI, pt. I, pp. 431–34.
4. Lamb, "Battles of Fort Fisher," pp. 278–79; Watson Diary, January 15, 1865; Lamb Diary, September 25, 1865; Lamb, "Battles of Fort Fisher," p. 286.

5. Deck Logs, USS *New Ironsides,* USS *Malvern,* January 15, 1865.
6. Leonard Thomas, pp. 8–9.
7. *London Illustrated News,* February 4, March 4, March 18, 1865; W. Stanley Hoole, *Vizetelly Covers the Confederacy* (Tuscaloosa, Ala.: Confederate Publishing, 1957), pp. 129–30; H. A. Wise to Captain George Wise, April 11, 1862, George Wise Papers, Manuscript Department, Duke University; Phillip Van Doren Stern, *They Were There* (New York: Crown Publishers, 1959), pp. 15–16.
8. Lamb, "Battles of Fort Fisher," p. 279; Fort Fisher Logbook, June 28, 1864.
9. Lamb, "Battles of Fort Fisher," p. 279; Benjamin Sands, p. 263.
10. *O.R.,* I, XLVI, pt. I, pp. 398, 419–21; Tanner, p. 12; "Task Before Them," pp. 40–41.
11. *O.R.N.,* I, XI, pp. 439, 446, 448, 454, 527; Deck Log, USS *Malvern,* January 15, 1865; Evans, p. 87; Grattan, "Under the Blue Pennant," Grattan Papers; *Battles and Leaders,* vol. IV, pp. 659, 662.
12. *O.R.N.,* I, XI, pp. 446–47, 454; *Battles and Leaders,* vol. IV, p. 657; *Dictionary of American Biography,* vol. III, pp. 13–14.
13. *O.R.N.,* I, XI, p. 439; James Merrill, pp. 466–67.
14. *O.R.N.,* I, XI, pp. 446–47, 494–95; *Battles and Leaders,* vol. IV, p. 659.
15. Ibid.; pp. 446, 450; *Harper's Weekly,* February 4, 1865; Gideon Welles to House Committee on Naval Affairs, February 17, 1868, Samuel W. Preston Papers, U.S. Navy Pension Records, National Archives.
16. *O.R.N.,* I, XI, pp. 446, 583.
17. *Battles and Leaders,* vol. IV, p. 659; *O.R.N.,* I, XI, pp. 446, 476, 510, 576–77.
18. *O.R.N.,* I, XI, pp. 446–47, 576–77.
19. Ibid., pp. 429–430, 576–78.
20. Ibid., pp. 576–83.
21. Ibid., pp. 429–30.
22. Ibid., pp. 429–30, 474; Evans, p. 87; "A Yankee's Account," p. 320.
23. "Task Before Them," p. 41; Grattan, "Under the Blue Pennant," Grattan Papers, p. 183; Lockwood, p. 687; Comstock, *Diary,* pp. 302–3.
24. Lamb, "Battles of Fort Fisher," p. 279.
25. Ibid.
26. Ibid.; *O.R.,* I, XLVI, pt. II, pp. 1062–65.
27. *O.R.,* I, XLVI, pt. II, pp. 1064–65.
28. Ibid.; "Defense and Fall of Fort Fisher," p. 359.
29. *O.R.,* I, XLVI, pt. I, pp. 439–42; Denson, p. 50.
30. Ibid., pp. 350–59; *Historical Times Illustrated Encyclopedia,* pp. 151–52.
31. Lamb, "Battles of Fort Fisher," p. 280; *Histories of Regiments and Battalions from North Carolina,* vol. II, pp. 638–41.
32. Ibid.; Lamb, "Battles of Fort Fisher," pp. 279–80; "Defense and Fall of Fort Fisher," p. 357; William Greer, "Recollections of a Private Soldier of the Army of the Confederate States," p. 24, William Robert Greer

Papers, Manuscript Department, William R. Perkins Library, Duke University.

33. Greer, p. 24; James F. Izlar Diary, January 15, 1865, Manuscript Collection, South Caroliniana Library, University of South Carolina.

34. James Izlar Diary, January 15, 1865, Manuscript Collection; Greer, p. 25.

35. Greer, p. 24; James Izlar Diary, January 15, 1865; William Valmore Izlar, *A Sketch of the War Record of the Edisto Rifles, 1861–1865* (Columbia, S.C.: State Company, 1914), pp. 107–8.

36. Lamb, "Battles of Fort Fisher," p. 280.

37. Ibid.; "Defense and Fall of Fort Fisher," p. 360.

38. *O.R.N.,* I, XI, pp. 446–47, 512–13; Curtis, "Capture of Fort Fisher," p. 37.

39. *O.R.N.,* I, XI, pp. 576–79.

40. Ibid., pp. 495–97; *The War of the 'Sixties,* ed. E. R. Hutchins (New York: Neale Publishing Company, 1912), p. 357.

41. *O.R.N.,* I, XI, pp. 576–82.

42. Ibid.

43. Ibid., pp. 429–30, 474; *Battles and Leaders,* vol. IV, p. 659.

44. *O.R.N.,* I, XI, pp. 882, 481, 889, 498, 518, 533, 537, 540–41, 552, 562, 564, 570; "Bloom" to "Louise," January 8, 1865, Joseph B. Osborne Papers, Manuscript Division, Library of Congress.

45. *O.R.N.,* I, XI, pp. 446–47; *O.R.,* I, XLVI, pt. I, p. 398; Deck Logs, USS *Malvern,* USS *New Ironsides,* January 15, 1865.

46. *O.R.N.,* I, XI, pp. 446, 498, 512, 576.

47. Ibid., pp. 426–34, 446–47, 498, 553; Francis Sands, p. 20; Buel, p. 332; "Bloom" to "Louise," January 18, 1865, Osborne Papers; Grattan, "Under the Blue Pennant," Grattan Papers, p. 183.

48. Grattan, "Under the Blue Pennant," Grattan Papers, p. 183; *Battles and Leaders,* vol. IV, p. 650; Lamb, "Battles of Fort Fisher," pp. 280–81.

49. Lamb, "Battles of Fort Fisher," pp. 280–81.

50. Ibid.; *O.R.N.,* I, XI, pp. 576, 578; James Merrill, p. 466; Evans, p. 88.

51. *O.R.N.,* I, XI, pp. 227, 435, 446, 449, 498, 527, 576; Francis Sands, p. 20.

52. Evans, p. 86; *O.R.N.,* I, XI, p. 532; Francis Sands, p. 21; Jack Coggins, *Arms and Equipment of the Civil War* (Garden City, N.Y.: Doubleday, 1962), pp. 32–38.

53. *O.R.N.,* I, XI, p. 546; Francis Sands, p. 20.

54. *O.R.N.,* I, XI, pp. 399, 449, 527; Grattan, "Under the Blue Pennant," Grattan Papers, pp. 139, 148, 178–85; *Harper's Weekly,* February 4, 1865; *List of Officers of the Navy of the United States and of the Marine Corps From 1775 to 1900,* ed. Edward W. Callahan (New York: L. R. Hamersly & Co., 1901), p. 440; Benjamin H. Porter Papers, Records of the Bureau of Naval Personnel, National Archives.

55. *Battles and Leaders,* vol. IV, p. 650; Lamb, "Battles of Fort Fisher," pp. 280–81.

56. Ibid.

57. Lamb, "Battles of Fort Fisher," p. 281; *Histories of Regiments and Battalions from North Carolina,* vol. II, pp. 641–42; *Battles and Leaders,* vol. IV, p. 650; Eldredge, p. 623; *O.R.N.,* I, XI, pp. 446, 512–13; Simms, p. 366.

58. *O.R.N.,* I, XI, pp. 552–54; Evans, p. 88.

59. Eldredge, p. 623; Evans, p. 89; Lamb, "Battles of Fort Fisher," p. 281; *O.R.N.,* I, XI, pp. 552–54.

60. *O.R.N.,* I, XI, pp. 552–54; Evans, p. 89; Eldredge, p. 623.

61. *Battles and Leaders,* vol. IV, p. 650; Lamb, "Battles of Fort Fisher," p. 281; Evans, pp. 88–89; Simms, pp. 366–67; *O.R.N.,* I, XI, pp. 526–27; William T. Cobb to "Dear Father," William T. Cobb Papers; Fort Fisher State Historic Site.

62. *O.R.N.,* I, XI, pp. 449, 527.

63. Ibid., pp. 446–47, 450–51, 500, 511; Gideon Welles to Committee on Naval Affairs, February 17, 1868, Samuel W. Preston Papers, U.S. Navy Military Service Records, National Archives.

64. *O.R.N.,* I, XI, p. 553; Evans, p. 89; Simms, pp. 366–67; *Battles and Leaders,* vol. IV, p. 660.

65. Ibid.; Evans, p. 90; "Bloom" to "Dearest Louise," January 18, 1865, Osborne Papers; *O.R.N.,* I, XI, pp. 533, 541, 552, 562, 564; Simms, p. 367.

66. *O.R.N.,* I, XI, pp. 495–97, 512–13, 560–61; Simms, pp. 366–67; Evans, pp. 88–89; *Battles and Leaders,* vol. IV, pp. 659–61.

67. *Battles and Leaders,* vol. IV, pp. 659–61; *O.R.N.,* I, XI, pp. 512–13, 553.

68. *O.R.N.,* I, XI, pp. 512–13; Simms, pp. 366–67.

69. Evans, pp. 88–92.

70. *O.R.N.,* I, XI, pp. 510–14; Grattan, "Under the Blue Pennant," Grattan Papers.

71. *O.R.N.,* I, XI, pp. 21, 471–72; James Tallentine Papers, U.S. Navy Military Service Records, Record Group 24, National Archives; David B. McComb to Commodore John Hope, South Atlantic Blockading Squadron Area File.

72. David B. McComb to Commodore John Hope, South Atlantic Blockading Squadron File; *O.R.N.,* I, XI, pp. 471–72; Eldredge, p. 606; Grattan, "Under the Blue Pennant," Grattan Papers, pp. 183–88.

73. *O.R.N.,* I, XI, pp. 495–500; *Battles and Leaders,* vol. IV, pp. 660–62.

74. *O.R.N.,* I, XI, pp. 443–48, 495–500, 503, 537; Evans, p. 95; Simms, pp. 367–69.

75. Simms, p. 367; *O.R.N.,* I, XI, pp. 495–500, 580–81; *Battles and Leaders,* vol. IV, p. 660; Lamb, "Battles of Fort Fisher," p. 281.

76. *O.R.N.,* I, XI, p. 523.

77. Ibid., pp. 495–500, 511–14.

78. Ibid., pp. 446–47, 498–99; Francis Sands, pp. 16, 23.

79. Francis Sands, pp. 16, 23; *O.R.N.*, I, XI, pp. 446–47, 495–500.
80. Francis Sands, pp. 16, 23; Simms, pp. 366–69; Evans, p. 90; *O.R.N.*, I, XI, pp. 443–47, 495–500, 528–29.
81. *O.R.N.*, I, XI, pp. 443–47; James Merrill, p. 467; *Battles and Leaders*, vol. IV, pp. 660–62; Lamb, "Battles of Fort Fisher," p. 281.

10

"The Air Seems Darkened with Death"

1. Lamb, "Battles of Fort Fisher," p. 281; *Battles and Leaders*, vol. IV, p. 650; Leonard Thomas, p. 10.
2. *O.R.*, I, XLVI, pt. I, p. 398; "Task Before Them," p. 40; Lockwood, p. 687.
3. "True History of the Army," p. 409; Deck Log, USS *Malvern*, January 15, 1865; "A Yankee's Account," p. 320.
4. Little, pp. 391–92.
5. *O.R.*, I, XLVI, pt. I, p. 398; Curtis, "Capture of Fort Fisher," pp. 36–37.
6. Curtis, "Capture of Fort Fisher," pp. 36–37; Comstock, *Diary*, pp. 302–3.
7. Adelbert Ames, "The Capture of Fort Fisher, North Carolina, January 15, 1865," *Personal Recollections of the War of the Rebellion*, ed. by A. Noel Blackman (New York: G. P. Putnam's Sons, 1907), p. 12; Dawson Journal, January 6–8, 1865; J. R. Hawley to Adrian Terry, June 1, 1896, Adrian Terry Papers, Terry Family Collection, Manuscripts and Archives Division, Sterling Memorial Library, Yale University; N. M. Curtis to Adrian Terry, May 30, 1896, Terry Papers; *Historical Times Illustrated Encyclopedia*, p. 11; Curtis, "Capture of Fort Fisher," pp. 33–38.
8. *O.R.*, I, XLVI, pt. I, p. 398.
9. Ibid.; Leonard Thomas, p. 9; *The Soldier of Indiana in the War for the Union* (Indianapolis: Merrill and Company, 1869), pp. 785–86; Isaiah Price, *History of the 9th Regiment of Pennsylvania Volunteer Infantry* (Philadelphia: n.p., 1875), p. 348; Lockwood, p. 687; "Task Before Them," p. 41.
10. "Task before Them," p. 41; Curtis, "Capture of Fort Fisher," p. 38; Howard Thomas, pp. 250–51.
11. *O.R.*, I, XLVI, pt. I, p. 398; Leonard Thomas, p. 9; "Task Before Them," p. 41; Curtis, "Capture of Fort Fisher," p. 38; George F. Towle to Adrian Terry, July 23, 1896, Terry Papers.
12. Ibid.; Howard Thomas, p. 251; Leonard Thomas, p. 9; Lockwood, p. 687.
13. "True History of the Army," p. 411; George F. Towle to Adrian Terry, July 26, 1896, Terry Papers.
14. *O.R.*, I, XLVI, pt. I, p. 398; Price, p. 349; "A Yankee's Account," p. 321;

Ames, pp. 11–12; George F. Towle to Adrian Terry, July 23, 1896, Terry Papers.

15. Ames, pp. 11–12; Curtis, "Capture of Fort Fisher," p. 38; "True History of the Army," p. 412; Dawson Journal, December 22–23, 1865.

16. *O.R.*, I, XLVI, pt. I, p. 398; Curtis, "Capture of Fort Fisher," pp. 38–39; Howard Thomas, p. 251.

17. Lamb, "Battles of Fort Fisher," pp. 282–83; Kinchen Braddy to Judge Z. T. Fulmore, March 25, 1901, Kinchen Braddy Papers, Civil War Collection, N.C. Department of Archives and History; *North Carolina State Troops*, vol. I, p. 226; "Task Before Them," p. 42.

18. Kinchen Braddy to Z. T. Fulmore, March 25, 1901, Braddy Papers; *North Carolina State Troops*, vol. I, pp. 273, 577; "True History of the Army," p. 410.

19. Kinchen Braddy to Z. T. Fulmore, March 25, 1901, Braddy Papers; "True History of the Army," p. 414.

20. Curtis, "Capture of Fort Fisher," p. 39; "Task Before Them," p. 42; Lockwood, p. 688; Howard Thomas, p. 251.

21. Curtis, "Capture of Fort Fisher," p. 39; Leonard Thomas, p. 11.

22. Hyde, pp. 122–23.

23. Ibid.; Howard Thomas, p. 251.

24. *O.R.*, I, XLVI, pt. I, pp. 398, 417; Curtis, "Capture of Fort Fisher," p. 39; Lockwood, pp. 688–89; Hyde, pp. 118–19; Comstock, *Diary*, pp. 302–3; "Task Before Them," p. 42.

25. "Task Before Them," p. 42; *Soldier of Indiana*, pp. 785–86; Beyer and Keydel, vol. I, p. 474.

26. *O.R.*, I, XLVI, pt. I, p. 417; Ames, p. 12; Comstock, *Diary*, pp. 302–3; "True History of the Army," pp. 413, 418.

27. Curtis, "Capture of Fort Fisher," p. 39; Comstock, *Diary*, p. 303; Hyde, pp. 118–19, "Task Before Them," p. 42; "A Yankee's Account," pp. 321–23.

28. Kinchen Braddy to Z. T. Fulmore, March 25, 1901, Braddy Papers; "Defense and Fall of Fort Fisher," p. 363; Lamb, *Colonel Lamb's Story*, p. 28.

29. Kinchen Braddy to Z. T. Fulmore, March 25, 1901, Braddy Papers; "A Yankee's Account," p. 322; Lamb, "Battles of Fort Fisher," pp. 283–84.

30. Kinchen Braddy to Z. T. Fulmore, March 25, 1901, Braddy Papers; Lamb, "Battles of Fort Fisher," pp. 283–84.

31. *From Antietam to Fort Fisher: The Civil War Letters of Edward K. Wightman, 1862–1865*, ed. Edward G. Longacre (Cranbury, N.J.: Associated University Presses, 1985), pp. 9–14, 24, 228–31, 241.

32. Lamb, "Battles of Fort Fisher," pp. 283–84; *North Carolina State Troops*, vol. I, pp. 313, 318.

33. Kinchen Braddy to Z. T. Fulmore, March 25, 1901, Braddy Papers; Lamb, "Battles of Fort Fisher," pp. 283–84; "A Yankee's Account," p. 323.

34. Ibid.

35. "A Yankee's Account," p. 323; Comstock, *Diary*, p. 303; Kinchen
     Braddy to Z. T. Fulmore, March 25, 1901, Braddy Papers.
36. "True History of the Army," pp. 413–14; Leonard Thomas, pp. 12–13;
     "A Yankee's Account," pp. 523–24; *Soldier of Indiana*, pp. 786–87;
     Hyde, pp. 119–20.
37. *The Memorial to Brevet Major General Galusha Pennypacker* (Phila-
     delphia: Pennypacker Memorial Commission, 1934), pp. 15–17; "True
     History of the Army," p. 413; Warner, *Generals in Blue*, pp. 365–66;
     Historical Times Illustrated Encyclopedia, p. 574; Galusha Pen-
     nypacker to Adrian Terry, June 6, 1896, Terry Papers.
38. "True History of the Army," p. 415; Leonard Thomas, p. 12; *O.R.*, I,
     XLVI, pt. I, p. 419.
39. *Histories of Regiments and Battalions from North Carolina*, vol. II, p.
     642; *North Carolina State Troops*, vol. I, p. 272; "True History of the
     Army," p. 415.
40. "True History of the Army," p. 415; *O.R.*, I, XLVI, pt. I, p. 420.
41. *O.R.*, I, XLVI, pt. I, p. 417; Dawson Journal, summation and entries for
     December 20, 1864–January 8, 1865; "True History of the Army," p.
     413.
42. Dawson Journal, summation; "True History of the Army," p. 413.
43. *O.R.*, I, XLVI, pt. I, pp. 403, 420; Price, pp. 354–56; Leonard Thomas,
     pp. 12–13; "A Yankee's Account," pp. 322–23; Beyer and Keydel, vol.
     I, p. 474.
44. Kinchen Braddy to Z. T. Fulmore, March 25, 1901, Braddy Papers; "A
     Yankee's Account," pp. 322–23; Comstock, *Diary*, p. 303.
45. Comstock, *Diary*, p. 303; Price, pp. 354–56; Leonard Thomas, pp. 12–
     13.
46. "A Yankee's Account," pp. 322–23; Curtis, "Capture of Fort Fisher,"
     pp. 39–40.
47. Curtis, "Capture of Fort Fisher," p. 39; Henry Clay McQueen Papers,
     Confederate Veterans' Talks, Lower Cape Fear Historical Society Ar-
     chives; Leonard Thomas, p. 14; *O.R.*, I, XLVI, pt. I, pp. 400, 416, 418.
48. *O.R.*, I, XLVI, pt. I, p. 400, 416; Curtis, "Capture of Fort Fisher," p. 39;
     Price, p. 355; "True History of the Army," p. 415; Leonard Thomas, p.
     13; Galusha Pennypacker to "My Dear Colonel Terry," June 6, 1896,
     Terry Papers; Adrian Terry, "Wilmington and Fort Fisher," unpub-
     lished manuscript, Adrian Terry Papers, Terry Family Collection, Ster-
     ling Memorial Library, Yale University. Note to p. 65; *West Chester
     Village Record*, January 31, 1865, February 18, 1865; Surgeon's Report,
     U.S. General Hospital, July 30, 1865, Galusha Pennypacker Papers,
     Historical Society of Pennsylvania.
49. *O.R.*, I, XLVI, pt. I, pp. 433–34; Lamb, "Defense and Fall of Fort
     Fisher," p. 348; *Histories of Regiments and Battalions from North
     Carolina*, vol. II, p. 802.
50. *Histories of Regiments and Battalions from North Carolina*, vol. IV, p.
     542.

51. Ibid., vol. IV, p. 542, vol. II, pp. 10, 802; *O.R.*, I, XLVI, pt. I, p. 424.
52. *Histories of Regiments and Battalions from North Carolina*, vol. II, p. 10, vol. IV, p. 542; "Defense and Fall of Fort Fisher," pp. 347–48.
53. A. W. Waddel, "Some Memories of My Life," McEachern-Williams Collection, Lower Cape Fear Historical Society Archives.
54. Mrs. T. C. Davis, "The Fall of Fort Fisher," *Confederate Veteran*, vol. XIII, no. 3 (March 1905), p. 131.
55. Robbins, John Davis, "The Second Battle of Fort Fisher," unpublished manuscript, McEachern-Williams Collection, Lower Cape Fear Historical Society; *Letters from the Colonel's Lady*, p. 10.

11

"Our Men Began to Waver"

1. *O.R.*, I, XLVI, pt. I, p. 440; Lamb, "Battles of Fort Fisher," p. 281; *Battles and Leaders*, vol. IV, pp. 650–51; James Izlar Diary, January 15, 1865.
2. *O.R.*, I, XLVI, pt. I, p. 438.
3. Lamb, "Battles of Fort Fisher," p. 281; *Battles and Leaders*, vol. IV, p. 650; James A. Montgomery Papers, Confederate Veterans' Talks, Lower Cape Fear Historical Society Archives; *O.R.*, I, XLVI, pt. I, p. 440.
4. *O.R.*, I, XLVI, pt. I, p. 440; *Battles and Leaders*, vol. IV, pp. 650–51; "Rocked in the Cradle of Consternation," p. 78.
5. "True History of the Army," p. 415; Curtis, "Capture of Fort Fisher," p. 40; Barrett, p. 277; Lamb, "Battles of Fort Fisher," p. 281; Denson, p. 42.
6. Kinchen Braddy to Z. T. Fulmore, March 25, 1901, Braddy Papers; Denson, p. 42.
7. *Battles and Leaders*, vol. IV, p. 651; Lamb, "Battles of Fort Fisher," p. 281.
8. Lamb, "Battles of Fort Fisher," pp. 281, 285; *Battles and Leaders*, vol. IV, pp. 651–52.
9. Ibid.
10. Watson Diary, January 15–16, 1865.
11. *Battles and Leaders*, vol. IV, pp. 651–52; Lamb, "Battles of Fort Fisher," p. 285.
12. Kinchen Braddy to Z. T. Fulmore, March 25, 1901, Braddy Papers; *Battles and Leaders*, vol. IV, pp. 651–52; Lamb, "Battles of Fort Fisher," p. 285.
13. Lamb, "Battles of Fort Fisher," p. 285; *Battles and Leaders*, vol. IV, p. 652.
14. Ibid.
15. John Bell Bouton, *A Memoir of General Louis Bell* (New York: n.p.,

1865), pp. 26, 28; George F. Towle to "My Dear Colonel," July 23, 1898, Terry Papers.

16. Bouton, pp. 5–28; *Dictionary of American Biography,* vol. I, p. 159.

17. Ibid.; Louis Bell Papers, Compiled Service Records of the 4th New Hampshire Infantry, National Archives; Bouton, pp. 5–28.

18. Bouton, pp. 5–28, 44.

19. Adrian Terry, "Wilmington and Fort Fisher," Terry Papers, p. 65; George F. Towle to "My Dear Colonel," July 23, 1898, Terry Papers; "Task Before Them," p. 43.

20. "Task Before Them," p. 43; Adrian Terry, "Wilmington and Fort Fisher," Terry Papers, p. 65; Bouton, pp. 28–29; "True History of the Army," p. 415.

21. Bouton, p. 29; Adrian Terry, "Wilmington and Fort Fisher," Terry Papers, p. 65.

22. *O.R.,* I, XLVI, pt. I, pp. 421–23.

23. Ibid.

24. *Battles and Leaders,* vol. IV, pp. 651–52; Lamb, "Battles of Fort Fisher," pp. 285–87.

25. *Battles and Leaders,* vol. IV, p. 652.

26. Ibid.

27. Ibid.

28. Ibid.

29. Ibid.

30. Lamb Diary, January 15, March 9, August 6, September 25, and October 12, 1865; *Battles and Leaders,* vol. IV, p. 652; *Histories of Regiments and Battalions from North Carolina,* vol. II, pp. 645–46.

31. *Histories of Regiments and Battalions from North Carolina,* vol. II, pp. 645–46; *O.R.,* I, XLVI, pt. I, pp. 437–38; *Battles and Leaders,* vol. IV, pp. 652–53.

32. *Battles and Leaders,* vol. IV, pp. 652–53; *O.R.,* XLVI, pt. I, pp. 437–38; *O.R.,* XLVI, pt. II, p. 1064.

33. *O.R.,* XLVI, pt. II, p. 1064; Lawrence Lee to John A. Reilly, November 21, 1983, Major James Reilly Papers, Archives Branch, U.S. Army Military History Institute; Sprunt, *Chronicles,* p. 361; *North Carolina State Troops,* vol. I, pp. 40, 75.

34. James Reilly Account of the Battles of Fort Fisher, W. L. DeRossett Papers, North Carolina Department of Archives and History; Kinchen Braddy to Z. T. Fulmore, March 25, 1901, Braddy Papers; James Izlar Diary, January 15, 1865.

35. Curtis, "Capture of Fort Fisher," pp. 39–41; *O.R.,* I, XLVI, pt. I, pp. 420–22.

36. Curtis, "Capture of Fort Fisher," pp. 39–41.

37. "True History of the Army," p. 418.

38. Curtis, "Capture of Fort Fisher," pp. 41–43; *O.R.N.,* I, IX, p. 454; Hyde, p. 120.

39. Curtis, "Capture of Fort Fisher," pp. 41–43; "Rocked in the Cradle of Consternation," p. 78.
40. Curtis, "Capture of Fort Fisher," pp. 41–42; David McComb to Commodore John Hope, South Atlantic Blockading Squadron Area File, National Archives.
41. Grattan, "Under the Blue Pennant," Grattan Papers; Samuel M. Zent to Adrian Terry, December 12, 1896, Terry Papers.
42. William A. Ketcham, "William A. Ketcham Reminiscences of Fort Fisher," William A. Ketcham Papers, Indiana Historical Society.
43. Curtis, "Capture of Fort Fisher," pp. 41–42; *O.R.*, I, XLVI, pt. I, pp. 420–21.
44. Ibid.
45. Ketcham, p. 39.
46. Ibid.; Reilly Account; Kinchen Braddy to Z. T. Fulmore, March 25, 1901, Braddy Papers; *North Carolina State Troops*, vol. I, p. 313; Curtis, "Capture of Fort Fisher," pp. 41–42.
47. Reilly Account; Kinchen Braddy to Z. T. Fulmore, March 25, 1901, Braddy Papers.
48. Curtis, "Capture of Fort Fisher," pp. 42–43; N. M. Curtis to Adrian Terry, May 30, 1896, Terry Papers.
49. Ibid.; Ames, p. 15.
50. Curtis, "Capture of Fort Fisher," pp. 42–43; N. M. Curtis to Adrian Terry, May 30 and June 6, 1896, Terry Papers.
51. N. M. Curtis to Adrian Terry, June 6, 1896, Terry Papers; Curtis, "Capture of Fort Fisher," pp. 42–43.
52. Curtis, pp. 42–44; N. M. Curtis to Adrian Terry, June 6, 1896, Terry Papers.
53. Ibid.
54. Samuel M. Zent to Adrian Terry, December 12, 1896, Terry Papers; Curtis, "Capture of Fort Fisher," p. 44.
55. Comstock, *Diary*, pp. 303–4; *O.R.*, I, XLVI, pt. I, p. 399.
56. Comstock, *Diary*, p. 304.
57. Ibid.; George F. Towle to Adrian Terry, July 23, 1896, Terry Papers.
58. *O.R.N.*, I, IX, p. 601; *O.R.*, I, XLVI, pt. I, pp. 399, 410; George F. Towle to Adrian Terry, July 23, 1896.
59. Ibid.; *O.R.*, I, XLVI, pt. I, pp. 399, 410, 424.
60. Comstock, *Diary*, p. 304; Curtis, "Capture of Fort Fisher," p. 45; *O.R.*, XLVI, pt. I, pp. 399, 410, 412–13, 424.
61. Comstock, *Diary*, p. 304.
62. Ibid.; *O.R.*, XLVI, pt. I, pp. 399, 410, 412–13; "True History of the Army," p. 417; *Stories of Our Soldiers* (Boston: *The Journal* Newspaper Co., 1893), p. 217.
63. "True History of the Army," p. 417.
64. Reilly Account; Lamb, "Battles of Fort Fisher," pp. 287–88; *O.R.*, I, XLVI, pt. I, pp. 410, 413–15.

65. Lamb, "Battles of Fort Fisher," pp. 287–88; *O.R.*, I, XLVI, pt. I, pp. 438–40; Denson, pp. 42–43.
66. Denson, pp. 42–43; Lamb, "Battles of Fort Fisher," pp. 287–88.
67. *O.R.*, I, XLVI, pt. I, pp. 411, 414–15; Little, pp. 399–400.
68. Little, pp. 399–400; *O.R.*, I, XLVI, pt. I, pp. 410–11, 414–15.
69. Reilly Account; Lamb, "Battles of Fort Fisher," p. 288; *O.R.*, I, XLVI, pt. I, p. 440; *Battles and Leaders*, vol. IV, p. 653; *O.R.N.*, I, IX, p. 365.
70. Reilly Account; *Battles and Leaders*, vol. IV, p. 653; *O.R.*, I, XLVI, pt. II, p. 1066.
71. Reilly Account; *North Carolina State Troops*, p. 247.
72. Lamb, "Battles of Fort Fisher," vol. IV, p. 288.
73. Lamb, "Battles of Fort Fisher," vol. IV, p. 288; *O.R.*, I, XLVI, pt. 1, pp. 438–39; *O.R.*, I, XLVI, pt. II, pp. 1071–73.
74. *O.R.*, I, XLVI, pt. I, pp. 411, 415, 444; Henry Benton Memoir, Henry Benton Papers, Manuscript Collection, N.C. Department of Archives and History; *Battles and Leaders*, vol. IV, p. 654.
75. Howard Thomas, p. 252; *Stories of Our Soldiers*, p. 218.
76. Grattan, "Under the Blue Pennant," Grattan Papers; Grattan Journal, Grattan Papers, January 15, 1865; Deck Log, USS *Malvern*, January 15, 1865; *O.R.N.*, I, XI, p. 444.
77. Evans, p. 98; Grattan, "Under the Blue Pennant," Grattan Papers.
78. Ibid.; Comstock, Diary, p. 305.
79. "Task Before Them," p. 43; Evans, p. 98; Grattan, "Under the Blue Pennant," Grattan Papers; William Cobb to "Dear Father," January 17, 1865, William Cobb Papers, Fort Fisher State Historic Site; "A Yankee's Account," p. 325.
80. Comstock, *Diary*, pp. 304–5; "Rocked in the Cradle of Consternation," p. 78; Benton Memoir, Benton Papers.
81. *O.R.*, I, XLVI, pt. I, pp. 410–15, 425; Little, pp. 399–400; "Task Before Them," p. 43.
82. Reilly Account; "Return of Major James Reilly's Sword," *Confederate Veteran*, vol. II, no. 4 (April 1894), p. 119; A. G. Jones, "About the Surrender of Fort Fisher," *Confederate Veteran*, vol. XXII, no. 1 (January 1914), p. 21; Charles H. Graves to Adrian Terry, August 5, 1897, Terry Papers.
83. *O.R.*, I, XLVI, pt. I, pp. 439–42, 446; *Battles and Leaders*, vol. IV, pp. 653–54.
84. Ibid.; *O.R.*, I, XLVI, pt. II, pp. 1065–74; *O.R.*, I, XLVI, pt. I, pp. 442–47.
85. Ibid.
86. *O.R.*, I, XLVI, pt. I, pp. 442–447; *Battles and Leaders*, vol. IV, pp. 653–54; Lamb, "Battles of Fort Fisher," pp. 288–89; "Defense and Fall of Fort Fisher," p. 365.
87. *Battles and Leaders*, vol. IV, p. 654; Lamb, "Battles of Fort Fisher," pp. 288–89; *O.R.*, I, XLVI, pt. I, pp. 442–47.
88. Reilly Account; "Return of Reilly's Sword," p. 119; Charles H. Graves to Adrian Terry, August 8, 1897, Terry Papers.

89. Charles H. Graves to Adrian Terry, August 8, 1897, Terry Papers; "Return of Reilly's Sword," p. 119; Lawrence Lee to John A. Reilly, November 21, 1983, Reilly Papers; Adrian Terry, "Wilmington and Fort Fisher," Terry Papers, pp. 74–75.

90. "Task Before Them," p. 43; *O.R.*, I, XLVI, pt. I, pp. 444–45; Francis Minot Weld, *Diaries and Letters of Francis Minot Weld*, ed. Sarah Swan Weld Blake (n.p., 1925).

91. *O.R.*, I, XLVI, pt. I, pp. 410, 425; A. G. Jones, "Delicate War Relic From Fort Fisher," *Confederate Veteran*, vol. XXII, no. 1 (January 1914), p. 21.

92. Ibid., pp. 21, 119; Charles H. Graves to Adrian Terry, August 8, 1897, Terry Papers; "True History of the Army," p. 419; *O.R.*, I, XLVI, pt. II, pp. 166; George F. Towle to Adrian Terry, July 23, 1898, Terry Papers; Adrian Terry, "Wilmington and Fort Fisher," Terry Papers, p. 35.

93. *O.R.*, I, XLVI, pt. I, pp. 394–400; Comstock, *Diary*, p. 365; "Task Before Them," p. 43.

94. "Task Before Them," p. 43.

95. Ibid.; Comstock, *Diary*, p. 305.

96. Ibid.

97. Adrian Terry, "Wilmington and Fort Fisher," Terry Papers, p. 83; "Task Before Them," p. 43; Comstock, *Diary*, p. 365.

12

"Wilmington Is Closed"

1. Deck Log, USS *Malvern*, January 16, 1865; Evans, pp. 98–99; Grattan, "Under the Blue Pennant," Grattan Papers.

2. Joseph Fernold to "Dear Louise," January 20, 1865, Joseph Fernold Papers, Southern Historical Collection, University of North Carolina; Andrews, *The North Reports the Civil War*, p. 618; *New York Tribune*, January 17, 1865.

3. Grattan, "Under the Blue Pennant," Grattan Papers.

4. Christian Fleetwood to "Dear Pop," January 21, 1865, Fleetwood Papers.

5. James J. Cleer to "Father and Mother," January 17, 1865, James J. Cleer Papers, Manuscript Department, William R. Perkins Library, Duke University.

6. "True History of the Army," p. 420; *O.R.*, I, XLVI, pt. I, p. 427; Samuel M. Zent to Adrian Terry, December 12, 1896, Terry Papers.

7. "Rocked in the Cradle of Consternation," p. 78; James J. Cleer to "Father and Mother," January 17, 1865, Cleer Papers; "True History of the Army," pp. 420–21; Fort Fisher Logbook; Joseph Fernold to "Louise," January 20, 1865, Fernold Papers; Francis Sands, p. 25.

8. Samuel M. Zent to Adrian Terry, December 12, 1896, Terry Papers; *O.R.*, I, XLVI, pt. I, pp. 426, 430–31.

9. *O.R.*, I, XLVI, pt. I, p. 430.

10. Deck Log, USS *Malvern,* January 16, 1865; "True History of the Army," p. 421; "Rocked in the Cradle of Consternation," p. 79; *O.R.*, I, XLVI, pt. I, pp. 425–31.

11. Howard Thomas, pp. 252–53.

12. Samuel M. Zent to Adrian Terry, December 12, 1896, Terry Papers.

13. Ibid.; *O.R.*, I, XLVI, pt. I, pp. 425–31.

14. Ibid.; "Rocked in the Cradle of Consternation," p. 79; *Battles and Leaders,* vol. IV, p. 654; Little, p. 401; *O.R.*, I, XLVI, pt. I, pp. 401, 403; Howard Thomas, pp. 253–54.

15. *New York Tribune,* January 18, 1865; James H. Clark, *The Iron-Hearted Regiment* (Albany, N.Y.: J. Munsell Co., 1865), p. 165; Howard Thomas, p. 253; "True Story of the Army," p. 421; *O.R.*, I, XLVI, pt. I, p. 401; Andrews, *The North Reports the Civil War,* p. 757; Little, p. 400.

16. *O.R.*, I, XLVI, pt. I, p. 969; *O.R.*, I, XLVI, pt. I, pp. 401, 405, 434; *O.R.N.*, I, XI, pp. 370–71, 444; *Battles and Leaders,* vol. IV, pp. 661–62; *New York Tribune,* January 18, 1865.

17. *O.R.*, I, XLII, pt. I, pp. 1008–9, 1023; *O.R.*, I, XLVI, pt. I, p. 434; *Battles and Leaders,* vol. IV, p. 661; Lamb, "Battles of Fort Fisher," p. 290; *Histories of Regiments and Battalions from North Carolina,* vol. II, pp. 649–50.

18. "Rocked in the Cradle of Consternation," p. 79; Taylor, p. 62; S. K. Wightman, "In Search of My Son," *American Heritage,* vol. XIV, no. 2 (February 1963), p. 68; *O.R.*, I, XLVI, pt. II, p. 157; *Philadelphia Inquirer,* November 18, 1881.

19. Deck Log, USS *Powhatan,* January 16, 1865; Evans, pp. 98–99; Grattan, "Under the Blue Pennant," Grattan Papers.

20. *Soldier of Indiana,* p. 789; Price, p. 356; William Izlar, p. 108.

21. James Izlar Diary, January 16, 1865; *History of Regiments and Battalions from North Carolina,* vol. II, p. 761; William H. Haigh Papers, Southern Historical Collection, University of North Carolina, p. 2; Leonard Thomas, p. 16.

22. Leonard Thomas, p. 16. Haigh Papers, pp. 2–3; James Izlar Diary, January 16–21, 1865.

23. Grattan, "Under the Blue Pennant," Grattan Papers; *O.R.*, I, XLVI, pt. I, p. 402; *O.R.*, I, XLVI, pt. II, p. 155; Welles, *Diary,* vol. II, p. 228; Little, p. 400; Comstock, *Diary,* pp. 305–6.

24. Comstock, *Diary,* pp. 305–6; Newton M. Curtis, *From Bull Run to Chancellorsville* (New York: G. P. Putnam's Sons, 1906), p. 374; *O.R.*, I, XLVI, pt. I, p. 402.

25. *O.R.N.*, I, XI, pp. 456, 519–22, 613; *Stories of Our Soldiers,* pp. 218–19.

26. *O.R.*, I, XLVI, pt. II, pp. 158–59; *Harper's Weekly,* January 28, 1865; *O.R.*, I, XLVI, pt. I, p. 402; *O.R.N.*, I, XI, pp. 458–59.

27. Welles, *Diary,* vol. II, pp. 226–29.
28. *New York Tribune,* January 18, 1865; *Harper's Weekly,* January 28, 1865.
29. Christian Fleetwood to "Dear Pop," January 21, 1865, Fleetwood Papers.
30. J. D. McGeachy to "Dear Sister," January 17, 1865, Buie Papers; *O.R.,* I, XLVI, pt. II, pp. 1070–73, 1078–79.
31. *O.R.,* I, XLVI, pt. I, p. 434; "Defense and Fall of Fort Fisher," p. 349.
32. *Wilmington Journal,* January 17, 1865.
33. James M. McPherson, *Battle Cry of Freedom* (New York: Oxford University Press, 1988), pp. 821, 838; Freeman, *Lee's Lieutenants,* vol. III, p. 638; "Resources of the Confederacy in February, 1865," *Southern Historical Society Papers,* vol. II, pp. 103–5; Alexander H. Stephens, *A Constitutional View of the Late War Between the States* (Chicago: National Publishing Co., 1868), vol. II, p. 619; *O.R.,* I, XLVI, pt. II, p. 1258.
34. McPherson, pp. 821–23; Stephens, p. 619; J. G. Randal and David Donald, *The Civil War and Reconstruction* (Boston: D. C. Heath and Co., 1961), p. 524; Clement Eaton, *Jefferson Davis* (New York: Free Press, 1977), pp. 259–60.
35. Ibid.; Randal and Donald, p. 513; McPherson, pp. 837–38; *Historical Times Illustrated Encyclopedia,* pp. 412–13; Haigh Papers, p. 3.
36. *O.R.,* I, XLVI, pt. II, pp. 1078–91; *O.R.,* I, XLVI, pt. I, pp. 434–35; Barrett, pp. 280–81; Alexander Torrey McLean, "The Fort Fisher and Wilmington Campaign: 1864–1865," master's thesis, University of North Carolina, 1969, pp. 65–66.
37. McLean, pp. 65–66; Barrett, p. 280; Denson, pp. 54–55; unsigned letter to "Kate," January 21, 1865, Buie Papers.
38. *O.R.N.,* I, XI, pp. 624–27; Barrett, pp. 281–84; *O.R.,* I, XLVI, pt. I, pp. 41–45.
39. *O.R.N.,* I, XII, pp. 31–34; Hagood, pp. 336–37; McLean, pp. 70–75; *Historical Times Illustrated Encyclopedia,* p. 831; Barrett, pp. 281–84.
40. Barrett, pp. 283–84; McLean, pp. 82–83; Joseph Hawley to "Hattie," February 28, 1865, Joseph R. Hawley Papers, Manuscript Division, Library of Congress; "Yankees Were Landing Below Us," ed. William N. Still, Jr., *Civil War Times Illustrated,* vol. XV, no. 1 (April 1976), p. 18.
41. McLean, pp. 82–83; Barrett, pp. 283–84.
42. Barrett, p. 284; Little, pp. 410–13; *North Carolina Civil War Documentary,* ed. W. Buck Yearns and John G. Barrett (Chapel Hill: University of North Carolina Press, 1980), pp. 91–92; Joseph Hawley to "Hattie," February 28, 1865, Hawley Papers.
43. Little, pp. 410–13.
44. Ibid.; *North Carolina Civil War Documentary,* pp. 91–92; Barrett, p. 284; Warner, *Generals in Blue,* pp. 219–20.

Epilogue

1. *Histories of Regiments and Battalions from North Carolina,* vol. II, p. 761; Haigh Papers, pp. 4–5. *North Carolina State Troops,* vol. I, pp. 171–73; ibid., vol. II, p. 761.
2. Haigh Papers, pp. 4–5.
3. James Izlar Diary, January 25–27, 1865; W. H. C. Whiting to Major General James Dix, January 27, 1865, Whiting Papers, Compiled Service Records.
4. Ibid.
5. *O.R.,* I, XLVI, pt. I, pp. 439–42.
6. Ibid., pp. 441–42.
7. "U.S.A. General Hospital, Fort Columbus, New York Harbor," Whiting Papers, Compiled Service Records; *Fort Fisher Expedition,* p. 108.
8. *North Carolina State Troops,* vol. I, pp. 173–74; James Izlar Diary, March 5, 1865.
9. "U.S.A. General Hospital, Fort Columbus, New York Harbor," Whiting Papers, Compiled Service Records; Denson, pp. 50–51; *New York Times,* March 11, 1865.
10. Denson, p. 51.
11. Ibid., pp. 51–52; *New York Times,* March 11, 12, 1965; W. H. C. Whiting File, Cemetery Records, Oakdale Cemetery, Wilmington, N.C.
12. Denson, pp. 49–50.
13. Warner, *Generals in Gray,* pp. 30–31; *Biographical Dictionary of the Confederacy,* p. 106; Introduction, Braxton Bragg Collection, Archives Department, Rosenberg Library; *Historical Times Illustrated Encyclopedia,* p. 75; Boatner, p. 78; *Battles and Leaders,* vol. IV, pp. 764–65; *New York Times,* September 28, 1876.
14. Warner, *Generals in Gray,* pp. 30–31; *Historical Times Illustrated Encyclopedia,* p. 75; Boatner, p. 78.
15. *Harper's Weekly,* February 4, 1865; *New York Tribune,* January 18, 1865; *O.R.,* I, XLVI, pt. II, p. 140; *O.R.,* I, XLVI, pt. I, p. 402; Captain E. Lewis Moore to Joseph Hawley, January 23, 1865, Hawley Papers.
16. Joseph C. Abbott to Joseph Hawley, January 23, 1865, Hawley Papers; Alfred H. Terry to Joseph Hawley, January 28, and 29, 1865, Hawley Papers.
17. Finan, p. 37; *New York Times,* December 20, 1890; Alfred H. Terry to Joseph Hawley, January 29, 1865, Hawley Papers.
18. Finan, p. 37; *Dictionary of American Biography,* vol. XVIII, pp. 378–79; Warner, *Generals in Blue,* p. 498.
19. *Dictionary of American Biography,* vol. XVIII, pp. 378–79; *New York Times,* December 17, 19, 20, 1890; Finan, pp. 43, 472.
20. Butler, pp. 1127–28.
21. *Dictionary of American Biography,* vol. XV, p. 88; *Fort Fisher Expedition,* pp. 87–104; James Merrill, pp. 470–74.
22. *Dictionary of American Biography,* vol. XV, p. 88; Butler, pp. 823–24.

23. *Dictionary of American Biography,* vol. XV, p. 88; Still, p. 46; *New York Times,* February 14, 1891.
24. *New York Times,* February 14, 1891.
25. *Fort Fisher Expedition,* pp. I–51.
26. *New York Times,* January 12, 1893; *Dictionary of American Biography,* vol. III, pp. 358–59.
27. Ibid.
28. Ibid.
29. Ibid.
30. Nash, p. 13; *New York Times,* January 12, 1893.
31. Comstock, *Diary,* pp. 305–6.
32. Comstock, *Diary,* pp. 387–90; *New York Times,* May 30, 1910; *O.R. Atlas,* plate LXXV; *O.R.,* I, XLVI, pt. I, p. 384.
33. *North Carolina State Troops,* vol. I, pp. 40, 75; Sprunt, *Chronicles,* p. 361; Lawrence Lee to John A. Reilly, November 21, 1983, Reilly Papers; "Return of Reilly's Sword," p. 119.
34. *North Carolina State Troops,* vol. I, pp. 226, 33; United States Census Schedule, Cumberland County, N.C., 1870, National Archives; Kinchen Braddy to Z. T. Fulmore, March 25, 1901, Braddy Papers.
35. Ibid., pp. 151–52; Warner, *Generals in Gray,* p. 58.
36. *Dictionary of American Biography,* vol. III, pp. 13–14.
37. *Historical Times Illustrated Encyclopedia,* vol. VI, p. 210; Robert Leckie, *The Wars of America* (New York: Harper & Row, 1968), vol. II, pp. 37–40; *New York Times,* January 6, 1912.
38. *Dictionary of American Biography,* vol. II, pp. 635–37; Roske and Van Doren, pp. 288–97.
39. *Dictionary of American Biography,* vol. I, pp. 23–24; Boatner, p. 1.
40. *Illustrated London News,* March 18, 1865; Hoole, pp. 132–33; *Historical Times Illustrated Encyclopedia,* p. 789.
41. Wightman, pp. 68–69.
42. *Historical Times Illustrated Encyclopedia,* p. 574; *Dictionary of American Biography,* vol. XIII, pp. 446–47; Galusha Pennypacker to Adrian Terry, June 1, 1896, Terry Papers; *New York Times,* October 2, 1916; War Department to Galusha Pennypacker, January 16, 1865, Galusha Pennypacker Papers, Historical Society of Pennsylvania; *West Chester Village Record,* November 14, 1865.
43. Bouton, pp. 31–37; *Dictionary of American Biography,* vol. I, pp. 159–60.
44. Warner, *Generals in Blue,* pp. 5–6; *Historical Times Illustrated Encyclopedia,* pp. 10–11; *New York Times,* February 5, 1897, April 14, 1933.
45. Ibid.
46. *New York Times,* February 5, 1897.
47. Ibid.; Ames, pp. 12, 18, 21, 23–24.
48. *New York Times,* February 5, 6, 1897; Ames, p. 21; *The Congressional Medal of Honor* (Forest Ranch, Calif.: Sharp and Dunnigan, 1984), pp. 707, 756; Curtis, *From Bull Run to Chancellorsville,* p. 374.

49. *New York Times,* February 5, 1897.
50. Ibid., May 6, 1897; Curtis, "Capture of Fort Fisher," p. 51; N. M. Curtis to Adrian Terry, February 22, 1897, Terry Papers.
51. Warner, *Generals in Blue,* p. 6; Adelbert Ames to "Blanche," August 15, 1898, Adelbert Ames Papers, Archives Branch, U.S. Army Military History Institute.
52. Warner, *Generals in Blue,* p. 6; *New York Times,* April 14, 1933.
53. Curtis, *From Bull Run to Chancellorsville,* p. 374; *Dictionary of American Biography,* vol. II, pp. 618–19.
54. Ibid.; *New York Times,* January 9, 1910, April 14, 1933.
55. Lamb Diary, January 23–March 21, 1865; *O.R.N.,* I, IX, pp. 714–15.
56. Madge Lamb Bilisoly to Louis Moore, August 4 and August 31, 1926, Louis T. Moore Collection, North Carolina Room, New Hanover County Public Library; Solon Carter, "Service with Colored Troops," *Civil War Papers* (Boston: Massachusetts Commandery of the Military Order of the Loyal Legion, 1900), vol. I, p. 176.
57. Lamb Diary, March 22–April 22, May 1–September 27, 1865; Baker, p. xix.
58. Ibid.
59. *The National Cyclopedia of American Biography* (James T. White & Co., 1891), vol. I, p. 274; Baker, pp. xix–xxxiii.
60. *Our Living and Our Dead,* vol. III, July–December 1875, pp. 100–105; *Colonel William Lamb Day,* p. 1; *Wilmington Messenger,* December 2, 1906; *Philadelphia Times,* November 18, 1881; *The American Heritage Century Collection of Civil War Art,* ed. Stephen Sears (New York: American Heritage Publishing Co., 1974), pp. 12–13.
61. Taylor, *Running the Blockade,* pp. 61–63; Baker, p. xxix; Photographs Collection, William Lamb Papers, William and Mary.
62. Baker, pp. xxvi–xxvii; "Biographical Note," Sarah Lamb Letters; Madge Lamb Bilisoly to Louis Moore, August 4, 1926, Moore Collection.
63. Ibid.; Baker, pp. xxviii–xxxv; "William Lamb," *Men of Mark in Virginia,* pp. 193–94.
64. Lamb Diary, March 4, March 23, 1909; Madge Lamb Bilisoly to Louis Moore, August 4, 1926, Moore Collection; Oscar Voorhees, "Colonel William Lamb and Phi Beta Kappa," *The Virginia Magazine of History and Biography,* vol. LIV, no. 3, 1946, pp. 218–32.
65. Reid, p. 39.
66. Ava L. Honeycutt, "Fort Fisher National Park Proposed, 1907–1910," *Lower Cape Fear Historical Society Bulletin,* n.d., Fort Fisher File, Lower Cape Fear Historical Society; *Hearing Before a Subcommittee of the Committee on Military Affairs of the House of Representatives on H.R. 9131, January 16, 1909* (Washington: U.S. Government Printing Office, 1909), p. 5.
67. *Hearing Before a Subcommittee, January 16, 1909,* pp. 3–12.
68. Ibid.; Honeycutt, "Fort Fisher National Park Proposed."
69. Robert Fales, "First Visit to Fort Fisher," unpublished manuscript, N.C.

Pamphlet File, North Carolina Room, New Hanover County Public Library; Thorndike Saville to U.S. Beach Erosion Board, September 5, 1931, Fort Fisher Collection, North Carolina Room, New Hanover County Public Library; T. R. Orrell to New Hanover County Board of Commissioners, January 11, 1928, New Hanover County Commissioners Minutes, 1928, North Carolina Room, New Hanover County Public Library; Olive Webster, "Fort Fisher: A Historic Site," unpublished manuscript, Moore Collection.

70. Louis T. Moore to "Aunt Cornie," March 31, 1937, Moore Collection; Forrest Rees to Andrew J. Howell, July 5, 1931, Fort Fisher Collection; A. L. Honeycutt, "Fort Fisher During World War II," unpublished manuscript, N.C. Pamphlet File, New Hanover County Public Library.

71. Richard Knapp, "North Carolina's State Historic Sites: A Brief History and Status Report," Official Report to the N.C. Department of Cultural Resources, 1985, Historic Sites Library, N.C. Department of Cultural Resources; Paul Kelly to N.C. Department of Conservation and Development, December 7, 1934, Fort Fisher Collection.

Bibliography

Manuscripts, Theses, and Official Records

ALDEN, ALONZO. Papers. Civil War Miscellaneous Collection, Archives Branch, U.S. Army Military History Institute.

AMES, ADELBERT. Papers. Archives Branch, U.S. Army Military History Institute.

The Atlas to Accompany the Official Records of the Union and Confederate Armies. Washington, D.C.: U.S. Government Printing Office, 1891.

BAKER, GERTRUDE. "The Diary of William Lamb, August 18, 1859–May 21, 1860." Master's thesis, The College of William and Mary, 1960.

BEEKER, HENRY JUDSON. "Wilmington During the Civil War." Master's thesis, Duke University, 1941.

BELL, LOUIS. Papers. Compiled Service Records of the 4th New Hampshire Infantry, National Archives.

BENTON, HENRY E. Papers. Manuscript Collection, North Carolina Department of Archives and History.

BETHAM, ASA. Papers. Manuscript Division, Library of Congress.

BLAIR, B. F. Papers. Civil War Miscellaneous Collection, Archives Division, U.S. Army Military History Institute.

BLAND, CHRISTOPHER. Papers. Compiled Service Records of the 36th North Carolina Artillery, National Archives.

BOLLES, CHARLES B. Papers. North Carolina Department of Archives and History.

BRADDY, KINCHEN. Papers. Civil War Collection, North Carolina Department of Archives and History.

BRAGG, BRAXTON. Collection. Archives Department, Rosenberg Library.

———. Papers. Manuscript Collection, the Western Reserve Historical Society.

BUIE, CATHERINE. Papers. Manuscript Collection, William R. Perkins Library, Duke University.

BUTLER, BENJAMIN F. Papers. Manuscript Division, Library of Congress.

CARTER, SOLON. Papers. Archives Branch, U.S. Army Military History Institute.

CARY, CLARENCE. Report. Manuscript Division, Library of Congress.

CIVIL WAR LETTERS. Lower Cape Fear Historical Society.

CLEER, JAMES J. Papers. Manuscript Department, William R. Perkins Library, Duke University.

COBB, WILLIAM. Papers. Fort Fisher State Historic Site.

Compiled Service Records. 4th N.C. Junior Reserves, 7th N.C. Junior Reserves, 8th N.C. Junior Reserves, 10th N.C. Artillery, 36th N.C. Artillery, 2nd S.C. Cavalry, 7th S.C. Cavalry, 21st S.C. Infantry, 25th S.C. Infantry, National Archives.

COMSTOCK, CYRUS B. Papers. Manuscript Division, Library of Congress.

CROMARTIE, JUNIUS. Papers. *Civil War Times Illustrated* Collection, Archives Division, U.S. Army Military History Institute.

DAWSON, RICHARD, W. Journal. Richard W. Dawson Papers, Manuscript Department, William R. Perkins Library, Duke University.

Deck Logs of the USS *Brooklyn,* USS *Fort Jackson,* USS *Juanita,* USS *Mahopac,* USS *Malvern,* USS *Monadnock,* USS *New Ironsides,* USS *Powhatan,* USS *Saugus,* USS *Tacony.* National Archives.

Demolay manuscript. Author's collection.

FALES, ROBERT. "First Visit to Fort Fisher." Unpublished manuscript, N.C. Pamphlet File, New Hanover County Public Library.

FERNOLD, JOSEPH. Papers. Southern Historical Collection, University of North Carolina.

FLEETWOOD, CHRISTIAN A. Diary. Manuscript Division, Library of Congress.

———. Papers. Manuscript Division, Library of Congress.

FONVIELLE, CHRIS JR. "To Forge a Thunderbolt: The Wilmington Campaign, February, 1865." Master's thesis, East Carolina University, 1987.

Fort Fisher Collection. North Carolina Room, New Hanover County Public Library.

The Fort Fisher Expedition: Report of the Joint Committee on the Conduct of the War, 38th Congress, 2nd Session. Washington, D.C.: U.S. Government Printing Office, 1865.

"FORT FISHER HISTORIC SITE." Raleigh: North Carolina Department of Archives and History, 1962.

FORT FISHER LOGBOOK. Military Collection—Civil War, North Carolina Department of Archives and History.

GRATTAN, JOHN W. Papers. Manuscript Division, Library of Congress.

GREER, WILLIAM ROBERT. "Recollections of a Private Soldier in the Army of the Confederate States." William Robert Greer Papers, Manuscript Department, William R. Perkins Library, Duke University.

HAIGH, WILLIAM H. Papers. Southern Historical Collection, University of North Carolina.

HAWLEY, JOSEPH R. Papers. Manuscript Division, Library of Congress.

Hearing Before a Subcommitee of the Committee on Military Affairs of the House of Representatives on H.R. 9131, January 16, 1909. Washington, D.C.: U.S. Government Printing Office, 1909.

HEBERT, LOUIS. Papers. Compiled Service Records of General and Staff Officers and Non-Regimental Enlisted Men, National Archives.

HONEYCUTT, A. L. "Fort Fisher During World War II." Unpublished manuscript, N.C. Pamphlet File, New Hanover County Public Library.

————. "Fort Fisher—Malakoff of the South." Master's thesis, Duke University, 1963.

IZLAR, JAMES F. Diary. Manuscript Collection, South Caroliniana Library, University of South Carolina.

KETCHAM, WILLIAM A. "William A. Ketcham Reminiscences of Fort Fisher." William A. Ketcham Papers, Indiana Historical Society.

KING, ASA. Papers. Confederate Veterans' Talks, Lower Cape Fear Historical Society Archives.

KNAPP, RICHARD. "North Carolina State History Sites: A Brief History and Status Report." Official Report to the N.C. Department of Cultural Resources, 1985. Historic Sites Library, N.C. Department of Cultural Resources.

LAMB, ELEANOR RUTH AND ORRE KNOX. Papers. Lower Cape Fear Historical Society.

LAMB, SARAH C. Letters. William Lamb Collection, Earl Greg Swem Library, The College of William and Mary.

————. Papers. William Lamb Collection, Earl Greg Swem Library, The College of William and Mary.

LAMB, WILLIAM. "Autobiography of William Lamb." William Lamb Collection, Earl Greg Swem Library, The College of William and Mary.

————. Diary. William Lamb Collection, Earl Greg Swem Library, The College of William and Mary.

————. "First Shot From Fort Fisher." William Lamb Papers, The College of William and Mary.

————. Papers. Compiled Service Records of Confederate General and Staff Officers and Non-Regimental Enlisted Men, National Archives.

LYBROOK COLLECTION. North Carolina Department of Archives and History.

McEACHERN-WILLIAMS PAPERS. Lower Cape Fear Historical Society.

McEwen, Eliza S. Papers. Manuscript Department, William R. Perkins Library, Duke University.

McLean, Alexander Torrey. "The Fort Fisher and Wilmington Campaign: 1864–1865." Master's thesis, University of North Carolina, 1969.

McNeil, Hector H. Papers. Manuscript Department, William R. Perkins Library, Duke University.

McNeil, Mary Margaret. Papers. Manuscript Department, William R. Perkins Library, Duke University.

McQueen, Henry Clay. Papers. Confederate Veterans' Talks, Lower Cape Fear Historical Society Archives.

Montgomery, James Alexander. Papers. Confederate Veterans' Talks, Lower Cape Fear Historical Society Archives.

Moore, Louis T. Collection. North Carolina Room, New Hanover County Public Library.

New Hanover County (N.C.) Commissioners Minutes, 1928, North Carolina Room, New Hanover County Public Library.

North Carolina Pamphlet File. North Carolina Room, New Hanover County Public Library.

Official Records of the Union and Confederate Navies in the War of the Rebellion. Washington, D.C.: U.S. Government Printing Office, 1880–1927.

Osborne, Joseph B. Papers. Manuscript Division, Library of Congress.

Pennypacker, Galusha. Papers. The Historical Society of Pennsylvania.

Porter, Benjamin H. Papers. Records of the Bureau of Naval Personnel, National Archives.

Porter, David D. Papers. Manuscript Division, Library of Congress.

Preston, Samuel W. Papers. U.S. Navy Military Service Records, National Archives.

———. Papers. U.S. Navy Pension Records, National Archives.

Reilly, James. James Reilly Account of the Battle of Fort Fisher. W. L. DeRossett Papers, North Carolina Department of Archives and History.

———. Papers. Archives Branch, U.S. Army Military History Institute.

Robbins, John Davis. "The Second Battle of Fort Fisher." McEachern-Williams Collection, Lower Cape Fear Historical Society.

Saunders, William J. Papers. Compiled Service Records of Confederate General and Staff Officers and Non-Regimental Enlisted Men, National Archives.

Scroggs, Joseph. Diary. Civil War Collection, Archives Department, U.S. Army Military History Institute.

Singleton, Spiers. Papers. Compiled Service Records of Confederate General and Staff Officers and Non-Regimental Enlisted Men, National Archives.

South Atlantic Blockading Squadron (SABS) Area File. National Archives.

South, Stanley. "Excavation of the Ruin of the House of the Keeper of the Light and William Lamb's Headquarters at Fort Fisher State Historic

Site." Unpublished manuscript, Historic Sites Division, North Carolina Department of Archives and History.

SPEED, THOMAS. Letters. Manuscript Collection, The Filson Club Historical Society.

TALLENTINE, JAMES. Papers. U.S. Navy Military Service Records, Record Group 24, National Archives.

TAYLOR, JOHN D. Papers. Manuscript Collection, North Carolina Department of Archives and History.

TERRY, ADRIAN. Papers. Terry Family Collection, Manuscripts and Archives Division, Sterling Memorial Library, Yale University.

———. "Wilmington and Fort Fisher." Unpublished manuscript, Adrian Terry Papers, Terry Family Collection, Sterling Memorial Library, Yale University.

United States Census Schedule, 1870. National Archives.

WADDEL, A. W. "Some Memories of My Life." McEachern-Williams Collection, Lower Cape Fear Historical Society Archives.

The War of the Rebellion: A Compilation of the Official Records of the Union and Confederate Armies. Washington, D.C.: U.S. Government Printing, 1880–1901.

WATSON, ROBERT. Diary. Manuscript Department, Cornell University.

WEBSTER, OLIVE. "Fort Fisher: A Historic Site." Unpublished manuscript, Louis T. Moore Collection, North Carolina Room, New Hanover County Public Library.

WHITING, W. H. C. File. Cemetery Records, Oakdale Cemetery, Wilmington, N.C.

———. Papers. Compiled Service Records of Confederate General and Staff Officers and Non-Regimental Enlisted Men, National Archives.

———. Papers. Manuscript Collection, North Carolina Department of Archives and History.

———. Papers. U.S. Army Military Academy Library, West Point.

WIGHTMAN, EDWARD K. Papers. Private collection of Dr. Henry B. Wightman, Ithaca, New York.

WILSON, CLYDE. "W. H. C. Whiting." Unpublished manuscript, history department, University of South Carolina.

WISE, GEORGE D. Papers. Manuscript Department, Duke University.

Books and Articles

ABBOT, WILLIS J. *Blue Jackets of '61.* New York: Dodd, Mead and Co., 1887.

ALEXANDER, EDWARD P. *Fighting for the Confederacy: The Personal Recollections of General Edward Porter Alexander.* Edited by Gary W. Gallagher. Chapel Hill: University of North Carolina Press, 1989.

ALMY, JOHN J. "Incidents of the Blockade." *War Papers Read Before the Military Order of the Loyal Legion, Commandery of the District of Columbia.* Washington, D.C.: Published by the Commandery, 1892.

The American Heritage Century Collection of Civil War Art. Edited by

Stephen Sears. New York: American Heritage Publishing Co., 1974.

AMES, ADELBERT. "The Capture of Fort Fisher, North Carolina, January 15, 1865." *Personal Recollections of the War of the Rebellion.* Edited by A. Noel Blackman. New York: G. P. Putnam's Sons, 1907.

ANDREWS, CUTLER J. *The North Reports the Civil War.* Pittsburgh: University of Pittsburgh Press, 1955.

ASHE, SAMUEL A. "Fort Fisher." *Confederate Veteran,* vol. XL, p. 250.

———. *History of North Carolina.* Raleigh: Edwards & Broughton Printing Co., 1925.

BARRETT, JOHN G. *The Civil War in North Carolina.* Chapel Hill: University of North Carolina Press, 1963.

Battles and Leaders of the Civil War. Edited by Robert U. Johnson and Clarence C. Buel. New York: Century Company, 1884.

BERRINGER, RICHARD, ET AL. *Why the South Lost the Civil War.* Athens: University of Georgia Press, 1986.

BEYER, W. F., AND KEYDEL, O. F. *Deeds of Valor from Records in the Archives of the United States Government.* Detroit: Perrien-Keydel Co., 1907.

Biographical Dictionary of the Confederacy. Edited by John L. Wakelyn. Westport, Conn.: Greenwood Press, 1977.

BOATNER, MARK MAYO III. *The Civil War Dictionary.* New York: David McKay & Co., 1959.

BOUTON, JOHN BELL. *A Memoir of Colonel Louis Bell.* New York: n.p., 1865.

BRADLEE, FRANCIS. *Blockade Running During the Civil War.* Salem, Mass.: Essex Institute Press, 1959.

BUEL, AUGUSTUS. *The Cannoneer.* Washington, D.C.: National Tribune, 1890.

BUTLER, BENJAMIN F. *Butler's Book.* Boston: A. M. Thayer & Co., 1892.

CADWELL, CHARLES K. *The Old Sixth Regiment.* New Haven: Tuttle, Morehouse and Co., 1950.

CARSE, ROBERT. *Blockade: The Civil War at Sea.* New York: Rinehart & Co., 1950.

CARTER, SOLON. "Service with Colored Troops." *Civil War Papers.* Boston: Massachusetts Commandery of the Military Order of the Loyal Legion, 1900.

CATALFO, ALFRED. *The History of the Town of Rollinsford, New Hampshire, 1623–1973.* N.p., 1973.

CATTON, BRUCE. *The American Heritage Picture History of the Civil War.* New York: American Heritage Publishing Co., 1960.

CHAITIN, PETER. *The Coastal War: Chesapeake Bay to Rio Grande.* Alexandria, Va.: Time-Life Books, 1984.

Civil War Naval Chronology. Washington, D.C.: U.S. Government Printing Office, 1971.

CLARK, JAMES H. *The Iron-Hearted Regiment.* Albany, N.Y.: J. Munsell Co., 1865.

COCHRAN, HAMILTON. *Blockade Runners of the Confederacy.* Indianapolis: Bobbs-Merrill Co., 1957.

COGGINS, JACK. *Arms and Equipment of the Civil War.* Garden City, N.J.: Doubleday, 1962.

Colonel William Lamb Day. Wilmington, N.C.: Carolina Printing Co., 1962.

COMSTOCK, CYRUS B. *The Diary of Cyrus B. Comstock.* Edited by Merlin E. Sumner. Dayton: Morningside House, 1987.

The Congressional Medal of Honor. Forest Ranch, Calif.: Sharp and Dunnigan, 1984.

CONNELLY, THOMAS L. *Autumn of Glory.* Baton Rouge: LSU Press, 1971.

CORNISH, DUDLEY TAYLOR. *The Sable Arm: Black Troops in the Union Army, 1861–1865.* Lawrence: University Press of Kansas, 1987.

CURTIS, NEWTON MARTIN. "The Capture of Fort Fisher." *Personal Recollections of the War of the Rebellion: Addresses Delivered Before the Military Order of the Loyal Legion of the United States, Commandery of Massachusetts.* Boston: Published by the Commandery, 1900.

———. *From Bull Run to Chancellorsville.* New York: G. P. Putnam's Sons, 1906.

DAVIS, JEFFERSON. *The Rise and Fall of the Confederate Government.* Richmond: Garrett and Massie, 1938.

DAVIS, MRS. T. C. "The Fall of Fort Fisher." *Confederate Veteran,* vol. XIII, no. 3 (March 1905).

"THE DEFENSE AND FALL OF FORT FISHER." *Southern Historical Society Papers,* vol. X. (August–September, 1882).

DEMEISSNER, SOPHIE RADFORD. *Old Navy Days: Sketches from the Life of Rear-Admiral William Radford, USN.* New York: Henry Holt and Co., 1920.

DENSON, C. B. *An Address Delivered in Raleigh, N.C. on Memorial Day (May 10) 1895, Containing a Memoir of the Late Major General William Henry Chase Whiting of the Confederate Army.* Raleigh: Edwards & Broughton Co., 1895.

DEROSSETT, WILLIAM LORD. *Pictorial and Historical New Hanover County and Wilmington, N.C., 1723–1938.* Wilmington: Wilmington Stamp and Printing Co., 1938.

Dictionary of American Biography. Edited by Allen Johnson and Dumas Malone. New York: Charles Scribner's Sons, 1928–1936.

DOWD, CLEMENT. *Life of Zebulon B. Vance.* Charlotte: Observer Printing and Publishing Co., 1897.

EATON, CLEMENT. *Jefferson Davis.* New York: Free Press, 1977.

ELDREDGE, DANIEL. *The Third New Hampshire, 1861–1865.* Boston: Stillings & Co., 1893.

EVANS, ROBLEY. *A Sailor's Log: Recollections of Forty Years of Naval Life.* New York: D. Appleton & Co., 1908.

FINAN, WILLIAM J. *Major General Alfred Howe Terry: Hero of Fort Fisher.* Hartford: Connecticut Civil War Centennial Commission, 1965.

FOOTE, SHELBY. *The Civil War: A Narrative.* New York: Random House, 1958.

FREEMAN, DOUGLAS SOUTHALL. *A Calendar of Confederate Papers.* Richmond: Whittet and Sheppersons, 1908.

————. *Lee's Lieutenants: A Study in Command.* New York: Charles Scribner's Sons, 1942.

From Antietam to Fort Fisher: The Civil War Letters of Edward K. Wightman, 1862–1865. Edited by Edward G. Longacre. Cranbury, N.J.: Associated University Presses, 1985.

HAGOOD, JOHNSON C. *Memoirs of the War of Secession.* Columbia, S.C.: State Company, 1910.

HALL, E. HEPPLE. "Reminiscences of the War: The Wilmington Expedition." *United States Service Magazine,* vol. IV (July 1865).

Hebe Centennial Program. Wilmington: Commercial Printing and Mailing Co., 1963.

The Historical Times Illustrated Encyclopedia of the Civil War. Edited by Patricia L. Faust. New York: Harper & Row, 1986.

Histories of the Several Regiments and Battalions from North Carolina in the Great War, 1861–'65. Edited by Walter Clark. Goldsboro, N.C.: Nash Bros., 1901.

HOLZMAN, ROBERT S. *Stormy Ben Butler.* New York: Macmillan Company, 1954.

HONEYCUTT, AVA L. "Fort Fisher National Park Proposed, 1907–1910." *Lower Cape Fear Historical Society Bulletin,* n.d. Wilmington, N.C.: Lower Cape Fear Historical Society.

HOOLE, W. STANLEY. *Vizetelly Covers the Confederacy.* Tuscaloosa, Ala.: Confederate Publishing, 1957.

HOWELL, ANDREW J. *The Book of Wilmington, 1730–1930.* Wilmington: n.p., 1930.

HYDE, WILLIAM L. *History of the 112th New York Volunteers.* Freedonia, N.Y.: McKinstry & Co., 1865.

IZLAR, WILLIAM VALMORE. *A Sketch of the War Record of the Edisto Rifles, 1861–1865.* Columbia, S.C.: State Company, 1914.

JOHNS, JOHN. "Wilmington During the Blockade." *Harper's New Monthly Magazine,* vol. XXXII, September 1866.

JONES, A. G. "About the Surrender of Fort Fisher." *Confederate Veteran,* vol. XXII, no. 1 (January 1914).

————. "Delicate War Relic From Fort Fisher." *Confederate Veteran,* vol. XXII, no. 1 (January 1914).

JONES, VIRGIL CARINGTON. *The Civil War At Sea.* New York: Holt, Rinehart, Winston, 1962.

LAMB, WILLIAM. "The Battles of Fort Fisher." *Southern Historical Society Papers,* vol. XXI.

————. *Colonel William Lamb's Story of Fort Fisher.* Carolina Beach, N.C.: Blockade Runner Museum, 1966.

————. "The Defense of Fort Fisher." *Battles and Leaders of the Civil War.*

Edited by Robert U. Johnson and Clarence C. Buel. vol. IV. New York: Century Company, 1884.

————. "The Heroine of Confederate Point." *Southern Historical Society Papers,* vol. XX, 1892.

LECKIE, ROBERT. *The Wars of America.* New York: Harper & Row, 1968.

Letters from the Colonel's Lady. Edited by Cornelius Thomas. Winnabow, N.C.: Charlestowne Preservation Trust, 1965.

List of Officers of the Navy of the United States and of the Marine Corps from 1775 to 1900. Edited by Edward W. Callahan. New York: L. R. Hamersly & Co., 1901.

LITTLE, HENRY. *The 7th Regiment of New Hampshire Volunteers in the War of the Rebellion.* Concord: n.p., 1886.

LOCKWOOD, H. C. "The Capture of Fort Fisher." *Atlantic Monthly,* vol. XXVII, May 1871.

LONG, E. B. *The Civil War Day by Day.* Garden City, N.Y.: Doubleday, 1971.

LORD, FRANCIS. *The Civil War Collector's Encyclopedia.* Columbia, S.C.: Lord Americana and Research, 1975.

LOSSING, BENSON J. "The First Attack on Fort Fisher." *The Annals of the War.* Philadelphia: Times Publishing Co., 1879.

MCELROY, JOHN. *Andersonville: A Story of Rebel Military Prisons.* Toledo, Ohio: D. R. Locke, 1879.

MCPHERSON, JAMES M. *Battle Cry of Freedom.* New York: Oxford University Press, 1988.

MCWHINEY, GRADY. *Braxton Bragg and the Confederate Defeat.* New York: Columbia University Press, 1969.

The Memorial to Brevet Major General Galusha Pennypacker. Philadelphia: The Pennypacker Memorial Commission, 1934.

Men of Mark in Virginia. Edited by Lyon G. Tyler. Washington, D.C.: Men of Mark Publishing Co., 1906.

MERRILL, JAMES M. "The Fort Fisher and Wilmington Campaign: Letters from Rear Admiral David D. Porter." *North Carolina Historical Review,* vol. XXXV, no. 4 (October 1958).

MOORE, LOUIS T. "The Heroine of Fort Fisher." *Confederate Veteran,* vol. XXXVII, no. 7, July 1929.

NASH, HOWARD P., JR. *Stormy Petrel: The Life and Times of General Benjamin F. Butler, 1818–1893.* Rutherford, N.J.: Fairleigh Dickinson University Press, 1969.

The National Cyclopedia of American Biography. James T. White & Co., 1891.

North Carolina Civil War Documentary. Edited by W. Buck Yearns and John G. Barrett. Chapel Hill: University of North Carolina Press, 1980.

North Carolina State Troops, 1861–1865: A Roster. Compiled by Louis H. Manarin. Raleigh: N.C. Department of Archives and History, 1966.

PARKER, JAMES. "The Navy in the Battles and Capture of Fort Fisher." *Personal Recollections of the War of the Rebellion Read Before the Mili-*

tary Order of the Loyal Legion, Commandery of New York. New York: Published by the Commandery, 1897.

PASHA, HOBART. *Sketches from My Life.* London: Longmans, Green & Co., 1886.

PORTER, DAVID D. *Incidents and Anecdotes of the Civil War.* New York: D. Appleton & Co., 1885.

———. *The Naval History of the Civil War.* Secaucus, N.J.: Castle Books, 1984.

PORTER, HORACE. *Campaigning with Grant.* Secaucus, N.J.: Blue and Grey Press, 1984.

PRICE, CHARLES, AND STURGILL, CLAUDE. "Shock and Assault in the First Battle of Fort Fisher." *North Carolina Historical Review,* vol. XLII, Winter 1970.

PRICE, ISAIAH. *History of the 9th Regiment of Pennsylvania Volunteer Infantry.* Philadelphia: n.p., 1875.

RANDAL, J. G., AND DONALD, DAVID. *The Civil War and Reconstruction.* Boston: D. C. Heath and Co., 1961.

REED, ROWENA. *Combined Operations in the Civil War.* Annapolis: Naval Institute Press, 1977.

REID, WHITELAW. *After the War: A Tour of the Southern States, 1865–1866.* New York: Harper & Row, 1965.

"Resources of the Confederacy in February, 1865." *Southern Historical Society Papers,* vol. II, pp. 103–5.

"Return of Major James Reilly's Sword." *Confederate Veteran,* vol. II, no. 4 (April 1894).

RIPLEY, WARREN. *Artillery and Ammunition of the Civil War.* Charleston, S.C.: Battery Press, 1984.

"Rocked in the Cradle of Consternation." Edited by Edwin S. Redkey. *American Heritage,* vol. XXXI, no. 6 (October–November 1980).

ROSKE, RALPH, AND VAN DOREN, CHARLES. *Lincoln's Commando: The Biography of Commander W. B. Cushing, USN.* New York: Harper & Brothers, 1957.

ROSS, MALCOLM. *The Cape Fear.* New York: Rinehart & Winston, 1965.

SANDS, BENJAMIN. *From Reefer to Rear Admiral.* New York: Frederick A. Stokes Co., 1899.

SANDS, FRANCIS. "A Volunteer's Reminiscences of Life in the North Atlantic Blockading Squadron, 1861–1865." *War Papers Read Before the Military Order of the Loyal Legion, Commandery of the District of Columbia.* Washington, D.C.: Published by the Commandery, 1894.

SCARF, J. THOMAS. *History of the Confederate States Navy from Its Organization to the Surrender of Its Last Vessel.* New York: Joseph McDonough Co., 1894.

SEITZ, DON C. *Braxton Bragg: General of the Confederacy.* Columbia, S.C.: State Co., 1924.

SELFRIDGE, THOMAS O., JR. *Memoirs of Thomas O. Selfridge, Jr., Rear-Admiral, USN.* New York: G. P. Putnam's Sons, 1924.

————. "The Navy at Fort Fisher." *Battles and Leaders of the Civil War.* Edited by Robert U. Johnson and Clarence C. Buel. New York: Century Co., 1884.

SIMMS, JOSEPH. "Personal Experiences in the Volunteer Navy During the Civil War." *War Papers Read Before the Military Order of the Loyal Legion, Commandery of the District of Columbia.* Washington, D.C.: Published by the Commandery, 1897.

SMITH, GUSTAVUS W. *Confederate War Papers.* New York: Atlantic Publishing and Engraving Co., 1884.

The Soldier of Indiana in the War for the Union. Indianapolis: Merrill and Company, 1869.

SOMMERS, RICHARD J. *Richmond Redeemed: The Siege at Petersburg.* Garden City, N.Y.: Doubleday, 1981.

SPRUNT, JAMES. *Chronicles of the Cape Fear River, 1660–1916.* Raleigh: Edwards and Broughton Printing Co., 1916.

————. *Tales of the Cape Fear Blockade.* Wilmington: Cornelius Thomas, 1960.

STEPHENS, ALEXANDER H. *A Constitutional View of the Late War Between the States.* Chicago: National Publishing Co., 1868.

STERN, PHILLIP VAN DOREN. *The Confederate Navy.* New York: Crown Publishers, 1962.

————. *They Were There.* New York: Crown Publishers, 1959.

STILL, WILLIAM. "Porter . . . Is the Best Man." *Civil War Times Illustrated,* vol. XVI, no. 2 (May 1977).

Stories of Our Soldiers. Boston: *The Journal* Newspaper Co., 1893.

"Story of the Powder Boat." *Galaxy Magazine,* vol. IX, January 1870.

TANNER, ZERA. "The Capture of Fort Fisher." *War Papers Read Before the Military Order of the Loyal Legion of the United States, Commandery of the District of Columbia.* Washington: Published by the Commandery, 1897.

"The Task Before Them." Edited by Edward G. Longacre. *Civil War Times Illustrated,* vol. XXI, no. 10 (February 1983).

TAYLOR, T. E. *Running the Blockade.* New York: Charles Scribner's Sons, 1896.

THOMAS, HOWARD. *Boys in Blue from the Adirondack Foothills.* Prospect, N.Y.: Prospect Books, 1960.

THOMAS, LEONARD. *The Story of Fort Fisher.* Ocean City, N.J.: n.p., 1915.

"A True History of the Army at Fort Fisher." Edited by L. R. Hamersly. *The United Service: A Monthly Review of Military and Naval Affairs,* vol. X. Philadelphia: L. R. Hamersly & Co., 1893.

TURNER, GEORGE E. *Victory Rode the Rails.* Indianapolis: Bobbs-Merrill Co., 1953.

The Uplift. Concord, N.C.: Concord Presbytery of the Presbyterian Church, U.S., vol. II, no. 2 (1910).

VOORHEES, OSCAR. "Colonel William Lamb and Phi Beta Kappa." *The Virginia Magazine of History and Biography,* vol. LIV, no. 3, 1946.

WALKLEY, STEPHEN. *History of the Seventh Connecticut Volunteer Infantry, 1861–1865.* N.p., 1905.

The War of the 'Sixties. Edited by E. R. Hutchins. New York: Neale Publishing Company, 1912.

WARNER, EZRA J. *Generals in Blue.* Baton Rouge: LSU Press, 1964.

———. *Generals in Gray.* Baton Rouge: LSU Press, 1959.

WATKINS, SAM R. *Co. Aytch: A Side Show of the Big Show.* Jackson, Tenn.: McCowat-Mercer Press, 1952.

WELD, FRANCIS MINOT. *Diaries and Letters of Francis Minot Weld.* Edited by Sarah Swan Weld Blake. N.p., 1925.

WELLES, GIDEON. *The Diary of Gideon Welles.* Edited by Howard K. Beale. New York: W. W. Norton & Co., 1960.

WIGHTMAN, S. K. "In Search of My Son." *American Heritage,* vol. XIV, no. 2 (February 1963).

WILLIAMS, T. HARRY. *Lincoln and His Generals.* New York: Alfred A. Knopf, 1952.

"A Yankee's Account of the Battles of Fort Fisher." *Our Living and Our Dead,* vol. I, September 1874–February 1875.

"Yankees Were Landing Below Us." Edited by William N. Still, Jr. *Civil War Times Illustrated,* vol. XV, no. 1 (April 1976).

Newspapers

Harper's Weekly
London Illustrated News
New York Times
New York Tribune
Philadelphia Inquirer
Philadelphia Times
West Chester Village Record
Wilmington Daily Herald
Wilmington Journal
Wilmington Messenger

Index

ABOUT THE AUTHOR

Rod Gragg is the author of five other works of nonfiction. One of them, *The Civil War Quiz and Fact Book*, was named as an alternate selection by the Book-of-the-Month Club. Another of his books, *The Illustrated Confederate Reader*, was chosen as a selection by the Military History Book Club and won the 1989 Douglas Southall Freeman Award for History. His work has appeared in *Civil War Times Illustrated*, *American West*, and other magazines. A former educator, he holds graduate and undergraduate degrees in history and journalism from the University of South Carolina. He and his family live in Conway, South Carolina.